Choice & Responsibility

Legal and Ethical Dilemmas in Services for Persons with Mental Disabilities

The New York State Commission on Quality of Care wishes to acknowledge the assistance and support of the van Ameringen Foundation, Inc., New York State Developmental Disabilities Planning Council, and Disability Advocates, Inc., in the publication of this monograph.

The New York State Commission on Quality of Care for the Mentally Disabled
99 Washington Avenue, Suite 1002
Albany, New York 12210-2895

ISBN 1-886702-00-4

Table of Contents

Contributors

IRA A. BURNIM, ESQ.
Legal Director
The Judge David L. Bazelon Center for Mental Health Law

JUDI CHAMBERLIN
Associate
National Empowerment Center

ELIZABETH J. CHURA
Director, Quality Assurance Bureau
New York State Commission on Quality of Care for the Mentally Disabled

FRED COHEN, ESQ.
Professor
School of Criminal Justice, State University of New York at Albany

MICHAEL R. DILLON, ED.D.
Director
Syracuse Developmental Services Office

DAVID FERLEGER, ESQ.
Attorney at Law

PHYLLIS GERBER
President
Friends and Advocates for Mental Health (FAMH)
Alliance for the Mentally Ill of Sullivan County

THOMAS R. HARMON
Director, Medical Review Investigations Bureau
New York State Commission on Quality of Care for the Mentally Disabled

MICHAEL KENDRICK
Associate Commissioner for Program Development
Massachusetts Department of Mental Retardation

MICHAEL J. KENNEDY
Training Associate
Center on Human Policy

ROBERT M. LEVY, ESQ.
General Counsel
New York Lawyers for the Public Interest, Inc.

DARBY J. PENNEY
Special Assistant to the Commissioner for Recipient Affairs
New York State Office of Mental Health

NANCY K. RAY, ED.D.
Director, Policy Analysis and Development Bureau, and Special Assistant
    to the Chairman
New York State Commission on Quality of Care for the Mentally Disabled

LEONARD S. RUBENSTEIN
Executive Director
The Judge David L. Bazelon Center for Mental Health Law

CHARLES E. SCHWARTZ, M.D.
Director
Psychiatric Consultation and Liaison Services
North Central Bronx Hospital

PAUL F. STAVIS, ESQ.
Counsel
New York State Commission on Quality of Care for the Mentally Disabled

SUSAN STEFAN, ESQ.
Associate Professor of Law
University of Miami School of Law

CLARENCE J. SUNDRAM, ESQ.
Chairman
New York State Commission on Quality of Care for the Mentally Disabled

RICHARD C. SURLES, PH.D.
Commissioner
New York State Office of Mental Health

E. FULLER TORREY, M.D.
Clinical and Research Psychiatrist
Public Citizen Health Research Group

Acknowledgments

This book would not have been possible without the contributions of many people, too numerous to all be individually recognized.

The people served by the Commission on Quality of Care and Disability Advocates, Inc.—persons with disabilities, their families and friends—provoked us into recognizing, confronting, and wrestling with the dilemmas in their lives as we sought to assist them. Provider agencies and their staffs contributed greatly to our understanding of the issues with candid discussions about their roles and responsibilities, and their own struggles to find the right balance between client aspirations and their obligations.

The staff of the Commission played a pivotal and ongoing role leading to this book. Their daily reporting from the front lines of the service delivery system continually reminds us of the rich and liberating potential of new approaches to individualized services and supports, and yet confronts us with the hazards of unbridled freedom. Their work shaped not only the case studies included in this volume but, with the help of staff from Disability Advocates, Inc., helped organize and stage the symposium held in Albany on June 21–22, 1994 from which most of the papers in this volume are drawn. While many Commission staff proofread drafts of the papers in this volume, special mention must be made of three individuals—Brenna Mahoney, Laurie Trojnor, and Rhonda Wallach—who painstakingly cite checked and proofed the final versions.

The financial support of the van Ameringen Foundation, Inc. and the New York State Developmental Disabilities Planning Council was indispensable to enabling Disability Advocates, Inc. and the Commission to organize the symposium and to publish this volume.

The exceptional work and patience of Kathy Runkle in working with documents in multiple word processing formats and transforming them into an elegant finished product deserves special recognition and thanks. Finally, I would like to acknowledge and thank Dr. Nancy Ray for her extraordinary contribution from the beginning to the end of this project, in helping to conceptualize it and to manage it to a successful conclusion.

Clarence J. Sundram

*To the Women and Men of the
Commission on Quality of Care*

INTRODUCTION

The past five years have been a period of unprecedented change in the service systems for persons with mental disabilities. For example, the implementation of the Medicaid Home and Community-Based Waiver, the commencement of the Community Supported Living Arrangement initiative, and the passage of seminal civil rights laws like the Americans with Disabilities Act and the Fair Housing Act Amendments have combined to reshape expectations of what is both possible and desirable in service systems, and to provide the flexibility in financing mechanisms to implement changes. The census of state institutions has continued to decline, while services in the community have continued to expand dramatically. In all of these changes there has been an increased stated emphasis on consumer choice and empowerment as a fundamental value in redesigning services and supports for community living.

These changes in the service systems have occurred during a period of fiscal distress in the states, one of the first casualties of which is staff training efforts. Thus, at a time when there has been a dramatic alteration in articulated policy and philosophy, there has been little opportunity to communicate systematically more than the language of these changes throughout large and complex service systems. Yet, such communication has been and remains vitally necessary. Not only are the policy changes profound in and of themselves, and a radical departure from the past assignment of roles and responsibilities between the servers and the served, but they have also occurred in an environment of mixed motives and other confounding developments. For example, while advocates and other leaders in the field of mental disabilities are moved by the opportunity to reverse a history of paternalistic decision-making that needlessly robbed many thousands of people of the right to control their own lives, the fiscal agents in Washington and the state capitals have seen in these changes new opportunities for cost cutting and have insisted that the implementation of the new policies be fiscally neutral or better. In doing so, they have helped limit the range of choices that can be financed since, in the bare-knuckled competition for funds, continuation of traditional services usually prevails over the development of new, nontraditional, and flexible services and supports that are essential for truly individualized planning.

In some states, rapid implementation of new community programs has been substantially influenced by a desire to conclude implementation of court orders in long-standing class action lawsuits and to thus terminate judicial supervision of the service system.

Finally, to add yet another element of confusion, during the past five years, several states have reduced or eliminated much of their regulation of services, have increased their reliance on nonlicensed and noncertified programs, and have delegated quality assurance functions to service providers. This movement has been in part a reaction to the excessive and largely misdirected regulatory structures developed for institutional programs and later indiscriminately extended to other services. The move to dismantle these regulatory structures has struck a responsive chord in an age when public skepticism about the competence and value of governmental services seems to be surging, and reducing governmental costs and eliminating governmental regulation are widely seen as desirable. Advocacy for a stronger role of state agencies in monitoring the safety and quality of services is seen in many quarters as depriving the individuals being served of autonomy and privacy, and an equal right to live their lives free of governmental interference. Yet, in responding to these concerns and dismantling regulatory structures, we seem to have thrown the proverbial baby out with the bathwater by often leaving staff who provide the newer community services and supports with indefinite standards and inadequate guidance. The historically high rates of staff turnover in front-line jobs in the service systems sometimes have resulted in delegating a broader range of responsibilities, which require both experience and judgment, to staff who have had too little time on the job to develop either.

These mixed motives and other changes have compounded the difficulty of clearly communicating the changed policies and expectations, of inculcating within vast human service organizations significantly different values than have guided the development of the community-based service systems over the past two decades, and of actually implementing person-centered services and supports.

To some extent, what has changed most is language. The seductive language of "choice" and "empowerment" is heard much more frequently, and services and supports are more often described as "individualized," as in "Individualized Service Environment." Sometimes the change in language has masked the sameness of the underlying reality which we have not found the ability or the will to change. For example, many of what are now called Individualized Residential Alternatives (IRAs) are the same residences that were called community residences and community-based ICF/MRs in the 1980s, and group homes in the 1970s. Some of the people living within them are the same as well, and the process of placing others within them remains largely unchanged. At other times, the change in language has communicated a message very different from what has been intended, and has taken the idea of choice and empowerment to the very edge of abandonment and abdication, and in some cases, over the precipice.

As an agency charged by law with investigating unnatural deaths and allegations of abuse and neglect on one hand, and advocating for the rights of individuals with disabilities on the other, the New York State Commission on Quality of Care regularly confronts these cases and often in their extreme forms—either where a calamity has occurred or when negotiations around client choices have failed. Regularly dealing with many cases in both categories has forced the Commission and its staff to wrestle with the issues of choice and responsibility, empowerment and protection—not as abstractions but in the context of real lives and real dilemmas. As we have struggled with these issues with the persons involved in the cases, consumers and providers, families and advocates, we have noted that there is little guidance available on reconciling rights and responsibilities and little consensus on the values or the process of thinking through them.

Out of these dilemmas and discussions came the idea for a symposium on the subject of *Choice and Responsibility: Legal and Ethical Dilemmas in Services for Persons with Mental Disabilities.* As we thought about these issues at the Commission, we realized that although the mental health and developmental disabilities service systems are distinct entities, with their own unique manifestations of the tension between empowerment and protection, there is value to a discussion of these issues in an environment which embraces the questions in their broadest form. With the cosponsorship of Disability Advocates, Inc., a public interest law firm that provides protection and advocacy services under contract with the Commission, the symposium was held in Albany, New York on June 21–22, 1994, and was attended by over 800 persons. With financial support from the van Ameringen Foundation, Inc. and the New York State Developmental Disabilities Planning Council, stipends were provided to sponsor the attendance and participation of primary consumers in the discussions.

This volume contains a collection of the principle papers and commentaries presented at the symposium, together with a few supplementary discussions of issues that we believed would be of interest to readers. Two caveats should be mentioned. First, while the Commission and Disability Advocates sponsored the symposium, and the NYS Developmental Disabilities Planning Council and the van Ameringen Foundation provided financial support for it, the views expressed in these papers are solely those of the authors. As will be apparent from reading the papers, several of the authors disagree with one another, sometimes vehemently. Second, while we are aware of the many different views about appropriate terminology to refer to people who have received services and supports from the mental health and developmental disabilities service systems, and recognize sensitivities about such terminology, we have not attempted to impose any consistent "correct" language, but have left it to the authors to resolve for themselves the issues about nomenclature.

This volume is organized into four sections. The first section provides broad perspectives on the issues of choice and responsibility from the varying vantage points of several observers who play different roles in the service systems. The Keynote Address, which provides a framework for a discussion of the issues of choice and responsibility, calls attention to the different types of choices people make; their consistency with known stable values of the individual; the types of risks entailed in decisions and the probability, severity, and duration of harm; and the nature of the interventions that ought to be considered in the case of imminent and nonimminent dangers.

The Keynote Address provides a decision-making matrix to guide thinking about how to reconcile the competing values of autonomy and safety. It is followed by commentary from Richard Surles, Ph.D., Commissioner of the NYS Office of Mental Health, who bluntly states that increased empowerment necessarily comes at the price of diminished protection. He nevertheless argues for increased empowerment of consumers and notes that the real constraints on empowerment may be less due to philosophical disagreements than the reality of scarce resources to offer a full range of choices.

Two recipients of services from the developmental disabilities and mental health service systems, Michael J. Kennedy and Darby J. Penney, respectively, call attention to the importance of self-direction in daily life. Mr. Kennedy reminds us of the importance of risk, of trying new things, of failure, as essential parts of normal growth that teach responsibility to the decision-maker. Ms. Penney notes that the most keenly felt infringements occur not in dramatic ways but in unnecessary control over the mundane decisions of daily life. Finally, Phyllis Gerber gives voice to the concerns of families who often find themselves the only real support system for a relative with a mental disability, and yet who have few rights of their own to information or to participation in decision-making.

These comments are followed by a point-counterpoint featuring E. Fuller Torrey, M.D. of the Public Citizens Health Research Group and Judi Chamberlin of the National Empowerment Project. Dr. Torrey argues that schizophrenia and manic-depressive illnesses are brain diseases that produce impaired logic and insight, and urges frank recognition of this reality. The failure to do so, he contends, has led to an extraordinary degree of self-inflicted harm and danger to others. He suggests several principles to guide decision-making about intervention in the decisions of persons with mental illness, urging that patients' "rights" not be the sole consideration. Instead, he suggests an "Ask Your Grandmother" test of common sense decision-making.

Judi Chamberlin rejects the validity of differential treatment of some citizens based on a diagnostic label of "mentally disabled." She argues against involuntary intervention in their decisions, holding that competence is in the eye of the beholder and that the essence of empowerment is the right to be wrong in the pursuit of happiness as one sees it.

From a broader perspective, Leonard S. Rubenstein notes that deinstitutionalization has been widely criticized as one of the most stunning public policy failures. Yet, he argues, this criticism disregards the magnitude and complexity of the societal and governmental changes needed to make this ambitious reform work, and has resulted in unrealistic yardsticks to measure its success. In the process, the dramatic contribution of this policy in creating a new concept of freedom for people with psychiatric disabilities and in spurring the development of innovative community services has been over-looked. Citing several recent developments in law, financing, and social policy, including recent proposals for national health care reform, Mr. Rubenstein asserts that these would never have happened without deinstitutionalization and that a fairer grade is neither "success" nor "failure," but "incomplete."

Finally, David Ferleger reflects on the place of choice in this debate. Reviewing the history of normalization, he notes that individual choice has always been regarded as one value, not the paramount value. The contemporary debate needs to keep sight of its origins and appreciate that normalization embraces many other values and interests including safety and protection from harm. Choices are circumscribed by substantive and procedural laws and social policies designed to protect the interests of the individual. Mr. Ferleger suggests several questions that should be asked to ascertain the authenticity of an articulated choice.

Section Two contains several of the theme papers from the symposium addressing the issues affecting the major domains of daily life.

Michael Kendrick discusses the dominant role of residential services and calls attention to the ways in which residential facilities, by whatever name they are called, are intentionally designed not to be a "home," and thus continue to devalue the lives of their residents. He identifies several sources of danger to residents and argues for the intentional development of appropriate safe-guards, and conscious attention to the ethical obligations of persons who provide services and supports to individuals with disabilities.

Two contributors discuss vocational and recreational services. Michael R. Dillon takes a line from an advertising jingle and suggests that consumers in developmental disabilities systems have an equal claim as the purchaser of a hamburger to "have it your way." He states that paternalistic and protective attitudes have been responsible for systematically depriving individuals with disabilities of their basic civil rights. Dr. Dillon observes that workers must assist persons with disabilities in the choice process, help expand their understanding of the range of choices, and be sensitive to the personal transformation that occurs in that process. To be responsive to consumer choice, the traditional hierarchy of agencies will have to change to shift greater authority to front-line workers to respond to consumer demands. When there is conflict between provider and consumer, ultimately, he argues, the customer is always right.

Elizabeth J. Chura calls attention to the central role that work and recreation play in determining the quality of life. These daily activities and our interactions with others in the environment have a major influence in shaping our character and making us the people we are, which in turn affects the choices we make. Conversely, our presence in this environment has a similar effect upon others. This understanding of work and recreation has profound implications for the manner in which we behave, and in which we support and assist persons with mental disabilities in making decisions. In essence, it requires an appreciation that choices about work and recreation are more than that; they are decisions about how to spend a life.

Two of the papers deal with the subject of health care. In the first, Charles E. Schwartz, M.D. discusses medical decision-making for persons with chronic mental impairments. He recounts the substantial history of poor medical care, undertreatment and overtreatment of persons with mental disabilities, and cites the need for advocacy to assure that such persons have access to high-quality medical care and to effective participation in medical decision-making, which may require finding an appropriate surrogate decision-maker. Using case examples, Dr. Schwartz suggests a step-by-step method for evaluating the capacity of patients to make informed medical decisions and for negotiating treatment options, noting that there is a fine line between respecting the patients' wishes and allowing them to make fatal mistakes because they do not fully comprehend the consequences of their actions.

Next, Robert M. Levy explores psychiatric decision-making in *Involuntary Treatment: Walking the Tightrope Between Freedom and Paternalism.* Mr. Levy's paper examines civil commitment and involuntary administration of psychotropic medications, providing both a historical context and a discussion of the current state of the law. He discusses how the legal system struggles to balance individual rights to liberty and the state's power and responsibility to confine and impose treatment on unwilling individuals to protect either their best interests or the interests of society.

The control of money in making the notion of choice a reality is the subject of a paper by Paul F. Stavis. This article suggests that it is time to seriously consider measures to enhance autonomy by changing who controls the money, resources, and property which the government now dedicates to care and treatment. With effective control of these funds, through the use of vouchers, for example, Mr. Stavis asserts that a person with mental disability can have much greater freedom by having many more choices in the myriad decisions of daily life. Where necessary, surrogate decision-makers with a genuine connection to the individual can help make decisions consistent with the person's preferences or best interests.

Some of the sharpest conflicts between individual choice and provider responsibilities arise in the context of sexual activity of persons with mental disabilities in institutions and community residential programs. Professor Susan Stefan's paper, *'Dancing in the Sky Without a Parachute': Sex and Love in Institutional Settings*, states that institutions must wrestle with these complex dilemmas, yet have few written policies to assist decision-making. She notes that institutional environments present many impediments to true choice. Professor Stefan recommends that all institutions develop comprehensive written policies regarding sexuality which: focus on recognizing and preventing sexual assaults and sexual abuse; promote responsibility and health in sexual activity; and recognize the right to sexual expression and voluntary sexual activity.

Ira A. Burnim observes that at the heart of the difficulty in dealing with issues of choice and responsibility is the recognition that the person has a mental disability. He asks: What is the relevance from the perspective of law and public policy of that fact? He reviews actions taken by legal advocates on behalf of persons with mental disabilities and notes that advocates are often arguing from two inconsistent perspectives. On one hand, they argue that disability is irrelevant and the person with a disability should be treated "like everyone else." Yet, on the other hand, they often argue that the disability *is* relevant and warrants special rights, privileges, benefits, and accommodations. Mr. Burnim discusses the options available for resolving this "dilemma of difference" and the implications of the choices.

Finally, Professor Fred Cohen discusses the issues of criminal responsibility that arise in dealing with the conduct of persons with mental disability.

He notes that, despite the availability of the insanity defense, many offenders with severe mental disabilities are sentenced to prison and that these numbers are increasing. The penal laws clearly "excuse" only a very small fraction of the criminal conduct of mentally disabled offenders and treat most of it as voluntary choices for which the actors are criminally responsible. Once in prison, however, even stricter rules of responsibility for conduct are followed, as disciplinary infractions and other violations typically have no insanity defense. Professor Cohen suggests that, as a matter of public policy, more efforts need to be made to divert from the criminal justice system offenders with severe mental disabilities who engage in minor criminal conduct, and to provide for their care and community protection in alternative community programs.

Section three addresses the role of quality assurance activities in helping to resolve the tension between choice and responsibility on an ongoing basis and in the concrete reality of real-life dilemmas confronted by servers and recipients in the service system. Nancy K. Ray's article, *Capitalizing on the Safety Net of Incident Reporting Systems in Community Programs*, notes that the newer types of individualized residential environments and work programs being created present more opportunities for recipients to make choices, to be independent, and to learn from mistakes. They also present different and often more serious risks. Dr. Ray argues that traditional quality assurance tools and particularly traditional incident reporting systems are ill-suited to either promote quality or safeguard against unreasonable risks in these newer environments which offer more independence and less continuous supervision. She suggests that incident reporting systems need to be designed to respect the greater expectation of privacy and autonomy in these environments. At the same time, their level and method of scrutiny—from definitions of reportable incidents, to methods of investigation, to composition of Incident Review Committees—must be recalibrated to provide reasonable assurances that incidents which expose individuals to substantial risks of serious harm are nevertheless reported, investigated and substantively addressed to protect residents from foreseeable harm. The article provides specific recommendations on how to accomplish such a design.

Section Four contains a compilation of case studies drawn from the files of the Commission. The lead study—*In the Matter of Jeff Kerwin*—depicts one person's journey through the service system, his quest to be free of the system's attempts to address his potentially life-threatening disability, the decisions reached by various providers at different junctures in his life, his family's perspective, and the circumstances of his death soon after he attained his goal: freedom from services he found too restrictive. The study, by Thomas R. Harmon, challenges the reader: What would you have done?

It is followed by several brief case studies, originally prepared for discussion at "practical" workshops at the symposium. These case studies are intended for use as teaching tools to bring the abstraction of the dilemmas of choice and responsibility into life. Several of the case studies are particularly well-suited for consideration in the context of Nancy K. Ray's article on incident reporting.

*   *   *

In organizing and sponsoring the symposium, it was our hope to begin a more public dialogue and discussion of the dilemmas and difficulties being confronted in private by workers on the front lines of the service systems as they seek to implement new visions of choice and empowerment for persons with mental disabilities. The overwhelming response to the symposium suggests that the need for such a discussion is keenly felt in service systems across the country. Over half the states were represented at the symposium and over 200 registrants had to be turned away for lack of space. It is our hope, through the publication of this volume, to carry the discussion to others who are wrestling with the same questions.

Clarence J. Sundram
Albany, New York
November 1994

SECTION ONE
CHOICE AND RESPONSIBILITY: PERSPECTIVES

1

A Framework for Thinking About Choice and Responsibility

Clarence J. Sundram, Esq.

The overwhelming response to the announcement for this conference suggests that we are all wrestling with profound dilemmas of choice and responsibility in the mental health and developmental disabilities service system and are looking for guidance in how to deal with them. At the Commission, our twin roles as advocates for persons with disabilities and as an agency charged with overseeing the operations of the service systems have forced us to see these dilemmas from different vantage points.

As advocates, we rejoice in the dramatic progress that has been made in both the developmental disabilities and mental health systems in recognizing the value of consumer choice as a cornerstone of the service systems. The voices of consumers have been actively sought out in the development of policy as never before, and the policies themselves place increasing emphasis on consumer participation, even consumer direction, aimed ultimately at a goal of consumer satisfaction.

This new policy of empowerment of consumers abandons long histories of unnecessarily paternalistic decision-making on behalf of people with disabilities that robbed many thousands of people of the joys and satisfaction of deciding for themselves how to live their lives. As we meet here today, we are on the uncomfortable cusp of change. While new policies are being enunciated, practice, as always, is slower to change. The transition from paternalism to empowerment is neither smooth nor seamless. There is a continual risk that existing roles, responsibilities, and understandings may disappear before the new safeguards are put in place. One of the key safeguards that has existed is the responsibility that program staff have felt for the welfare of people entrusted to their care—a responsibility that has been recognized to have constitutional dimensions in protecting such persons from harm.

In this period of transition and changing expectations and aspirations, we need to be conscious that it is not only the rights of consumers which are changing; it is also the rights and duties of the staff who work in our programs. To put it simply, if consumers now have the right and responsibility to make decisions and direct the services and supports they require, how does this change the role and responsibility of the staff of agencies and programs providing the services/supports? This question plays out in virtually every dimension of life from choosing a residence, to finding a suitable program, managing money, establishing personal relationships, and other activities.

Some have found it easier to surrender to the verbalization of choice than to wrestle with untidy questions and unclear answers.

Unfortunately, in espousing consumer empowerment we have tended not to confront these changes explicitly or to talk much about them or engage in the type of rethinking of roles and retraining that is essential if the changes in policy are to realize their full potential without unnecessary risk and harm.

As providers, consumers, advocates, or concerned family members, we are all struggling with new problems, ethical dilemmas, and confusion as the traditional anchors of settled roles and responsibilities seem to have floated away. Our thinking about these issues is prompted by the strong voices of energized consumers and self-advocates on the one hand, and occasional reports of stark tragedies which have occurred when safeguards have been removed, on the other. But most of us have not joined actively in the debate and discussion about the implications of these fundamental policy changes on our own roles and responsibilities. Some of us are concerned about wounding the sensibilities of others. We walk on eggshells, choosing our words carefully, fearful of offending or misspeaking or not being in touch with the evolving notions of acceptable language.

Others have concluded that it is simply no longer acceptable to question the limits of empowerment, to rethink aloud what are acceptable risks, and where lie the boundaries of choice, to seek safer middle ground. In the process they silently acquiesce in new responsibilities which they secretly fear, are confused by, and from which they retreat. Some have found it easier to surrender to the verbalization of choice than to wrestle with untidy questions and unclear answers.

It is plain that mental disabilities can and do make some people more vulnerable to harm, abuse, neglect, mistreatment, and exploitation. Cognitive limitations can make learning more difficult, more time-consuming, and less transferrable. And living long stretches of life without the opportunity to make decisions has placed many persons with mental disabilities at a disadvantage in immediately assuming the responsibility for making decisions about many areas of life in which they have had little experience.

So, while we applaud the leadership of mental health and developmental disabilities service systems for recognizing that sound public policy proceeds from empowerment and encouragement of persons with mental disabilities, we also need to be mindful of how much work lies ahead in making these policies work as intended.

The purpose of this symposium is to *begin* a discussion of these complex topics. I emphasize the word "begin." I don't want to create the impression that either I or any of the other speakers are coming here bearing stone tablets with definitive answers permanently etched. In fact, in the course of planning this symposium it has become clearer that such answers don't exist. In fact, there is considerable disagreement about what the questions are or should be. In putting this symposium together we have made a conscious effort to invite speakers with divergent views and experiences. With the help of the van Ameringen Foundation and the Developmental Disabilities Planning Council, we have actively solicited the attendance of primary consumers and families and direct care staff to participate in the discussions.

What we hope to accomplish is that we will all leave here with a fuller appreciation of the opportunities that are presented, the issues that are involved, the values with which we approach the questions, a commitment to forthrightly confront the dilemmas, and perhaps a framework for thinking through the problems.

> *Despite strong espousal of empowerment and choice by the leaders of mental health and developmental disability systems, these values have been slow to trickle down to the level of service delivery where there is often little of either.*

What Are the Problems?

First, despite strong espousal of empowerment and choice by the leaders of mental health and developmental disability systems, these values have been slow to trickle down to the level of service delivery where there is often little of either.

While consumers and families have had their expectations raised, the service systems still offer a limited menu of choices. All of us are familiar with the hundreds of ways the service systems are currently depriving persons of such elementary choices as where they live and with whom, who attends to their personal needs, who has access to the most private information about their lives, what they eat and when, and so on. Many of the complaints we receive from consumers are:

- about treatment in psychiatric facilities without consent and about a lack of choice and meaningful options upon discharge; and,
- about being forced to attend day programs or sheltered workshops they abhor as the price of maintaining a residential placement.

On the other hand, in our oversight work we have seen instances where staff either believed themselves powerless to protect individuals from a serious risk of harm or were simply unaware of options to inaction. For example:

- A young man with a history of substance abuse, depression, and suicide attempts was discharged after heroin detoxification to a residence for mentally ill chemical abusers. A month after his admission, he received a tuition reimbursement check for $800 and told staff that he intended to "split and get high." They attempted to dissuade him, but eventually gave him his check. He promptly left, rented a hotel room, purchased drugs, and was found dead the next day of an "acute mixed drug intoxication."

While consumers and families have had their expectations raised, the service systems still offer a limited menu of choices.

- A profoundly mentally retarded man was placed in a private home. It soon became apparent to staff from Protective Services that he was living in a small, filthy and barren room, spending his days seminude, sitting on a commode. His guardian appeared indifferent to his welfare. While professionals from several agencies dithered for a period of *years* about who should take responsibility, he suffered malnutrition, dehydration, decubitus ulcers, and gangrene which eventually caused his death. The reason for inaction? A lack of clarity about legal responsibility for decision-making.
- In yet another case, a 40-year-old autistic, nonverbal man lived in a community residence and attended day programs. Staff supervised him carefully because he would constantly seek food and coffee, rifling through garbage, stealing others' food, and drinking scalding hot coffee when he feared discovery. Once he learned to use transpor-

tation, he was allowed more freedom. He soon became a common
sight in the community—picking
through garbage, begging, urinating in public places. He became an
object of ridicule in the community
and gained over 30 pounds in a few
short months. Professional staff took
a hands-off approach to the devel-

Professional staff took a hands-off approach to the developing problems, citing the "dignity of risk" in his new found freedom.

oping problems, citing the "dignity of risk" in his newfound freedom.

- A severely mentally retarded resident of a community program was heard screaming in his bedroom. When staff responded, they found him trapped facedown between the mattress and the wall, with his underpants around his knees. He was yelling and crying and visibly angry as another resident was on top of him, pinning him down. The other resident's sweatpants were around his knees. This man has a history of sexual aggression against other residents and staff. Following staff intervention, they concluded that the incident was consensual, presumably because neither resident had been adjudicated as incompetent. Notably, staff concluded that neither resident had an understanding of sexual activity nor would they respond to or benefit from sex education.

- An elderly, long-term resident of a state psychiatric center was discharged to an adult home with a history of deficient services. By all accounts, including the patient's, he was content and well cared for in the center, and given his choice, would have opted to live out his years in its familiar environment. Soon after his admission to the adult home his condition began to deteriorate. His hygiene was poor, he developed a number of health complaints, and he became a frequent visitor to the local emergency room. Although his case manager, emergency room physicians, and hospital staff were all concerned about his deteriorating condition, no one was willing to help him find a more suitable place to live or to consider returning him to the psychiatric center until one could be found. Within a few months of his discharge, he died of medical complications.

- Another consumer, living in greater independence in a supported apartment and finally free of a representative payee, spent his SSI check on crack, prostitutes, and calls to a sex line. As a result, he didn't have money to pay his rent or to buy food for the month. The agency considered his nonpayment of rent as a choice. At first, they withheld

The Boy Scout motto: "Be Prepared" would be a good first step in today's Quality Handbook.

his personal needs allowance to pay back rent. But their eventual solution? Summary eviction from his apartment by placing all his belongings in garbage bags in the hallway. Presumably this was a lesson in normalization and consequences that, whatever its pedagogic value, left him homeless and broke.

The policy emphasis on choice and empowerment is long overdue, and we need to focus more on finding ways to promote informed, voluntary choices of people with disabilities, to provide options that allow them to meet self-identified needs, and to assist them in understanding the implications of decisions they want to make.

In the process, it is *essential* that we honestly ensure that we are eliciting *authentic* and *informed* choices of consumers and that we adequately prepare everyone, from agency managers on down, for the new responsibilities they will have to shoulder in respecting these choices and, as importantly, in challenging them when they expose the individual to unrecognized dangers. The Boy Scout motto: "Be Prepared" would be a good first step in today's Quality Handbook.

The preparation this time around is more complex than learning the regulatory requirements and black letter laws. Instead, we are entering a new world, like some of the private corporations that have prepared for a new era of business competition by throwing away their volumes of personnel manuals and replacing them with simple instructions like: "Employees are expected to use good judgment at all times." However, good judgment is a product of understanding the environment in which one is working, the values that are important, the risks that are present, and the outcomes

I think we have tended to be seduced by the power of the new application to people with disabilities of old ideas of equality, choice, autonomy, and inclusion to the point that we have relied more upon hope and belief than upon good judgment and careful planning to help make these ideas a reality.

that are desired. People make good judgment when they are prepared for and understand the judgments they must make, and their responsibility *to make them.*

I think we have tended to be seduced by the power of the new application to people with disabilities of old ideas of equality, choice, autonomy, and inclusion to the point that we have relied more upon hope and belief than upon good judgment and careful planning to help make these ideas a reality. In the process, we have failed to confront the reality that people with mental disabilities are individuals, each with his or her unique strengths, skills, experiences, and values that influence personal decision-making. Just as it was fundamentally wrong to assume the incompetence of everyone with a mental disability, it is equally misguided to assume that all such persons share equal knowledge, skill, and judgment in making decisions. Neither rigid notions of equality nor unbridled choice are likely to serve all people with mental disabilities well.

While a presumption of competence is a useful legal concept when one is ignorant about the capacities of another, it is no substitute for an assessment of strengths and needs that is a cornerstone of sound service planning.

I believe that in the process of implementing these profound changes, we have not recognized this reality enough and have paid insufficient attention to the changing management and professional responsibilities that should accompany the new role of consumers. We have failed to address squarely the responsibility of people working in human service systems to safeguard people who may be endangered by their limited abilities and life experiences. And this failure to directly deal with these central issues of professional responsibility is manifesting itself daily in demonstrable harm to people with mental disabilities.

In an era of individualized support environments, assuring quality will increasingly depend on the initial decisions about the nature of the living environment and the extent of the supports required for each person. If the supports and connections required for real integration are not carefully put in place, there is a risk that harm will occur and will remain undetected.

The foundation for a renewed understanding of professional responsibility in this changing service system is to emphasize the importance of truly individualized service planning. Our statutes and regulations are littered with mandates for such individualized planning. It is time to make them real. This means that staff working with consumers must make concerted efforts to learn the abilities, preferences, skills, and needs of the individual in developing a working relationship. While a presumption of competence is a useful legal concept when one is ignorant about the capacities of another, it is no substitute for an assessment of strengths and needs that is a cornerstone of sound service planning.

While we need to maintain a decent respect for the right of people with disabilities to make the decisions they can, to quote Judge Friendly, we ought not to leave our common sense at the door when we go to work.

Thus, implementation of these new policies requires not only paying attention to consumer preferences, choice, and satisfaction, but also carefully examining the decision-making knowledge and ability of the individual to assume the risks implicit in some choices.

While we need to maintain a decent respect for the right of people with disabilities to make the decisions they can, to quote Judge Friendly, we ought not to leave our common sense at the door when we go to work. People with severe cognitive limitations and limited life experience may want to make their own decisions and even believe they are making good decisions. They may unquestionably have the right, as we all do, to be dead wrong and make poor choices and mistakes, and hopefully to learn from them.

The greater the freedoms they enjoy, the greater will be the natural tension between their rights and the risks to them and to others involved in their lives, such as their children.

There are, unfortunately, no clear bright lines to mark the precise threshold at which outside intervention in their decision-making is acceptable or even obligatory for involved professionals. While laws define rights, they don't deal well with the ambiguity that is part of life.

In the past two decades, we have spent a great deal of effort training our staffs to comply with regulations. Our challenge now is to inculcate different values and train our staffs, not to look so much for prescriptive regulations that tell them what to do, but to apply judgment in balancing the value of consumer choice and empowerment with a responsibility to protect individuals from risks they may not comprehend due to limited cognitive ability or life experiences. These responsibilities may harken back to a more paternalistic time, but I think we need to be honest

While laws define rights, they don't deal well with the ambiguity that is part of life.

enough to recognize that many of the people being served have lived long stretches of their lives without choices or mentors to help guide them. They have thus not had the opportunity of guided learning about choices and boundaries, of having someone with an unquestioned commitment to them care enough to help them learn by taking measured risks or to challenge their decisions when they are thought to be unwise or harmful. They may not have

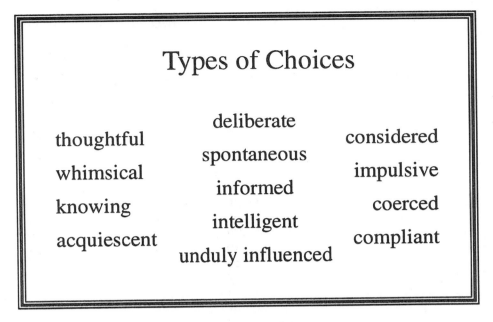

Figure 1-1

had much experience in learning the process and value of compromise in decision-making.

I would like to suggest a framework for thinking about the myriad issues that are presented. At the outset, I want to emphasize that this is a discussion about persons with mental disabilities who have a questionable capacity to make some types of decisions. The law is well settled that persons who are clearly competent have the right to make their own decisions despite the risks that may be involved.

In thinking about consumer choices, we need to recognize that there are many types of choices (Figure 1-1) with different degrees of voluntariness, knowledge, and intelligence. All of us often act on whims. We think about short-term benefits and less about long-term consequences. We make many spontaneous, impulsive decisions, and, truth be told, many of the joys of life and the most indelible memories we have are products of this type of decision-making rather than the more thoughtful, deliberate, and considered judgments we make.

We use different types of decision-making methods for different decisions, usually depending on what's at stake (e.g., buying an ice cream cone vs. changing jobs). And we may use different types of choices at different times (e.g., a dieter deciding on an ice cream cone).

One of the red flags that should prompt scrutiny about a choice is whether the choice itself and the manner in which it is made is consistent with what we know of the person's stable values and preferences.

Sometimes our decisions are not conscious decisions but acquiescence in the decisions or choices of another. Sometimes we do things against our better judgment because we are caught up in the moment.

My point is that, in thinking about choices of persons with mental disabilities, we need to be conscious of the fact that the choices all of us make run the gamut from ill-considered decisions that are inconsistent with our basic values and best interest, but which are a preference for the moment; to decisions that are impulsive and don't use the knowledge and intelligence we have, but which may be consistent with a life-style that values living on the edge; to decisions that are carefully calculated to weigh the pros and cons, that evaluate the information and knowledge and reach a considered judgment.

One of the red flags that should prompt scrutiny about a choice is whether the choice itself and the manner in which it is made is consistent with what we know of the person's stable values and preferences (Figure 1-2). Is it "in character" with him or her? How important is the choice/decision to the individual? This of course requires knowing the individual well enough to answer the question.

Examples of Consistent Values

moderation	caution	kindness
courage	self-esteem	ambition
justice	consideration	loyalty
altruism	risk-taking	honesty
prudence	industriousness	hope
piety		moral

Figure 1-2

Risk Assessment

Probability of Harm	Severity of Harm	Duration of Harm
None	None	None
Low	Minor	Brief
Moderate	Moderate	Temporary
HIGH	SERIOUS	PERMANENT
Unknown	Unknown	Unknown

Figure 1-3

The next set of considerations that plays a role in determining the importance of the choice at issue is the risk entailed in the choice (Figure 1-3). There are three different dimensions of risk—the *probability* that harm will occur, the *severity* of the harm, and the *duration* of the harm. The risks can range from a very low probability of slight and temporary harm to a high probability of serious and permanent harm (e.g., a person with poor motor coordination who chooses to hang glide) with many combinations in between.

In essence, this approach suggests that we think about each issue or situation as a matrix (Figure 1-4), with the risks arrayed on one axis and the choices, interests, and values of the individual on the other. While this approach does not offer mathematical precision in decision-making, it suggests that, when consumers' choices are clearly expressed and are consistent with known stable values and involve little or no risk to the consumer, the provider's responsibilities for scrutinizing such decisions are minimal and can be satisfied by an informal process. Many decisions of day-to-day living would fall into this category. These decisions of individuals with mental disabilities create great "teaching moments"—for staff to understand and appreciate the preferences and interests of the individual and, at the same time, to teach and to strengthen the individual's decision-making abilities.

When the consumer's choices are less clear or are inconsistent with known values and interests, but still involve little or no risk, the provider's responsi-

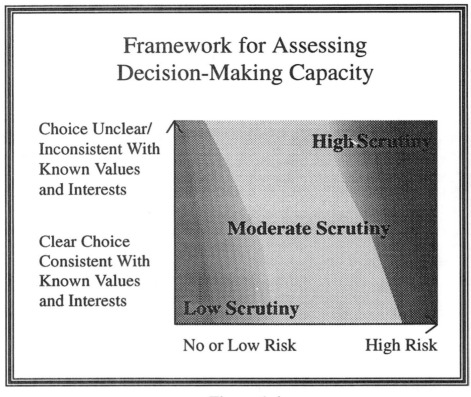

Figure 1-4

bility for assuring that the individual has in fact made a voluntary decision would rise, but could still be satisfied by an informal process (e.g., choosing to give away a modest amount of money to a stranger). Again, these types of decisions would create "teaching moments" about choice-making that would, over time, enhance the ability of the individual to make better choices, consistent with his values and interests.

As the risks inherent in a decision increase or as they are less clearly consistent with the known values and interests of the individual, the obligation of the provider to scrutinize the decisions will concomitantly increase, to assure that the decisions being made are voluntary and with understanding of the choices and options. The formality of the process of inquiry should likewise increase and involve individuals including professionals who know the consumer well.

At the other end of the continuum are decisions which clearly expose the consumer to serious risks and which appear to be inconsistent with the known values and best interests of the consumer. These would require careful scrutiny to determine whether the decision is being made voluntarily and with full knowledge of the risks and consequences and may require a formal review process.

Thinking about the issues presented within such a framework will require real relationships between the staff of our programs and the people they serve in order to understand where along the spectrum a particular problem falls.

Thinking about the issues presented within such a framework will require real relationships between the staff of our programs and the people they serve in order to understand where along the spectrum a particular problem falls. My guess is that, given the current state of implementation of the policies of choice and empowerment within the service systems, many of the issues we will be dealing with fall in areas where consumer choices are clearly expressed and involve little or no risk. Working with consumers to implement these choices offers the opportunity to deepen relationships, learn their values and interests, and explore their understanding of risks and consequences. The more successfully we carry out these tasks, the less likely it is that the decisions they make will fall within the red zone of high scrutiny with a formalized process of review.

But identifying the decisions as falling within the red zone of high risk and high scrutiny does not end the inquiry. What should the provider do?

If the situation presents an imminent risk of harm, it should be dealt with as an emergency where one acts to prevent harm and preserve the situation until other alternatives can be considered (Figure 1-5). If some type of coercive intervention is to be used, there must be a good reason to believe that some other judgment is clearly superior to the choice made by the consumer. In extreme cases, such decisions by an individual may prompt the provider to initiate formal proceedings to review the com-

---

Interventions
Imminent Risks of Serious Harm

- Immediate Action!
- Increase Supervision?
- Protective Orders?
- Restraint?
- Involuntary Intervention?
- Surrogate Decision-Making?

Figure 1-5

petence of the consumer and to secure surrogate decision-making (e.g., a person giving away *all* of his money and becoming destitute; choosing to forego low-risk medical treatment for a life-threatening condition).

If the risk of harm is not imminent, the provider can consider other methods of intervention from educational efforts about the risks and consequences, to an exploration of alternatives that might meet the consumer's interests and intent, to the implementation of safeguards to reduce the risks of harm (Figure 1-6).

It is clear to me from the cases I've seen that they present hard and challenging questions that force each one of us to confront our own values and to define the boundary lines beyond which we will seriously question other people's choices and intervene to protect them from harm, if necessary.

In closing, there is a rich promise in this new direction—one that recognizes the limits of regulation and inspection as tools to promote quality and one that relies instead on the choices and aspirations of the people being served, assisted by an engaged and supporting work force. What we will depend on more is what brings so many people to dedicate their lives to the helping professions—a sense of civic duty and a concern for the condition of other people's lives. With appropriate training and supervision of the workforce, and a clear understanding of their role and responsibilities in this changing world, there is no reason why persons with disabilities cannot be assisted and supported to take control of decisions about their lives, without undue risk of harm.

Interventions
Nonimminent Risks

- How Can Risks Be Minimized?
- Discuss Risks/Consequences?
- Provide Education/Training?
- Encourage Discussion With Friends/Family?
- Explore Other Choices/Alternatives?
- Add Safeguards?
- Provide Related Experiences With Lower Risks?

Figure 1-6

2

Free Choice, Informed Choice, and Dangerous Choices

Richard C. Surles, Ph.D.[1]

This conference falls within a great tradition in our field: the tradition of constantly reexamining the balance between liberty and security. I've witnessed this debate through several cycles of intensity, during which the pendulum swings back or forth between liberty and security with dramatic force and speed. Amazingly, at times like now, that pendulum seems to sharply swing both ways at once.

The conference is timely; a new cycle of intensity is clearly underway. One only need look at the front page of Friday's *New York Times*, which describes five bills to compel mental health treatment now before the New York State Legislature, including a bill to authorize an involuntary outpatient commitment demonstration.[2] The article discusses how an organization representing parents of persons with mental illness supports the outpatient commitment bill as a means to ensure the treatment of their relatives with mental illness. Meanwhile a group representing consumer/recipients vehemently opposes the bill as an infringement of their liberties.

But beyond the immediate legislative activity, the issue of liberty versus security is timely because of dramatic changes in the state's mental health system. The number of adult inpatients in state hospitals has dropped from a high of 93,000 in the late 1950s to its current census of about 9,700. At the same time, some 500,000 New Yorkers received mental health treatment last year. Clearly, we have radically transformed the mental health system from one where the primary focus of care was a hospital, to one where community care is the rule.

The implications of this shift in the locus of care for the debate on liberty versus security are great, and ironically pull in both directions. On one hand, involuntary hospitalization has become far more rare—it is now clearly the exception, not the rule. Less than 10% of all those served are subject to involuntary hospitalization.

On the other hand, the greater presence and visibility of persons with mental illness in communities has induced media and political leaders to focus on incidents of violence and the spread of homelessness, and to call for more measures to compel treatment.

Choice has proven to be an enormously important element in a recovery strategy, and has increasingly been integrated into the treatment of persons with mental illness.

In my view, neither camp has a monopoly on truth or justice. Clearly, we have to continue to strive to achieve a balance between maximizing liberty and promoting security. Yet if I have to align myself with one camp, I see myself as a partisan for greater liberty, greater freedom of choice. Let me mention three reasons.

In Support of Choice

The first, and most obvious reason to promote choice is the great value we in this society attach to personal autonomy—to the individualized pursuit of happiness. People make thousands of decisions, momentous and trivial, in the course of a day: when to get up, what to wear, what to eat, where to go. Over time people decide where to live, what work to do, what to do for recreation or entertainment. It is through these choices that we give our lives direction and meaning, and it is through these choices that we advance our own interests as we see them.

But the argument for enhancing freedom of choice has special force with respect to persons with mental illness. Until the recent past, mental illness had been portrayed as a chronic, irreversible condition, characterized by steadily decreasing capacity. With that predicate, policymakers focused on assuming more and more responsibility for the lives of persons with this disability.

Thus, a second reason is that we have learned that recovery is possible, and we are now transforming policies and treatments to vigorously promote that end. Choice has proven to be an enormously important element in a recovery strategy, and has increasingly been integrated into the treatment of persons with mental illness. Indeed, special training in areas of psychiatric rehabilitation teaches professionals the importance of choice and personal responsibility. So, the promotion of choice among persons with mental disabilities not only advances a basic value of our society, it also advances the rehabilitation of such persons.

A third reason to defend choice relates to the almost inevitable unevenness of decisions that deprive people of choice. I've become increasingly concerned about how we select who is involuntarily hospitalized and who isn't; who is involuntarily treated and who isn't; who has a representative payee and who doesn't; in sum, who we closely watch and who we don't closely watch. Some of our rules actually codify uneven-handedness. The discharge planning statute purportedly imposes a requirement to supervise the lives of patients discharged from state-operated hospitals, but not patients discharged from state-licensed psychiatric hospitals and inpatient units. Particularly in an era when a stay in a state hospital can be weeks, not years, I do not see the basis for attaching that supervisory duty to those leaving a state hospital who have rapidly responded to treatment.

But if we are to defend depriving people of liberties as basic as choice about hospitalization, treatment, and financial control, then a central tenet must be the similar treatment of people in similar circumstances.

In any case, in a large system, it is not possible to ensure complete uniformity and evenhandedness—even if the rules compelled it. But if we are to defend depriving people of liberties as basic as choice about hospitalization, treatment, and financial control, then a central tenet must be the similar treatment of people in similar circumstances.

I am inspired here by the example of now-retired Justice Harry Blackmun, who concluded that the death penalty was unconstitutional, not because the Constitution prohibited that punishment per se, but because states had proven themselves incapable of meting out such punishment equitably.

Limits on Choice

While choice is a cherished value in our society, it is not the only value. Let me briefly point out two competing values that can operate to constrain choices of persons with mental disabilities.

First, there is a strong societal interest in preventing a person from engaging in an activity that endangers his/her life or health—that is, in preventing a person from making a dangerous or self-destructive choice.

But the societal interest is not always an *overriding* interest. The question of whether an intervention is justified or not turns on several factors, including:

- the likelihood and degree of the danger;
- the person's ability to understand the likelihood and degree of the danger;
- whether the activity exposes others to some danger;
- the setting—that is, whether the person is in a hospital, the community, or elsewhere; and,
- the risk of intervening—that is, the risk that a compelling treatment or prohibiting patient choice will itself set back a person's recovery or lead to some other bad outcome.

To the extent we in the mental health system decide to expand the boundaries of recipient choice, that is, to allow greater self-determination and autonomy, we can expect bad choices and bad consequences, among them: injuries, rehospitalizations, and deaths.

So, for example, I mention two extreme cases. It would be appalling for the mental health system to forcibly intervene to prevent a person in the community with a mental disability from overeating or failing to get enough exercise. On the other hand, it would be equally appalling for a psychiatric hospital to decline to prevent an inpatient's effort to kill herself during a period of depression.

Of course, the problem cases are those in between. But the cases all illustrate one essential point. There is a direct trade-off between promoting choice and promoting safety. To the extent we in the mental health system decide to expand the boundaries of recipient choice, that is, to allow greater self-determination and autonomy, we can expect bad choices and bad consequences, among them: injuries, rehospitalizations, and deaths.

And, to the extent we in the Office of Mental Health promote choice and liberty, we can also expect sharp criticism from those oversight agencies, litigants, and others who see us as a guarantor against bad outcomes.

For example, consider the case of a former inpatient who, after discharge from a state hospital to an adult home, wants to be left alone and to have nothing to do with mental health providers or case workers. If a year later he becomes ill and dies or commits suicide, we can expect a Commission on Quality of Care report condemning the mental health system for failing to be more interventionist.

On the other hand, if the mental health system were more intrusive, and intervened over objection more readily in the lives of discharged persons, I'm sure we would be condemned by advocates, probably including the same Commission, for infringing on the liberties of citizens.

My point is that we cannot at the same time be more libertarian and more paternalistic. We cannot demand that the public mental health system ensure recipient choice and still guarantee recipient safety. It's not possible. If we are to promote choice, we have to be prepared to accept consequences. And, if we give priority to patient safety, we should give up the pretense of defending patient choice.

A second restraint on choice stems from the scarcity of resources. The stark fact of scarce resources constrains recipient choice in a multitude of ways.

Interestingly, while we have room to debate and move the boundaries of recipient choice on issues of safety, we probably have less ability to expand recipient choice when it confronts resource scarcity.

On the inpatient side, resource limits constrain the choice of facility a patient goes to, the doctor and other professionals he or she will see, the treatment offered, the daily activities offered, and so on.

On the community side, resources constrain the choice of outpatient treatment options, the choice of residential programs, and the choice of community support services. This is a fact of life.

Interestingly, while we have room to debate and move the boundaries of recipient choice on issues of safety, we probably have less ability to expand recipient choice when it confronts resource scarcity.

This leads to an ironic result in, say, the area of treatment options:

- the menu of treatments that patients can *decline* has grown significantly; and,
- the menu of treatments that patients can *accept* may soon be contracted significantly.

We have, as a result of court decisions and our own increased acceptance of the principles of patient autonomy, become increasingly supportive of treatment refusals. We have processes that allow for the refusal of antipsychotic medication and other mental health treatments, and we publicize and offer assistance to patients to create health care proxies and other advance directives.

At the same time, those who have been monitoring national health care reform efforts and their relation to mental health care know that, while most of the current proposals will extend health care coverage to a wider range of Americans, they will place new limits on benefits, particularly mental health benefits. There will likely be new caps, service exclusions, and co-pays. Those limits could significantly contract access to mental health services, particularly for persons with serious mental illness. Equally disturbing, health reform proposals threaten to divert resources from the mental health system to other health care systems (or to profits).

New York State has been working very hard on two fronts. We have sought to keep the mental health benefit as generous as possible. We are also attempting to preserve existing resources.

For our purposes today, I simply wanted to note that, in the area of treatment, recipient choice means not just the right to refuse treatment, but the right to have access to treatment from which to choose. I seek to protect both rights.

Endnotes

1. Commissioner, New York State Office of Mental Health. Commissioner Surles would like to acknowledge the assistance of Robert N. Swidler, Deputy Commissioner and Counsel to the New York State Office of Mental Health, in the preparation of these remarks.

2. Fonderaro, L. W. (1994, June 17). New York debates its rules for committing mentally ill people. *The New York Times*, p. A1. Ultimately, the New York State Legislature passed two bills in its 1994 session relating to involuntary hospitalization: (1) the involuntary outpatient commitment pilot bill (Chapter 560, Laws of 1994); and (2) a bill broadening the composition and powers of mobile crisis outreach teams (Chapter 678, Laws of 1994).

3

Customers Come First

Michael J. Kennedy

I think when we are talking about consumer choice and participation, we have to realize not every person with a disability has the same disability. We have to create the system for the individual and for years and years people have been trying to mold the person into the system—the system that already exists, and you can't do that.

First, some people might have more than one disability and they might need more support. And, the way I look at it is, if you can spend billions and billions of dollars sending people to the moon and to fight a Gulf War, then there's no reason why the money cannot be rechanneled so that the consumers can live as independently as possible.

Second, you got to take the consumers from the bottom and move them to the top because they know what their disabilities are. They know what their limitations are. I'll give you a perfect example: I can't do anything physical for myself. But that doesn't mean I can't direct my own aides and my own service to the

> *We have to create the system for the individual and for years and years people have been trying to mold the person into the system.*

way I need it. But for years the system has been saying, "Well, you're retarded; you don't know any better." Well, times have changed and who knows better than the consumers themselves?

For years I've been fighting not only for my own rights in the institution, but for the rights of people in institutions who are not heard of. And, many of those people are still not being heard from today. You know why? Because people have not taken the time to figure out a way to help them communicate. And yes, it's true they may not know what the choices are—but if you shut people away for years and don't give them the choice, naturally when they get the choice, they're going to be confused and they're going to take risks and that might be stupid and dumb. I'll tell you, I've done that. Since I moved out of the institution, I've made some mistakes; I fell flat on my face, but you know what? I learned from that. And hopefully the person will not make the same mistake twice.

But the service system has to allow us to make those mistakes. We're not saying that they're not trying to do a good job, but I think before you can do a good job, you have to have the people involved in making decisions for themselves. You have to realize not everybody is going to live their life like everybody else. Just because you

If you shut people away for years and don't give them the choice, naturally when they get the choice, they're going to be confused.

think you like something in your life, don't think that another person is going to like it because they may not. Once in a while it might be compatible with their desires, but that's not always going to be the case. And when you offer suggestions for a person about where they want to live or what they want to eat—just because they say, "No, I don't want that," don't say, "Okay, I'm gonna shut off your service because you didn't take our suggestions." You're not here for that! You're here to make sure that the person lives as independently as he or she possibly can. And, you don't have to like the way a person might live his life, but that's his own unique way of living his life.

There's a lot of things that I saw in the institution that I didn't like about how people were being treated. I took it upon myself to put my life in risk to make change for people with disabilities. If you want to learn to listen better, take yourself out of your perspective as a service provider. Put yourself in a

If you want to learn to listen better, take yourself out of your perspective as a service provider. Put yourself in a disabled person's shoes, whether it's mental illness or whether it's a physical disability, and ask how would you like your life to be like.

disabled person's shoes, whether it's mental illness or whether it's a physical disability, and ask how would you like your life to be like. Would you like everybody making your decisions? And would you like somebody lying to your parents and saying that everything's okay when it's not?

I went into the institution in 1965. They came to my house and they told my mother, "Well, if you keep him at home, you're going to be holding him back—he's not going to be able to get the skills and the opportunities that another person will get." Well, my mother being a new parent with three other children besides myself, she tried to do all the services herself with my father. And, when we went to the system to try and get help, the system was nowhere around. So she tried to do the best she could; as a result, she ended up having a nervous breakdown and I ended up going into the service system.

I'm glad I did in some ways, but I'd never go through it again, because it was pure hell. It was pure hell. And those of you might be out there saying, "Oh, there he goes again, on his bandwagon." Well, until you lived it, you have nothing to really feel how I feel. Those people who are stuck in institutions now, who are stuck in our residential services, they

> *I still make mistakes. But that's okay—I feel good about that—because I'm a human being. I'm not a disability.*

need to be heard from too, but before they do, they need to have the system to help them figure out a way to communicate. And they need to know that they can gain your trust in keeping their concerns, wants, and needs in mind. It might cost a lot of money in the long run to put them in a community and to give them the supports that they need. But I tell you, it's much much cheaper than putting them in institutions and nursing homes.

Like I said, if you can fight a Gulf War and you can send men to the moon, then you can reach in on that money. And you know what? I think that the consumers ought to be the ones that are handling the money. I am serious. Because they know what their needs are. They like to take risks just like anybody else. We make mistakes, and I still make mistakes. But that's okay— I feel good about that—because I'm a human being. I'm not a disability. And other people with disabilities—we're tired of being a statistic. And we want to be treated like everyone else. And, if it takes my last breath in the world, I will go down making sure that as long as I'm alive, that people with disabilities will have the best opportunity as anyone else sitting in this room.

For years we had to fight to get the basic rights just to have the freedom of speech. Now, it goes much more beyond that. There are a lot of good people in this field, but the thing is, when they go to hear from people with disabilities, they hear you, but they don't hear you, because they want to take the easy way out. They don't want to get off their cushy chairs and they don't want to take risks, and they don't want to bend the rules. Well, rules are made to be broken. And I think people need to start doing that.

If they could give more people with disabilities the opportunity to figure out a way to pay for their own services with the help of Mary Kay and so on and so forth, you're gonna see that our communities will be more receptive to them. They will be, because they have no idea what a disabled person has to go through in his or her life. For years I've had people come up and tell me, "You know, Michael, the reason why we react the way we do towards people with disabilities is because when I was growing up, my mother and father told me never to associate with them because you're gonna catch a disease!" That's why people with disabilities and people without disabilities need to start working together. And, it can't be all just the people with the disabilities trying to educate them. People without disabilities need to have an open mind and they need to work together, and they can't be afraid all the time. If people without disabilities are afraid of us, can you imagine how we feel with that? No sir!

So, I think even though we've come a long way, I think we really need to go out on a limb or step out of our comfort zone and start working together and making changes happen for people with disabilities all the way around. And, I mean *really* working together. And you don't need to like the way we live our lives—all you need to do is assist.

4

Choice, Common Sense, and Responsibility: The System's Obligations to Recipients

Darby J. Penney

I'm going to speak, primarily, as a person who has used mental health services on and off for the last thirty years and, secondarily, as a bureaucrat. I want to pick up on two themes that Clarence Sundram raised in his opening remarks. One of them is common sense and the other one is responsibility.

All too often common sense has not been a part of the discussion about choice for people with psychiatric diagnoses. The discussion has often been based on myths and stereotypes, unquestioned assumptions, and mistaken judgments about what those of us with diagnoses are capable of doing.

Those of us who feel that choice is a right—not a privilege to be afforded for good behavior—make a mistake when we let people who would like to slow down the move toward choice frame the issues around hypothetical examples or extreme situations that might happen once every ten years.

> *All too often common sense has not been a part of the discussion about choice for people with psychiatric diagnoses.*

Because for most of us who have received services, or who have been in hospitals and institutions and community residences and day programs, the truth is that most of the interference with choice actually occurs in much more mundane, routine noncrisis kinds of matters. Things like when we eat, when we're allowed to use the telephone, who we can associate with, and what we do with our time. And, while those issues don't have the "glamour" of the high-risk situations we hear about, I really believe that that's where most of us have felt the most intruded upon and where the lack of choice has really been a burden to us over the years. So if we deal in a common-sense way with choice in day-to-day situations, and we see that often staff don't *want* us to exercise choice, we have to wonder, how much of it is for staff's convenience? And, how often is it framed in those words that I think most of us have come to dread: "for your own good," or "in your own best interest"? And, how do professionals *know* what *our* best interests are? As Michael Kennedy pointed out earlier, *we* know that on a daily basis, in a gut way, that professionals who deal with dozens of clients don't.

Michael made a very good point when he noted that if those of us who receive services appear to lack good judgment at times, we really need to examine how much of that is due to the negative effects of learned helplessness and institutionalization, and how much of it may be due to a temporary or long-term extreme mental or emotional state.

Nonlabeled people get to exercise their judgment and, believe me, plenty of nonlabeled people make really dumb decisions every day and nobody—nobody—tries to move in.

There hasn't really been much research in that area, but most of us who have been in the system know that after a long time of other people making your choices for you, making you dependent, and not allowing you to make choices, your decision-making skills atrophy. And then staff say we're not competent to make choices—it's almost a matter of blaming the victim. The system has created groups of people who have had their volition taken away from them, who haven't been able to exercise their choices and who, therefore, may have forgotten how to do it. And all of a sudden the system turns around to them and says, "Okay, we've decided you're empowered, now go make choices." The system needs to take responsibility for how it has disempowered people, and help them get the supports they need to relearn those skills.

Nonlabeled people get to exercise their judgment and, believe me, plenty of nonlabeled people make really dumb decisions every day and nobody—nobody—tries to move in and say, "We're going to put you under house arrest because you went out and spent your money on a Jaguar instead of a Volkswagen."

People in the consumer/survivor/expatient movement often say that the mental health system treats us like children. But, frankly, I think that's an overgenerous assessment. If you think about good parenting, parents want children to grow up to become independent, to be able to make their own decisions. For most of us, the system hasn't done that. It has, in fact, not given us the opportunity to develop those skills or to keep practicing them if we already knew them, but instead has often taken that right away from us and, therefore, not prepared us the way a parent would prepare a child to go out in the world and be an adult.

This brings me to the theme of responsibility. I'd like to talk about the responsibility of staff and the responsibility of the mental health system. I think the system needs to seriously consider its responsibility in creating feelings of dependency and learned helplessness that interfere with people's abilities to make choices. The system not only has a responsibility *not* to continue to do that to new generations of people, but also to help and support the people who have been victims of that learned helplessness.

> *The system needs to seriously consider its responsibility in creating feelings of dependency and learned helplessness that interfere with people's abilities to make choices.*

Many of us who have used the system are more concerned about avoiding the negative effects of this system than we are in splitting hairs about what kind of services we want. One thing that we *do* want is protection and safety while we're in the system. It's ironic that a mental health system which has created institutional conditions that are often unsafe also sets itself up as the expert on what's a safe choice for recipients.

The Commission on Quality of Care recently released some studies on the effects of the use of restraint and seclusion, and one of the very troubling statistics in the report is that over a period of about ten years, over one hundred people have died in restraint and/or seclusion. If the mental health system paid as much attention to protection and safety in those kinds of circumstances as it does when it decides where we are allowed to live and if we are allowed to get a haircut, things would be a little more balanced.

> *It's ironic that a mental health system which has created institutional conditions that are often unsafe also sets itself up as the expert on what's a safe choice for recipients.*

Both professionals and recipients are trapped in a system that gives professionals too much responsibility and requires them to be accountable for too much. Professionals are often as unhappy about that situation as we are. A lot of times professionals don't know what to do; they can't guarantee success, yet they feel that society has placed them in a position where that's required of them.

Mental health professionals have a responsibility to examine how the situation was created and what their own responsibility in creating it was. How might we all pull ourselves out of this dilemma? I know that many professionals feel very burdened by this.

I had a discussion the other day at a conference with a psychiatrist. We were talking about my expectations the first time I voluntarily went to a psychiatric emergency room. He asked, "What did I expect to happen?" I said, "Well, I guess I naively expected somebody to do something or say something that would make me feel like I didn't need to kill myself." And he sort of recoiled from that and said, "It's not fair to expect that of us." He said, "It's not my responsibility to save your life." And I said, "Well your system has set up the expectation that that's where I go if I'm in that state. So, if you're not capable of doing that, your profession needs to rethink what you can offer me and what you can't offer me." He was very open to the idea that it's time to sit down and do that. In fact, he said it scares him to death when someone comes to him and says, "I want to kill myself," because he doesn't know what to do. And he would like to get away from that burden as much as I would like to get away from the burden of having someone lock me up if I say those words.

Both professionals and recipients are trapped in a system that gives professionals too much responsibility and requires them to be accountable for too much.

Choice is an integral part of the healing process. It's not just something that we can tack on to treatment when we feel it's convenient.

Finally, I want to talk about the idea that Ed Knight, who is the director of the Recipient Empowerment Project, calls the "healing power of choice." It is his contention that choice isn't just an add-on. That, in fact, if you talk to people who have recovered—whether we're talking about recovery from trauma, recovery from an extreme mental or emotional state, or recovery from learned helplessness and institutionalization—people who have recovered are people who have made choices on their own. Choice is an integral part of the healing process. It's not just something that we can tack on to treatment when we feel it's convenient. If choice isn't available, then healing cannot occur.

5

Empower Families, Too

Phyllis Gerber

I am a retired school teacher and have been involved as a family member and a family advocate for almost 20 years. I was a founding member of New York City's Friends and Advocates for the Mentally Ill and later of Sullivan County's Friends and Advocates for Mental Health, both affiliates of the Alliance for the Mentally Ill of New York State (AMI-NYS). I was a member of the early steering committee for AMI-NYS and have served on the AMI-NYS Board of Directors as vice-president and as president of AMI-NYS.

In those years, I have seen the system shift from an exclusionary mode regarding families, to a more accepting mode. I have seen the concept of confidentiality as used against involvement of families with their ill relatives' treatment brushed aside. I have seen the issue of choice for the recipient become, at least in theory, a part of the philosophical basis for treatment and for services. But the issues of choice have not been refined sufficiently, and the issue of professional responsibility

We want our relatives to be in a position to choose treatment, to have at least some control over the shape that treatment will take.

has not been extended to include accountability. In that regard, the Commission on Quality of Care has highlighted a very timely conference theme.

Choice for the recipient must go far beyond *choose* or *refuse*, that is, accept what is prescribed or recommended or refuse to accept it. In too many cases the *right to refuse* has been an escape clause for professionals or providers to shrug off responsibility.

Families have said: We don't want our relatives to die, figuratively, with their rights on. We want them to be treated, even if their impaired insight or impaired judgement causes them to refuse. But also, people refuse treatment because they want to be in control of their own lives. We want them to have every opportunity to be treated, *and* we want them to have control of their lives, both. This year the National Alliance for the Mentally Ill has adopted the phrase

"Treatment Works" for mental illness awareness week in the fall. Treatment does work. We want our relatives to be in a position to choose treatment, to have at least some control over the shape that treatment will take. They must participate in the development of choices. However, when individuals reject treatment because they are too impaired to make a rational choice, that choice must be made by others. Involuntary treatment must continue to be an option available for psychiatrists and for families to initiate. The definition for involuntary treatment should be *gravely disabled, period*. Families have not been fully permitted the role which physically incapacitated relatives' families have—that is, NEXT OF KIN can authorize life-saving psychiatric treatment. (To lose one's ability to tell reality from fantasy or to think rationally is indeed a loss of the ability to live in the real world.) Families need to have that right. Dangerousness ought not to be the criterion for involuntary hospitalization—grave disability should.

A stabilized, informed, and empowered consumer, participating fully and respected as a person first and foremost, has the best chance for recovery.

Now, back to the question of who's in charge. The recipient/consumer ultimately is the one in charge. You can't force recovery on people, although you can and should begin that process involuntarily, if necessary. One must want to get better and must become actively involved in the recovery process. A stabilized, informed, and empowered consumer, participating fully and respected as a person first and foremost, has the best chance for recovery. This is what recovered consumers have told us, and we must believe them. It is so common that so-called "noncompliant" recipients fall back again and again. Don't ask for compliance any longer. Ask for recipients to tell us what is relevant for them and what helps them. They must be empowered to take charge in choosing elements of treatment which enrich and enable them, and the rest of us must be facilitators as they themselves work toward recovery.

When choices are to be made, the families' opinions and perceptions, based on long-term knowledge, can be invaluable.

Families can be so important, both to the ill or recovered relatives, and to the professionals and other providers. When choices are to be made, the families' opinions and perceptions, based on long-term knowledge, can be invaluable. The support and advocacy which families can provide, the historical perspective, and the family ingredient (as we call it), should be sought, included, and given significant weight. When there is a relapse, families may be the first to notice; when there is a crisis, families should be believed and empowered to act. They too must be, at times, in charge.

The professionals, however, are in charge in terms of engaging, evaluating, prescribing, determining treatment modalities, and providing treatment. While these are their responsibilities, they also must accept responsibility for getting and keeping the consumers and the family partners in the process. The planning and developing, together, of realistic options from which consumer choices can be made is crucial, and not all of this is programmatic—it is humanistic and involves mainstream resources, as well as mental health resources.

Too often psychiatrists or therapists maintain an ivory tower philosophy, resulting in their being the last ones to know when things go wrong and then, I'm sorry to say, jump ship.

Staff in residential and community program settings must be used as a valuable resource. Sharing of all kinds of information will contribute towards the implementation of choices which have been made and the evaluation of whether they are working. Too often psychiatrists or therapists maintain an ivory tower philosophy, resulting in their being the last ones to know when things go wrong and then, I'm sorry to say, jump ship.

Finally, the ability of professionals, providers, families, and recipients to take charge cooperatively and with respect for each other, with as much information regarding the illness and the disabilities resulting therefrom, as well as the person's *talents and strengths and preferences*, may well determine the quality of life and the quality of treatment which will occur.

6

Protecting the Rights, the Person, and the Public: A Biological Basis for Responsible Action

E. Fuller Torrey, M.D.

One of the most clearly established functions of government is to protect and provide care for individuals who are physically or mentally disabled. The protection of mentally disabled individuals became incorporated as official policy in the United States in 1766 when Governor Francis Fauquier went before the Virginia House of Burgesses and requested funds to open a public psychiatric hospital. That hospital was utilized by individuals with all three major forms of mental disability: dementia, mental retardation, and serious mental illness.

Dementia is caused by brain diseases which impair cognitive functions and which are usually progressive; Alzheimer's disease is an example. Mental retardation may be caused by chromosomes, genes, birth injuries, infectious agents, metabolic defects, or other brain conditions which impair cognitive functions, usually during pregnancy or early in childhood. Serious mental illness, a category comprised primarily of schizophrenia and manic-depressive illness, is suspected of being caused by many of the same things which cause mental retardation, but differs in having an onset in early adulthood and in having a brain dysfunction predominantly of integrative functions of the limbic system.

It is now possible to measure abnormalities in brain structure and function on all three forms of mental disability: dementia, mental retardation, and serious mental illness. In schizophrenia, for example, one of the most commonly observed structural abnormalities is mild to moderate dilatation of the lateral and third ventricles on CT or MRI scans, which has been reported in over 100 controlled studies (Hyde et al., 1991). When patients who had never received medication were included in these studies, the results were the same, thereby proving that the dilatation is not a medication effect. Another structural

It is now clear, therefore, that schizophrenia and manic-depressive illness are brain diseases in exactly the same way that multiple sclerosis, Parkinson's disease, and Alzheimer's disease are brain diseases.

abnormality which is commonly found in schizophrenia is a moderately decreased size of the hippocampus and amygdala structures which are part of the limbic system. In one recently completed study of identical twins in which one has schizophrenia and the other is well, it was possible to identify correctly the twin with schizophrenia 80 percent of the time on the basis of hippocampus-amygdala size alone (Torrey et al., 1994). Changes in brain function are equally well established in schizophrenia, including metabolic function (e.g., as measured by PET scans), neuropsychological function (e.g., problem solving, abstract thinking), and neurological function (e.g., "soft" neurological signs); abnormalities in the last, for example, have been demonstrated in 25 separate studies, some of which included patients who had never been medicated.

It is now clear, therefore, that schizophrenia and manic-depressive illness are brain diseases in exactly the same way that multiple sclerosis, Parkinson's disease, and Alzheimer's disease are brain diseases. And it is our failure to fully realize and acknowledge this fact which has led to much confusion regarding choice and responsibility. For example, when Ms. Jones with Alzheimer's disease wants to take a walk in the snow without putting on shoes and socks, we do not let her do so because we recognize that her reasoning is impaired. Most of us have no difficulty in making such a decision for Ms. Jones and, in fact, we feel that we have a responsibility to do so. However, when a person with schizophrenia wants to do something equally absurd, many mental health professionals have great difficulty in saying that the person cannot do so and in making a more reasoned decision for the person. We invoke principles such as patients' rights, personal autonomy, and the right to lead an alternate lifestyle for the person with schizophrenia. However, we almost never invoke these same principles for Ms. Jones with Alzheimer's disease because they

The brain changes which accompany schizophrenia and manic-depressive illness produce two important deficits: impaired logic and impaired insight.

would appear absurd. They are often equally absurd for individuals with schizophrenia.

Impaired Logic and Insight

The brain changes which accompany schizophrenia and manic-depressive illness produce two important deficits: impaired logic and impaired insight. Impaired logic is one of the hallmarks of schizophrenia and is the basis for much delusional thinking, e.g., an individual who glances at you on the street is therefore thought to be a KGB agent sent to kill you. Impaired insight is the inability to realize that something is wrong with you. Two recent studies have attempted to measure insight in individuals with psychosis. In one of these, carried out by Dr. Anthony David and colleagues in London, 47 percent of inpatients with

It was reported "that nearly 60 percent of the patients with schizophrenia had moderate to severe unawareness of having a mental disorder."

schizophrenia and manic-depressive illness scored between 0 and 8 on an 18-point measure of insight (David et al., 1992). In the other study, done by Drs. Amador and Strauss in New York, it was reported "that nearly 60 percent of the patients with schizophrenia had moderate to severe unawareness of having a mental disorder" (Amador & Strauss, in press). There is also some evidence suggesting that impaired insight in schizophrenia is due to the disease process affecting frontal lobe function (Young et al., 1993).

Although both logic and insight are impaired in a significant percentage of individuals who have schizophrenia and manic-depressive illness, there are three complicating aspects to this impairment. First, most individuals will have *some* logic and *some* insight so that it is not an all-or-none phenomenon. Second, although logic and insight may be severely impaired, other aspects of brain function such as memory may be intact, thereby giving an impression of normalcy. And third, impairment of logic and insight may fluctuate over time even without medication, and may fluctuate widely when on and off medication. These fluctuations produce much confusion among mental health professionals when trying to sort out issues of choice and responsibility.

Some Proposed Principles

Recognizing that schizophrenia and manic-depressive illness have a biological basis equally as much as do dementia and mental retardation leads to some logical principles. These principles can be used to solve problems of choice and responsibility such as those posed in this conference. These principles include:

1. **Assess the person's logic and insight:** There are many neuropsychological tests for logic which can be done as part of a mental status exam. There are now also tests for insight which are easy to administer (Amador et al., 1993). These will establish a baseline against which the person's behavior can be judged. To use one example cited in the conference material, the person may well wish to go bungee jumping, but if they wish to try it without the cord, then you can be sure that their logic is impaired.

2. **Assess the person's underlying personality:** Brain diseases are equal opportunity diseases and affect all personality types. Our study of identical twins in which one was affected with schizophrenia or manic-depressive illness and the other was well, showed clearly that a person's underlying personality is minimally affected by the brain disease itself (Torrey et al., 1994). Thus when a person who is mentally disabled continues to smoke despite lung disease, or shoplifts, or is promiscuous, you should ask yourself whether or not the person would be doing the same thing if he/she had never gotten sick. For example, my sister, who has schizophrenia, has great difficulty managing her finances. She also had great difficulty managing her finances before she developed schizophrenia. And my mother and my other sister, neither of whom had schizophrenia, also had difficulty managing finances.

Do not blame all behavior on the mental disability. Some of it may just be the person's underlying personality.

There are two possible means of assessing a person's underlying personality to determine its relative role in causing troublesome behavior. One means is the use of formal personality tests such as the Minnesota Multiphasic Personality Inventory (MMPI) which can tell you, for example, whether the person is inherently a risk-taker (and thus would be likely to have gone bungee jumping) or inherently has sociopathic traits (and thus would be likely to have shoplifted). Using such personality tests may shed considerable light on whether the person's behavior is predominantly a product of his/her mental disability or of his/her underlying personality. The other means of assessing underlying personality is by knowing the person over a long period of time. This is feasible in treatment programs in which one professional or a team of mental illness professionals has responsibility for the same patients continuously for many years.

The most highly praised and effective example of this is the PACT model of continuous treatment teams originated in Madison, Wisconsin, and now found in many other states. In such situations where the team professionals have known the patients on

It is important to ask yourself whether the decision you are urging on a mentally disabled person is the person's wish or merely your *wish.*

their team for many years, the assessment of underlying personality versus effects of mental disability are much less problematic.

In summary, do not blame all behavior on the mental disability. Some of it may just be the person's underlying personality. This principle is especially helpful in assessing problems of sexual behavior.

3. **Assess your own philosophy:** Mental health professionals are notoriously liberal in their political beliefs and feelings about human rights. For that reason it is important to ask yourself whether the decision you are urging on a mentally disabled person is the person's wish or merely *your* wish. We are skilled at rationalizing one for the other. For example, when we defend a person's right to refuse medication which he/she needs to function in the community, are we really acting in the *person's* best interest or merely our own?

4. **Apply the Alzheimer's test:** When confronted with an ethical dilemma for a person with a mental disability, use Ms. Jones' Alzheimer's disease as a test case. For example, problems of confidentiality for individuals with schizophrenia should be assessed by comparing the options with what you would recommend for Ms. Jones. This will solve a surprising number of problems very quickly.

5. **Apply the ask-your-grandmother test:** Grandmothers represent common sense, a commodity which is in surprisingly short supply among many mental health professionals and lawyers. For example, when confronted with the problem of whether to tell one mentally disabled person that another mentally disabled person who is trying to seduce him/her is HIV positive and boasts of having unprotected sex, 99.9 percent of all grandmothers will say that you should of course tell

him/her. Only mental health professionals and lawyers have difficulty with such problems. [Many state laws do not incorporate this "grand-mother test" and specifically prohibit disclosure of a patient's HIV status. It is advisable to check the law in your state. Ed.]

6. **Remember that we have an obligation to not only protect a person's rights, but also to protect the person and the public as well:** "Rights" should not be reified as the *summum bonum*; they are simply an abstraction when removed from a human context. If the person or the public is at danger because of the person's mental disability, then we are obligated to utilize involuntary hospitalization, involuntary medication (including Norplant implants), conditional release, guardian-ship, outpatient commitment, assigned payeeship, and what-ever other mechanism is legally available and appropriate to protect the person and the public. Our failure to do so has resulted in an extraordinary number of self-mutilations, injuries to others, suicides, and homicides. For example, in a New York City study of individuals who push random people onto subway tracks in front of trains, it was reported that 19 out of 31 of the individuals doing the pushing were actively psychotic at the time (Martell & Dietz, 1992). It has been estimated that "the rate of children born to psychotic women has tripled since deinstitutionalization first began" (Seeman et al., 1990). And a study of women with chronic psychosis found that only one-third of the 75 children they had borne were being reared by the mothers (Coverdale et al., 1992). A 1992 study in a New York psychiatric hospital reported that 3.4 percent of all admissions diag-nosed with schizophrenia were HIV positive (Sacks et al., 1992). We are responsible for these failures, many of which have come from our propensity to reify the person's rights without considering the personal consequences for either himself/herself or others.

> We *are responsible for these failures, many of which have come from our propensity to reify the person's rights without considering the personal consequences for either himself/herself or others.*

7. **Recognize the need for asylums:** Most individuals with mental disabilities *can* live in the community *if* adequate outpatient services are provided. *However a small number cannot.* We must learn to

accept the fact that some of our community placements are failures because of some combination of mental disability and underlying personality. Such individuals should be returned to long-term inpatient facilities, asylums which protect both the individual and the public. Until we completely understand the causes and have definitive treatments for all mental disabilities, there will continue to be the need for a few asylums. Wishing it was otherwise will not change that reality.

References

Amador, X. F., & Strauss, D. H. (in press). Poor insight in schizophrenia. *Psychiatric Quarterly.*

Amador, X. F., Strauss, D. H., Yale, S. A., Flaum, M. M., Endicott, J., & Gorman, J. M. (1993). Assessment of insight in psychosis. *American Journal of Psychiatry, 159,* 873–79.

Coverdale, J., Aruffo, J., & Grunebaum, H. (1992). Developing family planning services for female chronic mentally ill outpatients. *Hospital and Community Psychiatry, 43,* 375–77.

David, A., Buchanan, A., Reed, A., & Almeida, O. (1992). The assessment of insight in psychosis. *British Journal of Psychiatry, 161,* 599–602.

Hyde, T. M., Casanova, M. F., Kleinman, J. E., & Weinberger, D. R. (1991). Neuroanatomical and neurochemical pathology in schizophrenia. In A. Tasman & S. M. Goldfinger (Eds.), *Review of Psychiatry* (Vol. 10). Washington: APA Press.

Martell, D. A., & Dietz, P. E. (1992). Mentally disordered offenders who push or attempt to push victims onto subway tracks in New York City. *Archives of General Psychiatry, 49,* 472–75.

Sacks, M., Dermatis, H., Looser-Ott, S., & Perry, S. (1992). Seroprevalence of HIV and risk factors for AIDS in psychiatric inpatients. *Hospital and Community Psychiatry, 43,* 736–37.

Seeman, M. V., Lang, M., & Rector, N. (1990). Chronic schizophrenia: A risk factor for HIV? *Canadian Journal of Psychiatry, 35,* 765–68.

Torrey, E. F., Bowler, A. E., Taylor, E. H., & Gottesman, I. I. (1994). *Schizophrenia and manic-depressive disorder.* New York: Basic Books.

Young, D. A., Davila, R., & Scher, H. (1993). Unawareness of illness and neuropsychological performance in chronic schizophrenia. *Schizophrenia Research, 10,* 117–24.

7

The Right to Be Wrong

Judi Chamberlin

I cannot speak from direct experience about the experiences of people labeled mentally retarded. But, as a person who has been diagnosed with what is called "severe mental illness" (a medical label which I do not accept as having anything meaningful to say about my life experiences), and as someone who chooses to deal with my periodic deep, suicidal depressions without psychiatric interventions, voluntary or involuntary, I believe that my views about choice and voluntariness are applicable to all people deemed incompetent by psychiatrists. Further, I think that any person, regardless of label (or unlabeled) who can express his or her own wishes and desires, no matter how irrational they may appear to others, deserves to have those wishes respected. People who are genuinely incapable of such expression probably fall beyond the scope of my argument. By genuinely incapable, I mean people who are comatose or otherwise unable to communicate, and I specifically exclude people who are clearly communicating what others may not want to hear.

Involuntary commitment, forced treatment, and psychiatric control over decision-making are really not complicated issues, despite the efforts to make them seem so. The fundamental question is this: Why do we take one group of people, those labeled "mentally disabled," and deny them the basic rights all other American citizens take for granted? We hear talk about "special needs," "vulnerabilities," "at-risk populations," and lots of other

Why do we take one group of people, those labeled "mentally disabled," and deny them the basic rights all other American citizens take for granted?

terms designed to obscure this fundamental question: Is it ethically justifiable to confine people against their will, to subject them to procedures against their will, or to overrule their life choices on the basis of an ostensibly medical diagnosis? I believe that until we frame this question properly, as a human rights question, we will continue to make the simple complicated.

Supposedly, we live in a society ruled by law. Just because we "know" someone is likely to commit a crime, we cannot put that person in jail. The reasons why we "know" that someone is a likely criminal often have to do with that person's membership in a class of people. The overwhelming amount of violent crime in this society, for example, is committed by young, urban, economically deprived males. At the same time, the majority of the members of this group do not commit crimes. Locking up someone just because he is a young, urban, poor male, in order to prevent crime, therefore, would be a vast injustice to the individual, and to society.

Let us look at the mental health system in the same way. We "know" that certain individuals are vulnerable to "mental illness." We also "know" that psychiatric interventions are what they "need." Is it justifiable, therefore, to ignore their expressed wishes and proceed on the basis of the superior wisdom of those who have the power to make the definitions and enforce the consequences? I believe that this, too, is a basic injustice.

If we are truly concerned with protecting people we may deem to be incompetent, surely we must zealously protect their right to pursue happiness as well as their right to be safe.

According to psychiatrists, most people at some point show some "symptoms" of "mental illness," and large numbers of people are seriously "ill," yet most of them manage quite well without psychiatric interventions. Most psychiatrists seem to think that a little psychiatry would be good for everyone, and that not knowing that you are "ill" is one of the "symptoms" of the "illness," and so people need to be coerced. But this is not the way things are supposed to work in a free society.

The ethical system (if I can call it that) that drives the involuntary treatment system is paternalism, the idea that one group (the one in power, not oddly) "knows" what is best for another group (which lacks power). The history of our civilization is, in part, the struggle against paternalism and for self-determination. People in power are always saying that they know what is best for those they rule over, even if those poor unfortunate individuals think they know best what they want. The powerful seldom cast their own motives in anything but benevolent terms. Rulers and slavemasters like to think (or to pretend) that their minions love them and are grateful to them, often having to ignore much evidence to the contrary. The struggle for freedom has always been seen by the powerful as a denial of the obvious truth of the superiority of the rulers.

The Declaration of Independence speaks of "life, liberty, and the pursuit of happiness," meaning that we all, as citizens, have the right—the inalienable right—to follow our own dreams. Among the most basic happinesses people seek are good and comfortable places to live, choice in daily activities, and satisfying companions for friendship and love. As the irrational, fallible human beings we are, our lives are an endless series of steps and missteps in pursuit of those dreams. Those who would over-rule, on the basis of "incompetence," the dreams of others, are usually concerned with safety issues, with little regard to happiness. If we are truly concerned with protecting people we may deem to be incompetent, surely we must zealously protect their right to pursue happiness as well as their right to be safe. Otherwise, we are prescribing one standard for so-called normals, which allows (and even celebrates) the primacy of the pursuit of happiness, and another, more sober and more severe standard, for those for whom we presume to decide their "best interest."

The primary issue is simply this: Who should define the needs and aspirations of a group, the members of that group, or those who claim superiority over them?

I think there are major parallels between the civil rights movement and the psychiatric survivor movement. Similarly, I think the same major parallels exist between the women's movement and the psychiatric survivor movement. In both instances, the primary issue is simply this: Who should define the needs and aspirations of a group—the members of that group, or those who claim superiority over them? The arguments that have been used, historically, to defend slavery and segregation have been the same as those used to deny women basic societal rights, such as the right to vote, own property, or control their own sexual and reproductive lives. And although there are still major disadvantages faced by ethnic minorities and women in our society, the principles of racial and sexual equality have become part of the ethical underpinnings of society.

But we are still in an era when people deemed mentally disabled are denied their basic rights to self-determination, on the basis that they are incapable of knowing their best interests or acting on them. The same paternalistic arguments are trotted out once again: special vulnerability, lack of intellectual capacity, a history of foolish actions, a demonstrated inability to care for oneself. Now they are clothed in the language of science, with diagnostic terms carrying supposedly moral weight.

This historic confusion of medicine and power skews our language and our thinking. We hear arguments for the "medical model"; that so-called "mental illness" is an illness like any other. If psychiatrists want to be like other doctors, I believe they should do as other doctors do—wait for patients to come to them, and treat those patients as free agents.

Historically, women, children, the insane, and petty criminals all were subjected to arbitrary control by those who supposedly knew what was best for them. Confinement and control were exercised for the protection of society, and institutions like poorhouses and workhouses were developed to keep such people out of mainstream society where, supposedly, they would victimize others or become victims themselves. Eighteenth-century "madhouses," nineteenth-century "insane asylums," and twentieth-century "psychiatric hospitals" are all derived from these roots. Now society claims that confinement in a psychiatric "hospital" is medical treatment, analogous to the medical treatment of physical illnesses, ignoring the very different historical roots and the very different ethical position of the two kinds of "patients."

Why do we deny the uninsured person who wants cancer surgery, for example, access to this treatment, while forcing treatment on a person diagnosed mentally ill?

No one wants to be ill. No one "chooses" to get cancer, or heart disease, or diabetes. But a person with one of these illnesses remains a free moral agent, who can choose to seek medical treatment, to enter a hospital, to undergo surgery or other medical procedures, or, equally important, can choose not to do so. The fact that a person has cancer (a real illness) does not give us, as a society, the right to lock that person up and treat him or her if that person's choice is to go to a faith-healer, or to ignore the situation. In fact, many people in this situation who want treatment can't get it because they don't have the money or the insurance coverage to pay for it.

Contrast the situation of the person who is diagnosed as "mentally ill" (a theoretical illness). Typically, the "illness" consists of behavior that the person may or may not find distressing, but which is distressing to people around him or her. This individual is not free to choose treatment or to reject it. This individual, too, may lack money or insurance coverage, but this does not serve as a barrier to subjecting the person to unwanted interventions. Clearly, something very different is going on here, despite the rhetoric of "illness" and "treatment." If it were really the same thing, why do we deny the uninsured person who wants cancer surgery, for example, access to this treatment, while forcing treatment on a person diagnosed mentally ill? It is public safety and social control that are the real reasons that mental patients are subjected to involuntary interventions while medical patients are not.

Supposedly, the difference is "competence." We allow people we deem competent to make irrational or wrong decisions, while assuming a paternalistic stance toward so-called "incompetents," to protect them from their own shortcomings. But I believe that competence, like beauty, lies very much in the eye of the beholder. Take, for example, teenagers who choose to smoke cigarettes. Almost by definition, teenagers are unable to judge long-term consequences, or to see themselves as old, and so many discount antismoking education that focuses on

> *It is public safety and social control that are the real reasons that mental patients are subjected to involuntary interventions while medical patients are not.*

the development of disease twenty or thirty years down the line. Are these teenagers incompetent, or are they simply showing some very human traits, putting current gratification above future considerations? I believe that in most so-called incompetent decision-making, this same process is at work, viewed through the lens, however, of a person's label. If you are considered normal, you have the right to be wrong.

Therefore, whether or not there is an underlying genetic or biochemical cause of "mental illness" is irrelevant. Despite all the research and all the theorizing, the schizophrenia gene or the schizophrenia germ has never been demonstrated. I believe that it never will; we can no more find the "cause" of complex human behavior in brain chemistry than we can find the "cause" of poetry. But even if they were real, biological diseases, psychiatrists wouldn't therefore derive the power to lock people up and treat them against their will, or to overrule their personal life decisions. These are legal, and ultimately moral decisions, not medical ones.

What, then, is the best way to help people who are confused, who are behaving in nonordinary ways, who seem to be out of contact with the ordinary world and society's expectations? This is another point where discussion usually gets muddled; opponents of involuntary psychiatric interventions are supposed to propose "alternatives," as if a better way to deal with these problems was the solution to the problem. It's like asking what the alternative is to slavery. Are opponents of slavery supposed to suggest "better" ways of "dealing with" a troublesome population? The ethical position toward slavery is to see it as a moral wrong, and freedom not as a "treatment" or an "alternative," but as a moral imperative. Similarly, the "alternative" to psychiatric domination is also freedom. Freedom does not mean that the problems of the former slave, or the former patient, disappear, but it does mean that the power over the individual that was formerly held by the slavemaster or the psychiatrist does disappear. Only then can people approach one another as equals, face difficulties, and search for solutions.

Defining a person's difficulties as psychiatric is a rejection of the reality of people's experiences. Psychiatric diagnosis is, in part, a process of de-contextualization, of denying the real meaning that supposedly dysfunctional behavior has to the individual. A person may behave in ways that other people can't understand, but ways which have meaning and value for that person in the context of his/her life. Turning behavior, thoughts, and feelings into "symptoms" actually gets in the way of understanding and helping. What is really helpful is contextualization, helping the person to understand that thoughts, feelings, and emotions do have meaning within the context of that person's own life and experiences. Unlike involuntary psychiatric treatment, this kind of real, individualized help is impossible without the active participation of the individual being helped.

Freedom does not mean that the problems of the former slave, or the former patient, disappear, but it does mean that the power over the individual that was formerly held by the slavemaster or the psychiatrist does disappear.

However, I am not going to talk today at any length about the self-help alternatives that have been developed by the psychiatric survivor movement as a way of helping people to deal with the pain that is often a significant part of life. That is another topic for another time. It is not the job of the psychiatric survivor movement to solve social problems that have led to the present unjust system. Instead, it is our job to serve as the moral focus of this debate, to represent the powerless in our struggle for fundamental justice. It is clear that we cannot leave our fate in the hands of lawyers, judges, and psychiatrists, who seem quite willing to sacrifice our freedom in the name of benevolent paternalism.

I want to say a few words about the Constitution, which I believe will eventually be interpreted to encompass the full citizenship of people labeled mentally disabled, and of others judged incapable of determining their own best interests. Let us not forget that the Constitution was written to define slaves as three-fifths of human beings, nor that the Supreme Court before the Civil War ruled that slaves were property that their masters had the right to pursue and that agents of the law were bound to turn over to their rightful owners. Let us not forget that fifty years later, after slavery was ended and the constitution amended, the Supreme Court ruled that segregation was constitutionally permissible, continuing to deny the basic equality of African-American citizens. It was not until 1954 that the Supreme Court finally ruled in favor of racial equality and equal rights for ethnic minorities. And it was not until the civil rights movement of the '50s and '60s that fundamental changes began to happen in race relations, because black people fought, and struggled, and died for their rights. Let us not forget, as well, that women were originally left out of the Constitution entirely. As our ideas of social justice have changed, the Constitution changes, too.

Our struggle is being fought...by many brave people who want...the chance to live our potentials, to take chances, to succeed, to fail, to try, to have opportunities, to make mistakes, to achieve, to change our minds, to be foolish, to pursue our dreams.

Psychiatric survivors, also, are fighting for our rights. We cannot wait for the lawyers and judges to decide when or if we are "ready" for freedom. Wanting to be free is not a delusion.

For all the people confined in psychiatric institutions against their will, for all the people confined in group homes and congregate living facilities, for all the people confined by the internal walls of forced drugging, for all the people confined by the lost memories and broken brains of electroshock, I say: "We will not wait!" Our struggle is being fought today, on many fronts, by many brave people, who want nothing more than the chance to live our potentials, to take chances, to succeed, to fail, to try, to have opportunities, to make mistakes, to achieve, to change our minds, to be foolish, to pursue our dreams.

Freedom is full of the risks and promises that are the essence of life itself. It is our goal; it is our right. It comes down to three fundamental questions: Will you stand with the forces of paternalism or the forces of freedom; will you honor our struggle; whose side are you on?

8

Reflections on Freedom, Abandonment, and Deinstitutionalization

Leonard S. Rubenstein

Deinstitutionalization has become synonymous not only with changes in mental health treatment over the past thirty-five years, but also with failed, even embarrassing social policy. This belief in its failure has become so powerful that one scholar recently wrote of an emerging consensus "that identifies deinstitutionalization as one of the era's most stunning public policy failures."[1] Deinstitutionalization has spawned shorter, even uglier words—"dumping" comes to mind—and is associated with homelessness, social disintegration, neighborhood deterioration, and violence. It has become fodder not only for dozens of books and articles, but exposés by the popular press that can always be inserted on a slow news day.

Deinstitutionalization has even become a metaphor for misbegotten social policy. In an editorial cartoon recently, one fellow says to another, "They're talking about welfare reform." The other responds, "Does that mean we'll be taking care of that guy lying in the gutter?" "No," the first responds, "we took care of him when we did mental health reform."

> *The sense that deinstitutionalization represents abandonment—even if it also represents freedom—has come to be the accepted starting point of any discussion of the subject.*

The sense of failure has been so pervasive that it even appears in the title of this session: "Deinstitutionalization: Appropriate Freedom or Irresponsible Abandonment?" The title seems to incorporate the view that deinstitutionalization has left people, literally, out in the cold. Our task is only to put a label on that result, as freedom or abandonment. To the institutional romantics who talk about asylums rather than snakepits, deinstitutionalization repre-

We cannot help but witness so many people with psychiatric disabilities relegated to the most marginal housing and grappling with lives of poverty and deprivation, as well as disability.

sents, at a minimum, the loss of the nonmedical functions of institutions, e.g., providing food, clothing, shelter, and protection from a hostile society. But the sense that deinstitutionalization represents abandonment—even if it also represents freedom—has come to be the accepted starting point of any discussion of the subject.

This common way of looking at deinstitutionalization is premised on society's inability to develop the infrastructure of community-based support services and housing responsive to the needs of the many people with serious psychiatric disabilities. We cannot help but witness so many people with psychiatric disabilities relegated to the most marginal housing and grappling with lives of poverty and deprivation, as well as disability. They are all too often denied access to services altogether or subjected to interventions not responsive to their needs. Government and privately operated services are fragmented, each with eligibility rules and application processes more byzantine than the next. Even people's liberty in a highly controlled board and care home may be scarcely greater than in a hospital ward.

This picture, if accurate, remains incomplete. The concept of abandonment fails to take into account the fact that deinstitutionalization represents a profound change in the way society responds to people with psychiatric disabilities. The process of deinstitutionalization required a fundamental alteration in the way society views and treats people with psychiatric disabilities and demanded creation of a system of social and support services in the community of a kind that never before existed for any group of people. I contend that it was the lack of appreciation of the very ambitiousness and profound change

Deinstitutionalization has given birth to a concept of freedom for people with psychiatric disabilities that transcends the liberty to be out of locked facilities.

required by this social policy that led both to unrealistic expectations for success and the deep sense of failure when the transformation required by deinstitutionalization did not materialize. At the same time, in the midst of this perceived failure, deinstitutionalization has given birth to a concept of freedom for people with psychiatric disabilities that transcends the liberty to be out of locked facilities.

I.

There have been many theories to explain how the conceptualization, planning, and implementation of deinstitutionalization were deeply, even maliciously flawed. The "naive psychiatrist" theory emphasizes how the enormous, misplaced hopes for antipsychotic medications, combined with overoptimism about the role community mental health centers would play in serving deinstitutionalized people, led to absurd expectations, soon to be dashed by programs more devoted to serving neurotic families than people with schizophrenia. The "finan-

The "lawyer conspiracy" argument blames reformist lawyers, motivated, we're told, by antipsychiatry and libertarian ideologies, and backed by imperial judges enamored of social engineering.

cial shell game" theory holds that states used federal Supplemental Security Income benefits as a way to transfer financial responsibility for people with serious mental illness to the federal government by removing them from state-funded institutions. The "lawyer conspiracy" argument blames reformist lawyers, motivated, we're told, by antipsychiatry and libertarian ideologies, and backed by imperial judges enamored of social engineering. Yet a fourth theory, "vanishing SROs," blames the failures of deinstitutionalization on social policies that destroyed the nation's housing infrastructure, particularly the stock of single room occupancy units necessary to provide homes for people who previously lived (or would today live) in institutions. The fifth theory, the "right-wing conspiracy," is a variant of the fourth. It emphasizes conservative social policies more generally, including cutbacks on disability benefits and state legislatures' stinginess in serving a powerless, disfavored group. Then there is the "edifice theory," emphasizing that states kept huge sums of money in state hospital systems, while starving community-based programs, even after most of the patients had left the buildings. Finally, the "transinstitutionalization theory" denies that deinstitutionalization took place at all; rather, it contends, people were placed in nursing homes, board and care facilities, or homeless shelters that have all the worst, deadening features of state psychiatric hospitals but none of their programs.

Some of these arguments are quite persuasive.[2] Others are little more than ideological axe-grinding. As Christopher Jencks points out, different explanations apply to different periods in the now 35-year history of deinstitutionalization.[3] Jencks and other critics, though, fail to understand the significance of a critical aspect of this history: Many of the problems associated with deinstitutionalization were apparent early on, especially after the almost 60% decline in hospital populations that took place between 1965 and 1975,[4] and during the course of a generation, concerted efforts have been made to address them.

By the mid-1970s government agencies,[5] the press, consumers, families, and professionals were all raising the alarm. Dr. Gerald Klerman observed that

> As a whole, patients in the community are "better but not well," and their limited capacity to lead independent social lives generates complex issues for public welfare, urban zoning, health care agencies and legal institutions. In some areas there are signs of backlash.[6]

The alarm was not ignored and we can no longer say that successful deinstitutionalization—by which I mean the development of adequate support services and housing for people with mental illness who live with freedom in the community—has not been attempted. While many of the problems identified in critiques of deinstitutionalization, including the loss of housing, inadequate funding of community-based services, and regressive federal social policy endure, these problems do not represent the whole story.

Despite the continuing power of facility-based labor unions and various other constituencies, the political power of those favoring heavy spending on institutions has dwindled.

That story must also recount the fact that many states are committing huge resources and tremendous energy to community-based services for people with serious mental illness. Despite the continuing power of facility-based labor unions and various other constituencies, the political power of those favoring heavy spending on institutions has dwindled. Virtually all state mental health agencies, no longer dominated by hospital superintendents, embrace community-based services for people with the most severe disabilities as their highest priority. One result is that the percentage of state-controlled funds tied up in institutions is gradually diminishing, and is now below 60%. At the same time, state and local investment in community-based programs has increased. During the 1980s, state-controlled spending on state institutions decreased 12% while spending on community-based programs increased by 33%.[7] Similarly, housing has become a major priority for many state and local mental health agencies, and they back this priority with staff dedicated to finding and even developing housing for people with serious mental illness. Spurred by the National Institute of Mental Health's Community Support Program and pressured by families and consumers, many community mental health centers have shifted their priorities toward seeking to serve people with serious mental disorders. Innovations in community-based services like assertive outreach, case management, and peer-run services have blossomed.

Barriers to providing services have fallen as well. During the 1980s, many of the anomalies and perverse incentives in the Medicaid and disability programs identified in the 1970s as serious obstacles to deinstitutionalization have been reformed, to the point where Medicaid has become a significant source of funds for community-based mental health services.[8] Disability benefit cutbacks that exacerbated the problems people with serious mental illness faced in the 1980s have been reversed.

Then, too, many of the perceived legal barriers to providing services to people with psychiatric disabilities in the community have proven to be nonexistent or have been addressed head-on. For example, the myth that legal restrictions on involuntary treatment perpetuate homelessness was punctured by the Federal Task Force on Homelessness and Serious Mental Illness, which concluded that "there is no empirical evidence to support the belief that changes in civil commitment law would provide a solution to the problems of homeless mentally ill."[9] Real legal barriers, particularly discrimination against people with mental disabilities in housing, fell with the enactment of the Fair Housing Amendments Act in 1988.

Deinstitutionalization represented the first time in history that society set out to permit and encourage people with serious mental illness and accompanying disabilities, most often poor, to live normal lives in normal communities.

And yet, in the face of these many changes and evidence of enormous effort, the rhetoric of abandonment remains compelling. Indeed, in light of the intensity of the effort, the persistence of the problems people with psychiatric disabilities face in gaining access to services reinforces the sense of failure. If deinstitutionalization has failed despite seriousness of purpose and concerted, dedicated effort, isn't that even more disappointing?

Maybe, though, we're asking the wrong questions and need to return to the most fundamental question of all, which is what did deinstitutionalization really set out to accomplish. This question is rarely asked because its answer seems so obvious: The purpose of deinstitutionalization was to change what some have referred to as the "locus of care" from the institution to the community. By the 1970s, this objective came to be described as movement to a less restrictive environment. A closer look, though, shows these statements of purpose are utterly inadequate to describe what deinstitutionalization really attempted in moving from "serving" someone in an institution to "serving" that person with supports in the community.

Deinstitutionalization represented the first time in history that society set out to permit and encourage people with serious mental illness and accompanying disabilities, most often poor, to live normal lives in normal communities. These were people, we must remember, who for centuries had been seen as pariahs, unfit, pitiable, or even subhuman. Whether viewed as worthy of sympathy and pity or hatred and contempt, segregation in the form of confinement or exclusion seemed entirely appropriate. Deinstitutionalization required a dramatic reversal: Now, the people society viewed as the mad women in the attic were suddenly to be brought not only into light, but also into the neighborhood. Deinstitutionalization represented a very painful, expensive, complex, and difficult struggle for society to come to grips with psychiatric disability in a way that respects human dignity.

Deinstitutionalization represented a very painful, expensive, complex, and difficult struggle for society to come to grips with psychiatric disability in a way that respects human dignity.

The move from institution to community represented far more than a change in the locus or restrictiveness of care. It required not just a change in the location of care, but the creation, out of whole cloth, of an entire support system that encompasses housing, income maintenance, work (often with support), medical care, psychiatric treatment, rehabilitation services, and much more, all for people who, by definition, have severe disabilities and might not jump at the idea of entering the "system." Multiple state and local mental health agencies, federal programs, nonprofit providers, housing agencies, health care financing agencies, and many more entities offering services, all of them short of resources and few with any history of connection to people with psychiatric disabilities, have to be coordinated to create a coherent program. They have to function smoothly together, with clear lines of responsibility, cooperate effectively even in lean budget times, and be responsive to individual needs. Where is the model for such a service system?

The implementation of the deinstitutionalization mandate departs not only from familiar bureaucratic precedents that focus on running discrete organizations, but assumes deep involvement in every aspect of the lives of individuals, in turn requiring a level of coordination and intervention over long periods of time virtually unknown in the social services field. In the world of social services today, the buzzword has become "service integration," but that integration has been the necessity for deinstitutionalization for decades.

Nothing like the effort at development of a comprehensive service system had even been attempted for any group before. Yes, there were settlement houses and child welfare agencies, but here was a concept that demanded that an adult be literally surrounded with services that had not been designed to be coordinated or integrated with one another, for which no agency possessed responsibility, and where the resources to pay for services were both scanty and spread thinly

Modern governments are relatively good (if not necessarily humane) at running institutions whose primary function is to control their inhabitants.

across many agencies. Even today, such systems are rare, especially if the people involved are poor or devalued. Fledgling efforts to design and finance systems for serving aging people in their homes and providing "wraparound" services to low-income families with young children are seen as requiring a frontal attack on traditional ways of organizing social services. Yet deinstitutionalization has needed this for decades.

Proponents, administrators, policymakers, and critics of deinstitutionalization, even today, have largely misunderstood the true nature of the mission on which they had embarked and have relied on an oversimplified concept of how deinstitutionalization could be successfully implemented. Modern governments are relatively good (if not necessarily humane) at running institutions whose primary function is to control their inhabitants. Like the military, they are rigidly centralized and hierarchal organizations. And even more convenient than the military, they sit in one physical location. The audience is captive. By contrast, as we see every day, community-based services are decentralized, fragmented, and nonhierarchal. The lack of recognition how deep and complex a transformation deinstitutionalization represents led to expectations which could not be quickly fulfilled, and when not met, brought charges of failure.

As the Cat in the Hat said, "And that was not all." Not only does successful deinstitutionalization require government bureaucracies to arrange for or provide all these services, but to do so in a manner that helps someone get better! Deinstitutionalization demands that these functions be performed in a manner that "engages" people rather than alienates them even as the service system subjects them to endless demands, waiting lists, programmatic rules and restrictions, and service models that thwart recovery and rehabilitation. Is it any surprise that people "placed" and "managed" to accommodate the very administrative difficulties of creating a system of community-based services become "treatment resistant"?

To put this point in perspective, it is worth looking at one of the most sophisticated efforts to devise and implement a well-functioning community services system for people with serious mental illness, the nine-city demonstration project funded by the Robert Wood Johnson Foundation. Before planning services, the designers believed they had to implement new governmental structures, including a local mental health authority with enough clout and resources to provide and coordinate the necessary

The task of deinstitutionalization demands change in the very way we organize our government.

services. In other words, before we start thinking about housing, income, services, supports, treatment resources, and the myriad other pieces of the community-services puzzle, the task demanded by deinstitutionalization demands change in the very way we organize our government. Even in a project rich in resources and technical assistance, this fundamental task proved, not surprisingly, time-consuming, politically complex, and difficult to achieve.[10] Political and bureaucratic leadership proved essential to the process. How much more difficult is it without the political clout of a foundation-funded project to take on entrenched forms of government?

To add to the difficulties of changing government organization and coordination, community-based services, unlike the state facilities they were supposed to replace, never proceeded with a defined and coherent source of financing. Indeed, many of the sources of funds captured for community-based services were designed for another purpose altogether, and to this day the best service programs have to be pieced together among state, federal, and local funds; SSI payments; Medicaid; federal, state, and local housing programs; and sometimes even private funds. The effort requires wizardry befitting a corporate takeover specialist. Often, those financing streams tend to defeat the very purposes and values for which deinstitutionalization stands. Robert Gettings has written an insightful article about a reform of Medicaid that permits funds originally designated for institutional care for people with developmental disabilities to be spent instead on community-based services. Despite the success many states have had in taking advantage of this waiver, Gettings points out that the structure of the financing

Deinstitutionalization has been attempted in an environment where many of the basic rehabilitative and support services necessary to make it work are excluded from mainstream health financing.

scheme, itself designed to promote community-based services, tends to undermine the very values on which those services are premised.[11]

Even more extraordinary, deinstitutionalization has been attempted in an environment where many of the basic rehabilitative and support services necessary to make it work are excluded from mainstream health financing. Virtually no private health insurance policy, for example, covers psychiatric rehabilitation, nonhospital-based crisis intervention, or case management; neither does Medicare. Medicaid has only begun to cover these services, and they are subject to the nightmare of Medicaid's restricted eligibility rules, stingy reimbursement rates, and byzantine administrative structures.

Part of the reason for this exclusion was the stigma against and devaluation of people with mental illness. I suspect, though, that the very lack of awareness of the need to develop new structures to enable people with psychiatric disabilities to be fully integrated in the community contributed to the problem. States were responsible for running long-term institutions for people with psychiatric disabilities, and it might seem to follow that they continue to be the dominant source of funds for services in an era of deinstitutionalization. This approach not only excluded people with psychiatric disabilities from mainstream health coverage, but guaranteed that funding for a critical health service would be subject to the annual or biannual appropriations wars in ev-

Yet another unanticipated complexity is that the "community" did not embrace deinstitutionalization, no matter how well services were organized.

ery state legislature. Michael Perlin has explored the consequence of this choice, that deeply hostile popular and political attitudes about people with mental illness, the poor, and racial minorities deprived people with psychiatric disabilities of funding for services and led as well to programs more concerned with coercion against devalued people than to the development of services necessary to help them survive.[12]

Yet another unanticipated complexity is that the "community" did not embrace deinstitutionalization, no matter how well services were organized. In a recent survey, 48% of respondents said they would not welcome group homes or other facilities for people with mental illness in their communities. Demographically, the strongest opposition group was composed principally of the more affluent and well-educated members of the community,[13] precisely

Substance abuse appears to significantly increase the risk of violence by people with mental illness, which in turn inflames communities against locating services for any *people with mental illness in their midst.*

the group with the greatest political skills. Recent enactment of legislation supported by "liberal" members of Congress permitting segregation of people with mental illness in public and assisted housing[14] underscores, if underscoring is needed, how difficult it is to shift from institutions to communities as the "locus of care."

As if the process were not difficult enough, demographic and social trends have made implementation of deinstitutionalization even more complicated. Members of the baby boom generation reached the age of onset of major mental illness just as deinstitutionalization got seriously underway, and an epidemic of crack and other street drugs makes the task of serving people even more vexing. Substance abuse appears to significantly increase the risk of violence by people with mental illness,[15] which in turn inflames communities against locating services for *any* people with mental illness in their midst.

An appreciation of the requirements of deinstitutionalization should lead us to rethink the concept of abandonment. The idea of abandonment is a moral and political judgment that does not take into account the enormity and difficulty of the task presented and, in the

It is a serious mistake, though, to forget that deinstitutionalization virtually set out to build a new civilization from scratch.

context of the long history of institutionalization, the relatively short time we have been at it. Demands for funds, coordinated services and housing, and respect for people with psychiatric disabilities must continue, and the pain of those people deeply hurt in the process cannot be ignored. Shortsightedness, overselling, and even bad faith have been far from absent. Moreover, in retrospect, we can see ways to have avoided some, if not all, of the anguish and degradation of those who have suffered.

It is a serious mistake, though, to forget that deinstitutionalization virtually set out to build a new civilization from scratch. Never before in our history had the effort been tried to develop programs based on the idea that people with disabilities are part of the community. That it has been a struggle is undeniable. But misleading the public and politicians that the transformation should have been easy can only lead to more cynicism, dispiriting rhetoric, and in the end, true abandonment.

II.

What about the other side of the equation? Has deinstitutionalization brought an increase in freedom? I believe it has, again in ways unanticipated by its proponents and opponents alike.

Recall that I argued that one of the goals of deinstitutionalization was to change the way in which society views and treats people with psychiatric disabilities. Deinstitutionalization has led to a wondrous change in the very idea of freedom for people with psychiatric disabilities, beyond the conventional sense of freedom, i.e., to live outside the walls of a hospital as one wishes without state interference. That new idea of freedom has become expressed in cliches like empowerment and self-determination, but it really amounts to seeing people with mental illness not as afflicted objects to be fixed, but as people struggling to make sense of, and recover from, their pain. This freedom means encouraging others to see them not as labels or diagnoses, but as people seeking to participate in the life of the community, taking responsibility for their lives.

Much of the movement for patients' rights in the 1970s came directly from the civil rights movement, where the concept of freedom had itself been transformed in just this way. The origins of the civil rights movement began, of course, in enslavement, a deprivation of freedom and liberty in the most physical sense. At the time the modern civil rights movement took shape, physical enslavement was long gone, but the concept of freedom was just as powerful. Martin Luther King's most famous speech recited a dream of freedom, concluding with a phrase harking back to the days of slavery, "Free at last."

Deinstitutionalization has been most successful, in building and nurturing the possibility for people with psychiatric disabilities to be seen as fully human and fully worthy of respect for that humanity.

What was this freedom? In fact, we know quite well what he meant: equal participation in civic life through voting, equal opportunity in employment and in housing, and more profoundly still, equal rights to make choices about, and take responsibilities for one's life without the limitations imposed by prejudice, discrimination, and diminution. The absence of freedom meant not only physical bondage, but perpetual dependence on the decisions and good will of others.

These ideas of freedom, though, have been missing from the debate about deinstitutionalization, which has focused on the freedom only to be out of a locked ward. And yet it is in this sense that deinstitutionalization has been most successful, in building and nurturing the possibility for people with psychiatric disabilities to be seen as fully human and fully worthy of respect for that humanity. The field of mental retardation is far ahead in finding a way to express this idea. It has seized on the concept of "community membership." replacing "client" with "citizen," and following these concepts, began seeking to design supports to enhance the person's own goals rather than to provide services to change behaviors according to professionally determined criteria.[16] Similarly, in mental health, services must begin with the individual as a person, not as an object. The growing consumer movement in mental health has made its fundamental demand to determine the way services are designed and implemented. This means appreciating the person's struggle with the pain of the disorder as well as dealing with its outward symptoms. This approach does not negate traditional interventions like medication and other therapies, but it very much changes the approach professionals take to their interactions with people.

This may sound very abstract, but it has enormous implications for life in the real world. For example, for years we talked about appropriate settings, a continuum of housing, or levels of restrictiveness, or whatever jargon was popular at the time. The approach was based on categorizations of people based on diagnosis and level of functioning. The program models that were created as a result of these categories worked for some people. But they did not work for many others because this approach lacked attention to what the individual with mental illness wanted for himself or herself, how the type of living arrangement met personal goals, how the person balanced choices about independence and loneliness, and what trade-offs in housing (e.g., more space/ worse neighborhood) the person was willing to make. It built in requirements for frequent and often traumatic moves from one residential program to another as the person got better or worse, or simply reached the program's time limitations. In short, it ignored all the preferences and decisions about housing anyone seeking a place to live would otherwise make. It precluded the person from taking responsibility. It fostered dependence. It was distinctly unfree. Now, as more expansive ideas of freedom are taking hold, housing is not seen as a "placement" made by professionals, but as a life choice driven by the consumer and constrained only by the market.

Deinstitutionalization has not yet brought this freedom to flower. In big urban mental health systems and small rural ones, programs strained by lack of resources and mind-sets dominated by expectations of professional and patient roles, render the journey to freedom a long one. The debate over health care reform shows how great resistance is, even to providing stable financing for community-based services.

Deinstitutionalization is not a choice between freedom and abandonment. It represents a struggle for freedom and for a system of services that is harder to develop than anyone envisioned.

The very difficulties of making the transition away from institutional confinement gets in the way of this freedom. Without deinstitutionalization, though, it would not even have been possible to conceive of this idea of freedom for people with psychiatric disabilities. It is a vast accomplishment, and it will influence the very structure of the services to be developed in the future.

III.

Deinstitutionalization is not a choice between freedom and abandonment. It represents a struggle for freedom and for a system of services that is harder to develop than anyone envisioned. We have been at it for more than thirty years and cannot be satisfied with its results, nor can we forget those who have suffered in the process. It remains the worthiest of causes—not failed, but uncompleted.

Endnotes

1. DAVID A. ROCHEFORT, FROM POORHOUSES TO HOMELESSNESS: POLICY ANALYSIS AND MENTAL HEALTH CARE, at 214 (1993).

2. The literature on deinstitutionalization is enormous. A thorough and compelling review is ANN BRADEN JOHNSON, OUT OF BEDLAM (1990). *See also* Rochefort, *supra* note 1; Michael Perlin, *Competency, Deinstitutionalization and Homelessness: A Study in Marginalization*, 28 HOUS. L. REV. 63 (1991). On the early history of the federal policy related to deinstitutionalization, *see* HENRY A. FOLEY & STEVEN SHARFSTEIN, WHO CARES FOR THE MENTALLY ILL? (1983). On homelessness generally, *see* P.H. ROSSI, DOWN AND OUT IN AMERICA: THE ORIGINS OF HOMELESSNESS (1989).

3. CHRISTOPHER JENCKS, THE HOMELESS (1994).

4. The year-end census for state psychiatric hospitals declined from 475,202 in 1965 to 191,395 in 1975. *See* AMY A. SIBULKIN & CHARLES A. KIESLER, MENTAL HOSPITALIZATION (1987).

5. U. S. GEN. ACCOUNTING OFFICE, RETURNING THE MENTALLY DISABLED TO THE COMMUNITY: GOVERNMENT NEEDS TO DO MORE HD 76–152 (1977).

6. Gerald Klerman, *Better But Not Well: Social and Ethical Issues in the Deinstitutionalization of the Mentally Ill*, 3 SCHIZOPHRENIA BULL. 617 (1977).

7. Theodore C. Lutterman & Vera L. Hollen, *Changes in State Mental Health Agency Revenues and Expenditures Between Fiscal Year 1981 and 1990, in* CENTER FOR MENTAL HEALTH SERVICES AND NATIONAL INSTITUTE FOR MENTAL HEALTH, MENTAL HEALTH, UNITED STATES (1992).

8. CHRIS KOYANAGI & HOWARD GOLDMAN, INCHING FORWARD, NAT'L. MENTAL HEALTH ASSN. (1991).

9. FEDERAL TASK FORCE ON HOMELESSNESS AND MENTAL ILLNESS, OUTCASTS ON MAIN STREET (1992).

10. M.F. Shore & M. Cohen, *The Robert Wood Johnson Foundation on Chronic Mental Illness: An Overview*, 41 HOSP. AND COMMUNITY PSYCHIATRY 1212 (1990); H.H. Goldman, et al., *Form and Function of Mental Health Authorities at RWJ Foundation Program Sites: An Overview*, 41 HOSP. AND COMMUNITY PSYCHIATRY 1222 (1990).

11. R. Gettings, *The Link Between Public Financing and Systemic Change in* CREATING INDIVIDUAL SUPPORTS FOR PEOPLE WITH DEVELOPMENTAL DISABILITIES 155–170 (V.J. Bradley et al. eds., 1994).

12. PERLIN, *supra* note 2.

13. A. Borinstein, *Public Attitudes Toward Persons with Mental Illness*, 11 HEALTH AFF. 186 (1992).

14. Housing and Community Development Act of 1992, Pub. L. No. 102–550.

15. *See* E. Mulvey, *Assessing the Evidence of a Link Between Mental Illness and Violence*, 45 HOSP. AND COMMUNITY PSYCHIATRY 663 (1994).

16. V. Bradley & J. Knoll, Shifting Paradigms in Services to People with Developmental Disabilities (1990) (unpublished manuscript, on file with the Administration on Developmental Disabilities, Washington, D.C.).

9

The Place of "Choice"

David Ferleger, Esq.

Introduction

Dorothea Lynde Dix, in her 1843 address to the Massachusetts Legislature exposing the plight of people who were poor, disabled, and in government care, declared: "Familiarity with suffering, it is said, blunts the sensibilities, and where neglect once finds a footing other injuries are multiplied."[1]

In considering the organization and implementation of services for people with retardation, I would like to suggest that we take care not to elevate "choice" above other values. An unbalanced emphasis upon choice risks, recalling Dix's words, multiplication of the neglect to which people with retardation have been subjected for too long.

The current desire to see "choice" as a dominant theme in both individual planning and system design is likely to be temporary, and to be superseded by other themes as we move to another stage in the realization of normalization, that of integration.[2]

Just as the theme "quality control" was superseded by "quality assurance" and "quality enhancement,"[3] so "choice" will later be seen in context as a small, albeit important, part of ensuring quality,

> *An unbalanced emphasis upon choice risks, recalling Dix's words, multiplication of the neglect to which people with retardation have been subjected for too long.*

responsive services to people who are in our communities.

Some writers, perhaps enamored of the philosophical connections between "choice" and "freedom" or perhaps connecting liberation from institutions with some notion of freedom, seem to extol "choice" as a value supreme to others. For example:

> Choice, personal freedom, and personal empowerment are the rubrics that, perhaps more than any other, signal the presence of the new way of thinking or the new paradigm in the design of supports to people with disabilities.[4]

The purpose of this essay is to reflect on the limitations of choice as a guide for decision-making at the individual, service provider, and systems levels. I do not intend to discuss the subject in all its ramifications, but merely to provide an initial basis for critical examination.

Energizing this examination is a current tendency in practice which justifies what I would label deprivation or denial of services, or violation of rights, of people with retardation based on invocation of "choice" as a guiding principle. For example, people are denied individual habilitation planning, or even a case manager, (in a system where a plan and case management is prerequisite to any assistance at all) because they are said to have chosen to give up such assistance. People are denied a job or meaningful activity during the day or evening because they are said to choose otherwise. People's homes and bedrooms, and daily life choices, are barren and devaluing, all based on what is said to be "choice."

The notion that primacy should be given to the articulated choices of people with retardation or their surrogates presupposes that they are at liberty to exercise choices among many options.

As in Herman Melville's story, *Bartleby the Scrivener*, unqualified deference to the preference "not to" leads to isolation, devaluation, and harm.

I consider "choice" from several perspectives:

- the relationship of choice to the real world options available to people with retardation;
- the relationship between choice and other values;
- the relationship between choice and the law; and,
- the relationship between choice and the chooser.

My purpose is not to describe all the limitations of choice in retardation services, but rather to assist people with retardation, and their advocates, friends, supporters, and service providers, with perceiving and beginning to understand those limitations.

"Choice" and Real World Options

The notion that primacy should be given to the articulated choices of people with retardation or their surrogates presupposes that they are at liberty to exercise choices among many options. Otherwise, they are like the magician's volunteer, compelled always to choose the "force card" from the card deck, while imagining that any one of the fifty-two cards was a possible outcome.

At least five categories of obstacles limit the available options: a) the persistence of institutions, b) the persistence of abuse and mistreatment, c) the effect of class, stigma, and the nature of bureaucracies, d) the inadequacy of many community programs, and e) respecting choice and perpetuation of neglect.

A. PERSISTENCE OF INSTITUTIONS

In his detailed prescription of the meaning of the normalization principle in the United States, Gunnar Dybwad twenty-five years ago asked the question, "The Old Institution: Renovate or Discard?" He answered that fixing the institution "is at best ill advised, and at worst unfeasible, and a poor service to the residents now housed in such institutions."[5] Many have come to that conclusion since that time.

Viewed from one perspective, there has been tremendous progress in implementation of this "discarding" of institutions. Between 1950 and 1970, more public retardation facilities were added than in any other period in United States history, and the number of people with retardation in public institutions grew from 116,828 in 1946 to its peak of 193,188 in 1967, a 65% increase which was nearly twice the rate of increase in the general population; by 1988, the number had decreased to 91,440 (Table 1).[6] Since 1970, 44 institutions for people with retardation have closed or are scheduled to close.[7] In New York, the institutional population dropped from a high of 20,000 to about 7,000 a few years ago.[8]

Although many people with retardation are now enjoying the fruits of life in the community, many more remain in large congregate institutions.

If the question asked is, where have people gone to, the answer may be jolting for some of us. Among people remaining in large institutions, there are more in private institutions than in public institutions.

From June 30, 1982 to June 30, 1991, the number of people in large private ICF/MRs *increased* by 9,311, while there were 31,830 fewer people living in large state-operated ICF/MRs.[9]

Large private institutions have replaced the large public institutions. Although many people with retardation are now enjoying the fruits of life in the community, many more remain in large congregate institutions. Three-quarters of the funding from the federal ICF/MR program, the principal fiscal support for deinstitutionalization, in fiscal year 1985 provided for institutional, not community, placements.[10]

Residential Facilities for People With Mental Retardation United States, 1988

Type of Facility	Number of Clients
Public Institutions	91,440
Congregate (16 or more beds)	
Large Private Facilities	46,351
Private Nursing Homes	50,606
TOTAL	96,957
Small (less than 16 beds)	
Public ICF/MRs	3,355
Private ICF/MRs	23,949
Other Residences	125,557
TOTAL	152,861

Table 1

We continue to use institutions for a majority of people with retardation receiving residential services. Institutions remain available for new admissions. The persistence of institutions, and their continued consumption of massive fiscal resources, are major inhibitors of the major reallocation which would be needed to enable free choices to be made.

B. PERSISTENCE OF ABUSE AND MISTREATMENT

For many decades, we have recognized the abuse and mistreatment to which we subject people with disabilities. We have long been familiar with the abuse and neglect so prevalent in institutions.[11-13]

Both in institutions and in community programs, abuse and neglect continue to harm people with retardation.[14-16]

Beyond the spectacular abuse, there is a day-to-day form of mistreatment which has changed little for many people from Burton Blatt's characterization years ago. "The ordinary condition is boredom more than brutality, legal abuse more than illegal assault, and a subtle degradation rather than a blatant holocaust."[17]

Everyday lives, blessed with large and small choices, cannot be obtained by people with retardation without surmounting many obstacles, many of which have little to do with the retardation system itself.

C. COMMUNITY "OPTIONS," ECONOMICS, MINORITIES, STIGMA, AND BUREAUCRACIES

Everyday lives, blessed with large and small choices, cannot be obtained by people with retardation without surmounting many obstacles, many of which have little to do with the retardation system itself.

People with retardation and other disabilities are more likely to be poor, unemployed, underemployed, and to be denied economic benefits and status which are accorded to people without disabilities. Women with disabilities fare worse than men with disabilities; members of ethnic and racial minorities encounter greater barriers than nonminorities.[18] While there may be little which can be done in the short run to rectify the resulting inequitable distribution of services and wealth, and the stigma which attaches to disability, it is important to keep sight of these issues when one examines choices which are made by or for people with disabilities.

The negative valuation of the social status of people with retardation results in individuals being confronted at virtually every turn with restrictions on choice.

The negative valuation of the social status of people with retardation results in individuals being confronted at virtually every turn with restrictions on choice. Applying for a job or housing, ordering food in a restaurant, or seeking friends, for example, are all occasions on which stigma and stereotypes may make it impossible for a person to "choose" options which nondisabled people take for granted.

There is a menu of service styles available today including a variety of individual supports, independent and semi-independent living, foster care, group homes, and the like. This variety creates an illusion of choice. There is an "insidious danger of assuming that the development of multiple placement options has led to matching clients with the facility most appropriate" for the person.[19]

> *There is no doubt that people with retardation who have moved to the community from institutions are in most cases flourishing.*

In addition, bureaucratic program restrictions inhibit effective exercise of choice. John O'Brien and Connie Lyle O'Brien have pointed out that consumer choice is severely inhibited, if not altogether precluded, by government agency control of service structures:

> However, most people with developmental disabilities who live outside their families' homes or residential facilities now depend on a supported living agency because current public policy severely restricts people's option to control their share of available funds. And even when people with disabilities gain full control of available cash—as the authors believe they should—it is reasonable to assume that some people will probably choose the convenience of purchasing services from a supported living agency over the investment of time required to self-manage a personal support system.[20]

Contradictory service system assumptions result in continued devaluation of people served in the community. For example, some people who live in and control their own homes nevertheless "spend their days in mindless, segregated activities."[21]

D. COMMUNITY "OPTIONS": OUT OF THE FRYING PAN

There is no doubt that people with retardation who have moved to the community from institutions are in most cases flourishing. They are working, have homes and friends, and are participating in their communities. They are learning from others and, perhaps of greater importance, are enriching their neighborhoods and towns.

For many, however, there has been, in Burton Blatt's prophetic phrase, a "reformation to sameness."[22] We have established many baby institutions which, although relatively small and located in the community, may grow up to be larger and more oppressive. Some residences have routines and an ambiance in which boredom, routinization, and compliance are the primary elements. Some community "services" are so abusive and neglectful as to recall the institutions for observers as well as clients.

An example of the "out of the frying pan, into the fire" aspect of community services is the status of former residents of the Pennhurst institution, a facility closed in 1987 under a court order. During the day, even in a community in which the individuals are protected by the landmark court order, most people spend most of their time in segregated "day activity" and sheltered workshop programs. Class members in the Pennhurst case in Philadelphia, by provider agency, spend 81% to 100% of day service hours in segregated settings. Only

Excessive respect for the abstract notion of "choice" can lead to the perpetuation of neglect or to an increase in the risk of neglect and other harms.

1.4% are in what is nominally called "community integrated employment" and, of those, the majority are not paid and not actually working.[23]

The court found in 1994 that the abuse/neglect investigation system is inadequate, the medical care provided is insufficient, and that individuals in the community are not being provided the individual planning and other services to which they are entitled.[24-25]

Thus, although in terms of many aspects of personal growth, individuals do relatively well in the community, they sometimes do so despite the failure of the government or provider agency to ensure that needed conditions and safeguards are in place. In such situations, true exercise of "choice" is adventitious.

E. RESPECTING CHOICE AND PERPETUATION OF NEGLECT

Excessive respect for the abstract notion of "choice" can lead to the perpetuation of neglect or to an increase in the risk of neglect and other harms. As I discuss in the next section, choice must be kept in context, and other values (sometimes competing and sometimes complementary) must be weighed in the balance.

In 1864, Dr. Edouard Seguin emphasized that affirmative encouragement is a responsibility of the teacher of people with retardation. Seguin's religiously motivated interest in people with retardation encouraged his development of sensory, muscular, and speech training as the methods for what is today called habilitation. If we can set aside for the moment his negative characterizations and language which would not be acceptable today, his words are an interesting reminder from more than a century ago that respect for "choice" cannot ignore the need for a proactive relationship with people with disabilities:

> The incessant volition of the moral physician urges incessantly the idiot out of his idiocy into the sphere of activity, of thinking, of labor, of duty and of affectionate feelings; such is the moral treatment. The negative will of the idiot being overcome, scope and encouragement being given to his first indications of active volition, the immoral tendencies of this new power being repressed, his mixing with the busy and living world is to be urged on at every opportunity. This moral part of the training is not something separate, but is the necessary attendant and super-addition upon all the other parts of the training, whether we teach him to read, whether we play with him the childish game, let our will govern his, if we will enough for himself, he shall be become willing too.[26]

Unchanneled deference to choice can be an excuse for neglect. It is easier to go along with choices which mean less work, less expense, less relationship, or less caring than it is to truly assist someone in identifying the larger universe of options, exploring those options, and coming to grips with the struggle to realize a choice truly made or the disappointment of the impossibility of realizing the choice.

"Choice" and Other Values

A. CHOICE IN CONTEXT

How we value and articulate choice has changed, even during the "modern" era of services for people with retardation. Before government funding for community services, for example, "choice" meant simply providing parents with a choice of community, services; the emphasis was on the locus of care, community or institution.[27] Today, with community life more differentiated, choice often means such things as selection of types of services (independent living, apartments, group homes, etc.), particular opportunities for employment or other day activity, and uses of leisure time.

It is easier to go along with choices which mean less work, less expense, less relationship, or less caring than it is to truly assist someone in identifying the larger universe of options.

Although "choice" (or its sister concept, "empowerment") is described by some as a transcending or unifying value, replacing others such as normaliza-tion or rights or habilitation, those who articulate what is now being called a "new paradigm" do not give such preeminence to "choice." In-stead, they recognize that the present emphasis on participation of people

> *Normalization does not exclude respectful response to the choices of individuals.*

with retardation as full citizens, and in relationships with others, is inherent in the normalization first articulated twenty-five years ago.[28]

Valerie Bradley describes a three-stage process: the institutionalization era ending in the mid-1970s, the community development era beginning at that time, and the "third and emerging stage is the era of community membership, which is marked by an emphasis on functional supports to enhance inclusion and quality of life as defined by physical as well as social integration."[29]

"No single categorical principle has ever had a greater impact on services for mentally retarded persons than that of normalization."[30] Codified in a Danish statute in 1959, the concept was explained in 1969 by Niels Bank-Mikkelsen, Director of the Danish Service for the Mentally Retarded, as embodying "a basic right to receive the most adequate treatment, training, and rehabilitation available and to be approached in an ethical fashion."[31-32]

Bengt Nirje, then director of the Swedish Parents Association for Mentally Retarded Children, defined normalization as "making available to the mentally retarded patterns and conditions of everyday life which are as close as possible to the norms and patterns of the mainstream of society."[33] We have generally accepted the normalization as the "one unifying principle" which, as it evolves, "expresses the aims, attitudes and norms implied in quality work for and with the mentally retarded."[34] The principle applies to all people with retardation, regardless of level of disability or residential setting, and is "useful in every society, with all age groups, and adaptable to social changes and individual development."[35] Therefore, "it should serve as a guide for medical, educa-tional, psychological, social and political work in this field, and decisions and actions made according to the principle should turn out more often right than wrong."[36]

Normalization does not exclude respectful response to the choices of individuals. Its early formulation explicitly recognized this: "The normaliza-tion principle also means that the choices, wishes, and desires of the mentally retarded themselves have to be taken into consideration as nearly as possible, and respected."[37]

There are values embodied in normalization other than choice. Nirje's formulation of twenty-five years ago includes:

- normal rhythm of the day;
- normal rhythm of life, including participation in the regular society;
- normal rhythm of the year;
- opportunity to undergo normal developmental experiences of the life cycle, with maximum contact with a normal rather than a deviant society;
- respect for choices, wishes, and desires of the individual;
- life in a world including men and women;
- enjoyment of normal economic standards and work opportunities; and,
- standards for physical facilities the same as those for ordinary citizens.

In addition to "choice" as an explicit central element of the normalization principle, the other elements imply acceptance and encouragement of individual choice. For example, integration with the society as a whole increases knowledge of options and the consequent opportunity to choose among homes, friends, and activities. Decent living conditions and economic power expand one's choices as well.

One response to the normalization principle has been to seek structures for acting responsively and responsibly, with the person (rather than the professional team, or the family, or the government) at the center of attention.

Wolf Wolfensberger's redefinition of normalization emphasized social integration and directed attention to the obstacles preventing it. Normalization is:

> Utilization of means which are as culturally normative as possible, in order to establish, enable, or support behaviors, appearances, and interpretations which are as culturally normative as possible.[38]

Interaction with the community is key. "Ultimately, integration is only meaningful if it is social integration; i.e., if it involves social interaction and acceptance, and not merely physical presence."[39] The 1983 reformulation of normalization as "social role valorization" continued to pay close attention to the roots of devaluation of people in our society, and mechanisms to end that devaluation.[40]

E. CHOICE AND PERSON-CENTERED PLANNING

One response to the normalization principle has been to seek structures for acting responsively and responsibly, with the person (rather than the professional team, or the family, or the government) at the center of attention.

Such person-centered planning of necessity has called upon us to focus on choice, both because those assisting in the planning need to listen to the choices made by the individual and, in many cases, to aid in the choice-making.

Choice has high visibility in person-centered planning:

> Many people with disabilities have been denied the life experience and opportunity needed to make informed choices. We have suppressed expressions of choice by consistently failing to honor the expressions of choice that are made. Where people have not been trained into passivity, they have been forced into rebellion and their expressions of choice have been distorted in the process. The effects of the disability have been used as an excuse to make choices *for* people. * * * With these individuals, efforts must focus on understanding the individual. Person-centered planning efforts simply provide a structured process by which this understanding can be achieved.[41]

None of those leaders who have developed person-centered planning have elevated choice above the other values inherent in normalization.

None of those leaders who have developed person-centered planning have elevated choice above the other values inherent in normalization; all, in fact, take as the fundamental base all the elements of normalization and all recognize how easy it is for the person to be dropped from the center of the planning. For example, Beth Mount warns:

> When the system takes over the futures planning process, the activity immediately loses its power, flexibility and responsiveness, quickly becoming one more intrusive, insensitive and ineffective activity. When people lacking strong person-centered values are given the power to conduct a procedure that has no potential to change the system of which it is a part, then futures planning becomes one more way to process people through a series of empty and meaningless rituals.[42]

C. RESPECTING CHOICE AND NEGATING VALUED LIVES

Some people might suggest that normalization did not pay sufficient attention to choice and that therefore normalization should be superseded by a new unifying principle—"choice." It is said by some that, since a person with retardation might choose, for example, to not work or to live in a large segregated group home, or to dress abnormally, or to spend time in segregated activities, one must accept this "choice" as part of normalization or accept it as a limitation on normalization.[43]

Acquiescence in such "choices" is a destructive elevation of choice among other values which constitute the normalization or social role valorization principle. As Wolfensberger has pointed out:

> Thus, for the largest number of devalued persons, the *right not to be different* in certain dimensions of living is actually a much more urgent issue than the right to be different. When we recall that the overwhelming response of society to devalued people is segregation, expressed partially by its confinement of vast numbers of citizens to institutions and partially by sequestering devalued people in other nonnormative settings, we realize that the right not to be segregated and institutionalized (which is almost equivalent to being made different, or more different) is really a bigger issue than the restrictions of individual choice, which, left to itself, would more often than not result in a choice of something that would fall within the range of the cultural norm anyway.[44]

Some people with retardation may deliberately choose nonnormative ways of life, or of dress, or the like. The exercise of such choice is itself culturally normative. Friends and supporters of the person would respond in the same ways in which we respond for others in our lives or in our care. "First, one pursues the line of persuasion, pedagogy, modeling and other forms of culturally normative social influence to steer a person toward a course of action one desires. Second, one imposes coercion only where one would do so legally in the larger societal context, i.e., where one would do so with other (valued) citizens of the same age. Third, one chooses the least restrictive alternative, if one does coerce."[45]

Choice is not enough. Seymour Sarason warned that the choice option ignored the social context and could rob the larger community of the benefits of integration.

Choice is not enough. Seymour Sarason in 1969 noted the limitations of simply allowing parents to have "freedom of choice" to place children with retardation wherever they wished. Although he recognized this would allow use of some small residential facilities as an alternative to needless institutionalization, he warned that the choice option

When we consider the value of choice, we must do so in the context of the other values which inform our society in general, and services for people with retardation in particular.

ignored the social context and could rob the larger community of the benefits of integration:

> As a reaction to our present way of handling residential care, the proposal has merit. However, I must express the serious reservation that the proposal perpetuates the tendency to think primarily in terms of the retarded child and not in terms of the possible relationships between the field of mental retardation and other community needs and problems. To the extent that a plan for residential care does not reflect the systematic exploration of the alternative ways in which it can be related to other community needs and problems—that is to say, truly integrated with the activities of diverse groups and settings in the community—to that extent the field of mental retardation and the larger social community will be robbed of the benefits they can derive from one another.[46]

When we consider the value of choice, we must do so in the context of the other values which inform our society in general, and services for people with retardation in particular. Otherwise, we are perverting the principle of normalization either through misunderstanding or through failing to articulate compromises which result from inadequate resources or will.[47]

"Choice" and the Law

A. PERSONAL RIGHTS

Rights have many sources in our culture, ranging from enforceable enactments of legislatures to organizational expressions of desiderata. For people with retardation, there have been many declarations of rights by the United Nations, American Association on Mental Deficiency, and other groups.[48–50] Courts have set standards for treatment.[51–58] Legislatures have articulated standards as well.[59–61]

Common to those expressions are rights to education; training; habilitation; medical treatment; humane care; protection from harm, abuse and exploitation; and the right to the least restrictive individually appropriate environment.

Profoundly relevant to the degree of freedom which a person with disabilities may express and implement are rights to economic security, a decent standard of living, and employment.

Included in some rights declarations—and profoundly relevant to the degree of freedom which a person with disabilities may express and implement—are rights to economic security, a decent standard of living, and employment. For example, the United Nations 1971 Declaration of General and Special Rights of the Mentally Retarded provides, "The mentally retarded person has a right to economic security and to a decent standard of living. He has a right to productive work or to other meaningful occupation."[62] The 1993 United Nations Standard Rules on the Equalization of Opportunities for Persons With Disabilities provides for "equal opportunities for productive and gainful employment in the labour market." For caretakers of people with disabilities, the Standard Rules provide for "income support and social security protection."[63] The 1973 AAMD rights include the "right to gainful employment, and to a fair day's pay for a fair day's labor."[64]

For those rights which are enforceable, there is an affirmative duty on the government in the United States to either provide services or to ensure that there is no violation of those rights. For example, retardation institutions must provide treatment and protection from harm to those who live there.[65] Rights in the community post-institutionalization are also protected; a state may not end its duty to people it has incarcerated simply by discharging them to community programs.[66–71]

A person with retardation may not give up an important right casually. The "choice" to surrender such a right may not be freely or easily made.

B. CHOICE AND WAIVER OF RIGHTS

A person with retardation may not give up an important right—for example, a right to an individual treatment plan or a right to habilitation or a right to community services—casually. The "choice" to surrender such a right may not be freely or easily made.

The legal obstacle to the exercise of this rights-waiving choice arises from the requirement that a choice which rejects such an important right is permitted only after the occurrence of procedures designed to examine that choice. Understandably, a decision to accept a benefit is assumed to have been freely made; however, a decision to reject important benefits is seen as subject to such a likelihood of misunderstanding or possible undue influence that it is not permitted absent safeguards.

The rights discussed above are personal rights and are possessed by the individual. In one illustrative and influential case, for example, state and local governments sought to demonstrate compliance with a court order by showing that community services were adequate for the vast majority of the plaintiff class. The federal court of appeals, agreeing with the trial court, found that, because the right to adequate habilitation extends to each person individually, the government defendants were in contempt unless each and every class member's rights were implemented. Compliance is measured person-by-person.[72]

Fundamental legal principles require that waiver of a right be knowing and with awareness of both the nature of the right and the consequences of waiver.

Fundamental legal principles require that waiver of a right be knowing and with awareness of both the nature of the right and the consequences of waiver. For example, when a person is subject to proceedings to commit him or her involuntarily to a mental institution, the right to have a hearing and to be present may be waived only with the approval of the court.[73–74] In many jurisdictions, a person with retardation may not be sterilized without a hearing and a judicial determination approving the surgery.[75]

While, generally, there is no affirmative right to receive services when one is not in an institution,[76] there is a growing body of law which provides some protection of a right to community services in some circumstances. Some courts ground the right on the general right to treatment for people in or leaving institutions; others find a source in state law, and still others adopt and enforce settlement agreements between the parties.[77–80] One recent settlement requires California to reduce the population of four institutions by 2,000 residents over five years.[81] Regardless of the source of the right, it is no small matter for the individual to give it up. Even the existence of an arguable right gives a person leverage in negotiating for governmental aid.

If a person is purportedly choosing to give up a right or benefit which is important, such as a community home or the right to an individual habilitation plan and its implementation, then the waiver should be reviewed through a fair hearing process in which the person has an advocate who presents the point of view which favors retention of the benefit.

C. EXCLUSION OF OPTIONS

One does not have the ability under the law to choose anything one wishes. Some options are excluded or forbidden, either in the interest of the community's overall welfare or as a result of governmental authority to set priorities and allocate its resources.

One does not have the ability under the law to choose anything one wishes.

Generally, we permit a person to choose among alternative services. "If several alternative service options exist for a given client, and if all these alternatives can be considered rightful, it is widely accepted that the client has the right to choose which option or even combination of options should be implemented."[82] However, the "rightfulness" of the options is subject to change.

The federal and state governments have the authority to exclude certain treatment options for people with retardation. This may result from funding decisions (for example, extending financial aid or health benefits to certain types of care) or from a fiat simply shutting down an institution or a program.[83–87]

There are other "options" for life choices which are flatly forbidden, even absent any government involvement. For example, peonage (forced and uncompensated labor) is forbidden, as is sexual abuse, and subjection of people with retardation to secret or unconsented dangerous experimentation.

There are likely to be choices which, for one reason or another, the law denies to a person with retardation even in the face of a demand from the person or a representative. In some states, the choice of an institution may not be available. In others, a particular program model may be denied.

The degree of scrutiny with which the law views a distinction targeting people with retardation will vary depending on the consequences to the person of denial. Martha Minow, explains:

> [T]he premise is that relationships between people are what matter, and attributions of difference that build obstacles to such relationships are suspect. Isolation itself may contribute to false views of difference that impede or obstruct relationships, and isolation of a powerless minority group by a powerful majority should raise special suspicions for a court that focuses on relationships and power.[88]

"Choice" and the Chooser

A choice may be attributed to the person with retardation which is not the choice of that person. There often is another "chooser" who, in the background or quite directly, actually makes or directs the choice.

While we may sometimes accept surrogate or *sub silentio* choice-making, such acceptance should be conscious and should acknowledge that, from the perspective of the person subjected to the choice, it is imposed. The greater the social and personal distance between the chooser and the chosen-for, the greater is the likelihood of the choice being false or mistaken.

A. PARENTS' CHOICE

Parents of people in institutions often choose continued institutional care and vigorously reject community placement. A 1985 study found that 58.2% of parents would not approve of placement under any circumstances.[89] The phenomenon is nothing new. "A corollary of our present ideological confusion is the strong but inappropriate ideology prevalent today that parents have a right to decide whether to keep a retarded child or whether to divest themselves of it. The literature is replete with this implication, or with explicit statements that, 'the placement decision is the parents.'"[90]

> *The greater the social and personal distance between the chooser and the chosen-for, the greater is the likelihood of the choice being false or mistaken.*

One cannot accede to parental opposition because, first, it may not be in the interests of the person in the institution, and, second, there are serious limitations on the parental view which arise from misunderstanding of community services, anxiety about the unknown, and other factors. Many parents who initially disagree with placement change their minds and become supporters after placement occurs. At the least, the parents' decision-making is quite complex.[91–93]

One court deferred to parental decision-making with regard to minors for whom professionals have chosen community placement where evidence on a preferable setting is found to be conflicting, and where the pro-community decision was that the new home would be "more beneficial."[94] In that case, the trial court had ordered placement but the appeals court found that the parent's views, while not sufficient to automatically veto placement, had not been afforded sufficient consideration.

B. GOVERNMENTS' CHOICE

The absence of a mandate for community services for all in the United States results in state and local government making choices about who to serve. Such governmental choices restrict what is available, leaving the person with retardation to make a forced "choice," not a free choice. It is important that we not mistake one type of choice for another.

Such governmental choices restrict what is available, leaving the person with retardation to make a forced "choice," not a free choice. It is important that we not mistake one type of choice for another.

A 1992 federal court decision examined in detail how Rhode Island, then in the process of closing its one institution, handled in its Medicaid Plan what the court called its "shortage of space in private and small public ICF-MRs." The court found that one's chance of receiving an ICF-MR bed depended on "good timing and luck" as a "natural characteristic of any shortage of goods under price regulation." Because the state offers all eligible people the choice of the institution, there was no violation of Medicaid law.[95]

In Kansas, counties contract with private providers for community services. A county embroiled in a dispute with one provider called Terramara terminated its contract with the agency which had provided a work activity center, housing, and other services. Terramara's clients were given just over 45 days to either switch to the new contracted provider which the county had just formed, Flinthills, Inc., or to lose any preference for being served by Flinthills. A court upheld the county's ability to force this "choice" on the clients of Terramara who, in the county's view, could choose to continue at Terramara but only at the person's own cost.

A federal court in a lawsuit challenging the provider-switch in Kansas recognized that the plaintiffs (individuals with retardation) "have fundamental constitutional rights to live where and with whom they choose, to pursue employment through workshops, to associate with their friends, to live in group housing arrangements as provided by Terramara, and to make fundamental choices affecting their lives."[96]

In our system, the government cannot be relied on as a provider or source of funds for services. About 181,835 people in the United States are on "waiting lists" for retardation services.[97] In terms of the numbers of people affected, federal, state, and local governments, which determine eligibility and make allocations, are the primary choosers of who gets what.

C. PROVIDERS' CHOICE

Service providers often have a limited number of options for the people they serve; the public agencies which fund such providers often require a person to be served by a particular agency based on geography or the happenstance of a contract award.

> *In terms of the numbers of people affected, federal, state, and local governments, which determine eligibility and make allocations, are the primary choosers of who gets what.*

Thus, if the provider has group homes and apartments, for example, the person's choice is between those two options. If the provider has a day habilitation program, a sheltered workshop, and a mobile janitorial service, the person's choice would be limited to those possibilities.

Despite the virtually overwhelming control which rests with the provider, the person's unchosen residence or program may nevertheless be denominated the person's "choice," A recent federal court decision illustrates the situation. Allied Health Care, Inc., operator of two community homes in Louisiana, claimed that zoning restrictions violated the Fair Housing Act. The homes, which had been duplexes, were renovated into single-family homes, and then Allied had opened an "internal passageway" between the two homes. Local zoning law restricted each of the two homes to four unrelated persons each, for a total of eight. Allied intended to operate with six persons in each home, for a total of twelve.[98]

Although Allied professed adherence to normalization, its explanation for the need for a twelve-bed site was based on Allied's claim (supported by the court) that it could not operate with fewer residents because "payments received from Medicaid and SSI" would not offset the expenses. The court determined that there was no violation of the Fair Housing Act's prohibition on discrimination against people with disabilities because the zoning ordinance "has the practical effect of limiting the ability of the mentally handicapped to reside in the residence of their choice in the community." However, the court cites no evidence that any person actually made a choice to live in the twelve-bed site, and no person with a disability was a party to the lawsuit.

A contrary court decision, one which correctly recognizes that a provider cannot exercise a choice for residents which limits integration, rejected a challenge to a zoning ordinance which precluded placement of residential facilities within 1,320 feet of existing facilities.[99] Familystyle had thirteen homes on one street, four homes on another street, and other homes as well. It sought to occupy one home with 13 residents, another with six and another with four. Specifically finding that the zoning rule does "not prohibit mentally ill persons from renting or buying a home within 1,320 feet" of another home (thus respecting an individual's personal choice), the court upheld the restrictions as applied to a "facility provider":

> The state has determined that a proper setting is one which is, as much as possible, in the mainstream of the community. Forcing new residential facilities to locate at a distance from other facilities by its very terms prevents the clustering of homes which could lead the mentally ill to cloister themselves and not interact with the community mainstream. Because the state and local laws prohibit this clustering effect, they do further the goal of integrating the handicapped into the community.

D. PROFESSIONALS' CHOICE

Related to the influence of providers on general program-type choices is the often determinative choosing which is performed by professionals.

> Just as persons with disabilities may have limited opportunities to exercise personal choice and autonomy on a daily basis, it is also quite unusual for them to be actively involved in the development of their service plans (e.g., educational, habilitation programs). * * * Far too often, educational, residential, and vocational placements reflect the choice of well-meaning parents and staff rather than the preferences of the individual with the disability.[100]

During the 1980s there was a significant professionalization of retardation services, with interdisciplinary teams and other bodies assigned to make choices for people.[101-102] Professionals continue to wield considerable authority and to make choices for people in their charge, and the law often upholds that authority.[103-104]

E. NEIGHBORHOODS' CHOICE

Communities to which people with retardation are returning sometimes oppose development of community homes. Estimates of opposition to about 25% to 35% of residences underestimate the extent of opposition because they do not include those homes which fail to open or close early.[105] While, over time, opposition decreases and support increases, regardless of the neighborhood's initial opposition,[106] the potential for opposition surely affects siting choices by governments and private providers.

E. RESPECTING CHOICE AND CHOOSING THE CHOOSER

Clearly, the preferred chooser is the person with retardation. Unfortunately, however, he or she is most typically the subject or victim of other people's choices. For those individuals who presently cannot express choices themselves, we must turn to various surrogate alternatives for both decision-rules and for specific decisions.

It is not sufficient simply to accede to parental desires for children or to turn over decisions wholesale to guardians of adults, or to professionals, providers, or others. Whatever decision-maker is permitted to speak for the individual to make a specific decision, it is essential that the decision-maker be bound by decision-rules, and decision-processes, which reflect the imperative that "choice" be exercised in accordance with the principles of normalization and social role valorization and, thus, in favor of options which reflect physical and social integration, and culturally normative results.

Where the person's wishes are not known directly, efforts can usually be made to ascertain those wishes indirectly, both from the person and those who know the person well.[107–108]

Where decisions are made which are so important that they have irreversible results, or will deny habilitation or other treatment, or will affect such basic interests as a person's liberty, the waiver of a person's rights should not be entrusted to a surrogate decision-maker alone, but should be reviewed by a court, with the individual represented at the hearing by an advocate assigned to argue *against* the waiver of rights.[109]

Regardless of our individual roles in the lives of people with retardation, it is essential to turn toward those people who are identified variously as consumers, clients, or who are advocating for themselves. From the first gatherings of such groups in the 1970s, the demands of such organizations have been for the same things required by the normalization principle and the rights enunciated by the United Nations and by the courts: community services rather than institutions, paid employment, maximum self-sufficiency, ability to choose helpers and services, involvement in policymaking.[110]

> *Where the person's wishes are not known directly, efforts can usually be made to ascertain those wishes indirectly, both from the person and those who know the person well.*

Conclusion

Elevation of "choice" above other elements of normalization inevitably shortchanges the people who we serve. Their choices are often restricted by the deprivations to which we have subjected them or by denial of real-life experience with the options which we present to them.

People are also presented with fake or insincere opportunities to choose. Where a government agency or contracted provider has a short predetermined menu of alternatives, meaningful choice is not possible. For a person who wants a job, a choice of which sheltered workshop station to sit at is not a real choice. For a person who wants her own home, a choice between group homes, or a choice of bedspread, is not a real choice. In those situations, we have a tendency to retrospectively endorse such a fake choice as a real one, forgetting the narrowing of options over which the individual has no control.

For a person who wants a job, a choice of which sheltered workshop station to sit at is not a real choice.

If the goal is to enable and assist people to have access to a valued life and a valued culture, then we need to ask ourselves questions on each occasion where we believe we are providing, presenting, or witnessing a "choice." Kristjana Kristiansen and others have begun to articulate these issues.[111] I would contribute these questions:

- What frame of reference is being used?
- How do we assist people in obtaining access to a better frame of reference when making choices?
- What is life like for other people of the same age, interests, and goals? How do the prospective choices enable that life?
- Is the suggested choice likely to invite, risk, or perpetuate neglect or other harm?
- Who is the most vulnerable in the situation? Who is at risk if particular choices are made? Who will be left out?
- Who is the chooser? Why is this the chooser in this situation? What voice does the subject of the choice have? Why does he or she not have a greater or determinative choice?

With these questions both in mind and in practice, perhaps we can begin to see the place of choice.

Endnotes

1. D.L. Dix, Memorial to the Legislature of Massachusetts (1843), *in* 1 THE HISTORY OF MENTAL RETARDATION: COLLECTED PAPERS, at 6, 3–30 (M. Rosen et al. eds., 1976).

2. K. Grunewald, Speech given at the World Federation for Mental Health, Dublin (1971), *in* CREATING INDIVIDUAL SUPPORTS FOR PEOPLE WITH DEVELOPMENTAL DISABILITIES (V.J. Bradley et al. eds., 1994).

3. K. Moore & D. Ferleger, Evolutions in Advocacy 1960–1994, People With Developmental Disabilities in the United States, Presentation at conference, Beyond Normalization Toward One Society for All (June 3, 1994) in Reykjavik, Iceland.

4. B.C. Blaney & E.L. Freud, (1994). *Trying to Play Together: Competing Paradigms in Approaches to Inclusion Through Recreation and Leisure*, *in* CREATING INDIVIDUAL SUPPORTS FOR PEOPLE WITH DEVELOPMENTAL DISABILITIES, at 245, 237–253 (V.J. Bradley et al. eds., 1994).

5. G. Dybwad, *Action Implications: USA Today*, *in* CHANGING PATTERNS IN RESIDENTIAL SERVICES FOR THE MENTALLY RETARDED, at 423, 383–428 (W. Wolfensberger & R. Krugel eds., 1969).

6. J.W. TRENT, JR., INVENTING THE FEEBLE MIND: A HISTORY OF MENTAL RETARDATION IN THE UNITED STATES (1994).

7. *Id.*

8. D. Corcoran, *Nameless Headstones for the Forgotten Mentally Retarded*, N.Y. TIMES, Dec. 9, 1991, at B12.

9. K.C. LAKIN ET AL., RESIDENTIAL SERVICES FOR PERSONS WITH MENTAL RETARDATION AND RELATED CONDITIONS: YEAR ENDING JUNE 30, 1991 (1993).

10. TRENT, *supra* note 6 (citing Braddock, 1987).

11. D.J. VAIL, DEHUMANIZATION AND THE INSTITUTIONAL CAREER (1967).

12. W.D. White & W. Wolfensberger, *The Evolution of Dehumanization in Our Institutions*, 7(3) MENTAL RETARDATION 5–9 (1969).

13. TRENT, *supra* note 6.

14. Halderman v. Pennhurst State Sch. and Hosp., 1994 WL 150371 (E.D. Pa. Mar. 28, 1994).

15. Lelsz v. Kavanagh, 673 F. Supp. 828 (N.D. Tex. 1987).

16. S. SCHWARTZ, ANNOTATED LIST OF DAMAGE CASES FOR PERSONS WITH MENTAL DISABILITIES (1994).

17. B. BLATT, EXODUS FROM PANDEMONIUM, at 79, (1970).

18. R. Traustadottir et al., *Community Living: A Multicultural Perspective, in* CHALLENGES FOR A SERVICE SYSTEM IN TRANSITION 405–426 (M.F. Hayden & B.H. Abery eds., 1994).

19. K.C. Lakin et al., *Deinstitutionalization and Community Adjustment: A Summary of Research and Issues, in* DEINSTITUTIONALIZATION AND COMMUNITY ADJUSTMENT OF MENTALLY RETARDED PEOPLE, at 391, 382–412 (R.H. Bruininks et al. eds., 1981).

20. J. O'Brien & C.L. O'Brien, *More than Just a New Address: Images of Organization for Supported Living Agencies, in* CREATING INDIVIDUAL SUPPORTS FOR PEOPLE WITH DEVELOPMENTAL DISABILITIES, at 119, 109–140 (V.J. Bradley et al. eds., 1994).

21. *Id.* at 125.

22. BLATT, *supra* note 17.

23. K. Moore, *Vocational and Day Services: Summary Data—Pennhurst Plaintiff Class in Philadelphia*, presented at trial, *Halderman v. Pennhurst State Sch. and Hosp.*, (E.D. Pa. Dec., 1993).

24. Halderman, *supra* note 14.

25. S. Gant, *Report and Recommendations: Status of Philadelphia Class Members*. Filed with the court in *Halderman v. Pennhurst State Sch. and Hosp.* (E.D. Pa. Feb. 19, 1991).

26. E. Seguin, Origin of the Treatment and Training of Idiots (1864) *in* 1 THE HISTORY OF MENTAL RETARDATION: COLLECTED PAPERS, at 159, 151–159 (M. Rosen et al. eds., 1976).

27. R.E. Cooke, *The Free Choice Principle in the Care of the Mentally Retarded, in* CHANGING PATTERNS IN RESIDENTIAL SERVICES FOR THE MENTALLY RETARDED 359–365 (W. Wolfensberger & R. Kugel eds., 1969).

28. V.J. Bradley, *Evolution of a New Service Paradigm, in* CREATING INDIVIDUAL SUPPORTS FOR PEOPLE WITH DEVELOPMENTAL DISABILITIES 11–32 (V.J. Bradley et al. eds., 1994).

29. *Id.* at 13.

30. R.C. SCHEERENBERGER, A HISTORY OF MENTAL RETARDATION: A QUARTER CENTURY OF PROMISE, at 116, (1987).

31. N. Bank-Mikkelsen, *A Metropolitan Area in Denmark: Copenhagen*, *in* CHANGING PATTERNS IN RESIDENTIAL SERVICES FOR THE MENTALLY RETARDED 227–254 (W. Wolfensberger & R. Kugel eds., 1969).

32. Dybwad, *supra* note 5.

33. B. Nirje, *The Normalization Principle and Its Human Management Implications*, *in* CHANGING PATTERNS IN RESIDENTIAL SERVICES FOR THE MENTALLY RETARDED, at 181, 181–194 (W. Wolfensberger & R. Kugel eds., 1969).

34. *Id.*

35. *Id.*

36. *Id.*

37. *Id.* at 184.

38. W. Wolfensberger, *The Definition of Normalization: Update, Problems, Disagreements and Misunderstandings*, *in* NORMALIZATION, SOCIAL INTEGRATION AND COMMUNITY SERVICES, at 80, 71–115 (R. Flynn & K. Nitsch eds., 1980).

39. W. WOLFENSBERGER, THE PRINCIPLE OF NORMALIZATION IN HUMAN SERVICES (1972). Toronto, Canada: National Institute on Mental Retardation.

40. W. Wolfensberger, *Social Role Valorization: A Proposed New Term for the Principle of Normalization*, 21 MENTAL RETARDATION 234–239 (1983).

41. M. Smull & A.J. Danehy, *Increasing Quality While Reducing Costs: The Challenge of the 1990s*, *in* CREATING INDIVIDUAL SUPPORTS FOR PEOPLE WITH DEVELOPMENTAL DISABILITIES, at 67, 59–78 (V.J. Bradley et al. eds., 1994).

42. B. Mount, *Benefits and Limitations of Personal Futures Planning*, *in* CREATING INDIVIDUAL SUPPORTS FOR PEOPLE WITH DEVELOPMENTAL DISABILITIES, at 103, 97–108 (V.J. Bradley et al. eds., 1994).

43. R. Neumeyer et al., *Leisure-Related Peer Preference Choices of Individuals With Down Syndrome*, 31 MENTAL RETARDATION 396–402 (1993).

44. Wolfensberger, *supra* note 38, at 93.

45. Wolfensberger, *supra* note 38, at 110.

46. S.B. Sarason, *The Creation of Settings, in* CHANGING PATTERNS IN RESIDEN-
    TIAL SERVICES FOR THE MENTALLY RETARDED, at 357, 341–357 (W.
    Wolfensberger & R. Kugel eds., 1969).

47. W.T. McCord, *From Theory to Reality: Obstacles to the Implementation
    of the Normalization Principle in Human Services*, 20(6) MENTAL RETAR-
    DATION 247–253 (1982).

48. UNITED NATIONS, DECLARATION OF GENERAL AND SPECIAL RIGHTS OF THE
    MENTALLY RETARDED (1971).

49. UNITED NATIONS, THE STANDARD RULES ON EQUALIZATION OF OPPORTUNITIES
    FOR PERSONS WITH DISABILITIES (1993).

50. American Association on Mental Deficiency, *Rights of Mentally Retarded
    Persons*, 11(5) MENTAL RETARDATION 56–58 (1973).

51. Wyatt v. Stickney, 344 F. Supp. 387 (M.D. Ala. 1972).

52. Wyatt v. Stickney, 773 F. Supp. 1508 (M.D. Ala. 1991).

53. Halderman v. Pennhurst State Sch. and Hosp., 446 F. Supp. 1295 (E.D. Pa.
    1974).

54. Halderman, *supra* note 14.

55. Lelsz, *supra* note 15.

56. Lelsz v. Kavanagh, 783 F. Supp. 286 (N.D. Tex. 1991), *aff'd*, 983 F.2d
    1061 (5th Cir.), *cert. denied*, 114 S. Ct. 287 (1993).

57. NYARC v. Carey 393 F. Supp. 715 (E.D.N.Y. 1975).

58. NYARC v. Carey, 492 F. Supp. 1099 (E.D.N.Y. 1980).

59. Developmentally Disabled Assistance and Bill of Rights Act of 1975
    reprinted in *Rehabilitation and Developmental Legislation*. Washington,
    DC: U.S. Gov't.

60. D. Ferleger & P. Boyd, *Rights and Dignity: The Supreme Court, Congress
    and People With Disabilities After Pennhurst*, 5 W. New Eng. L. Rev. 327
    (1983).

61. Americans with Disabilities Act of 1990, 42 U.S.C. § 12101 *et seq.*

62. United Nations, *supra* note 48.

63. United Nations, *supra* note 49.

64. AAMD, *supra* note 50.

65. Youngberg v. Romeo, 457 U.S. 307 (1982).

66. Thomas S. v. Morrow, 781 F.2d 367 (4th Cir. 1986).

67. Thomas S. v. Flaherty, 699 F. Supp. 1178 (W.D.N.C. 1988), *aff'd*, 902 F.2d 250 (4th Cir.), *cert. denied*, 111 S. Ct. 373 (1990).

68. Clark v. Cohen, 794 F.2d 79 (3d Cir. 1986).

69. Wyatt, *supra* note 52.

70. Jackson v. Fort Stanton Hosp. & Training Sch., 757 F. Supp. 1243 (D.N.M. 1990), *rev'd in part*, 964 F.2d 980 (10th Cir. 1992).

71. Halderman, *supra* note 14.

72. Halderman v. Pennhurst State Sch. and Hosp., 901 F.2d 311 (3d Cir. 1990), *cert. denied*, 111 S. Ct. 140 (1990).

73. Lessard v. Schmidt, 349 F. Supp. 1078 (E.D. Wisc. 1972).

74. Lynch v. Baxley, 386 F. Supp. 378 (M.D. Ala. 1974).

75. S. Stefan, *Whose Egg Is It Anyway? Reproductive Rights of Incarcerated, Institutionalized and Incompetent Women,* 13 NOVA L. REV. 405 (1989).

76. DeShaney v. Winnebago County Dep't of Social Servs., 489 U.S. 189 (1989).

77. S.H. v. Edwards, 886 F.2d 292 (11th Cir. 1989).

78. Jackson, *supra* note 70.

79. Arnold v. Dep't of Health Servs., 160 Ariz. 593, 775 P.2d 521 (1989).

80. Lelsz, *supra* note 56.

81. Coffelt v. Dep't of Developmental Servs., No. 916401, slip op. (Cal Super. 1994).

82. W. Wolfensberger, *A New Approach to Decision-Making in Human Management Services, in* CHANGING PATTERNS IN RESIDENTIAL SERVICES FOR THE MENTALLY RETARDED, at 369, 367–381 (W. Wolfensberger & R. Kugel eds., 1969).

83. Baccus v. Parrish, No. 3:92-CV-0666-H (N.D. Tex. November 29, 1993), appeal *appeal filed*, No. 94-10017 (5th Cir.).

84. Wimber v. Dep't of Social & Rehabilitation Servs. 1994 WL 192039 (D. C. Kan. April 13, 1994).

85. Lelsz, *supra* note 56.

86. D. FERLEGER & P. BOYD, ANTI-INSTITUTIONALIZATION: THE PROMISE OF THE PENNHURST CASE, STAN. L.R. 717–752 (1979), *reprinted in* NORMALIZA-TION, SOCIAL INTEGRATION AND COMMUNITY SERVICES 141–166 (R. Flynn & K. Nitsch eds., 1980).

87. D. Ferleger, *Anti-institutionalization and the Supreme Court*, 14 RUTGERS L.J. 595–635 (1983).

88. M. Minow, *When Difference Has Its Home: Group Homes for the Mentally Retarded, Equal Protection and Legal Treatment of Difference*, 22 HARV. C.R.-C.L. L. REV. 111–189 (1987).

89. S. SPREAT ET AL., ATTITUDES TOWARD DEINSTITUTIONALIZATION: A NATIONAL SURVEY OF FAMILIES OF INSTITUTIONALIZED MENTALLY RETARDED PERSONS (1985).

90. W. Wolfensberger, Will There Always Be an Institution? II. The Impact of New Service Models, *in* 2 THE HISTORY OF MENTAL RETARDATION: COL-LECTED PAPERS, at 424, 415–424 (M. Rosen et al. eds., 1976) (article originally appeared in MENTAL RETARDATION, 9(6): 31–38.)

91. J.W. CONROY & V.J. BRADLEY, THE PENNHURST LONGITUDINAL STUDY: A REPORT OF FIVE YEARS OF RESEARCH AND ANALYSIS (1985).

92. S.A. Larson & K.C. Lakin, *Parent Attitudes about Residential Placement Before and After Deinstitutionalization: A Research Synthesis*, 16 J. OF THE ASS'N FOR PERSONS WITH SEVERE HANDICAPS 25–38 (1991).

93. J.W. Conroy, *Reactions to Deinstitutionalization Among Parents of Mentally Retarded Persons, in* LIVING AND LEARNING IN THE LEAST RESTRIC-TIVE ALTERNATIVE 141–152 (R.H. Bruininks & K.C. Lakin eds., 1985).

94. Halderman v. Pennhurst State Sch. and Hosp., 707 F.2d 702 (3d Cir. 1982).

95. King v. Fallon, 801 F. Supp. 925 (D.R.I. 1992).

96. Wimber, *supra* note 84.

97. M.F. Hayden & P. DePaepe, *Waiting for Community Services: The Impact on Persons with Mental Retardation and Other Developmental*

Disabilities in CHALLENGES FOR A SERVICE SYSTEM IN TRANSITION 173–206 (M.F. Hayden & B.H. Abery eds., 1994).

98. Parish of Jefferson v. Allied Health Care, Inc., 1992 WL 142574 (E.D. La. June 10, 1992).

99. Familystyle of St. Paul, Inc. v. City of St. Paul, 728 F. Supp. 1396 (D. Minn. 1990).

100. B.H. Abery, *A Conceptual Framework for Enhancing Self-Determination, in* CHALLENGES FOR A SERVICE SYSTEM IN TRANSITION 345–380 (M.F. Hayden & B.H. Abery eds., 1994).

101. M.W. Krauss, *On the Medicalization of Family Caregiving* 31(2) MENTAL RETARDATION 78–80 (1993).

102. Moore, *supra* note 3.

103. Youngberg, *supra* note 65.

104. Jackson, *supra* note 70.

105. M.M. Selzer & G. Seltzer, *Community Responses to Community Residences for Persons Who Have Mental Retardation, in* LIVING ENVIRONMENTS AND MENTAL RETARDATION (S. Landesman & P. Vietze eds., 1987).

106. *Id.*

107. Mount, *supra* note 42.

108. Smull, *supra* note 41.

109. In re Biscardi, No. 86P1126-G1 (Bristol Probate and Family Court, Massachusetts October 25, 1993).

110. Scheerenberger, *supra* note 30.

111. K. Kristiansen, Responsibility and Quality Assurance in a Collapsing Welfare System, Presentation at conference, Beyond Normalization Toward One Society for All (June 3, 1994) in Reykjavik, Iceland.

Section Two
The Context for Considering Choice
and Responsibility

10

Some Significant Ethical Issues in Residential Services

Michael Kendrick

Introduction

Residential services play a dominant role in overall control of the lives of clients. The well-being of residents can be dramatically helped or hurt by the character of the services and those who work in them. The range of ethical issues that may be faced is substantial since virtually all aspects of life are affected by one's home life. What has been selected here for discussion are merely some of these issues. While the issues selected are important, they are presented here only in the briefest forms.

Often the whole character of a human enterprise may turn on a single choice. So it is with residential services that their eventual identity may be massively dependent upon what their sponsors conclude in practice is best for clients. If they choose the wrong path, it is quite possible that thousands of lives can be harmed. Similarly, if a constructive path is chosen, great good can follow. Thus, it is very important that the crucial day-to-day ethics of residential services not be taken as automatically self-evident and beneficial.

Ethics are often reduced to decision rules concerning choices and conduct. While this view has validity, it ignores that ethics draw for their authority on the deeper values of society. Often these values are embedded in everyday culture as "taken for granted" assumptions and beliefs. These values will eventually summate into practical ethics whether these are recognized as such or not. This paper will examine five selected examples of ethical matters that rest deeply in the current culture of residential services. While they are referred to here as "issues," they may actually not be treated by many as a problem in everyday life. In this way they reveal themselves to be "settled" matters.

This paper will first examine the current character of our residential services from the vantage point of whether they help provide genuine homes for people and whether the act of providing service detracts from this sense of

home. Secondly, the clients of most services may be endangered by being
subject to either the harmful effects of services themselves or the general
hazards of community life.

The same essential house, apartment, or condominium can for one person be a "home," yet for another, it can be a "program site" or "facility." The difference is not merely one of vocabulary, but of two quite dramatically different concepts and realities.

This will be presented with a
view toward discerning
whether intentional safe-
guards may be needed.
Thirdly, the paper will examine what may be at stake
if a developmental mentality
gives way to a custodial one.
Fourth, client choice will be
examined from within the
web of conditions that influence its eventual expression. Finally, the often
hidden use of clients as involuntary participants in a wide variety of well-
intended, but not necessarily advantageous, experiments will be examined.

A "Home" or a "Facility"

It matters immensely what a thing really is as opposed to what it may seem
to be. The same essential house, apartment, or condominium can for one
person be a "home," yet for another, it can be a "program site" or "facility."
The difference is not merely one of vocabulary, but of two quite dramatically
different concepts and realities. We are tempted by the superficial similarities
(i.e., the same house) into thinking that in social, psychological, legal, and moral
dimensions the contexts are similar. Yet a "facility" is not a "home" even though
it may aspire to maintain as much of the idea of "home" as may be possible.

"Home" as we commonly use the idea can simply be something like
"household" or "dwelling." Yet for most people, "home" goes much further
in that it refers to a place of considerable personal, intimate meaning. It is the
place where we are most ourselves, surrounded by those closest to us and
where we are most able to achieve privacy. While few people have identical
senses of what is and isn't important in the cluster of meanings involved in our
common sense of "home," few would disagree that there is indeed a rich
meaning to what most people mean by "home" in our culture.

"Facility" is a quite different matter than "home." It is a programmatic
term intended to describe a resource for the dispensation of some form of
treatment rendered under agency and professional authority. A "facility"
needn't be a "home" (in the normative sense of the word) even though people
reside there. This can also be seen in the common administrative description

of residential institutions as "facilities." Most people can readily distinguish the difference between homes and facilities when such facilities and groupings are larger than the size of most ordinary people's homes. Even mini-institutions may quickly be recognized as facilities. Where it becomes more difficult is when the size, grouping, and general appearance of a household is within the range of what is normative. Under these circumstances, the things that make it a facility can be so subtle that it may be hard to immediately identify the elements of both. Nonetheless, it is not purely a "home" even at this point. This is because the characteristics of the home are nonnormative on many other less obvious dimensions beyond those of grouping size and household appearance.

Perhaps the most important distinguishing factor to note is whether the home is indeed that of the person(s) who reside there. In this sense, did they elect to live there or was the place selected for them by others? At issue is whether they exercise some normative sense of sovereignty over the home typical of that enjoyed by most citizens. Specifi-

Putting in familiar personal furniture and decorations may make a nursing home room more "homey," but it cannot make it a home.

cally, there should be no confusion as to whose home it really is. For many clients of services, the home isn't really theirs, but rather is controlled by others—typically agencies or other corporate bodies. Ownership may be less the issue than personal dominion over one's place of residence. To be one's home, such dominion need not be absolute in the sense that it may be shared with others, yet the understanding that it is authentically "your place" should not be in dispute.

Another useful distinction that can illuminate the essential character of a dwelling is whether it is a home or "home-like." The intent to make a home a real home is quite antithetical to the commitment to creating a "home-like" substitute. By definition, a "home-like" entity is, at essence, intentionally not a home. As such, it represents an unambiguous resolve to intentionally compromise the normative concept of home. Putting in familiar personal furniture and decorations may make a nursing home room more "homey," but it cannot make it a home. This is because at its most fundamental level, a nursing home is intentionally a program.

Many residential settings can be distinguished from homes by whether they are, at their core, private rather than public places. In the normative sense of "home," one's dwelling is essentially private property even if one rents. This is not so with residential programs in that the place is subject to public oversight and management in ways not done in regards to private homes. Perhaps the most obvious of these is the regulation of access to the home of the resident. In residential services, it is not uncommon for a wide range of persons associated with the program to have access to the dwelling. This is most noticeable in larger programs or heavily staffed programs. Some managers reduce this invasiveness through rules that require the residents' permission before access is granted. Still, this is a difference that does not actually change the essential status of the dwelling from public to private. Of course, for most clients, the place they live in is unapologetically public in nature.

Few of us would normally have people placed in our home under the will and direction of others. Yet, that is essentially what is done when we staff residential programs.

In most cases, a residential setting is in actuality the private-appearing expression of a public activity, i.e., running a residential program. The setting is often selected by the agency, partially paid for out of program funds or even owned outright by the agency, managed as an agency asset, registered publicly as a program site, presented in agency promotional material as the agency's, managed and maintained by agency personnel, disposed of by the agency when no longer of programmatic utility, etc. As a consequence, it is a fiction to pretend that this type of setting is, in fact, private. It is much more accurate to see it as an instrumentality of interests other than those of the resident. In most cases these interests are ultimately public. Even those programs managed by so-called private agencies still render the site to be something other than the private home of the resident.

An additional dimension of usurpation of the private character of the homes of residents is the lawful intrusion into the home by various regulatory and public safeguarding groups. Their right to inspect the home comes from the essential identity of the setting as a facility for programmatic activity. Whether this oversight is licensing, certification, quality assurance, human rights monitoring, or whatever, may not matter as much as the status of these activities, and the invasiveness they represent is simply not normative in private homes. These practices are permissible only when the activities in the home characterize it as a publicly sanctioned service.

Few of us would normally have people placed in our home under the will and direction of others. Yet, that is essentially what is done when we staff residential programs. These staff often insist on a whole range of staff accoutrements, accessories, and activities such as offices, staff parking, staff meetings, residential logs, safes and other locked cabinets, various required programmatic rituals, e.g., "group," house meetings, etc. Not untypically, the staff are not persons recruited, selected, managed, and disposed of by the resident, but are unmistakably the agents and employees of other interests. As remarkable as it may seem, these patterns are so taken for granted as necessary compromises with the concept of "home" that few persons even stop to consider what things might be like if the concept of "home" were wholeheartedly pursued and edified.

Clearly, if the vast majority of people can manage to have a genuine home, why is it that persons designated as clients of services must forfeit this possibility? In part, it derives from the social devaluation of the clients. Few normative courtesies and considerations are granted to those who are deemed lowly in society. A condition of receiving service which is not usually explicitly stated, but nonetheless is in effect, is that once you are a client, you must abide by the rules of your caretakers. You are beholden to them through your "neediness." As such, a kind of programmatic domination gets created whereby the persons served lose their ability to direct their own lives. Instead, the server and serving organization take its place. This conquest is often portrayed as a voluntary surrender of autonomy and control, but it is rarely ever done explicitly enough to pass most reasonable tests of consent. Thus, this process of takeover might be better portrayed as an assumption of control by the serving authority over the person, even if such a stance was not recognized consciously by either the client or the server. Nevertheless, the public typically expects service providers to be "in charge" and holds such providers to a standard of judgement commensurate with their presumed custodial obligations, i.e., "duty of care." In this way a lower standard of "home" is accorded to socially devalued persons who become clients of a service provider.

A second possible reason that the concept of home is so readily sacrificed is that it is either not thought to be of any particular importance intrinsically to persons with disabilities or it is not a primary consideration in rendering assistance to people. "Home" in this sense is treated as a "frill" of no particular importance that can be gotten to once the more important programmatic work is done. If the people being served are socially devalued or stigmatized, it may well be assumed that they do not deserve to be treated as well as most citizens would expect. In all likelihood, they will be treated less well than others by giving very little standing to many other normative human needs—not only that of "home."

These preceding speculations as to why "home" may be denied to clients of services focus largely on societal views of the client. It is also possible that another contributing factor is that the socialization and outlook of professionals and leaders in the field do not prepare them to see the importance of not only "home," but a wide range of other universal human needs. Certainly in the general field of disability, it often has been difficult and divisive to get the field to adopt normalized life-style goals (e.g., community living, integration, etc.) for clients. Consequently, it is highly possible that at least some of those leaders and professionals in the field are either doubtful that "home" can be achieved as a practical matter, or are actively resistant to the proposition. When a field is dominated by a view of clients as pathologically or irreversibly different, it is understandable that the dominant residential model will not be normative and probably significantly deficient. As the field moves towards a view of clients as being people like all other people, one can expect the growth of residential patterns that are closer to what is typical for most people, i.e., "home."

> *As the field moves towards a view of clients as being people like all other people, one can expect the growth of residential patterns that are closer to what is typical for most people, i.e., "home."*

The Probable Endangerment of Clients and the Need for Appropriate Intentional Safeguards

Most clients of human services are in a disadvantaged position in society. Most are poor, lack power and powerful allies, often are from groups which are socially devalued, etc. It is quite reasonable to portray them as vulnerable to being treated less well than most citizens. In fact, persons with disabilities are disproportionately at risk of abuse and mistreatment in comparison to their nondisabled peers. As a consequence, it is useful to see such persons as living an existence of relative endangerment or heightened vulnerability to socially constructed and patterned mistreatment. In this sense, their mistreatment is neither random nor anomalous, but is better understood as organized and systematic. Obviously, a group's risk factors are not necessarily fulfilled in the experience of a given person.

Logically, if one lives a life filled with probable dangers, one learns to live defensively so as to better the odds that some misfortune does not befall oneself. The actions one takes constitute a safeguarding strategy which may have multiple and complementary components. Taken together, these measures reduce the likelihood of bad things happening. If for instance one lives in an area with high crime rates, one travels about with various precautions; one's home is made secure; help is organized to be nearby if needed; one avoids certain high-risk situations or behaviors, etc. Thus, heightened risk does not necessarily translate into negative consequences if one's intentional safeguards

Persons who have never been deprived of their credibility through misleading stereotypes may have trouble perceiving the problems recipients of mental health services have in being taken seriously.

are substantial enough to compensate for the level of danger present. Proper safeguarding may not be foolproof, but it does provide a positive, constructive, and feasible response to living with societally induced endangerment.

Many residential service providers fail to fully recognize the degree to which clients are more vulnerable to mistreatment, abuse, or neglect. This may simply be due to the naive and wishful assumption that human service clients are "just like everybody else," when it is patently clear that they labor under disadvantages which are not shared by more privileged persons and classes. While it is true that their needs as human beings are like those of everyone else, they must cope with the additional burdens of being disadvantaged or devalued in society. Persons who have never been deprived of their credibility through misleading stereotypes may have trouble perceiving the problems recipients of mental health services have in being taken seriously.

A second and major source of endangerment for such clients arises from their reliance on services and the control of many aspects of their lives by service providers. "Services" are often portrayed by their practitioners in largely positive and enabling terms. Such depictions are not completely without merit in that a good deal of inspirational and even heroic conduct occurs in human services, much as it does in all walks of life. However, such virtue cannot be institutionalized to the degree that it would substantiate the utopian fantasy that all services are consistently noble. The more earthly reality is that services are subject to the same forces of decadence, imperfection, entropy, dysfunctionality, and perversity that have been evident in human experience through the ages. Whether it is an attractive notion or not, human services are deeply flawed by all manner of shortcomings. In this sense, they are indeed "human" services.

The implications for clients who are now highly vulnerable to the errors, limitations, and transgressions of imperfect services are as numerous as the dangers that each specific shortcoming may create. For instance, if services are poorly conceived as to what clients really need, it is highly probable that the service will miss the mark and provide service that is unneeded or even harmful. Similarly, if the model of service is reasonably valid, but those implementing it are unmotivated, corrupt, or simply incompetent, the service will still shortchange or perhaps even injure the client. Similarly, if a venal administrator surreptitiously thieves from the private funds of clients, a trust will have been breached that results in a loss to the persons affected. In all of these instances and in multitudes of others, the central point is not just that services are flawed and clients are vulnerable to the resulting effects; rather, the central ethical preoccupation should be on assuring such clients the greatest degree of appropriate safeguarding feasible. By this, it is not meant that all well-intended safeguards are likely to be effective or appropriate, since many safeguarding measures are themselves flawed and insufficient. The more important point is that good service is not possible or realistic without good safeguards against the intrinsic limitations of the service itself.

For residential services, the implication is that clients should be provided the means or context by which they can most optimally benefit from both society and services. However, this must be done in such a way as to ensure that the least harm comes from the engagement. This obligation derives not only from the abstract principle that the server must ensure safety and security, but also from the practical necessities

Whether it is an attractive notion or not, human services are deeply flawed by all manner of shortcomings. In this sense, they are indeed "human" services.

of living in a world where bad things happen disproportionately to clients, and many of these are partially, if not wholly, preventable and reducible. The server is not being of much service if the client remains weighted with endangerments that could have been avoided or limited through astute service practices.

A further dimension of the problem of realistic safeguarding is the reality that services do not "per se" exist solely or even primarily for the exclusive benefit of the client. Services are suffused with a variety of legitimate and not so legitimate vested interests whose needs, preferences, priorities, values, and outlook may substantially clash or compete with that of the clients. Competing and conflicting interests may well adopt practices that are actually detrimental to the client. Given that most clients are not well positioned to struggle against more powerful interests, it is predictable that their ability to alone prevail against these forces is severely limited. As such, most services, quite routinely, may not be solely "consumer driven," but rather "interest driven." The common facile posturing that "only the clients' interest matters" cannot possibly be true even if it were our fervent wish.

One clearly essential proactive safeguarding preoccupation must be the defense of clients against other interests that may unfairly prevail over theirs. Put into other terms, it is the question of, "Whose service is it anyways?" Given that other interests may overwhelm those of the clients, thoughtful service providers must confront the question: To whom do they owe their greatest loyalty? For instance, is it one's employer, the funder, families, one's agency, one's profession, the client, one's col-

Given that other interests may overwhelm those of the clients, thoughtful service providers must confront the question: To whom do they owe their greatest loyalty?

leagues, etc.? It is noteworthy that the server's own personal vested interest may collide with that of the client. This is the normal and quite ancient challenge of addressing one's inherent conflicts of interest. However, if the server believes it to be imperative to faithfully ally with the client against legitimate or other vested antiethical interests, which might further disadvantage the client, such fidelity to clients may occasionally cost people their jobs.

Custodial or Developmental Ethics

As has been indicated earlier, there is a widespread tendency in services that results in clients becoming objects of custodial care. Custodialization may have many advantages in that it ensures that clients of services are maintained in safety and in healthy circumstances. Given the atrocities found in "bad" custodial situations, it is possible to recognize a "good" custodialization. Nonetheless, human beings are much more than insensate bodies requiring civil, hospitable, and clean accommodation. Being "in the community" is no insulation from becoming custodialized, though this brand of it might be usefully distinguished as a neo-custodialism.

Perhaps the most obvious universal of human needs is "to have a life"; to grow and to not waste one's potential. This can express itself as a search for challenge, a love of learning and stimulation, a hunger for experience, an impatience with tedium, a delight in novelty, or whatever. This stirring indicates in people a propensity towards development and growth that must somehow be answered. The ethic that would guide such a quest would necessarily have at its foundation a view of clients as having such a potential, a practical grasp of the many ways such a need might be addressed, and a resolve not to lapse into a nondevelopmental posture, i.e., to retreat to merely a custodial or maintenance-oriented outlook. Choices do exist in daily life in residential programs. Clearly some of these choices will be far more developmental in outlook than others.

As has been noted, socially devalued persons may have a particular difficulty in having their humanity and potential recognized. If they are not actually seen as valuable human beings, then it is probable their lives and what might be accomplished in them will be discounted. If the conclusion is that they are not a priority for a developmental investment, then it will follow that they will be impoverished and deprived, if not outright neglected or harmed. Given that many clients of services do not reach their realistic potential, it is logical that sufficient developmental investments were not made. Such persons may quite accurately be seen as suffering from a lack of developmental commitment beyond that experienced by most people. Happily, the sustained neglect of people can be substantially reversed, even at a late age. It must be recognized nonetheless that this is predicated on the presence of persons and organizations with a developmental ethic.

While custodial and developmental ethics are not mirror images of themselves, it is crucial to note that a thoroughgoing developmental ethic will require a great deal more of people in a service role than simply providing custody alone. Consequently, a developmental orientation may indeed be more taxing overall. This burden of development may well be offset by the delights and joys of being part of a life-giving and enriching growth experience. Even so, it would be unwise to inordinately diminish the very real costs of development. Doing nothing may indeed be easier. Development is effort and, thereby, is harder to do.

Custodial functions do not necessarily preempt developmental ones, though each may constrain the other. Nonetheless, an indifferent custodial outlook may well place a premium on the wrong things, resulting in a thwarting of the client's will, a deprivation of opportunity and encouragement, and a hostility to a wholesome ambition. In many instances, custodial imperatives do drive out or diminish developmental ones—much like many organizations whose maintenance activities easily extinguish essential growth experiences. One of the worst aspects of unrepentant custodialism is the injury that can come to people through the callous paternalism of professionals, agencies, and governments who "know best" already and can no longer learn from, be guided by, and respond to the emergent reality of the clients' lives. Growth would require a partnership between clients and others that is undermined by a disregard for the essential dignity of people wanting to control their own lives. Yet for many people to grow, there must be the engagement of their will, their convictions, and their efforts.

The Context of Client Choice

While it has become commonplace for people to abstractly favor client "choice," it is not necessarily the case that what is meant by this sentiment is

"Choice" is not freestanding as it is always embedded in a web of both visible and unseen conditions that shape the nature of its enactment.

particularly obvious or even wholesome. Like all incantations, its true function may be more to reassure either the speaker or listener as to their virtue than to bespeak a promise or obligation. It is imperative to examine the ways in which client choice is discussed in order to see which version of "choice" one ultimately can favor. Behind each slogan of "choice" lies quite variable epistemologies: These are created not only by differing philosophical assumptions, but as well by the milieu within which such choices are eventually made. "Choice" is not freestanding as it is always embedded in a web of both visible and unseen conditions that shape the nature of its enactment.

An instructive example of the effect of milieu or environment may be seen where institutionalized persons are given "choice" over which foods they might prefer or which television show they would like. While the availability of choices may be a relative improvement, it is notable that the choices they might exercise are always subject to the initiative and approval of the authorities who control their life circumstances. Also noteworthy are all the choices not offered or even considered. For instance, what of the choice of one day leaving the institution and living in the community? Conceivably, one could have a life where one isn't beholden to the authorities as to which choices are "on the table."

A second instance is where it is assumed that persons are well-informed and thus make choices fully aware of what they are gaining or relinquishing. Choice without a full grasp of its implications may not be "choice" so much as self-directed decision-making in the framework of poor advice, information, or guidance. Such a concern may be most acute in instances where the decision-maker is impaired in competency to comprehend matters, poorly supported, or advised and/or mistaken. Even very astute persons can make foolish decisions if they are given and trust plausible but distorted versions of reality.

A third instance is where "choice" is bound up in agency practices that themselves constrain the quality of decision-making that may be ultimately possible. For instance, when the client has no access to outside advice and advocacy, he/she may well be unconsciously led to prefer options that are agreeable to those who surround him/her. When the process of making choices is articulated and institutionalized by the system, rather than the people themselves, it is quite possible that a process will be devised that is not particularly suitable for many clients. A common example of this can be found in the myriad individual program planning schemes that proliferate. These systems may only be as good as the people who show up for the meeting— even though their rhetoric and operational premises are that the planning team thinks only of what is best for the person. As indicated elsewhere in this paper, this pretense belies the underlying conflicts of interest, commitments, and talent of those in attendance, quite apart from the substantial influence of their frailties and true degree of loyalty to the client. In fact, in some instances the co-planners may be persons the client has no choice but to accept, e.g., their mandated case manager, etc.

For many persons, "choice" contains within it an obligation to honor all wants expressed by a person, whether these are sensible, meritorious, or otherwise advantageous.

Another instance is the clash between needs and wants. For many persons, "choice" contains within it an obligation to honor all wants expressed by a person, whether these are sensible, meritorious, or otherwise advantageous. The server may not begin with a sense of obligation to the client such that he/she would challenge the client's inclinations if those were seen by the server to lead to poor outcomes. Under these conditions, the server would have no scruples supporting even ill-informed choices as long as it is "what the client wants." A more eloquent defense for the transparent neglect of the client's true needs couldn't be found. A different approach would be to assume that the client's wants, needs, and best interests may be in conflict, and it may well benefit the client to be made aware of these conflicts, as well as the wide array of choices that are possible in his best interests. It may well anger clients to be challenged, but it may ultimately mean that whatever choices they eventually make are done with a clearer sense of what is at stake.

Beyond this point, there may well be both danger and value in a server arguing a case for a specific choice not currently favored by the client. The server may well be trying to convey important aspects of the situation not fully grasped or accepted by the client. A timid or understated argument may lack the compelling quality needed to impress some clients with the import of a matter. The danger is obviously one of choosing to influence—not just inform—the client. Many staff are uncomfortable with the thought that they might actually have legitimate values, opinions, and insights that can and should be conveyed to clients. They be-

The original creators of our residential institutions were like many people today in that they were so enthused for change and had few scruples as to what they were asking from the people whose lives would be captured in their experiment.

lieve they have no right to stand for anything whatsoever for fear that it may deprive clients of their right to choice through this untoward imposition or assertion of their judgement. As such, they resolve the resulting dilemma by themselves becoming people without convictions and principles, at least insofar as sharing these with the client is concerned. A quite different resolution to the matter would be to be scrupulous in ensuring that the client makes the eventual decision, but is afforded a process whereby the person is exposed, through a genuine dialogue, to matters or aspects that do not necessarily originate with the client.

The Unrecognized, Widespread, and Incessant Use of Clients as Involuntary Fodder for Human Service Experimentation

Services are a cultural phenomena in that they typically mirror the preoccupations of the broader society. Consequently, they are constantly changing as various fads, ideologies, and technologies wash through them. Not uncommonly, service systems get enamored of seemingly novel models and often install them on a wholesale basis. Whether these practices are particularly valuable to clients may not be as interesting as the fact of the continuous adoption of largely untested practices. As often as not, the purveyors of change are astonishingly well-motivated and convinced that their clients will fare better under their "new" regime. The original creators of our residential institutions were often passionate progress-minded reformers who had no inkling of what the real world would actually do with their notions. They were like many people today in that they were so enthused for change and had few scruples as to what they were asking from the people whose lives would be captured in their experiment.

Sadly, clients of services have had to endure countless thousands of intrusions into their lives of the concepts, ideologies, practices, and vested interests that get created by each successive reform. When these reforms do not eventually fulfill their originators' high hopes and degenerate into much less, it is extraordinarily rare that such innovators return to apologize and compensate those who were subjected to such tinkerings with their lives. Many clients, if they live long enough, will have been witness to and enfleshed by dozens of such experiments. Apparently, it is their duty to cooperate with the infatuations of their service masters.

The difficulty is not that we human beings are endlessly drawn to search for a better way or that we are moved by passions for improvement. It is that we do not often recognize that we are using clients to address our own needs and preoccupations. Clients at such times become "tabula rasa" to meet our psychic, professional, and societal needs. Occasionally, the blithe rendering of them to the status of experimental fodder is argued as "for their own good." The journals and conferences are full of often breathless reports of the latest experiment and its promising contribution to human service improvement. Such experimentation is so common and taken for granted that their status as trials using real human beings is obscured. It is not just that formalities like consent are overlooked that make these innovations worrisome. Rather, it is the wholesale use of one group by another that should be worrying. Staff do not readily become the toys of clients. It is not so easy to say that the reverse is untrue. Where power, authority, and legitimacy are not evenly divided, there lies the possibility of the misuse of these advantages unless they are constrained by suitable ethics.

Part of the difficulty is that unrestricted human service experimentation often only generates concern when it is formally called experimentation. The rules in many states regarding formal experimentation with human subjects are often quite a serious counterweight to client harm. Nonetheless, if the experiment is called something else, it actually does not look to most people to be experimentation. Instead it is seen as an ordinary part of program development and modification. For instance, most groupings of clients in residential settings do constitute an experiment in how well people will get along, yet this practice seems an innocuous and routine part of service delivery, although it could affect people's health and safety every bit as much as a medication trial. It would be useful to occasionally stand back from our daily habits of the service world and to consider them in the light of what we are subjecting clients to.

Not all innovations, of course, lack merit, but a culture of indifference to the claims of clients to not be used must force us beyond the specific innovation to the underlying moral, political, and economic context within which such experiments come into being. It is an ethical matter whether we have the right to assume such a command over people's lives that we can instill a never-ending progression of "improvement" upon them. Surely something is amiss when there is absolutely no widespread obligation to seek to protect clients from the untoward effects of such experimentation, however well-intentioned it may be. Our human service culture seems confused and uncertain as to how to best conduct itself to ensure that the dignity and well-being of clients is not transgressed. This confusion, coupled with the ardent desire for much-needed change, produces a brew that sanctions and rewards progress, or at least the appearance of it. It needs to be tempered by the kinds of ethics that do not presume that good intentions are all there is to reality.

Conclusion

The clients of human services cannot be defined properly just by the view of them held by service providers. Their human identity both precedes and transcends the identity ascribed to them by services and their processes. Foremost in this is their universal identity as human beings. In this they are entitled to all the dignity and respect normally extended to all persons. Residential services must resolutely commit themselves to not create a standard of treatment for their clients that is less than or perversely different from that accorded to the most valued of citizens in our community. To do otherwise is to risk the institutionalized degradation of persons who become clients. This in turn requires rigorous ethics on the part of residential services to ensure that their "clients" do not lose just by becoming recipients of services but, in fact, prosper.

11

Consumer Choice is
the American Way

Michael R. Dillon, Ed.D.

Why is it that so often in the field of developmental disabilities, consumer choice is paired with notions of unrealistic demands and even dangerous consequences?

Does Burger King wring its hands in terror over the vast possibilities inherent in someone "having it their way?" Are they overwhelmed with requests for culinary disaster? What liabilities exist for a pickle in a milk shake?

> *Consumer choice should not be a foreign concept to us as service providers in this great land of opportunity.*

What is it about consumer choice that seems to generate negative reactions from many well-meaning providers?

Too often simple, safe, and valued consumer choices are responded to with a whole list of "what ifs" sung like a litany chanted in a monastery.

The choice: "I'd like to go to church tomorrow."

The response: "What if it rains tomorrow?"

"What if you get up too late?"

"What if there's not enough staff?"

"What if the sky falls?"

Such a litany spoken in a monotone and with a consistent cadence is guaranteed to send sound waves which penetrate the head of the listener and result in immediate feelings of regret for having raised the issue at all.

Consumer choice should not be a foreign concept to us as service providers in this great land of opportunity.

Indeed, our society proclaims the rights of the individual above almost any other. Whether real or myth, the image of individual choice is the reputed energy that fuels our free enterprise system.

As a people, we are loath to restrict the rights of self-expression no matter how outrageous. And it is only recently that we have begun to impose restrictions on individual actions which result in environmental exploitation.

Hence, the better mousetrap will emerge, the inferior will diminish, only when people can genuinely exercise their rights based upon good information on which to make their choices. These concepts are basic to our way of life.

Our history is one of paternalism, protection, and control. It stems from a view of disabilities which emphasizes deficits, not assets.

Yet sadly, this has not been the case in human services and in the area of developmental disabilities in particular. Our history is one of paternalism, protection, and control.

It stems from a view of disabilities which emphasizes deficits, not assets. And, those deficits are sought only within the individual and not within a nonresponsive environment in which a person finds oneself.

In the name of protection and control, our society has perpetrated the most heinous crimes on the persons it seeks to serve, such as the recent revelations concerning the radiation of food in an institution for the mentally retarded.

The very classes of people that our society sought to protect have been the most exploited and deprived—our children, the elderly, those with disabilities, the poor. Yes indeed they have been specially treated, but how well? Our newspapers remind us daily of the abuse and misuse of vulnerable persons. We should not be surprised by these acts of personal victimization because we live in a society where, by

We have created segregated housing and specialized transportation for our elderly which separates this vulnerable group and further stigmatizes them.

law and practice, these same vulnerable groups are systemically segregated, educated, and victimized.

For example, we would be guilty of assault and battery and sued if we treated our neighbor the way we can legally treat our children.

We have created segregated housing and specialized transportation for our elderly which separates this vulnerable group and further stigmatizes them. Need I describe the devastating effects of "trickle down" economics on those in poverty? One only has to look at the conditions in our inner cities to see that the trickle dried up long before it hit those streets.

So what does this have to do with developmental disabilities and choice? It has everything to do with them because under the guise of protection, persons with disabilities have been systematically denied their basic civil liberties.

Segregated in housing, in school, in work, at play, and even sometimes in places of worship, persons with disabilities are only now emerging and striving for full participation in all areas of community life.

The very same agents who have sponsored those past "benevolent" protections are now cast as primary supports to persons reaching to achieve inclusion and self-actualization. Those of us who just yesterday made decisions, often of a most personal and intimate nature on behalf of persons with disabilities, are now to be directed by those same people we so ably directed. This is an enormous transformation with profound implications for both person and provider.

Those of us who made decisions, often of a most personal and intimate nature on behalf of persons with disabilities, are now to be directed by those same people we so ably directed. This is an enormous transformation.

Some may choose to trivialize this fundamental power shift by denying it or by frequently referencing through extreme examples of absurd and impossible choices. This is done in many ways. Choices are offered in only perfunctory ways geared to elicit agreement with the status quo. "You want to continue in this program, don't you?" Or it is offered with little option, "You can choose to stay in the program or quit."

Basically, the person is cued to accept the available choice or is offered only one acceptable option.

The transformation inherent in consumer choice requires change on the part of the person and the service agent.

The frequent referral to absurd or impossible choices is geared to call into question the legitimacy or competency of the choice process itself. "When asked what job he wanted, John said he wanted to be President, or Jet Pilot, or Workshop Supervisor"...or something else equally unreal. You get the picture. By focusing on the unrealistic choices, we diminish the credibility of the choice process.

It is unfair to characterize a person or indeed a group based on the exceptions or extreme examples. After all, how many of us harbor similar unrealistic visions in our secret selves. The choice process is far more complex than is the response to simple multiple choice selection. The transformation inherent in consumer choice requires change on the part of the person and the service agent. This change can only happen if it is approached with all due sincerity and respect. There is much to learn on the part of all parties involved. The issues and lessons are many and the outcomes for us all are worth our efforts to change.

We should always bear in mind that every freely conceived choice followed by appropriate action, constitutes, to a certain extent, a new beginning, a new point of departure that may set in motion an entire series of sequences. These can lead to outcomes that could never have been originally envisioned. It is often only with hindsight that we can see what significance an apparently simple choice may have had on our later lives. How many careers in physical therapy began with an errant bicycle crash and a broken leg, a cast, and subsequent therapy exercises?

So often, we examine choice at the end stage, the culminating moment, and fail to understand

Not only must we assist the individual through the choice process, but recognize that through this process we all change and grow to become what we were not before.

the full complexities of the process that has led to that choice. If we are to fully support individual choice, then we must be sensitive to this personal transformation of as yet unknown dimension. Not only must we assist the individual through the choice process, but recognize that through this process we all change and grow to become what we were not before. It is dynamic.

This process is not without risk. All elements cannot be foreseen. It is evolving. It is a process in which subsequent choices are based on the outcome of earlier choices. What begins as an apparently unrealistic aspiration will often be modified based on experience. One's interest in being a football coach could well lead to exposure to a whole range of options in recreation or other tangential areas.

There are several significant issues crucial to supporting persons with developmental disabilities as they make decisions about vocational and leisure options. Some of these issues are person-centered and others are agency-centered. How these are recognized and addressed can have enormous impact on how effective will be our support.

Sadly, many persons with developmental disabilities have had little opportunity to make personal choices. So often, when confronted by choice, individuals will seek to state, not what may be their own personal desire, but rather what they perceive to be the "correct" choice or the choices that others would like to hear. It takes some effort to get beyond this "hypercompliant behavior" and get to a level of sharing real personal hopes, wants, and desires.

For others, it is equally clear that many have very narrow ranges of experiences on which to base their choices.

If one's only experience with a ball is that you can roll it, then one's idea of ball play is very limited. The knowledge and experience that a ball can be kicked, dribbled, or hit opens up vastly greater possibilities.

Many people with a narrow base of life experiences actively resist new and different options. It would indeed be a mistake to just accept that as the individual's choice.

This lack of experience across the board is the biggest challenge confronting persons as they make choices, a lack which can only be made up by gaining new life experiences. It is never too late. The degree to which a person gains new experiences places that person in a better position to evaluate them and to use them to consider future choices. How can someone have "informed choice" if he/she has little experience in considering options, and little history in dealing with the consequences? For example, when an individual is on a bus, he/she must decide at which stop to get off. Missing the stop results in the person walking to the right stop. Experiencing such consequences convinces us to pay great attention to the right bus stop.

Many people with a narrow base of life experiences actively resist new and different options. It would indeed be a mistake to just accept that as the individual's choice. I would suggest the opposite—that, in fact, the person *has* no choice because of his/her limited experiences. We have a responsibility to expose people to the excitement of new challenges and opportunities. This perhaps should be our major task and one that will require as much strategic planning as we have expended in skill-acquisition activities. Nor can

Each aspect of one's life offers countless opportunities for honing one's choice-making skills. These opportunities must be capitalized upon.

we compartmentalize these experiences by our traditional artificial program concerns, such that vocational planning is only concerned with work experience. In fact, often career interest is generated by social or leisure experiences. It is important that a more holistic view of life experience be considered.

In order to assist persons in gaining greater experience and ability in making choices, this should be an important consideration in all planning and activities. From meal planning, preparation to actual consumption, the individual should be assisted to make the many choices involved and then aided to assess the outcomes. It should be remembered that what is incidental learning for one might require a more structural methodical approach for another.

Each aspect of one's life offers countless opportunities for honing one's choice-making skills. These opportunities must be capitalized upon. Therefore, these are not just the concerns of the teacher or therapist, they should be the concern of all, including family, friends, and supporters.

Leisure time and recreational opportunities offer wonderful situations for natural reinforcement for choice-making and for experiencing the growth and exhilaration of accomplishing something for the first time.

To be responsive to consumer choice, the traditional top-down hierarchy of agency administration has to change. Direct care workers and line staff need the authority to be able to respond to consumers.

By their very nature, leisure and recreational activities are typically more self-directed. Usually the primary reason for participating is the intrinsic enjoyment of the activity itself. While this is not always true, it is true of these activities, probably more than any other class of activities.

From the choices and successes that one experiences here, the seed for future work and other leisure opportunities can grow.

Similarly, a family's or a friend's own social, vocational, and business interests can often become the catalyst for social, vocational, and work aspiration of the individual. How can an agency help translate these possibilities into new opportunities? The relationships that one has with others will also frequently be the basis for choice and exploration. One's brother or friend did it and enjoyed it, so will I, maybe.

Nothing is forever. Decisions to do, or to participate, can be of short or long duration, but they do have value. These decisions provide experiences that can lead to new choices and new alternatives which would not have been possible before. Seize the opportunity. Alexander Graham Bell was an educator of persons with hearing impairments, but that did not prevent him from seeing the larger use of his invention—the telephone.

So, too, choices and experiences in one area may have unexpected consequences later.

Furthermore, these opportunities do not always arise conveniently during the "six hours" of the program day. They occur at night and on weekends too. How do we support the individual during these times? The service provider does have an important role here as well. While family and friends continue the natural supports which assist the person, too often the agency support is absent, and growth opportunities are lost.

Another consequence of our past models of services is attributable to the past preponderance of segregated services. Very often, experiences which occur in segregated settings are not easily transferred to existing inclusive community activities.

It becomes most important to assist individuals to function in the real-life, typical community setting. Training does not easily transfer from the workshop cafeteria to a line at McDonald's during rush hour. There is no substitute for these real-life community-based experiences.

Human service agencies need to market themselves to the individual, to customize their service directly to the person's needs, wants, and desires. This is not just rhetoric, it is hard work.

In order to effectively support individuals as they make decisions about their lives, we also need to examine how we, ourselves, must be transformed.

To be responsive to consumer choice, the traditional top-down hierarchy of agency administration has to change. Direct care workers and line staff need the authority to be able to respond to consumers who are actively seeking to make choices about their own lives.

It becomes increasingly important for the direct line staff to have the freedom to flexibly interact with the person in ways which respect the choices and orientation of the individual.

Instead of "directive according to the book," direct line staff need to support and respond according to the hopes, needs, and desires of the person.

Much can be learned from the renewed emphasis on the customer in American business today. It is not only Burger King who seeks to know their customers.

Too many of our human service organizations are absorbed with their own view of themselves and of the world, instead of being concerned with what others want and ask of them.

An agency must start by listening to its customers. They begin by hearing the customers' requirements, their needs, and their expectations. From this, individualized services are developed to satisfy those needs.

This sounds easy—but it is not. Our history conditions us to look at the service recipient as passive, an object to be treated or acted upon. This objectifies the person, it depersonalizes and devalues also.

It is axiomatic today in American business that in order to succeed, the focus be on quality, and that means meeting customer requirements.

Human service agencies must center everything they do on those they serve. They need to market themselves to the individual, to customize their service directly to the person's needs, wants, and desires. This is not just rhetoric, it is hard work.

In the past, work and leisure options were offered to persons based solely on what the agency had procured. To be responsive, agencies need to reach out and procure the kinds of work and leisure options that persons request. Agencies also need to become more responsive to consumer choice, even to offering flexible hours of service and convenient locations, as opposed to today's usual condition of one schedule, one place fits all.

It will be found that people tend to make choices that benefit themselves, that agencies can do things differently, that sincere people can differ, and that through mutual respect and compromise, more effective alternatives, never before considered, may be found.

There has been a long-standing expressed value towards single providers of services in a given locality. With a focus on consumer choice, it is imperative that multiple providers of services be available. Only in this way will consumers be able to learn how to make important choices of by whom, and how, they wish to be served.

Competiveness will lead to innovation. The better mousetrap will emerge. Consumer choice will drive services in directions that the majority of consumers choose.

Certainly conflicts exist today. They occur often as a result of our limitations: limitations of resources, of abilities, of creativity, and of will.

We cope with these conflicts as best we can. The change may be one of expectation. The expectation to change may shift from the person to the agency.

And finally, we arrive at the question raised in the original title, *When Consumer Choices Don't Match Provider Expectations: Who Makes The Decision in Rehabilitative Services?*

Yes, there will be conflict between person and provider. But unless something is radically wrong, these conflicts will be in the minority and will result in more positive, dynamic change. Conflict should only suggest that more work must be done by the person and provider together, to refine, explore, and pursue new possibilities.

An agency cannot do what is impossible or immoral or illegal. No consumer can demand otherwise. Yet in a situation where there is only one agency, that agency is burdened by a conflict of self-interest. Is the option chosen really impossible, immoral, or illegal, or just that the provider has deemed not to do it, since the consumer has no other alternative? Ultimately, the consumer should make the final decisions. In an open system, another provider who can perform might be chosen.

As both consumer and provider strive to deal with authentic choice, lessons will be learned. It will be found that people tend to make choices that benefit themselves, that agencies can do things differently, that sincere people can differ, and that through mutual respect and compromise, more effective alternatives, never before considered, may be found.

Hold the pickle! Hold the onion! Have it your way in Human Services today.

12

3,650 Hours A Year: Considerations for Spending Vocational and Recreational Time

Elizabeth J. Chura

The question of how to help persons with mental disabilities arrange for vocational and recreational activities which enhance the quality of their lives is one that has been raised more recently than debates on some other essential questions, such as if and how to support persons with challenging behaviors or medical conditions in the community. Because it is a relative latecomer, the dialogue surrounding the issue has often been circumscribed by rhetoric indigenous to the current controversy involving choice and responsibility, and the quality of the discussion has suffered.

While discussion of choice is a valid and necessary component of a thoughtful look at the issue, it too frequently leads to an uncreative process and an unsatisfactory product. Limiting the focus of the discussion to the issue of choice hampers meaningful and useful discourse because it nearly always pits the "pro-choice" and the "yes-but" factions against one another and reduces the discussion to a question of whether to placate or support (depending on your position) this person who has expressed a strong preference in the matter.

> *In a world where many of us spend more awake time with our coworkers than we do with family, spouses, and children, it is little wonder that the quality of our work life is so significant a determinant of the quality of our life.*

Alternately, some unanimously "pro-choice" planning sessions so trivialize the topic that a listener would believe that the decisions reached would have no more consequence than deciding between watching "Jeopardy" or "Wheel of Fortune."

In a world where many of us spend more awake time with our coworkers than we do with family, spouses, and children, it is little wonder that the quality of our work life is so significant a determinant of the quality of our life in general. It is axiomatic that if we are happy at work, that goes a long way toward making us happy in general. Our crowded workdays make the few hours of recreation time all the more precious and charge them with the expectation that they will provide us with opportunities for taking pleasure in favorite pastimes, for discovering new things to enjoy, and for nurturing relationships. These high expectations—a distortion of the work ethic that sanctions a "you are what you do" measure of a person's worth—often focus our attention and energies on finding a suitable *activity* for someone to work or play at. A broader context for these decisions, I believe, would be useful.

The environment of our daily activities shapes our very character, and from this character—disciplines and virtues—will come our life choices.

A good match between our daily activities and our wants, needs, and talents is more than a hedge against misery. It plays a major role in making us the kind of person that we are, and it thereby influences the decisions and choices we make in all other aspects of our lives. The environment of our daily activities shapes our very character, and from this character—disciplines and virtues—will come our life choices. More precisely, the people in our work and recreation environments become our community, and we each fashion who we are by our interactions with our community. Put more succinctly and pleasingly, "Our character is a gift from others."[1]

An appreciation of the role of the environment, and particularly the people sharing the environment with me, compels a recognition of the converse. If I am shaped by those with whom I interact, then I must be exercising the same influence on them. Sharing responsibility for the character of others and acknowledging their role in shaping mine is not an idea that goes

The people in our work and recreation environments become our community, and we each fashion who we are by our interactions with our community.

down easily, especially to Americans. We have a proud history of individualism and still thrill to anthems recalling that, "I did it my way." But in any quiet minute the interconnectedness of our lives rings true.

Looked at this way, what one does—the activity—becomes only one consideration, but who one does it with and where, are equal considerations because our real freedom, our taking over the work of becoming the men and women we are capable of, depends on it.

There are formidable challenges inherent in this understanding of work. On a personal level, there is the responsibility for my actions and attitude attendant to an appreciation that I am shaping the character of others, as well as being shaped by them. And, there are professional challenges in making recommendations and finding positions and activities for persons with developmental disabilities and mental illnesses consistent with this perspective. Additionally, there are challenges in finding ways to share this understanding with those individuals, and in teaching them skills and shaping attitudes that are consistent with this view.

> *Sometimes kneading principles—working the ideas, stretching and poking at them, and testing their limits with real situations—clarifies them and helps us apply them guilelessly.*

*   *   *

Sometimes kneading principles—working the ideas, stretching and poking at them, and testing their limits with real situations—clarifies them and helps us apply them guilelessly. These short sketches are offered with the hope that they will provide a starting point for looking at employment and leisure time decisions within the broader context described above. Some are success stories; some are stories which are still unfolding.

❑ "Laura"

Laura is a young woman who has worked all of her adult life in a sheltered workshop where she is known for being gregarious and a bit of a busybody. Counselors have spent endless hours over the years trying to stop Laura from fussing over coworkers and "mothering" them. Laura can write her name and name letters and numbers; she cannot read and cannot tell you what kind of work she would like to do. She is much more articulate about her preferences for recreational activities. In a beginning-stage effort to find her competitive employment, her job counselor has set up work samplings as a grocery packer, kitchen helper in a fast-food restaurant and, most recently, as an office helper doing filing and sorting.

Laura's family believes the job sampling choices could not have been better picked for failure. Laura's job counselor counters with the idea that any experience is useful because it expands Laura's choice-making options.

❏ "Randy"

Randy has a mental health problem which has prevented him from keeping a job that he liked in the past. Either he was fired rather quickly, or he felt the job had no purpose, and he stopped going to work. Randy now works as a Rehabilitation Program Aide. In that capacity, he assists psychiatric patients in an inpatient setting, working under the direction of other ward staff. He is particularly good at motivating patients to participate in scheduled programs and activities and as a co-leader for certain group sessions. In addition, Randy has weekly on-the-job training sessions and attends a weekly vocational support group which gives him the opportunity to discuss work experiences and build community with others doing the same job.

❏ "Maria" and "Peter"

Maria and Peter have both recently moved out of a developmental center and are both of retirement age. Maria hates staying home all day, saying that daytime TV is boring. Peter, on the other hand, wants to live in the country, by himself (or with one other person perhaps), and walk in the fields and smoke his pipe.

Maria has begun attending a senior day care center which is integrated with a day care program for children. She is enjoying herself immensely. Peter is staying home alone with a single staff member.

Marion, the caseworker for each of these individuals, is under strong pressure to entice Peter into Maria's program for fiscal reasons and because "It doesn't look good for him to be doing absolutely nothing."

❏ "Andy"

Andy's hyperactivity and severe mental retardation have made it difficult for him to attend to tabletop tasks at the day program. Since he moved into the community within the last few months from a developmental center, he has received one-to-one programming at his home. This training has included activities to teach him what is dangerous in a home (e.g., a hot stove), how to eat using utensils, and how to greet people (in his enthusiasm, he has a handshake that feels like it will crush your hand). His stay-at-home program has also given him plenty of opportunities to intersperse these activities with walks in the neighborhood and playing in the yard.

Reviewers have criticized the program because Andy is not doing what adults in the community typically do—he is not leaving his home to go to work.

❑ "George"

George is 48 years old, in good health, and has worked all of his life in a sheltered workshop where he is one of the top wage-earners. His program team is split over his announcement that he does not want to work or go to day program any longer. He says that he gets enough spending money living at the community residence, has simple needs and wants, and does not want to work.

❑ "Andrew"

Staff in a quiet, segregated day program classroom defend Andrew's sheltered but isolated program, noting that they have plenty of time to develop relationships with the pro-

Appreciating that persons with disabilities, like all of us, will both shape and be shaped by their work and recreational environments, necessitates that we give professional attention in helping these individuals develop work skills and coping skills.

gram participants and that the relationships among the individuals are more harmonious because of the minimal external stimuli.

Casemanagers visiting the program believe everyone looks just too "comfortable" and no one is growing. No program participants have any complaints.

*   *   *

Appreciating that persons with disabilities, like all of us, will both shape and be shaped by their work and recreational environments, necessitates, as mentioned earlier, that we give professional attention in helping these individuals develop work skills and coping skills. Professionals in the field of developmental disabilities and vocational rehabilitation are very good at teaching people discrete skills. This aspect of training will not likely be shortchanged. We do need to work, however, on teaching and encouraging persons with mental disabilities to *exercise* the coping skills that we all use and which assist us in interacting in the workplace in such a way that we are positive influences on the characters of coworkers. The coping strategies identified below are some that we use frequently. The intent of the list is only to spark an appreciation of how very commonly we use them and how almost impossible we sometimes make it for persons with mental disabilities to use them.

❏ **Opting Out**

This is simply saying, "No, thank you," to the suggestion of an activity that one doesn't want to engage in at the time, even though one may generally enjoy the activity. While going bowling may usually be fun, it is an excruciatingly painful activity if one has a head-ache, and it is incompatible (at least to most people) with thinking through a problem. For some people with mental disabilities, if it's bowling night, everybody in the house goes bowling. Consequently, people go despite wanting to opt out, sometimes nudged by the added guilt that in exercising one's right to stay home, nobody will be able to go.

Persons with mental disabilities are often taught that it is fine and good to talk over these kinds of feelings with a counselor, but not to share them with coworkers.

❏ **Postponing**

Most of us have jobs that have high-concentration tasks and low-concen-tration tasks and, at least some of the time, we get to choose which activity to do when. This ability not only relieves stress, but also results in a better work product, one could argue. This autonomy is seldom available to workers with mental disabilities because their jobs are often monotonous repetitions of the same act or, if there are varied tasks, someone has developed a rigid schedule for doing them which, like a menu of luncheon specials, does not allow for substitutions.

❏ **Talking It Over**

At its best, commiserating with colleagues relieves individual stress and oftentimes helps us develop a more positive perspective on things. At the very least, it lets us know we are not alone in our misery. Persons with mental disabilities are often taught that it is fine and good to talk over these kinds of feelings with a counselor, but not to share them with coworkers. Similarly, we frequently and unnecessarily institutionalize the process when dealing with persons with mental disabilities and call it a therapy group. We need to break this pattern and affirm, in its proper context, a community-building coping strategy which we all use.

❑ Psychological and Somatic Stress Reducers

Whole sections of bookstores are devoted to various stress-reducing activities. Professionals need to be familiar with these and choose those most likely to benefit the individual he/she is working with. Physical exercise and/or a change of scenery for a few minutes are work enhancers we almost all use. Micro vacations through the mental imaging of ourselves in peaceful, pleasant surroundings and other relaxation techniques are also helpful to people to varying degrees.

Persons with mental disabilities have a right to expect those of us who profess to help them to exercise thoughtful professional judgement.

❑ Assertiveness Training

We have done a good job of teaching persons with mental disabilities compliance. With few safety valves for pent-up anxiety and anger, it is no wonder that these individuals "blow up" or are cranky at work. Helping someone say what is on his/her mind in a socially acceptable way is a must for a peaceful work life.

❑ Paid Vacations, Sick Leave, and Holidays

These most common and, in the case of holidays and vacations, the most looked forward to of breaks are not available to many individuals with mental disabilities in workshops.

*   *   *

As stated earlier, my purpose is not to provide a checklist of tools with which to equip persons with mental disabilities; it is to emphasize that an appreciation of the importance of decisions around how to spend one's time brings with it the responsibility to think about how to make people most comfortable and able to be their best selves.

In conclusion, persons with mental disabilities have a right to expect those of us who profess to help them to exercise thoughtful professional judgement. This means, in helping persons make decisions about their work and recreation, that we view these decisions in a broader context that acknowledges that they are extremely important to an individual and to every single person around him/her. This is not only a matter of how to spend 3,650 hours a year, but how to spend a life.

Endnotes

1. Hauerwas, S. (1983). *The peaceable kingdom* (p. 45). Notre Dame, IN: University of Notre Dame Press.

13

Medical Decision-Making for People with Chronic Mental Impairments

Charles E. Schwartz, M.D.

A Fundamental Problem: Poor Medical Care

Any discussion of issues relating to medical decision-making for people with chronic mental impairments must begin with the recognition that these individuals have traditionally received terrible medical care. Multiple studies have thoroughly documented the alarmingly high rate of undiagnosed medical problems in individuals with significant mental disabilities. In a review by Erwin Koranyi (1980) of a dozen studies conducted over a 40-year period involving some

> *Multiple studies have thoroughly documented the alarmingly high rate of undiagnosed medical problems in individuals with significant mental disabilities.*

4,000 mentally disabled persons, approximately half had major medical illnesses, and in one-half to three-quarters of these individuals, the major medical illnesses went unrecognized. Poor medical care occurs both in public institutions and in community-based residential and outpatient care settings.

Undertreatment

In psychiatric outpatient settings, Hall and colleagues (1978) found in their study of 658 patients that 9.1% had medical disorders that might be producing the patients' psychiatric symptoms and that three-fourths of these disorders had been unrecognized. Koranyi (1979) reviewed some 2,090 outpatients and found that 43% had one or more medical illnesses; referring psychiatrists had missed 50%; referring medical physicians had missed 33%. In self-referred and social agency-referred patients, where almost 100% had one or more illnesses, some 46% had gone unrecognized. Koranyi further found that 18% of the medical disorders were causing the psychiatric symptoms, 51% were exacerbating them, and 31% were serious but unrelated.

When they studied 100 patients in psychiatric inpatient settings, Hall and colleagues (1981) found that 46% of patients had previously unrecognized medical illnesses that directly caused or exacerbated their psychiatric symptoms. An additional 34% of patients had unrecognized serious co-existing medical problems. In fact, only 20% of the psychiatric inpatients were free of significant undetected medical problems.

Martin and colleagues (1985a, 1985b) demonstrate the unfortunate consequences of poor medical care. In their seven-year follow-up study of 500 individuals with chronic mental impairments, it was found that the mortality rate was twice that of matched individuals who were not significantly mentally disabled. And, in several investigations conducted by the New York State Commission on Quality of Care for the Mentally Disabled concerning the

At the other extreme, individuals with significant mental disabilities also run the risk of being inappropriately overdiagnosed and overtreated.

deaths of individuals residing in group homes for developmentally disabled persons, it was found that the individuals were exhibiting symptoms of diseases which claimed their lives, but the symptoms were mistakenly attributed to "behavioral problems" or emotional factors.

❑ **Example**

Ms. R., a 63-year-old woman with mild mental retardation was transferred from one group home to another. Soon after the transfer she began to complain of abdominal pains, and she refused to eat. Known to be a "picky eater," staff thought that she was just nervous over the recent move. Even when she experienced bouts of vomiting in the following days, administrative and nursing staff, without the benefit of ensuring a full physical examination, concluded she had a "nervous stomach" and was anxious over the recent transfer. On the fourth day after the move, she vomited what appeared to be black fluid and was taken to the hospital. She arrived unresponsive and died shortly thereafter. The cause of death was septic shock and gastro-intestinal bleeding due to an abdominal catastrophe.

Overtreatment

At the other extreme, individuals with significant mental disabilities also run the risk of being inappropriately overdiagnosed and overtreated. For example, it is widely recognized that elderly patients with dementia who enter acute medical/surgical facilities may be subjected to an array of invasive diagnostic tests and therapeutic procedures, the risks and adverse consequences of which, including significant discomfort, are much clearer than the benefits.

❑ Example

A physician approached a surrogate medical decision-making panel in New York State on behalf of a 74-year-old profoundly retarded individual who lacked the capacity to consent to medical care and had no relatives. The physician sought permission to perform a cystogram, a biopsy of the prostate, a transurethral resection of the prostate, a craniotomy, and an insertion of a gastrostomy tube for feeding. The request for the procedures was denied by the panel as being medically futile; the patient was semicomatose with terminal brain cancer.

Contributing Factors

Why does this inappropriate under- and, at times, over-medicalization occur? Hoffman and Koran (1984) describe "disease-related, patient-related and physician-related factors."

By "disease-related factors," Hoffman explains that many medical disorders may first or most prominently present with changes in mental status. In addition, many symptoms can be associated with either medical or nonorganic mental disorders, e.g., weakness, fatigue, gastrointestinal complaints, anorexia, shortness of breath, anxiety, depression, and hallucinations.

> *Physicians may have subconscious emotional biases that mentally impaired patients are subhuman and not really people, or may find those patients frightening reminders of the tenuousness of their own mental health.*

❑ Example

Mr. J., an 80-year-old gentleman with dementia living at home with his wife, is brought to the hospital because he is up all night "ranting and raving and sitting by an open window, driving his wife crazy." On medical evaluation, however, he is discovered to have congestive heart failure with orthopnea and paroxysmal nocturnal dyspnea. What was initially mistaken for psychopathology was physiological in nature; due to fluid back-up in the lungs, Mr. J. could not lie flat and would periodically awaken and need to sit bolt upright at the window in the acute air hunger characteristic of severe congestive heart failure.

"Patient-related factors" include the off-putting appearance and behaviors of some individuals with mental disabilities, particularly those individuals who are not receiving appropriate assistance with these matters. As Hoffman puts it, "A malodorous, dirty, and obstreperous patient discourages close, prolonged, and careful scrutiny." In addition, persons with serious mental disabilities may be unable to provide good medical histories and may be uncooperative with examinations and tests. As Jonathan Borus (1987) points out, "Almost one-half of public sector mental health patients studied [in studies like those quoted above] did not participate due to lack of cooperation...."

"Physician-related factors" include an all-too-common aversion to individuals with mental disabilities. Physicians are often unsympathetic and sometimes frankly frightened by these patients. Physicians may have subconscious emotional biases that mentally impaired patients are subhuman and not really people, or may find those patients frightening reminders of the tenuousness of their own mental health. Physicians may even irrationally fear contagion. In consequence, physicians may too often perform inadequate evaluations like the classic hasty "medical clearance" of patients presenting for psychiatric care, and grossly underdiagnose and treat.

❑ Example

Ms. I., a young woman with a chronic mental illness, was admitted to the surgical service after swallowing glass. She was followed by the surgical house staff without any surgical intervention despite psychiatry's repeated misgivings. In retrospect, the director of the surgical service stated that this approach had been dangerous, and surgery ought to have been performed to remove the glass before it passed through narrow segments of the gastrointestinal tract.

Conversely, physicians may be overly zealous and aggressive out of reaction formation to their hidden distaste, out of a failure to see the patients as fully human, and out of the absence of a counterbalancing capable voice representing the patient and saying "No" where appropriate.

It is sometimes thought that all individuals who agree to medical treatment are capable of making that decision, and that only those who refuse need psychiatric evaluation. In fact, patients who accept medical intervention may be as incapable of making their own informed medical decisions as patients who refuse it, and we should always consider whether they are capable of making such decisions.

Need for Advocacy

What is clear is that individuals with chronic mental impairments need advocates to help them negotiate their successful passage into and through the medical care system. Such advocates must insure that patients are fully informed of their needs and options, given sound expert medical advice, and heeded when they are capable of making their own decisions. Advocates must insure that medical care is accessible and of high quality. And finally, when patients are incapable of making their own decisions, such advocates must see that appropriate surrogate decision-making is set into motion.

Making Medical Decisions

Decisions about medical screening, diagnosis, and treatment are often complex. While many medical interventions may be of great benefit, others may not. For many conditions, there is simply no effective treatment available, or the potential risks may outweigh potential benefits. Going to great lengths to identify and/or treat such conditions may be counterproductive. Similarly, patients, or their surrogate decision-makers, may have decided not to undergo invasive treatments, such as surgery, under any circumstances. Getting diagnostic information that can lead only to a recommendation for clearly undesired surgery is not worthwhile. Diagnostic tests should be obtained only when the information will be of some benefit.

When patients are not capable, appropriate surrogates must make informed medical decisions for the mentally impaired.

□ **Example**

A 75-year-old male has clearly stated that he would not undergo coronary bypass surgery or angioplasty under any circumstances. Coronary angiography would be of dubious value to this patient.

When deemed capable, persons who happen to have a mental disability, like all patients, should make their own informed medical decisions. Judge Benjamin Cardozo clearly established this principle in a precedent-setting 1914 New York Court of Appeals decision in the case of *Schloendorff v.*

Society of New York Hospital: "Every human being of adult years and sound mind has the right to determine what shall be done with his own body; and a surgeon who performs an operation without his patient's consent commits an assault."

Just because a patient carries a diagnosis of a mental disability does not mean that he/she is incapable of informed medical decision-making.

❑ **Example**

> A patient with a diagnosis of chronic schizophrenia is admitted to the medical hospital with a breast lump. Incorrectly assuming that the patient is incapable of making an informed decision because she is mentally ill, the medical team discusses a proposed biopsy with the family instead of with the patient.

Even the patient deemed incapable of making informed decisions is humanly entitled to be told as much as he/she can understand and to be prepared as fully as possible for any interventions. Decisional incapacity is no excuse for not talking to the patient.

When patients are not capable, appropriate surrogates must make informed medical decisions for the mentally impaired. (The determination of an appropriate surrogate is a complex legal issue that is outside the scope of this chapter.) Where possible, surrogates should follow the principle of substituted judgment. In other words, knowing the patient, his/her life story, values, and previously stated opinions, the surrogate should try to determine what the patient would want to do now if he/she could speak for himself/herself. If this is not possible, surrogates should follow the principle of *best interest*: that is, given all the facts about the patient, the medical condition, and potential risks and benefits of intervention, what is in the patient's best interest? Where possible, "substituted judgment" is the preferred method of decision-making, not only because it most closely follows the patient's wishes, but also because it unburdens a surrogate decision-maker, who does not have to decide for the patient, but only speak for him/her.

In addition, even the patient deemed incapable of making informed decisions is humanly entitled to be told as much as he/she can understand and to be prepared as fully as possible for any interventions. Decisional incapacity is no excuse for not talking to the patient. Information, preparation, and support are not only humane, but may facilitate cooperation.

Evaluation of Capacity for Informed Medical Decision-Making

Only the most severely mentally impaired individuals—those who are completely out of touch with reality, unable to grasp basic concepts, and unable to clearly articulate their understanding and preferences—are categorically incapable of making their own informed medical decisions.

❏ Example

A mentally retarded individual is admitted to the hospital and is found to be disoriented to time and place and unable to answer simple questions or follow simple commands, and only speaks occasional words.

Most individuals with mental impairments, however, are capable of at least some informed medical decisions. This capacity may vary over time and may vary across different decisions. Therefore, except for the most profoundly impaired, capacity evaluations must be decision specific.

In determining capacity, a heavy emphasis is placed on the word "informed." The first step, accordingly, is to give the patient adequate information.

- Why is a medical intervention being proposed, i.e., what is the problem, concern, or diagnosis?
- How is the proposed intervention supposed to help? What is the potential benefit?
- What is the likelihood of that benefit?
- How might the proposed intervention hurt, i.e., what are the potential adverse consequences or risks?
- What is the likelihood of the adverse consequence(s)?
- What will happen if the intervention is not done, i.e., risks/adverse consequences?
- How likely are these?
- Are there any alternatives?
- If so, what are *their* potential risks and benefits?

The second step in the evaluation process is to have the patient repeat all of the information critical to making a decision and then to explain the reasoning behind his or her decision.

In this explanation, the physician/health care provider should not be neutral, but should express his/her expert opinion, i.e., what he/she believes the patient ought to do. For health care professionals to respectfully provide their views may in fact be quite persuasive.

❑ **Example**

Mr. R., a 36-year-old patient with advanced AIDS and mild cognitive impairment, was admitted following a first seizure with new slurring of speech. The patient wished to leave against medical advice to go home. On evaluation by a Consultation-Liaison psychiatrist who had known the patient previously, the patient was found to be clear-headed and in possession of the necessary facts. The psychiatrist then told Mr. R. that he was able to make his own decision, but that if he were in Mr. R.'s situation, he would stay for a CT scan because of the seizure and slurred speech. The patient stayed.

The second step in the evaluation process is to have the patient repeat all of the information critical to making a decision and then to explain the reasoning behind his or her decision. This allows the provider to assess the patient's retention of needed information and capacity to integrate that information to arrive at a logically consistent decision—whether the same as the provider's or not; the patient does have a unique set of values and point of view.

Although this second step seems awkward, it may be done as follows: "In order for you to make this important medical decision, I as your doctor (provider) need to know that you understand what the issues are so that you can make a good decision for yourself. I presented them to you a few minutes ago, and now I need to ask you to present them to me so that I am sure you understand."

How much a patient needs to understand and articulate to be deemed capable depends on the complexity, potential benefits, and potential risks of what is being proposed. In other words, *standards for judging capacity vary*.

Roth and colleagues (1977) propose an approach to the varying standard and situations which they illustrate graphically (see Figure 1).

SITUATION A

If a patient is agreeing to an intervention that is likely to be highly beneficial relative to its risk ("favorable risk/benefit ratio"), that patient needs to demonstrate a relatively low level of knowledge in order to be deemed capable. Vaccinations, many noninvasive diagnostic tests, emergency or life-saving invasive procedures, and invasive procedures that the vast majority of individuals would readily agree to under the circumstances fall into this category.

❑ **Example**

A patient with a diagnosis of chronic schizophrenia comes in with signs and symptoms suggestive of acute appendicitis. After the doctor explains the medical situation, including the risks, the patient says that he understands that

Risk/Benefit Ratio

	Favorable Risk/Benefit Ratio	Unfavorable/ Questionable Risk/Benefit Ratio
PATIENT AGREES	**A** Low Standard for Capacity Determination	**C** High Standard for Capacity Determination
PATIENT REFUSES	**B** High Standard for Capacity Determination	**D** Low Standard for Capacity Determination

Figure 1

he may have appendicitis, that taking care of it right away and having surgery is important, and that surgery has some risks that he can't really specify despite having just heard about them.

This patient knows enough to be capable of making a decision under the circumstances.

❑ Example

A 21-year-old woman with mental retardation is found to be pregnant after a rape and is admitted for a termination of pregnancy (T.O.P.). The patient is quite aware that she has been raped and that she wants the doctors to make sure she does not have a baby. She points repeatedly at her lower abdomen. She cannot say much about how the rape relates to the baby or about what the T.O.P. entails, but is repeatedly consistent in her point of view and is supported unanimously by family and physicians.

As in the above example, this patient also knows enough under the circumstances to be deemed capable of making her own decision.

SITUATION **B**

If a patient *refuses* a highly beneficial intervention as described in Situation A, the patient must demonstrate a much higher level of knowledge about the issue at hand to be deemed capable.

❑ **Example**

A 45-year-old white female with chronic schizophrenia living in a group home is discovered to have a right breast lump on examination, and she refuses evaluation.

Her understanding requires close scrutiny before deeming her to be making a fully informed decision to refuse.

❑ **Example**

Mrs. L., a 45-year-old female in labor, is told that her fetus is showing mild distress with uterine contractions. Mrs. L. tells her obstetrician that under no circumstances will she ever agree to undergo a Caesarian section. On evaluation she is suspicious of the University Hospital and wonders whether her fetal monitoring is in part "an experiment." Mrs. L. is, however, quite clear and consistent that she has never had any surgery, never will, and does not believe her baby to be in any danger. Even if the doctors are right and she and/or her baby

If a patient agrees to a questionably beneficial intervention, or one whose benefit is heavily counterbalanced by its risks, that patient must demonstrate a high level of knowledge about the issue at hand to be deemed capable.

may die, Mrs. L. says that she would not have surgery because it is against her personal values. She is aware of the report by her doctor of mild fetal distress. Her husband reports that his wife is in her usual state of mental health and that this is her lifelong philosophy and that he concurs and completely supports her.

Because of her clarity and consistency and the unequivocal statement by her spouse as to her usual state of mental health and long-term values, this patient was judged capable to refuse treatment.

SITUATION C

If a patient agrees to a questionably beneficial intervention, or one whose benefit is heavily counterbalanced by its risks, ("unfavorable or questionable risk/benefit ratio"), that patient must demonstrate a high level of knowledge about the issue at hand to be deemed capable. Interventions of this kind include:

- diagnostic tests where information will not alter care;
- controversial or experimental interventions;
- invasive interventions for terminally ill patients;
- invasive interventions for individuals who have profound mental impairments and a severely compromised quality of life;
- interventions that have significant potential for adversely affecting long-term functioning and quality of life (e.g., colostomy or loss of limbs); and,
- interventions that many individuals would refuse under the circumstances.

> *If a patient refuses a questionably beneficial intervention, the patient needs to demonstrate a lower level of knowledge to be deemed capable.*

❑ **Example**

A 62-year-old man with chronic schizophrenia is admitted to the hospital with inoperable lung cancer and asked to participate in a randomized trial of an experimental chemotherapy protocol involving four drugs and a 25-page consent form. The patient turns to the last page and quickly signs, saying, "Whatever you say, Doc."

This patient's capacity to give informed consent should be carefully evaluated despite his cooperativeness and the physician's desire to try to heroically help the patient and advance scientific knowledge about cancer and its treatment.

SITUATION D

If a patient refuses a questionably beneficial intervention as described in Situation C, the patient needs to demonstrate a lower level of knowledge to be deemed capable.

❑ Example

Mrs. D., a 49-year-old female with schizophrenia is diagnosed as having a brain tumor possibly representing metastatic spread from breast cancer diagnosed and treated with mastectomy three years before. She is offered and refuses brain surgery to remove the tumor. On three different interviews, Mrs. D. says that she is in the hospital, but doesn't know why. Each time after being reminded of the brain tumor, Mrs. D. immediately says ,"Oh, yes," and goes on to say she thinks it is related to her breast cancer and that she does not want any surgery because she feels it will not help and may leave her impaired.

Determining that a refusing patient is incapable of making an informed decision does not mean that the patient should be forced to undergo the intervention he/she has refused.

Because (a) the intervention was of questionable benefit, (b) the patient expressed knowledge of her condition and a possible adverse outcome of the procedure, and (c) the patient consistently refused surgery, she was deemed to be capable of making this decision despite some elements of cognitive impairment.

Again, note that "Agreers" as often as "Refusers" require close scrutiny as to their capacity to make informed medical decisions (Situations B and C).

When the "Incapable" Patient Refuses Treatment

If the patient is capable of making an informed decision then he/she has every right to agree or refuse.

If the patient is incapable of such a decision but agrees to treatment, then appropriate surrogate decision-maker(s) should make a "substituted judgment" or "best interest" informed decision. If the surrogate agrees, then the patient should undergo the proposed intervention.

Clearly, the most difficult situation arises when a patient who is incapable of making his or her own medical decisions refuses treatment.

Determining that a refusing patient is incapable of making an informed decision does not mean that the patient should be forced to undergo the intervention he/she has refused. All that such a determination should mean is that an appropriate surrogate makes the decision, which can be a complex and difficult process.

In medical emergencies, incapable refusals should be overridden. In fact, in medical emergencies there may be little time to make capacity determinations as the patient's life may be in danger.

In nonemergency situations, the likelihood of short- and long-term benefit, adverse outcomes, patients' values, and quality of life issues are important factors in deciding how to proceed.

There are three possible options:

- the surrogate may decide to honor the patient's refusal;
- the surrogate may try to persuade the patient to agree to the recommended intervention, or at least to cooperate with tests and/or treatments; and,
- the surrogate may decide to override the patient's refusal and force the patient to undergo the medical procedure because it is in the patient's best interest.

The following examples may help to illustrate a variety of approaches to this most difficult group of patient situations.

□ **Example 1: Honoring the Refusal**

Ms. M., a 55-year-old female with a diagnosis of chronic schizophrenia, was admitted from a community residence with pneumonia and newly discovered diabetes. The patient insisted that the only treatment she would accept was IM penicillin and that any other suggestion was made only because the doctors were being paid by a drug company. The medical house staff was appalled at her choice. By history, Ms. M. was a chronically noncompliant, difficult patient in her residence.

For diagnostic tests with a high likelihood of benefit (e.g., the ruling in or out of a life-threatening infection) and low likelihood of adverse outcome (e.g., lumbar puncture), the patient must meet a very high standard to be deemed capable of refusing.

In the hospital she appeared to be physically well without fever, chest pain, or shortness of breath. On interview, Ms. M. was adamant and would not listen to or reliably repeat any information in conflict with her point of view. She was judged incapable of making her own medical decisions. The psychiatric consultant suggested that a course of IM penicillin be administered as an initial approach because she looked so well clinically, and she was so adamant in her refusal, that imposing some different treatment would most likely involve physical and/or pharmacologic restraint. The consultant suggested that if her condition declined, appropriate steps should be taken to make a surrogate decision to treat Ms. M. with a more appropriate antibiotic against her wishes.

This case illustrates that compromises may need to be made in the medical care of the incapable but refusing patient. These compromises need to be well thought out in terms of their risks and benefits. Plans to change the approach in the event of a decline in the patient's medical condition must be incorporated in such compromised care approaches.

❑ **Example 2: Overriding the Patient's Refusal**

Mr. M. is a 39-year-old male with a history of chronic mental illness who is brought to the hospital from a residence with a fever of 102 degrees and an increase in his usual psychiatric symptoms coupled with some new confusion. In the emergency room he refuses a lumbar puncture (L.P. or "spinal tap"). On evaluation he has trouble concentrating, which suggests possible delirium. Mr. M. insists that he doesn't want a spinal tap, but can't say why. He can offer no explanation of why the spinal tap is being proposed despite being told clearly that his doctors need to make sure that he doesn't have meningitis. He is judged incapable of making this decision, and because of the emergency nature of the situation, the consultant urges that the medical team sedate Mr. M. and perform the L.P. immediately.

Several elements deserve highlighting in this case. First, for diagnostic tests with a high likelihood of benefit (e.g., the ruling in or out of a life-threatening infection) and low likelihood of adverse outcome (e.g., lumbar puncture), the patient must meet a very high standard to be deemed capable of refusing. Furthermore, in an emergency situation, appropriate steps should be taken to override the incapable patient's refusal and proceed with medical care.

Finally, when the medical problem is abnormal brain functioning (e.g., trouble concentrating or delirium, as in this case), and the patient refuses evaluation, it is generally in the patient's best interest to override that refusal (which may be the product of a brain pathology) and proceed with the evaluation.

❑ **Example 3: Honoring the Patient's Refusal, with Adverse Consequences**

A 45-year-old-female with chronic schizophrenia (previously mentioned on page 144) refused further evaluation of a right breast lump found on routine physical examination while residing in her community residence. Six years later, she is admitted to the hospital with a large breast mass and a possible metastasis to her upper arm seen on a routine chest X-ray. The patient currently agrees to a biopsy and appears to understand that she might have cancer.

The tragedy of this case is that the patient might not have been capable of making an informed refusal six years ago. If so, her refusal should not have been taken at face value, especially given the possible life-threatening consequences of failing to act at that time. Simple steps like repeated discussions with the patient and the involvement of significant others and staff members close to the patient to try to gain her agreement might have been useful. She could have been encouraged to undergo a mammogram and/or repeated breast exams during subsequent menstrual cycles. If she continued to refuse, an appropriate surrogate should have considered authorizing a mammogram or biopsy under sedation over her objections.

Aggressive work with the incapable refusing patient and aggressive thinking by appropriate surrogate decision-makers should be the hallmarks of care when disease presents early and has a high likelihood of cure.

Diagnosis of early breast cancer at that time could have changed her attitude and she might have agreed to definitive treatment and possible cure of her cancer. Many individuals with mental disabilities actually function well in the face of a concrete, definitive, external threat to their lives. They may function better than they function routinely or when confronted with more theoretical health issues.

Unfortunately, we will never know what the outcome of more vigorous efforts might have been. Some six years later, she is now a metastatic cancer patient with a poor prognosis who is finally agreeing to a diagnostic evaluation —much too little and much too late.

Aggressive work with the incapable refusing patient and aggressive thinking by appropriate surrogate decision-makers should be the hallmarks of care when disease presents early and has a high likelihood of cure.

□ **Example 4: Gaining the Patient's Cooperation**

Mrs. M. is a 60-year-old divorced female who lives with her sister and works as a filing clerk for New York City. She has a history of hypertension, congestive heart failure, and chronic paranoid schizophrenia, and was admitted to the medical service for evaluation of a 40-pound weight loss over six months and severe iron deficiency anemia.

History of Present Illness

Mrs. M. had been noted to be anemic approximately one year prior to admission and was noncompliant with outpatient medical evaluation, refusing stool guaiacs and gastrointestinal work-ups for months. Prior to admission, Mrs. M. told her medical clinic doctor that she was "not eating at home" because of "feculent water in the apartment which occasionally also smells of urine." The clinic doctor also discovered that Mrs. M. had been noncompliant with antipsychotic medication and psychiatric follow-up for approximately seven months.

The physician sent Mrs. M. to the emergency room, where she was noted to be "guarded, irritable...blunted...positive for paranoid delusions—believes she hears voices of her sister and co-workers coming through the walls and ceilings trying to torment her." She was described as having "no understanding of her medical condition, unable to evaluate consequences of refusal of treatment." The psychiatrist in the emergency room suggested that "the patient be treated medically as necessary."

Mrs. M.'s sister reported that since the patient had stopped her Haldol seven months before, she had steadily decompensated. She stopped sleeping at night, began talking and cursing to herself, stopped talking to her sister, stopped eating, and became very restless. Her sister stated that although the patient had continued to work until a few days prior to admission, Mrs. M. had "never been this bad before" and "couldn't come home in this condition."

On admission, Mrs. M. expressed concern about "going along with the doctors," but couldn't give any details, said she "wasn't worried" about her health, and "didn't want to die." After a simple explanation of her medical condition—severe iron deficiency anemia and its dangers and need for evaluation—the patient was unable to repeat any of this information. Mrs. M. admitted to some "confusion" and "trouble getting her thoughts together."

The psychiatric consultant concluded that it would be tragic for this patient to leave without a work-up for a potentially life-threatening condition, noting, "She is severely psychiatrically impaired and not capable of making critical medical decisions for herself."

Initial Approach

Mrs. M. was placed on constant observation (i.e., staff with her at all times) to minimize the chance of self-injury and elopement. She was started on Haldol and Cogentin to try to control her psychotic symptoms.

The consultant suggested that diagnostic and therapeutic interventions deemed emergencies should be done with or without Mrs. M.'s assent and cooperation. Nonemergency interventions should be done with the family's consent and, if at all possible, with Mrs. M.'s cooperation. If, however, she continued to actively resist intervention, the consultant suggested that the medical team consider overriding her refusal, using appropriate surrogate decision-making channels.

Hospital Course

On Hospital Day 5, Mrs. M. was able to repeat that she might have internal bleeding or a malignancy, but she refused a diagnostic work-up, saying only that her "mind is telling me to stick to my decision" even though it might mean "the difference between living and dying."

As her medical attending noted on Day 7, Mrs. M. needed "an UGI series, barium enema or colonoscopy. These tests require active patient cooperation and cannot be done in this patient even if she were heavily sedated." With this in mind, the psychiatric consultant recommended considering tests that could be done under sedation—for example, bone marrow, CT scan, ultrasound.

The consultant recommended taking "an extremely firm approach with patient—no asking about procedures, no asking her to sign consent form (she is incapable and sister will do this). Please just tell her when necessary procedures are scheduled and let's see what happens." On Day 16 the patient gave her first stool sample for guaiac testing ever.

After her physicians were unable to reach her sister, they obtained administrative consent (i.e., permission for an emergency procedure granted by senior facility personnel in situations where the patient cannot consent and relatives cannot be contacted) for a barium enema. On Day 27 she went for a barium enema and cooperated, but was full of stool, so the study couldn't be completed. On Day 28 she refused prep, but on Day 29 she again cooperated with a barium enema, which was grossly negative, but inadequate due to presence "of residual stool throughout colon."

On Day 33 the consultant again described his suggested management approach to the medical team: "Be firm and definitive with patient—give her warning of upcoming procedures but don't ask her (sister will give informed consent); firmly and gently and confidently tell her."

On Day 34 Mrs. M. uneventfully underwent a pelvic sonogram, which showed uterine fibroids.

On Day 35 Mrs. M. told her night mental health aide that her older sister "wants to control my life." Mrs. M. went on to say, "I have my own interests and desires and can manage my own affairs."

On Day 39 a gynecological exam was negative; Mrs. M. was cooperative, but refused a rectal examination.

On Day 41 Mrs. M. fully cooperated with the colonoscopy prep—she drank the required one gallon of prep solution!

On Day 42 Mrs. M. cooperated and underwent a taxing upper endoscopy and colonoscopy done in one session. A right ascending colon lesion was discovered and biopsied, and Mrs. M. was transferred to the surgery service on Day 43 when the biopsy reading showed "infiltrating moderately differentiated adeno-carcinoma."

On Day 45 she told the psychiatrist that her surgery was to be Tuesday or Wednesday, but stated she was unaware of the nature of the operation and that she didn't want to know because, "It might make me nervous."

On Day 47 the psychiatric consultant became aware that surgery for Mrs. M.'s colon cancer might entail a temporary or even permanent colostomy. There was no guarantee that the cancerous colon could be resected with full restoration of normal bowel function. Mrs. M. might not simply have a scar on her abdomen, but might have to live with a colostomy. This led the consultant to rethink his approach to clinical decision-making and management in this case, concluding that it was important to try to increase Mrs. M.'s participation. He told the surgical team that in his opinion, "The patient should be given full information. If patient continues to be vague, but passively cooperative, then best decisions in her interest must be made by family and the physicians. If, however, patient adamantly refuses, with possible adverse surgical outcomes like colostomy in mind, then we may very well want to involve other parties—Bioethics Committee, etc., in decision," and may want to honor her refusal.

The surgical resident and psychiatrist collaborated and gave Mrs. M. full information. The consultant wrote in his note that the patient was initially "upset at the prospect of possible colostomy but a few minutes later was just lying passively in bed."

On Day 51 the psychiatrist again discussed surgery with Mrs. M. and her sister. Mrs. M. was "completely unaware of cancer and any details of surgery at all. All she reported was an awareness of a 'tumor' and 'some' surgery." The psychiatrist again told Mrs. M. in some detail about the diagnosis of her cancer, its prognosis, the proposed treatment, and the possibility of a colostomy. "Patient declined to express any opinion and is passively awaiting surgery."

The psychiatrist asked the surgical nurses to discuss colostomy and have Mrs. M. meet a patient with one if possible. The psychiatrist further suggested an abdominal CT scan to rule out metastatic disease preoperatively, noting, "If cancer has spread, we might not push surgery; if not spread, would push."

On Day 52 the psychiatrist again spoke with Mrs. M., now scheduled for surgery the next day, to give her a final opportunity to participate actively in planning her treatment. Mrs. M. told him she was "aware" of surgery and "reports she has no questions about it at this time."

Fifty-six days after her admission, Mrs. M. had an uneventful right colon resection with end-to-end anastomosis restoring normal bowel function, requiring no colostomy. Constant observation was discontinued postoperatively, as Mrs. M. had been calm and cooperative for a number of days.

Mrs. M. recovered uneventfully and on Day 63 the pathology report came back "19/19 mesenteric nodes (-) for cancer," strongly suggesting that the cancer had been caught early enough so it had not yet spread and that surgery had cured the cancer. Mrs. M. agreed to return to the outpatient psychiatry clinic for follow-up care and to accept Visiting Nurse and Home Health Aide Services at home with her sister. The Haldol dosage was decreased, and Mrs. M. was discharged after a 71-day hospitalization.

This case illustrates an integrated approach to managing the care of a patient who is incapable of making informed medical decisions and is refusing treatment. Simply honoring her rejection of a potentially life-saving diagnosis and treatment would have been inappropriate. On the other hand, overriding her refusal and evaluating and treating her against her wishes was neither fully practical nor desirable.

Working together, the psychiatric consultant, the medical physicians, and the family decided that the way to approach this situation was, first, to have family, acting as a surrogate, make appropriate informed medical decisions, and second, to gain the patient's cooperation in implementing these decisions. The first steps were to ensure her safety by providing constant supervision and to treat her psychosis by restarting antipsychotic medication. The next step was to adopt the strategy of, "Don't ask, tell"— firmly, gently, and repeatedly informing her that there would

Ultimately, the advocates must walk a fine line between respecting the patients' wishes and allowing them to make fatal mistakes because they do not fully comprehend the consequences of their actions.

be a work-up and proceeding with the tests without asking for her permission (which she was judged to be incapable of giving). This strategy was formulated based upon the clinical experience that many patients object verbally but ultimately cooperate physically with medical care that is in their best interest.

Once the diagnosis of cancer was made and treatment decisions needed to be made, the strategy had to change. The diagnostic tests might have caused some temporary discomfort, but had no lasting effects. Surgery, however, might leave the patient not only with a scar, but with a colostomy, a major change in body image and functioning.

The psychiatric consultant devised a new strategy. The patient was not asked to consent, but was repeatedly given complete information, actively invited to ask questions, and given an opportunity to refuse if she chose.

A "best interest" approach to surrogate decision-making still argued strongly for surgery, but the risk of an adverse outcome was substantial enough to require an increase in the patient's participation in decisions about her care.

As this case illustrates, individuals with chronic mental impairments need advocates in the medical system. It is the advocate's role to:

- understand the medical issues which the patient faces;
- inform and evaluate the patient to determine if he or she is capable of making informed medical decisions;
- insure high quality medical care in a system which often poorly serves individuals with significant mental disabilities; and,
- develop strategies for that most difficult group of patients, especially those who are incapable of making their own informed medical decisions, but who refuse needed care.

Ultimately, the advocates must walk a fine line between respecting the patients' wishes and allowing them to make fatal mistakes because they do not fully comprehend the consequences of their actions.

References

Annas, G. J. (1994). Legal issues in medicine: Informed consent, cancer, and truth in prognosis. *The New England Journal of Medicine, 330,* 223–225.

Appelbaum, P. S., Lidz, C. W., & Meizel, A. (1987). Exceptions to the legal requirements: Incompetency. In *Informed Consent: Legal Theory and Clinical Practice* (pp. 81–111). New York: Oxford University Press.

Auerbach, V. S., & Banja, J. D. (1993). Competency determinations. In A. Stoudemire & B. S. Fogel, (Eds.), *Medical Psychiatric Practice: Volume II* (pp. 515–535). Washington, DC: American Psychiatric Press.

Borus, J. F. (1987). The other part of the elephant: Mental disorder screening in primary health care settings and physical disorder screening in psychiatric settings. *Medical Care, 25*(Suppl.), 100–102.

Goldney, R. D., & Bottrill, A. (1980). Attitudes to patients who attempt suicide. *Medical Journal of Australia, 2,* 717–720.

Hall, R., Gardner, E, Popkin, M. K., Lecann, A. F., & Stickney, S. K. (1981). Unrecognized physical illness prompting psychiatric admission: A prospective study. *American Journal of Psychiatry, 138,* 629–635.

Hall, R., Popkin, M., Devaul, R. A., Faillace, L. A., & Stickney, S. K. (1978). Physical illness presenting as psychiatric disease. *Archives of General Psychiatry, 35,* 1315–1320.

Hoffman, R. S., & Koran, L. M. (1984). Detecting physical illness in patients with mental disorders. *Psychosomatics, 25,* 654–660.

Irwin, M., Lovitz, A., Marder, S. R., Mintz, J., Winslade, W. J., Van Putten, T., & Mills, M. J. (1985). Psychotic patients' understanding of informed consent. *American Journal of Psychiatry, 142,* 1351–1354.

Koran, L. M., Sox, H. C., Sox, C. H., & Marton, K. I. (1987). Detecting physical disease in psychiatric patients. *Medical Care, 25*(Suppl.), 99–105.

Koran, L. M., Sox, H. C., Marton, K. I., Moltzen, S., Sox, C. H., Kraemer, H. C., Imai, K., Kelsey, T. G., Rose, T. G., Jr., Leven, L. C., & Chandra, S. (1989). Medical evaluation of psychiatric patients: I. Results in a state mental health system. *Archives of General Psychiatry, 46,* 733–740.

Koranyi, E. K. (1979). Morbidity and rate of undiagnosed physical illnesses in a psychiatric clinic population. *Archives of General Psychiatry, 36,* 414–419.

Koranyi, E. K. (1980). Somatic illness in psychiatric patients. *Psychosomatics*, *21*, 887–891.

Loewy, E. H. (1987). Sounding board: Treatment decisions in the mentally impaired. *The New England Journal of Medicine*, *317*, 1465–1469.

Martin, R. L., & Cloninger, R. (1985). Mortality in a follow-up of 500 psychiatric outpatients II. Cause-specific mortality. *Archives of General Psychiatry*, *42*, 58–66.

Martin, R. L., Cloninger, R., Guze, S. B., & Clayton, P. J. (1985). Mortality in a follow-up of 500 psychiatric outpatients I. Total mortality. *Archives of General Psychiatry*, *42*, 47–54.

Perl, M., & Shelp, E. E. (1982). Sounding board: Psychiatric consultation masking moral dilemmas in medicine. *The New England Journal of Medicine*, *307*, 618–621.

Roth, L. H., Meisel, A., & Lidz, C. W. (1977). Tests of competency to consent to treatment. *American Journal of Psychiatry*, *134*, 279–284.

Schloendorff v. Society of New York Hospital, 211 N. Y. 125, 105 N. E., 92 (1914).

Shouten, R. S., Groves, J. E., & Vaccarino, J. M. (1991). Legal aspects of consultation. In N. H. Cassem, (Ed.), *Massachusetts General Hospital handbook of general hospital psychiatry* (3rd ed.) (pp. 619–638). St. Louis, MO: Mosby-Year Book.

Stone, A. A. (1981). The right to refuse treatment: Why psychiatrists should and can make it work. *Archives of General Psychiatry*, *38*, 358–62.

Strain, J. J., Rhodes, R., Moros, D. A., & Baumrin, B. (1993). Ethics in medical-psychiatric practice (1993). In A. Stoudemire & B. S. Fogel, (Eds.), *Medical Psychiatric Practice: Volume II* (pp. 585–607). Washington, DC: American Psychiatric Press.

14

Involuntary Treatment: Walking the Tightrope Between Freedom and Paternalism

Robert M. Levy, Esq.

No area of mental disability law is likely to arouse more controversy than involuntary treatment. Whether in the form of civil commitment, the forcible administration of medication, or the imposition of mandatory outpatient programs, coerced treatment creates a conflict between the individual's fundamental right to liberty and government's twin powers to shield helpless citizens from harm and to protect society from danger. The intensity of this controversy is magnified by the importance of the interests at stake and the absence of several key due process safeguards that traditionally have protected mentally typical people facing confinement or the deprivation of the right to bodily integrity.

This paper will examine civil commitment and involuntary medication, providing both a historical context and a brief description of the current state of the law.

Involuntary Commitment

The Supreme Court has termed involuntary commitment a "massive curtailment of liberty."[1] Individuals are held under lock and key,

> *Coerced treatment creates a conflict between the individual's fundamental right to liberty and government's twin powers to shield helpless citizens from harm and to protect society from danger.*

viduals are held under lock and key, separated from family and friends, deprived of personal privacy and subjected to the possibility of forced treatment with highly intrusive neuroleptic drugs that alter thought processes and can have serious and potentially irreversible side effects. Commitment infringes the right to liberty, to freedom of association, to travel, to freedom from unreasonable searches and seizures, and to bodily autonomy. Yet, unlike criminal defendants, people facing commitment can be preventively detained for behavior that violates no law, because the confinement is to an institution, not a prison, and the purpose is said to be treatment, not punishment.

The state has two sources of authority for involuntary commitment: its *parens patriae* power and its police power. *Parens patriae* literally means "Father of his country; parent of his country. In England, the King. In the United States, the state as sovereign—referring to the sovereign power of guardianship over persons under disability...such as minors and insane and incompetent persons."[2] The concept of *parens patriae* developed in feudal England, not so much to protect people with disabilities as to protect the King's property interests, and later those of his noblemen. It is only comparatively recently that this power has been invoked to justify involuntary institutionalization and the nonconsensual treatment of people with mental disabilities. In the United States, the *parens patriae* power first came into wide use as a justification for involuntary treatment in the mid-nineteenth century, when a "cult of asylum swept the country,"[3] and psychiatrists claimed that "moral treatment" in a remote institutional setting "held the secret to the cure of insanity."[4]

> *Civil commitment is a profound abridgement of individual liberties that has continuing consequences after release.*

The *parens patriae* power authorizes the state to intervene in the lives of people who lack the capacity to take care of themselves, such as minors, the elderly, and people with mental disabilities. The theory is that the state has an obligation to protect the interests of those who cannot do so themselves, even if this means overriding their decisions and, in some cases, confining them involuntarily for their own good. Without a finding of incapacity, however, there is no justification for such an interference with the right to personal autonomy that is otherwise guaranteed to all persons "of adult years and sound mind."[5] The *parens patriae* power is typically used to commit people whose mental disability makes them dangerous to themselves.

By contrast, the purpose of the police power is to protect society from potential harm. Criminal laws and public health codes that authorize compulsory vaccinations[6] or quarantines of people with contagious diseases[7] are among the most common exercises of this power. In the mental health context, the police power is typically invoked to commit people whose mental disability poses a danger to others. Unlike criminal defendants, people facing police power commitments can be confined without proof that they violated the criminal law, or, under some state laws, evidence that they committed a dangerous act.

Civil commitment is a profound abridgement of individual liberties that has continuing consequences after release. In addition to the massive curtailment of liberty during confinement, inmates also suffer from a lasting stigma thereafter that can impair their ability to obtain employment, housing, education, and other opportunities. Because commitment infringes so deeply on fundamental rights, individuals are entitled to strict due process safeguards limiting the reach of state control to situations where the state interest in curbing dangerous behavior is truly compelling and outweighs personal liberty interests.

Until the nineteenth century, there were very few public institutions for people with mental disabilities in America. Although the first institution in the colonies devoted exclusively to mental disabilities was established in 1773,[8] few others were built during the next sixty years. The first institution for people with mental retardation was not authorized until 1848, when Massachusetts approved a school for "pauper idiots."[9] Lumping "fools" and "lunatics" together with vagabonds, beggars, and other social outcasts, eighteenth century America dealt with mental disorders "as a problem of containment, not treatment."[10] People with mental disabilities were expected to look to their families for support. Many lived at home, some were boarded out to private households or confined in almshouses and jails, while others were banished from towns along with paupers and wandered the countryside.[11] In eighteenth century New York, for example, a succession of laws provided that an "idle wandering vagabond" could be summarily confined to a house of corrections, whipped, or deported out of the jurisdiction.[12]

Lumping "fools" and "lunatics" together with vagabonds, beggars, and other social outcasts, eighteenth century America dealt with mental disorders "as a problem of containment, not treatment."

A wave of change swept the country in the decades before the Civil War, born of the conviction that institutions could cure "lunatics" and sufficiently train "idiots" to enable them to lead productive lives in their communities. For people with mental illness, champions of institutions hailed the creation of places of peace and order, seeing in them true asylums, isolated from the frenzy and disorder of the cities, that would cure insanity by bringing a quiet "discipline to the victims of a disorganized society."[13] In their view, civilization itself was the cause of mental illness, and there was a "constant parallelism between the progress of society and the increase of mental disorders."[14]

This optimism eventually faded as no cure was found for many of the residents who had been admitted with such high hopes. Soon more than half of the inmates of these institutions were classified as incurable, and by the 1860s it became clear that the asylum was not the panacea it had been presumed to be. As institutions filled with people deemed incurable, they inevitably became more custodial. Their new mission was to protect society from what was widely perceived as the unpredictable violence of the mentally disturbed and to stop the spread of madness by quarantining people with mental illness.[15] Ultimately, the asylum became "a dumping ground for social undesirables,"[16] with a significant immigrant and poor population. "The convenience of confining these people," Rothman concludes, "even without the possibility of cure, made the institution worth supporting after its original purpose was no longer attainable."[17] Then, as now, institutions became at least in part the repositories of unresolved social problems.[18]

Institutions for people with mental retardation fared no better. Their populations swelled as more and more residents were deemed untrainable and their parents refused or were unable to take them home. By the end of the nineteenth century, there were more custodial institutions than educational facilities for mentally retarded people.[19] With the advent of the eugenics movement at the turn of the century, mental retardation was increasingly seen as the cause of crime, poverty, and insanity, all of which were said to be passed inevitably from one generation to another. The eugenicists' solution called for the use of involuntary commitment laws to enforce the strict segregation of

Due process precludes the commitment of harmless, mentally ill people simply because they are dirty or unattractive, they have a diminished quality of life, or their presence at large is objectionable to some members of society.

mentally retarded people from society at large, in order to prevent them from propagating and thereby "nearly extinguish their race."[20]

Even after the hysteria of the eugenics movement receded in the 1930s and 1940s, the segregation continued, in part, because there were no real community alternatives to institutions. It is only since the 1970s that large, chronically understaffed and overcrowded state institutions have become suspect, slowly giving way to smaller, normalizing community facilities modeled after private homes.

Following the Supreme Court's landmark ruling in *O'Connor v. Donaldson*,[21] courts and legislatures across the country have established stringent standards for commitment, requiring proof of a mental disability which poses a substantial threat of serious harm to one's self or others. As a general rule, the threat of harm must be real and present[22] and the proof of dangerousness clear and convincing.[23]

Although civil commitment had been practiced in the United States for over 200 years, *O'Connor* was the first case in which the Supreme Court considered the constitutional boundaries of the commitment process.[24] The Court ruled that, "A State cannot constitutionally confine a nondangerous individual who is capable of surviving safely in freedom by himself or with the help of willing and responsible family members or friends."[25] Due process precludes the commitment of harmless, mentally ill people simply because they are dirty or unattractive, they have a diminished quality of life, or their presence at large is objectionable to some members of society. In tones that presaged the homelessness crisis a decade later, the Court admonished:

> May the State confine the mentally ill merely to ensure them a living standard superior to that they enjoy in the private community? That the State has a proper interest in providing care and assistance to the unfortunate goes without saying. But the mere presence of mental illness does not disqualify a person from preferring his home to the comforts of an institution. Moreover, while the State may arguably confine a person to save him from harm, incarceration is rarely if ever a necessary condition for raising the living standards of those capable of surviving safely in freedom, on their own or with the help of family or friends.
>
> May the State fence in the harmless mentally ill solely to save its citizens from exposure to those whose ways are different? One might as well ask if the State, to avoid public unease, could incarcerate all who are physically unattractive or socially eccentric. Mere public intolerance or animosity cannot constitutionally justify the deprivation of a person's physical liberty.[26]

There is relatively little controversy over the mental disability component of the commitment standard, apart from some grumbling about the definitions of "mental illness" in various state statutes, which often tend to be vague[27] or circular. The seriousness of the disability must be such that it renders the individual dangerous to self or others and requires treatment in a confined setting.

A few states maintain the additional requirement that the person be incapable of making a rational decision whether to accept treatment,[28] on the theory that *parens patriae* commitments require a finding of incapacity to make treatment decisions and the presence of mental illness alone "does not mean that an individual is deprived of all of his capacity to make rational decisions."[29]

> *The definition of dangerousness, however, is among the most elusive concepts in mental disability law.*

The definition of dangerousness, however, is among the most elusive concepts in mental disability law. Most statutes provide minimal definitions and leave it to clinicians and the courts to fill in the details. There is relatively little caselaw on point, because decisions at commitment hearings tend to be oral. Moreover, when an appeal is taken, the amount of time necessary to have the case heard and decided is frequently so great that most patients have already been discharged and their appeals dismissed as moot before a decision is rendered.

Dangerousness is a prediction about a person's future behavior. Alexander Brooks has written that the term can be broken down into at least four component parts: 1) the magnitude of harm; 2) the probability that the harm will occur; 3) the frequency with which the harm will occur; and 4) the imminence of the harm.[30] By weighing the various factors, he suggests, one can make a judgment whether an individual is dangerous. For example, a trivial harm that is unlikely to take place would not constitute dangerousness, whereas a serious harm that is highly likely to occur right away would.

Most states require a finding of some substantial likelihood of serious physical harm to self or others.[31] Dangerousness to self or others is generally demonstrated through prior acts, attempts or threats of physical violence, or expert predictions of future harmful conduct. The danger to self need not be active or self-inflicted, but also encompasses the inability to survive safely outside of an institution, even with the help of others.[32] Mere self-neglect, however, is not

> *Although most state statutes contain an imminent harm requirement, they do not provide a precise definition of the term, leaving it to clinicians and the courts to decide whether the proper period is a matter of hours, days, or even weeks.*

enough. Due process precludes the commitment of people who, albeit poor, ill-clothed, or disturbed, are nevertheless able to obtain the bare essentials to enable them to survive in the community.[33]

The anticipated danger must be imminent, not remote or speculative.[34] For example, it is improper for a psychiatric outreach team to commit a mentally ill homeless woman who is surviving safely on the streets, simply because it fears that she will deteriorate in the coming months and become unable to care for herself. Although most state statutes contain an imminent harm requirement, they do not provide a precise definition of the term, leaving it to clinicians and the courts to decide whether the proper period is a matter of hours, days, or even weeks.

"When it comes to predicting violence, our crystal balls are terribly cloudy," reports Dr. John Monahan, one of the leading experts on the prediction of future violent behavior. "The research indicates that clinicians are better than chance at predicting who will be violent, but they are far from perfect. The problem is there is no standard procedure and the field lacks a solid research base for knowing which factors to rely on."[35]

There is a substantial body of research documenting the inability of psychiatrists to make reliable predictions of future dangerous behavior.

There is a substantial body of research documenting the inability of psychiatrists to make reliable predictions of future dangerous behavior.[36] Indeed, even the American Psychiatric Association has recognized some of the limitations of psychiatric expertise in this area, stating that the "unreliability of psychiatric predictions of long-term future dangerousness is by now an established fact within the profession."[37] In a review of the scientific research that became a classic in its field,[38] Dr. Monahan concluded that two out of three clinical predictions of future dangerousness are wrong,[39] that is "of every three people predicted to be violent, only one is discovered to be violent over the ensuing five years."[40]

Ironically, despite the unreliability of psychiatric expertise in this area, courts have been reluctant to increase due process safeguards to reduce the risk of error. The most egregious example was a death penalty case in which the Supreme Court held that, even if clinical predictions were inaccurate two-thirds of the time, psychiatrists could testify as expert witnesses on the prediction of future dangerousness.[41] The American Psychiatric Association, among others, had urged the court to vacate a death sentence and preclude psychiatrists from testifying as experts in this area because their testimony is so unreliable and prejudicial as to violate due process.[42] This decision has been the target of well-justified criticism.[43]

Similarly, the Court relied in part on the "lack of certainty and the fallibility of psychiatric diagnosis" in rejecting a "proof beyond a reasonable doubt" standard at civil commitment hearings, because it found that "there is a serious question as to whether a state could ever prove beyond a reasonable doubt that an individual is both mentally ill and likely to be dangerous."[44] The Court observed that it is very difficult for an expert psychiatrist to "offer definite conclusions about any particular patient."[45] It was precisely because of the uncertainty of psychiatric opinions,

> *It was precisely because of the uncertainty of psychiatric opinions, and the serious deprivation of liberty that could result from them, that the Court was asked to strengthen the safeguards at commitment hearings to protect against erroneous confinement.*

and the serious deprivation of liberty that could result from them, that the Court was asked to strengthen the safeguards at commitment hearings to protect against erroneous confinement.

There is a split among the jurisdictions as to whether commitment can rest upon a mere prediction of future harm, without evidence of an actual act, attempt, or threat of dangerous behavior. An "overt conduct" requirement is a necessary safeguard because, standing alone, psychiatric predictions of future dangerousness are too arbitrary and unreliable to justify confinement. Without recent evidence of dangerous threats or conduct, many harmless people will be erroneously committed. Such evidence could include, for example, a threat to commit suicide, an attempt to throw a child in front of a car, or the mere act of sleeping uncovered on the sidewalk in sub-zero weather, wearing only shorts and a tee shirt. An overt conduct requirement makes particular sense in the case of police power commitments, that is, commitments for the protection of society, not the individual. In such cases it is unreasonable to forbid the confinement of a mentally typical person who has not committed a criminal act, while allowing the incarceration of a person with mental disabilities for the same conduct. In both circumstances, the individual suffers a serious deprivation of liberty in order to prevent harm to the public. One cannot say that the presence of a mental disability makes the prediction of future dangerousness without actual overt conduct more reliable. Indeed, it may be easier to predict the future dangerous behavior of a mentally typical person with a long history of violent acts than that of a person with a mental disability with no such history.

A number of courts have ruled that state commitment statutes were overly broad or unconstitutionally vague without a recent overt act requirement.[46] Some more recent decisions have declined to require this standard.[47] For example, while conceding that "in most cases a somewhat more reliable prediction [of future dangerous behavior] can be made if there is a history of a recent overt act," one court found that there are instances where a psychiatrist can determine from a clinical examination that a person is reasonably likely to harm herself or others. Although these cases "may be relatively few," the court reasoned, "they are not insignificant" and to adopt an overt act requirement would render the state "powerless to protect the mentally ill person and society in these cases."[48] However, the same could be said for certain people without a mental disability, yet the Constitution does not condone their preventive detention. The existence of such a double standard for the police power confinement of people with mental disabilities betrays society's failure to accord people with mental disabilities the rights we take for granted in the criminal justice system when detaining individuals who present a threat to society, as well as the mistaken notion that people with mental disabilities tend to be more dangerous than other, similarly situated members of society. At present, somewhat less than one-half of the state commitment statutes include an overt act requirement.

> *The doctrine of the least restrictive alternative is based on the constitutional principle that, in pursuing legitimate state interests, the government must use means that least restrict fundamental personal liberties.*

The doctrine of the least restrictive alternative is based on the constitutional principle that, in pursuing legitimate state interests, the government must use means that least restrict fundamental personal liberties.[49] In the context of civil commitment, this means that the state may not involuntarily institutionalize an individual if less restrictive settings will suffice. For example, if release to the care of family or friends, the provision of outpatient services, or even a period of residence in a supervised community facility were sufficient to enable a person to survive safely in the community without endangering others, then commitment would be unconstitutional.[50]

Virtually every state has incorporated this doctrine into its commitment laws,[51] and numerous courts have mandated it as a matter of constitutional due process.[52]   The Supreme Court relied on this principle in *O'Connor v. Donaldson* in formulating its ruling that it is unconstitutional to confine...nondangerous individuals who are "capable of surviving safely in freedom, on their own or with the help of family or friends"[53] and explicitly referred to *Shelton v. Tucker*, the Court's first modern decision setting forth the doctrine.[54] As a federal appeals court noted,[55] "The principle of the least restrictive alternative consistent with the legitimate purposes of a commitment inheres in the very nature of civil commitment, which entails an extraordinary deprivation of liberty...."[56]

There has been relatively little litigation surrounding the commitment standard for people with developmental disabilities. Because the individual liberty interests of mentally ill and mentally retarded people are virtually identical, as are the state interests in providing them treatment and preventing harm, the author believes that there is little principled justification for adopting different commitment standards for either of these two groups.[57] Thus, if an individual can live safely in freedom and is not dangerous to self or others, involuntary commitment is unconstitutional, regardless whether the person suffers from mental illness or mental retardation.

> *"In reality, the states are using the fiction of 'voluntariness' for most institutionalized persons with mental retardation to avoid judicial scrutiny of individual placement decisions."*

At least two courts have reinterpreted broad state commitment laws for people with developmental disabilities to bring them into harmony with the dangerousness standard enunciated in *O'Connor v. Donaldson*[58] and other cases involving mental illness. They permit commitment only if a person has a developmental disability and is dangerous to self or others.[59] Although some states have adopted a dangerousness standard, others still authorize confinement upon a mere finding of a need for treatment, in contradiction of *O'Connor*.[60] These statutes will likely be the subject of future litigation.

Many states also institutionalize adults with developmental disabilities as voluntary or "nonobjecting" patients without a finding of dangerousness to self or others. A significant number of these people, however, are severely or profoundly retarded and have no capacity to consent to their placement in large, congregate care institutions.

This practice has aroused some controversy. As James Ellis writes, "In reality, the states are using the fiction of 'voluntariness' for most institutionalized persons with mental retardation to avoid judicial scrutiny of individual placement decisions."[61] The result, according to Ellis, is that people can "get 'lost' and 'forgotten' in mental retardation institutions."[62] Ellis suggests that the Supreme Court's decision in *Zinermon v. Burch*,[63] could alter this practice. In *Zinermon*, the Court held that a mental hospital could be held liable for confining as a voluntary patient a man who lacked the capacity to give informed con-

> *The mere fact that a person has no home is not sufficient grounds for commitment, unless she has a mental disability and is dangerous to herself or others.*

sent. Similarly, a California court held that a "nonobjecting" adult with developmental disabilities who was incompetent to consent to institutionalization could not continue to be confined without a hearing to determine whether she was dangerous to herself or others and required placement in a state institution.[64]

Homelessness and Mental Disabilities

The same standard for commitment applies to homeless people as to everyone else. The mere fact that a person has no home is not sufficient grounds for commitment, unless she has a mental disability and is dangerous to herself or others.

During the 1980s, there was an explosion in the number of homeless people in the United States, fueled by a scarcity of affordable housing, and the destruction of low-income housing;[65] a drop in the real value of wages and welfare benefits compared to inflation;[66] the reduction in government benefits;[67] chronic unemployment in the inner cities, particularly among minority youths;[68] and the failure to develop community mental health services and housing for people discharged from public institutions.[69]

Efforts to determine the demographics of homelessness have been fraught with uncertainty, often relying on small samples and anecdotal reports. Estimates of the homeless population nationwide have ranged from the figure of 250,000–350,000, put forward by the U.S. Department of Housing and Urban Development in 1984, to 2.2 million, suggested by the Community for Creative Nonviolence, a Washington advocacy group, in 1982.[70] In 1990, the Census Bureau conducted what has been termed "the largest and most ambitious" survey of its kind,[71] counting homeless people in the nation's 200 largest cities. It found 230,000 homeless people living in shelters, on streets, or in other nonresidential locations—a figure that has been attacked from all sides for overlooking many street homeless and even entire shelters.[72] A more recent study examined records of shelter admissions during the past five years in New York City and found that 239,425 people, or 3.3 percent of the city's population had spent some time in city shelters during that period.[73]

Despite the general belief that a majority of homeless people suffer from serious mental illness, studies suggest that it is families with children that make up the largest subgroup of the homeless. A report issued by the United States Conference of Mayors in December 1993 concluded that families with children comprise approximately 43 percent of the homeless population nationwide and a staggering 75 percent of homeless people in New York City.[74]

Estimates of the homeless mentally ill are frequently misleading because they often rely on surveys that focus on the streets and shelters, locations where homeless families are less likely to be.[75] The best estimates of the prevalence of major mental illness among the total homeless population range from 15 to 40 percent, depending on the definition of mental illness and the nature of the group sampled.[76]

Many homeless people live on the streets. Some fear going to shelters, which they see, with some justification, as unsafe, overcrowded, and in certain cases breeding grounds for communicable diseases such as tuberculosis. Others prefer their privacy, while still others are too disordered to seek shelter on their own. In the mid-1980s the presence of homeless people living in public places began to arouse strong public reactions, from compassion to outrage and disgust. Street homelessness became a quality of life issue for both the homeless, who suffered serious privations, and for a significant segment of the public, who watched with dismay the transformation of their sidewalks and parks into what they viewed as unsightly and unsanitary encampments.

Most city and state governments were unable, or unwilling, to allocate enough of their scarce resources to provide adequate food, shelter or permanent housing for the homeless. Faced with pressure to help the homeless and protect the quality of life of its more fortunate citizenry, some localities began to focus their efforts on the homeless mentally ill. In many quarters this group had become the focal point of compassion and distaste as the most visible example of a problem that had hitherto appeared insoluble.[77]

Perhaps the best known initiative to involuntarily commit homeless people began in New York City in 1987, when Mayor Edward I. Koch ordered psychiatric outreach teams to comb the streets in search of mentally disordered individuals. At the same time, New York created a 28-bed unit at Bellevue Hospital to provide special care for the homeless people brought in by these teams. Although New York State law prohibited involuntary confinement without a finding of mental illness and imminent dangerousness, the City issued a directive authorizing the detention of homeless people who, although not imminently dangerous, were deemed by a psychiatrist to be likely to become so at an unspecified future date.

One of the first people to be confined was a homeless woman who called herself Billie Boggs.[78] Although she had survived safely on the street for more than a year, eating regularly, maintaining good health and keeping warm next to a hot-air vent, she was forcibly removed from the sidewalk on Manhattan's Upper East Side where she lived, injected with Haldol, and involuntarily confined in the special locked ward for homeless people. Calling herself a political prisoner, Boggs challenged her confinement.

Calling herself a political prisoner, Boggs challenged her confinement. She argued that she was not imminently dangerous to herself or others and, although her lifestyle was neither aesthetically pleasing nor socially acceptable, she had demonstrated she could survive safely in freedom.

Boggs argued that she was not imminently dangerous to herself or others and, although her lifestyle was neither aesthetically pleasing nor socially acceptable, she had demonstrated over a year and a half that she could survive safely in freedom and therefore must be released. Relying upon the Supreme Court's warning in *O'Connor* that the state could not confine the harmless mentally ill to improve their standard of living or shield the public from eccentric or objectionable behavior,[79] she claimed that her continued detention violated due process. She conceded that she had urinated and defecated on the sidewalk, because there were no accessible toilets, but asserted that this was not a proper basis for commitment. Any violation of criminal or public health laws, she urged, should be addressed in another setting.

The City countered that Boggs' mental condition was steadily deteriorating. It noted that she had burned money, thrown a sandwich and a milk carton at a psychiatrist, yelled epithets at delivery men, and once walked into Second Avenue against the light. Although she had survived on the street until then, she was likely to be dangerous to herself in the future. To the City, the "most fundamental issue in the case"[80] was whether Boggs was mentally ill, because it was "less likely" that a mentally ill person will survive on the street.[81]

The hearing judge ruled that Boggs' confinement was unconstitutional:

Freedom, constitutionally guaranteed, is the right of all, no less of those who are mentally ill...Whether [Billie Boggs] is or is not mentally ill, it is my finding...that she is not unable to care for her essential needs. I am aware that her mode of existence does not conform to conventional standards, that it is an offense to aesthetic senses. It is my hope that the plight she represents will also offend moral conscience and rouse it to action. There must be some civilized alternatives other than involuntary hospitalization or the street.

[T]he mayor's program is a first step in the right direction towards helping the homeless mentally ill. [Billie Boggs], however, does not fall within the ambit of that program.[82]

In many ways, civil commitment in the age of homelessness has become a modern-day surrogate for the criminal vagrancy laws that the Supreme Court ruled were unconstitutional in the early 1970s.

A split intermediate appeals court reversed in a 3-2 decision,[83] and the New York Court of Appeals dismissed the case as moot after the City released Boggs when a lower court denied its request to medicate her against her will.[84] Despite the prediction of her Bellevue psychiatrist that she would deteriorate and become suicidal within three days of her release, Billie Boggs went to a supported hotel in Manhattan, where she remained for more than five years.

The Boggs case reflects the deep divisions in our society concerning the proper treatment of mentally ill homeless people. It also illustrates the role that involuntary commitment has increasingly been asked to play in addressing the consequences of unresolved social issues, such as the lack of affordable housing and the dearth of less restrictive community mental health services. In many ways, civil commitment in the age of homelessness has become a modern-day surrogate for the criminal vagrancy laws that the Supreme Court ruled were unconstitutional in the early 1970s.[85]

Involuntary Treatment

There is perhaps no right more basic than the right to control what happens to one's own body. Variously referred to as the right to bodily integrity, the right to privacy, the right to personal autonomy, and the right to determine the course of one's own medical treatment, this right is at the heart of our society's concept of personal liberty. As New York's highest court has observed:

> In our system of a free government, where notions of individual autonomy and free choice are cherished, it is the individual who must have the final say in respect to decisions regarding his medical treatment in order to insure that the greatest possible protection is accorded his autonomy and freedom from unwanted interference with the furtherance of his own desires.[86]

It is a well-established principle of the common law that any unwanted bodily intrusion or physical contact is considered an assault or a battery. In the words of Justice Benjamin Cardozo: "Every human being of adult years and sound mind has a right to determine what shall be done with his own body [.]"[87] Although in New York and most other states every adult is presumed to be competent unless there is a judicial determination to the contrary,[88] people with mental disabilities do not always enjoy the benefit of this presumption.

The doctrine of informed consent requires that patients be provided sufficient information before consenting to a test, treatment, or procedure, in order to make a competent, informed, voluntary, and understanding decision whether or not to consent. At a minimum this means that patients must be told of: 1) the risks and benefits of the proposed treatment or procedure; 2) any side effects or complications; 3) the likelihood of improvement with and without the treatment, including an explanation of the kinds of improvement that should be expected; and 4) any alternative treatment methods. As a prerequisite to giving informed consent, a patient must have the capacity to make a reasoned decision whether to accept or refuse the proposed procedure.[89]

The doctrine of informed consent applies to every competent adult. The existence of a mental disability, by itself, does not disqualify an otherwise competent person from exercising this right. As a general rule, all adults are presumed competent and remain so unless a court makes a finding of incompetency or partial incompetency. Although some states have treated an involuntary commitment order as a finding of a lack of capacity to refuse mental health treatment, such as psychotropic

Logically, the principles of informed consent apply equally to the treatment of people with mental disabilities. In reality, however, there is often a double standard where mental disabilities are concerned.

drugs, a growing number of states have rejected this analysis and require a separate judicial finding of incapacity before an involuntary patient can be treated without consent.[90] In New York, the presumption of competency continues even after an order of involuntary commitment. As the New York Court of Appeals explained with regard to mental illness:

> Indeed, it is well accepted that mental illness often strikes only limited areas of functioning, leaving other areas unimpaired, and consequently, that many mentally ill persons retain the capacity to function in a competent manner.[91]

To give competent consent, a person must be able to make a reasoned decision whether to accept or refuse a proposed procedure. It is the individual's ability to weigh the relevant factors, not the advisability of the decision, that determines competency. Because one of the purposes of informed consent is to enhance personal autonomy, patients have broad latitude to make choices which reflect their personal values. For example, a competent patient diagnosed with cancer of the larynx may reject life-prolonging surgery, because it removes the voice box, and radiation treatment, because of its painful side effects, and choose no treatment at all because, despite a hastened death;

More often than not people with mental disabilities are singled out from other patients and denied even the most basic information needed to make choices about their treatment, regardless of their capacity to decide for themselves.

this course offers what the patient considers to be a better quality of life. A person is not incompetent merely because the decision deviates from what the majority of patients would do, is not in the patient's best interests, or contradicts the doctor's advice.

The doctrine of informed consent is the cornerstone of the legal safeguards that protect patients receiving medical treatment. Logically, the principles of informed consent apply equally to the treatment of people with mental disabilities. In reality, however, there is often a double standard where mental disabilities are concerned. Although some states require informed consent before the administration of psychotropic medication or electro-convulsive therapy,[92] more often than not people with mental disabilities are singled out from other patients and denied even the most basic information needed to make choices about their treatment, regardless of their capacity to decide for themselves.

New York is a case in point. The regulations of the State Office of Mental Health (OMH) enumerating the procedures for which informed consent is required in psychiatric facilities include major medical treatment, but not the administration of psychotropic medication—perhaps the single most common form of inpatient psychiatric treatment.[93] Similarly, OMH regulations do not list the right to informed consent among the rights of psychiatric patients.[94]

> *People who disagree with the recommendations of their psychiatrist are often said to lack "insight" into their condition and, consequently, the capacity to make treatment decisions.*

Those familiar with facilities for people with mental disabilities know that an individual's decision is rarely questioned so long as it agrees with the doctor's. A psychiatrist recommending psychotropic drugs, such as Haldol or Thorazine, will generally accept an individual's consent without further ado, but is likely to challenge the competency of a person who refuses treatment. People who disagree with the recommendations of their psychiatrist are often said to lack "insight" into their condition and, consequently, the capacity to make treatment decisions. Such a conclusion is legally unsound unless the individual also lacks the capacity to make a reasoned decision about treatment. This is particularly true in states like New York where court decisions have built upon the common law principles of informed consent to create a right of medical autonomy that includes the right of competent, involuntarily committed persons to refuse antipsychotic medications.[95]

By the same token, it is improper to presume the competency of people who raise no objection to treatment, if they do not have the capacity to weigh the risks and benefits.[96]

One way to enhance the ability of people with mental disabilities to participate in their own health care decisions is through the use of advance directives. Advance directives, such as living wills and health care proxies, enable individuals with decision-making capacity to indicate their treatment preferences, or designate another person to make decisions for them, in the event that they become incompetent to do so at some future time. Each of the 50 states has now enacted statutes governing living wills, the appointment of health care agents, or a combination of the two. Some of these statutes define health care broadly to include treatment for a mental condition.[97] Minnesota has enacted an advance directive law exclusively for psychiatric treatment.[98] These laws are coming into increasing use as health care planning tools for people with mental disabilities.[99]

Although much has been written on the subject, there is no standard test for determining competency. The key question is whether the person understands the nature of the proposed treatment, its risks and benefits, alternative forms of treatment, and the prognosis with and without the recommended treatment.

To be valid, consent must be freely given, without threats, intimidation, or coercion. Pressure to consent can be direct, such as a threat to initiate commitment proceedings if the person does not agree to a particular treatment. The pressure can also be more subtle, especially in a setting where individuals are dependent on staff for their basic needs and know that privileges can be granted or withheld at the staff's discretion.[100]

Refusing Medication

Drugs are the most common form of treatment in psychiatric facilities and are often prescribed as well for people with mental retardation who have aggressive or self-abusive behaviors.[101] Antipsychotic drugs, also known as neuroleptics or major tranquilizers, and lithium are the medications most frequently used to treat major mental illness. The most commonly prescribed antipsychotic drugs are Thorazine, Haldol, Prolixin, Navane, Mellaril, and Compazine. Introduced into psychiatry in the early 1950s, neuroleptics have been hailed by their proponents as short-

For all their usefulness, antipsychotic drugs are far from being the antibiotics of mental illness. Unlike antibiotics, these drugs do not cure mental illness—they control symptoms.

ening hospital stays, reducing symptoms, and enabling individuals who would otherwise have spent much of their lives in institutions to live in less restrictive community settings. As the Supreme Court has explained, their purpose is to "alter the chemical balance in a patient's brain, leading to changes, intended to be beneficial, in his or her brain processes."[102] They are widely used to treat psychoses, particularly among people diagnosed with schizophrenia. Many of these drugs can be administered by pill or injection, and can easily be given over the person's objections.

For all their usefulness, antipsychotic drugs are far from being the antibiotics of mental illness. Unlike antibiotics, these drugs do not cure mental illness—they control symptoms. They are most effective at reducing psychotic thinking, hallucinations, delusions, and paranoia. Antipsychotics are also used as heavy duty tranquilizers to reduce hyperactivity, agitation, and aggressiveness. Although many physicians believe that antipsychotics are at their best in treating schizophrenia, where they can help decrease both the florid symptomatology and the rate of relapse, the former Chief for the Studies of Schizophrenia at the National Institute of Mental Health has cautioned that "symptom reduction by itself is not synonymous with successful treatment" and has suggested that the most disabling aspects of schizophrenia may be beyond the reach of treatment with drugs.[103]

There has been considerable debate over the efficacy of antipsychotic drugs, as well as over the care with which they are prescribed. Although there is general agreement that certain neuroleptics can help control the symptoms of schizophrenia, and that lithium can help manage manic depression, there is not universal agreement as to the effectiveness of these drugs in treating other conditions. The dispute over the uncertainty of psychiatric diagnoses also affects decisions about medication. For example, one court found that "even the value of psychotropic drugs as a means of controlling symptoms of mental illness (as opposed to their use as a cure for such disorders) often depends upon the accuracy of the diagnosis as to what disorder the patient suffers from, and there is wide recognition that such diagnosis is a less than precise art."[104]

Even where drug treatment is statistically most effective, as in the treatment of schizophrenia, and the diagnosis is properly made, it may be difficult to predict with any certainty whether a particular individual will respond positively, negatively, or not at all to a given drug. It may not be easy to determine which drug is best for a given set of symptoms[105] or which dosage should be prescribed for a particular patient.[106] Further compounding this difficulty, doctors in large institutions, as well as private settings, may not have access to the patient's prior history or the time to study it carefully, and may be unaware of past diagnoses, the effectiveness of prior treatments, or any side effects.

The critical question is whether the individual is fully informed of the risks and benefits of the drugs, and of any alternative treatments, and is permitted to exercise informed consent.

Despite their potential therapeutic benefits, antipsychotic drugs also have an undeniable dark side, for they can produce severe, painful, and at times debilitating side effects that are potentially as disabling as the conditions they are prescribed to treat. The toxic effects of these drugs are well documented in the scientific literature[107] and run the gamut from minor irritations[108] to severe muscular side effects[109] to irreversible damage to the central nervous system and even death.[110]

The most serious, common side effect of antipsychotic drugs is tardive dyskinesia, a neurological syndrome characterized by involuntary, rhythmic, and often grotesque movements of the face, lips, tongue, fingers, hands, legs, and pelvis. Most cases of tardive dyskinesia appear after at least six months of drug use;[111] however, some patients have developed this syndrome after only a few months on antipsychotics.[112] Once discovered, tardive dyskinesia is considered irreversible in two of every three cases, even after the patient ceases taking the medication.[113] There is no proven cure for persistent tardive dyskinesia at this time. Continuing the use of antipsychotics after the onset of tardive dyskinesia can exacerbate the condition.[114]

> *As a matter of dignity and personal autonomy, persons with decision-making capacity should have the right to make what could be a difficult decision with lasting consequences.*

The prevalence of tardive dyskinesia is staggering and is now beginning to spawn damages litigation. The Supreme Court has noted that between ten and twenty-five percent of all patients treated with antipsychotic drugs display the symptoms of tardive dyskinesia.[115] Estimates of tardive dyskinesia among chronic or institutionalized persons run even higher.[116]

Despite the potential side effects of most drugs used in mental hospitals, the vast majority of hospitalized psychiatric patients are on a drug regimen which they are encouraged to maintain once they leave the institution. There is, of course, nothing inherently objectionable about taking neuroleptic medication. There are sound reasons why a competent person with mental illness might choose or reject treatment with antipsychotic drugs, just as a cancer patient might elect chemotherapy, radiation, surgery, or no treatment at all for a malignancy. The weighing of risks and benefits is ultimately a matter of personal values.

As Alexander Brooks aptly observed:

> The decision whether or not to accept drugs is for many patients a difficult one in which the patient is often between Scylla and Charybdis. It is difficult for some patients to know which is worse, the illness itself or the side effects of medication.[117]

The critical question is whether the individual is fully informed of the risks and benefits of the drugs, and of any alternative treatments, and is permitted to exercise informed consent. As a matter of dignity and personal autonomy, persons with decision-making capacity should have the right to make what could be a difficult decision with lasting consequences.

The extent of such a right, however, depends on one's admission status and can vary from state to state. Outpatients generally have a right to refuse medication, unless a court has declared them incompetent or subjected them to an outpatient commitment order. Most states extend this right to voluntary and informal patients, who can leave the institution,[118] unless the facility takes steps to have them committed.

Involuntary patients, however, are a more complicated matter. For years proponents of forced medication argued that involuntary commitment constitutes a judicial determination of incapacity to make decisions about treatment.[119] More recently, many states have enacted civil rights laws declaring that involuntary commitment did not, in itself, suspend individual rights or render patients incompetent to exercise them. One of the most basic of these rights is the "fundamental right to make decisions concerning one's own body."[120]

The fact that a person has a mental illness does not necessarily signify an inability to make a reasoned decision whether to take medication.

Coupled with this greater respect for individual rights is what one court has termed "the nearly unanimous modern trend in the courts, and among psychiatric and legal commentators to recognize that there is no significant relationship between the need for hospitalization of mentally ill patients and their ability to make treatment decisions."[121] The fact that a person has a mental illness does not necessarily signify an inability to make a reasoned decision whether to take medication. It is well established that mental illness can impair one area of functioning while leaving others intact.[122] Nor does a person's ability to survive safely outside an institution or her propensity for violence to others necessarily affect her capacity to make treatment decisions inside a hospital. Unless a court makes a separate finding at the commitment hearing that the person lacks the capacity to make treatment decisions, an order of commitment, by itself, should not constitute such a finding.

Virtually every court that has considered this issue has found that involuntary patients have a protected interest in refusing treatment, based on either the common law doctrine of informed consent or state or federal constitutional law.[123] Typically, the source of the constitutional right is the liberty interest in the due process clause of the fifth and fourteenth amendments to the federal constitution, triggered by the drugs' potential for altering thought processes and hampering physical mobility. It is no coincidence that these drugs are also known as "chemical restraints." Because antipsychotic drugs can affect the will and the mind of the subject,[124] the First Amendment right of free speech,[125] including the right to generate thoughts, as well as the constitutional right cf privacy, are also implicated. Former Supreme Court Justice Louis Brandeis eloquently expressed the principles underlying these rights in 1928:

> The makers of our Constitution undertook to secure conditions favorable to the pursuit of happiness. They recognized the significance of man's spiritual nature, of his feelings and of his intellect. They knew that only a part of the pain, pleasure and satisfactions of life are to be found in material things. They sought to protect Americans in their beliefs, their thoughts, their emotions and their sensations. They conferred, as against the Government, the right to be let alone—the most comprehensive of rights and the right most valued by civilized men.[126]

The key elements comprising the right to refuse medication are: 1) the standard for evaluating whether a person may be medicated involuntarily; and 2) the process for deciding whether that standard has been met. Although some of the details may vary from one jurisdiction to another, there are essentially two models for making these decisions: a "medical" model and a "legal" or "informed consent" model.

Under the medical model, the decision whether an involuntary patient can be forced to take antipsychotic drugs is a question of professional expertise rather than personal autonomy. The inquiry is whether medication is medically appropriate to treat and control a mental illness that has caused the person to be dangerous to self or others and thereby require involuntary confinement. Although the Supreme Court has not directly ruled on a case defining the standards and procedures for the forced treatment of civilly committed persons,[127] some courts have applied the medical model framework set forth in *Youngberg v. Romeo*[128] in analyzing this issue.[129]

> *Because antipsychotic drugs can affect the will and the mind of the subject, the First Amendment right of free speech, including the right to generate thoughts, as well as the constitutional right of privacy, are also implicated.*

This analysis is best illustrated by the decision of the Second Circuit Court of Appeals in *Project Release v. Prevost*,[130] which applied *Youngberg* in upholding New York's involuntary treatment regulations against a constitutional challenge. The New York rules allowed doctors almost complete discretion to medicate involuntary patients. A person who disagreed with the doctor's decision could "object to" and "appeal," but not *refuse* treatment with psychotropic drugs. The ultimate decision whether to medicate by force was vested in doctors and administrators at the hospital or the State Office of Mental Health. The regulations provided absolutely no standards for making this decision, but simply gave carte blanche to hospital employees to "review" the individual's objection, "consider the appeal and make a decision."[131] It was not even necessary to find that the medication was needed to prevent harm to self or others, that the individual lacked the mental capacity to make a treatment decision, or that there was no less intrusive alternative to the drugs.

Applying the *Youngberg* test, the Second Circuit found that the individual's "interest in being free from bodily restraint" was satisfied if "professional judgment was in fact exercised."[132] A doctor's decision to medicate an unwilling person is presumptively correct unless it was "such a substantial departure from accepted professional judgment, practice, or standards as to demonstrate that the person responsible actually did not base the decision on such a judgment."[133] Thus, unless the doctor has committed malpractice, the decision will be sustained. There is no room in this equation for personal choice, no matter how well-reasoned the individual's decision, how serious the drugs' potential side effects, or how appropriate other, less intrusive therapies may be—even if a dozen doctors are enlisted to testify that medication is not necessary.

> *Under the legal, or informed consent, model, the decision whether to override an involuntary patient's treatment objections can only be made by a court, based on a strict interpretation of the state's* parens patriae *and police powers.*

As for procedures, the court found that there should be an opportunity for a hearing and review of the individual's objections, but that due process did not require more than allowing the patient to voice objections to supervising hospital personnel.[134] Without independent decision-makers or a strict legal standard, the appeal process became a rubber stamp for the doctor's decision.

Under the legal, or informed consent, model, the decision whether to override an involuntary patient's treatment objections can only be made by a court, based on a strict interpretation of the state's *parens patriae* and police powers. Typically, this model relies on state constitutional law and entails a two-step process. In order to outweigh the individual's fundamental liberty interest in bodily autonomy, the state must demonstrate a compelling[135] or "overwhelming"[136] state interest. This generally requires either an emergency, where forced medication is necessary to prevent a danger to self or others within the institution, or a judicial declaration of incapacity to make the treatment decision at issue. Because there is a general presumption that involuntary commitment does not render individuals incompetent to make treatment decisions,[137] this model bars forced drugging without a judicial determination of incapacity, except in emergencies.

The mere fact that an involuntarily confined person may arrive at a different conclusion from the treating psychiatrist does not make that decision any less competent.

Even if the court finds that the individual lacks the capacity to refuse the medication, it is the court, not the doctor, who makes the final decision. Some courts apply a "substituted judgment" analysis, in which they attempt to put themselves in the incompetent person's shoes and determine what the individual would have decided, if competent.[138] Others attempt to determine what would be in the patient's best interests and weigh such factors as the risks and benefits of the proposed treatment, the prognosis and the individual's expressed wishes. Under either analysis, the courts must pay careful attention to less restrictive alternatives. Even when ordering forced medication, judges have the power to scrutinize the number and type of medications to be administered, and their dosage, to ensure that the treatment is narrowly tailored to the individual's needs. Using a substituted judgment analysis, the Massachusetts Supreme Judicial Court has even extended the right to refuse treatment to legally incompetent people whose guardians seek an order to administer medication.[139]

Finally, the legal model provides a full panoply of procedural protections, including a hearing, the right to counsel, and the right to have the need for involuntary medication proved by clear and convincing evidence.[140]

The New York Court of Appeals' decision in *Rivers v. Katz*[141] best illustrates the difference between the medical and legal models. Applying a strict legal analysis, *Rivers* struck down on state constitutional grounds the same New York regulations that the Second Circuit had upheld under a federal constitutional, medical model analysis.

The legal model has several advantages over the medical model. First, it recognizes that, except in emergencies, competent individuals—not doctors —have the right to weigh the therapeutic benefits of the drugs against their serious and potentially irreversible side effects. The mere fact that an involuntarily confined person may arrive at a different conclusion from the treating psychiatrist does not make that decision any less competent. After all, it is the individual who will endure the consequences long after the clinician has left the scene.

Second, the legal model establishes clear standards and procedures for overriding an individual's treatment decision, rather than leaving it to the unfettered discretion of a psychiatrist. This is critical in view of the historic overuse of these drugs and their potential for abuse. As one psychiatrist has written:

> Placing unbridled discretion in the hands of a single clinician has often led to unskillful and at times unfortunate use of medications. This is particularly true in some of our public facilities, which historically have had difficulties recruiting and supporting competent clinicians.[142]

Antipsychotic medications have been overprescribed,[143] prescribed as punishment,[144] and administered for the convenience of staff.[145]

Finally, the legal model affirms that people with mental disabilities are entitled to the same judicial safeguards of their medical autonomy as other individuals.

One promising model for enhancing the autonomy of competent individuals who anticipate the possibility of forced treatment is an advance directive such as a living will or a health care proxy. Such documents preserve the individual's wishes for a time when his or her capacity to make treatment decisions is called into question and have been recognized by courts in states such as New York.[146] They enable people with mental disabilities to exercise increased control over their lives and plan for their health care in the event they lose the capacity to make decisions for themselves.

One promising model for enhancing the autonomy of competent individuals who anticipate the possibility of forced treatment is an advance directive such as a living will or a health care proxy.

Despite the fears of many institutions that a right to refuse drugs would create chaos and harm people who need treatment, studies of facilities that have implemented such a right have generally found that drug refusals were relatively rare and easily handled. Not only does such a right not impair overall treatment, but one study of drug refusals at a Massachusetts hospital observed that in some cases it actually yielded positive advantages, and "the feared epidemic of refusals did not materialize."[147] A more recent study of drug refusal in Massachusetts found that "fewer than 8% of patients refused medication, over half of those reaccepted medication voluntarily, just under a quarter had their refusals respected by clinicians, and the remainder had their refusals overturned in court."[148]

> *A fully developed network of voluntary treatment resources is one of the essential prerequisites to the constitutionality of a system that allows forced treatment.*

In fact, studies, observations of judicial hearings and interviews with practitioners suggest that courts deny most patients' objections to medication.[149] The explanation appears to be a combination of judicial reluctance to override professional judgment and the informal, prehearing resolution of a percentage of clear cases where patients obviously have the capacity to withhold consent to the medication.

Conclusion

The legal system has struggled for years to strike a balance between individual liberty and the state's power to impose treatment on unwilling individuals to protect their "best interests" or those of society. All too often, involuntary measures are selected by default, because of the unavailability of less restrictive alternatives, such as housing, community services, and programs designed by and for consumers. From both a civil liberties and a therapeutic perspective, a fully developed network of voluntary treatment resources is one of the essential prerequisites to the constitutionality of a system that allows forced treatment. If individuals are not offered appropriate outpatient treatment options, then the least restrictive alternative becomes a hollow principle.

Governments throughout the country have justly been criticized for their failure to develop an adequate network of outpatient treatment resources. In states like New York, for example, citizens have endured several decades of promises that community mental health services would be developed in sufficient numbers to meet the needs of people with mental illness. Although some steps have been taken to improve the quantity and quality of these services, they are still highly inadequate. There can be no meaningful, voluntary system of less restrictive alternatives until this goal has been accomplished.

Endnotes

1. Humphrey v. Cady, 405 U.S. 504, 509 (1972).

2. BLACK'S LAW DICTIONARY (5th ed. 1979).

3. DAVID J. ROTHMAN, THE DISCOVERY OF THE ASYLUM: SOCIAL ORDER AND DISORDER IN THE NEW REPUBLIC 130 (Little, Brown & Co. 1971).

4. *Id.* at 133.

5. Schloendorff v. Society of New York Hosp., 211 N.Y. 125, 129, 105 N.E. 92 (1914).

6. *See, e.g.,* Jacobson v. Commonwealth of Massachusetts, 197 U.S. 11 (1905).

7. A contemporaneous example of the exercise of this authority is the detention of people with multiple drug-resistant tuberculosis. Indeed, the involuntary confinement of people with communicable diseases is subject to all of the due process safeguards applicable to the commitment of people with mental disabilities, including the requirement that there be no equally effective, less restrictive alternative to protect the public health. *See, e.g.,* Greene v. Edwards, 263 S.E.2d 661 (W. Va. 1980); New York City Health Code, 24 R.C.N.Y. tit. II § 11.47 (adopted March 1993).

8. SAMUEL J. BRAKEL ET AL., THE MENTALLY DISABLED AND THE LAW 13 (American Bar Found. 3d ed. 1985).

9. STANLEY S. HERR, RIGHTS AND ADVOCACY FOR RETARDED PEOPLE 17 (D.C. Heath 1983).

10. *Id.* at 19.

11. Lessard v. Schmidt, 349 F. Supp. 1078, 1086 (E.D. Wis. 1972).

12. HERR, *supra* note 9, at 16. Herr writes that it was not until 1827 that New York State forbade the confinement of people with mental illness in jails, prisons, or houses of correction. *Id.* at 17.

13. ROTHMAN, *supra* note 3, at 138.

14. *Id.* at 112, quoting Isaac Ray, one of the leading medical superintendents of the pre-Civil War period in America.

15. *Id.* at 286.

16. *Id.*

17. *Id.* at 283.

18. For further discussion of the use of institutions to compensate for society's failure to adequately address social problems such as the lack of affordable housing, *see infra* p. 11 for a discussion of homelessness and mental disabilities.

19. Herr, *supra* note 9, at 22.

20. Anne Moore, The Feeble-Minded in New York, a Report Prepared for the Public Education Assoc. of NY 3, 89–92 (United Charities Bldg. 1911); cited in Herr, *supra* note 9, at 23.

21. 422 U.S. 563 (1975).

22. *See, e.g.*, Lessard v. Schmidt, 394 F. Supp. 1078, 1094 (E.D. Wis. 1972); Scopes v. Shah, 398 N.Y.S.2d 911, 913 (3d Dep't 1977) (due process requires finding that the person to be committed poses "a real and present threat of substantial harm to himself or others").

23. Addington v. Texas, 441 U.S. 418 (1979).

24. The case involved a 55-year-old man who was committed to the Florida State Hospital at Chattahoochee in 1957 and kept there for nearly 15 years without treatment, although he had never been dangerous to himself or others, was capable of earning a living outside the hospital, and had received offers to live in a responsible halfway house or with a former college classmate who was willing and able to provide for his welfare. The superintendent rejected each of these offers, insisting that Donaldson could only be released to his parents, who, as the superintendent knew were "too elderly and infirm" to care for him and indeed were never even informed of the availability of the halfway house. Upon his release, Donaldson immediately obtained a responsible job in hotel administration. *O'Connor*, 422 U.S. at 568.

25. *Id.* at 576.

26. *Id.* at 575 (citations omitted).

27. Challenges to the imprecision of the definition of mental illness in state statutes are generally unsuccessful. For example, in rejecting the claim that the definition of mental illness in Utah's commitment statute was unconstitutionally vague and overly broad, a Utah federal court noted that "the field of mental health is not one that lends itself to extremely precise

definitions. To require a degree of precision that the current science cannot afford would be futile." Colyar v. Third Judicial District Court, 469 F. Supp.424, 434 (D. Utah 1979).

28. *See, e.g., id.* at 431–32.

29. *Id.* at 431.

30. ALEXANDER D. BROOKS, LAW, PSYCHIATRY & THE MENTAL HEALTH SYSTEM 680 (1974).

31. Although a few states permit confinement for dangerousness to property, it is doubtful that the state's interest in protecting property is an appropriate justification for such a serious deprivation of liberty. While leaving this ultimate question open, the highest federal court to consider this issue struck down a Hawaii statute that authorized commitment for danger to any property, regardless of its value or significance, noting that it would improperly allow commitment for threatening to shoot a trespassing dog. It did not say what, if any, property interest might be significant enough to warrant commitment. Because so few states have such a provision, there has been little litigation on this issue.

32. *See, e.g.,* O'Connor v. Donaldson, 422 U.S. 563 (1975).

33. *See, e.g.,* the Supreme Court's admonition in *O'Connor,* 422 U.S. at 535, that the Constitution prohibits the use of institutionalization to raise an individual's standard of living or to protect the public from eccentric or unattractive behavior, if the individual has the capacity to survive safely in the community.

34. *See, e.g.,* Lessard v. Schmidt, 394 F. Supp. 1078, 1094 (E.D. Wis. 1972).

35. Quoted in Elisabeth Rosenthal, *Who Will Turn Violent? Hospitals Have to Guess,* N.Y. TIMES, Apr. 7, 1993, at A1.

36. *See, e.g.,* JOHN MONAHAN, THE CLINICAL PREDICTION OF VIOLENT BEHAVIOR (U.S. Dep't Health & Human Servs. 1981); Bruce Ennis & Thomas Litwack, *Psychiatry and the Presumption of Expertise: Flipping Coins in the Courtroom,* 62 CAL. L. REV. 693 (1974). This is not to say, however, that there is no relationship between mental disorder and violent behavior. Although "the vast majority of individuals with serious mental illness are not violent and are not more dangerous than individuals in the general population," there is a "subgroup of such individuals" who are "more dangerous." E. Fuller Torrey, *Violent Behavior by Individuals with Serious Mental Illness,* 45 HOSP. & COMM'Y PSYCHIATRY 658 (1994).

Monahan has reached a similar conclusion. John Monahan, *Mental Disorder and Violent Behavior*, 47 Am. Psychol. 511–521 (1992)(cited in Torrey, *supra* note 36, at 658).

37. Brief for *Amicus curiae* A.P.A. at 12, Barefoot v. Estelle, 463 U.S. 880 (1983).

38. Monahan, The Clinical Prediction of Violent Behavior, *supra* note 36, at 49.

39. *Id.* at 13, quoting Monahan.

40. *The Clinical Prediction of Dangerousness: An Interview with John Monahan, Ph.D.*, reprinted in 10 Currents Affective Illness No. 6, June 1991, at 7.

41. Barefoot v. Estelle, 463 U.S. 880 (1983).

42. *Amicus curiae* brief *Barefoot*, 463 U.S. 880.

43. Monahan, for example, stated: "Courts have been willing to accept remarkably low levels of predictive accuracy...So, if one out of three is sufficient to justify execution, then one might imagine that a significantly lower level of predictive accuracy could justify less draconian interventions." *The Clinical Prediction of Dangerousness: An Interview with John Monahan, Ph. D., supra* note 40, at 7.

44. Addington v. Texas, 441 U.S. 418, 429 (1979).

45. *Id.*

46. *See, e.g.*, Stamus v. Leonhardt, 414 F. Supp. 439, 451 (S.D. Iowa 1976); Doremus v. Farrell, 407 F. Supp. 509, 514–15 (D. Neb. 1975); Lynch v. Baxley, 386 F. Supp. 378, 391 (M.D. Ala. 1974); Lessard v. Schmidt, 349 F. Supp. 1078, 1093 (E.D. Wis. 1972).

47. *See, e.g.*, Project Release v. Prevost, 722 F.2d 960, 973 (2d Cir. 1983); Colyar v. Third Judicial Dist. Ct., 469 F. Supp. 424, 434 (D. Utah 1979).

48. United States *ex rel.* Mathew v. Nelson, 461 F. Supp. 707, 711 (N.D. Ill. 1978) (three-judge court).

49. *See, e.g.*, Shelton v. Tucker, 364 U.S. 479 (1960) (Arkansas statute requiring public school teachers to list all organizations to which they belonged or contributed was unconstitutional because state had less drastic means for pursuing its interest in monitoring fitness of teachers).

50. There has been some debate whether a commitment is invalid if a less restrictive setting would be appropriate but none is available. Virtually every court that has considered the issue has ruled that the doctrine applies only to alternatives that are actually available.

51. RALPH REISNER & CHRISTOPHER SLOBOGIN, LAW AND THE MENTAL HEALTH SYSTEM 683 (2d ed. 1990). ("As of 1985, at least forty-seven states required that involuntary patients be committed to treatment in the least restrictive setting." Ingo Keilitz et al., *Least Restrictive Treatment of Involuntary Patients: Translating Concepts into Practice*, 29 ST. LOUIS U. L. REV. 691, 708 (1985).)

52. *See, e.g.*, Suzuki v. Quisenberry, 411 F. Supp. 1113, 1132–33 (D. Haw.1976); Lynch v. Baxley, 386 F. Supp. 378, 392 (M.D. Ala. 1974); Lessard v. Schmidt, 349 F. Supp. 1078, 1095–96 (E.D. Wis. 1972); Kesselbrenner v. Anonymous, 305 N.E.2d 903 (N.Y. 1973) (federal and state constitutional grounds).

53. O'Connor v. Donaldson, 422 U.S. 563, 576 (1975).

54. *Id.* at 575.

55. Lynch v. Baxley, 744 F.2d 1452 (11th Cir. 1984).

56. The doctrine of the least restrictive alternative also extends to other aspects of commitment, such as transfers from open to secure units in an institution, *see* Covington v. Harris, 419 F.2d 617 (D.C. Cir. 1969); *Kesselbrenner,* 305 N.E.2d 903, and decisions about forced treatment; *see, e.g.*, Rivers v. Katz, 504 N.Y.S.2d 74, 78 (1986).

57. The United States Supreme Court's decision in *Heller v. Doe*, 113 S.Ct. 2637 (1993), is not to the contrary. In *Heller*, the Court ruled that a Kentucky statute requiring proof beyond a reasonable doubt for the commitment of people with mental illness, but only clear and convincing evidence for the commitment of people with mental retardation, and permitting family members and guardians to participate as parties at commitment hearings for people with mental retardation but not for people with mental illness, did not violate the equal protection clause of the fourteenth amendment. Although justifying the statute's disparate procedural safeguards for these two groups on what it concluded was the special nature of mental retardation (a lifelong, relatively static condition with an early onset that is easier to diagnose), this decision did not suggest that different *standards for commitment* were appropriate. Nowhere did the Court say that a finding of dangerousness is not required for the commit-

ment of people with mental retardation. Rather, it observed that the ease of diagnosis and the static, relatively predictable nature of mental retardation justify a lower standard of proof, in contrast to mental illness, which may be manifested by sudden past behavior which may not be a sufficient predictor of future conduct.

58. 422 U.S. at 563.

59. *See, e.g.*, Matter of Harry M., 468 N.Y.S.2d 359 (2d Dep't 1983) (due process permits involuntary commitment of mentally retarded persons only upon showing of danger to self or others and lack of less restrictive alternatives); Kinner v. State, 382 So.2d 756 (Fla. App. 1980) (commitment only appropriate for persons who are dangerous to self or others or lack the capacity to evaluate for themselves the risks of freedom and the benefits of institutionalization). *But see* Matter of Vandenberg, 617 P.2d 675 (Or. 1980) (upholding Oregon statute authorizing commitment of "mentally deficient" persons provided that they meet the American Association of Mental Deficiency's definition of mental retardation and that institutionalization "is the optimal available plan" and "is in the best interest of the person and the community").

60. BRAKEL ET AL., *supra* note 8, at 37–39.

61. James Ellis, *Decisions by and for People with Mental Retardation: Balancing Considerations of Autonomy and Protection*, 37 VILL. L. REV. 1779, 1809 (1992).

62. *Id.* at fn. 124 (citing Clark v. Cohen, 794 F.2d 79 (3d Cir. 1986), *cert. denied*, 409 U.S. 962 (1986) (woman confined 30 years despite requests for release).

63. 494 U.S. 113 (1990).

64. *In re Hop*, 623 P.2d 282 (Cal. 1981).

65. *See generally* Robert M. Levy, *Should the Homeless Have a Right to Counsel?*, BRIEF, Summer 1989, at 7–8 ("The deepening housing crisis is the product of a number of factors, which include the low vacancy of affordable housing; the continued loss of low-income housing through conversion, abandonment and deterioration; the steep decline in the stock of public housing; and the displacement of low-income people through the process of gentrification."). *See also* U.S. GEN. ACCOUNTING OFFICE, HUMAN RESOURCES DIV., HOMELESSNESS: A COMPLEX PROBLEM AND THE FEDERAL RESPONSE (1985) (30 percent of all Americans earning half or less of the median income paid 70 percent of their income in rent in 1983).

56. *See, e.g.*, Celia W. Dugger, *Study Says Shelter Turnover Hides Scope of Homelessness*, N.Y. TIMES, Nov. 16, 1993, at A1 (The value of the monthly rental subsidy to families on welfare has declined by 42 percent since 1972, while the real cost of housing has risen.). *See also* Levy, *supra* note 65, at 7–8; *More of Homeless Are Now Families*, N.Y. TIMES, Dec. 22, 1993, at A18 (Unveiling a report on Hunger and Homelessness in American Cities, the co-chairman of the United States Conference of Mayors reported in 1993 that there was "a significant number of working poor among the homeless," and noted that thirty percent of adults requesting food assistance in 1993 were employed.); and Wicker, *infra* note 68, at A31 (Figures from a 1986 Census Bureau Report showed that 41.5 percent of the poor in America had a job in 1985 and that the working poor were the fastest growing segment of the poverty population: 18.9 million—up 33 percent from 1979.).

57. In 1981 the Reagan Administration adopted procedures that caused over 350,000 people to lose their Supplemental Security Income (SSI) benefits. Many of these people had mental disabilities. Perlin writes that, "While these cutbacks have diminished in the face of public outrage and congressional response, there is no question that the reduction of disability benefits was a significant factor in the increase in the number of homeless persons." MICHAEL L. PERLIN, MENTAL DISABILITY LAW: CIVIL AND CRIMINAL § 7.25, at 686 (1989).

58. *See* Tom Wicker, *Always With Us*, N.Y. TIMES, Nov. 19, 1987, at A31.

59. D. CULHANE ET AL., PUBLIC SHELTER ADMISSION RATES IN PHILADELPHIA AND NEW YORK CITY: THE IMPLICATIONS OF TURNOVER FOR SHELTERED POPULATION COUNTS (Fannie Mae Office Hous. Research 1993) (citing MARTHA R. BURT, OVER THE EDGE: THE GROWTH OF HOMELESSNESS IN THE 1980s (Russell Sage Found. 1992); PETER H. ROSSI, DOWN AND OUT IN AMERICA: THE ORIGINS OF HOMELESSNESS (University of Chicago Press 1989); and Kim Hopper & Jill Hamberg, *The Making of America's Homeless: From Skid Row to New Poor, 1945–1984, in* CRITICAL PERSPECTIVES ON HOUSING 12 (R.G. Bratt et al. eds., 1986)).

70. CULHANE ET AL., *supra* note 69, at 2.

71. *Id.* at 3.

72. *Id.*

73. Dugger, *supra* note 66, at A1. A similar study of Philadelphia shelter admissions found that 3 percent of that city's population had spent time in

its shelters during the same period. *Id.* The authors of the studies estimated that more than 2 million Americans may become homeless at one time or another during a given year. *Id.*

74. *More of Homeless Are Now Families, supra* note 66, at A18.

75. The public is also generally less aware of homeless families because they are less visible than single, homeless people with mental illness or substance abuse problems, who are more often to be found on the streets and in public places.

76. *See, e.g.*, NEW YORK ST. DEP'T SOC. SERVS., HOMELESSNESS IN NEW YORK STATE: A REPORT TO THE GOVERNOR AND THE LEGISLATURE (1988); *Fear and Dependency Rub Shoulders in the Shelters*, N.Y. TIMES, Nov. 4, 1991, at A1, B2 (survey of 202 New York City shelter residents in 1990 found 21.5% had received counseling services for an emotional problem or nervous condition); H. Richard Lamb & John A. Talbott, *The Homeless Mentally Ill: The Perspective of the American Psychiatric Association*, 256 JAMA 498 (1986) (The most sound studies indicate that the prevalence of major mental illness is about 40% among the total homeless population.).

77. For example, in the late 1980s, the *New York Times* began running occasional editorials that discussed the plight of the mentally ill homeless and referred to New York City as Calcutta on the Hudson.

78. Although her real name was Joyce Brown, she preferred to be known as Billie Boggs, after the television personality Bill Boggs in order to elude her family's efforts to find and confine her.

79. O'Connor v. Donaldson, 422 U.S. 563, 575 (1972).

80. Respondents' Brief at 24, Matter of Boggs, 520 N.E.2d 515 (N.Y. 1988).

81. *Id.* at 11.

82. Matter of Boggs, 522 N.Y.S.2d 407, 412–13 (Sup. Ct. N.Y. County 1987).

83. 523 N.Y.S.2d 71 (1st Dep't 1987).

84. 520 N.E.2d 515 (N.Y. 1988), *rearg't denied*, 524 N.E.2d 879, *appeal dismissed*, 70 N.Y.2d 981, 526 N.Y.S.2d 429, 521 N.E.2d 436 (1988).

85. *See, e.g.*, Papachristou v. City of Jacksonville, 405 U.S. 156 (1972).

86. Rivers v. Katz, 504 N.Y.S.2d 74, 78 (1986).

87. Schloendorff v. Society of New York Hosp., 211 N.Y. 125, 129, 105 N.E. 92 (1914).

38. *See, e.g.*, GEORGE J. ANNAS, THE RIGHTS OF PATIENTS 89 (Southern Illinois Univ. Press 1989); Winters v. Miller, 446 F.2d 65, 68 (2d Cir. 1971).

39. The doctrine of informed consent applies whenever there is an inherent risk of injury or death that the patient might not be aware of, there are alternative procedures, or the probability of success is low. It applies to a broad range of medical procedures, including the administration of medication, diagnostic tests and major or minor surgery. *Id.* at 87–88. In practice, however, as discussed later in this paper, many states do not require informed consent for the administration of psychotropic medication to people with mental disabilities.

90. *See, e.g.*, Rogers v. Commissioner, Dep't of Mental Health, 458 N.E.2d 308 (Mass. 1983); *Rivers*, 504 N.Y.S.2d at 79 ("The nearly unanimous trend in the courts and among psychiatric and legal commentators is to recognize that there is no significant relationship between the need for hospitalization of mentally ill patients and their ability to make treatment decisions.") (citations omitted).

91. *Rivers*, 504 N.Y.S.2d at 79.

92. *See, e.g.*, Minn. § Stat. 253B.03 (6)(b) (as amended by 1991 Minn. Laws, Ch. 148) (informed consent required for administration of electro-convulsive therapy and psychotropic medication, but *not* for treatment for mental retardation).

93. 14 N.Y.C.R.R. 27.9.

94. 14 N.Y.C.R.R. 27.5.

95. *See, e.g.*, *Rivers*, 504 N.Y.S.2d 74 (1986).

96. The practice of providing intrusive treatment to nonobjecting people who lack the capacity to consent not only violates the doctrine of informed consent, but may well violate federal due process. In *Zinermon v. Burch*, the U.S. Supreme Court ruled that it was unconstitutional for a hospital to admit as a voluntary patient a person who lacked the capacity to consent to inpatient status. 494 U.S. 113 (1990). The principles of *Zinermon* logically apply as well to people who lack the capacity to consent to other forms of inpatient treatment for a mental disability.

97. *See, e.g.*, N.Y. Pub. Health L. § 2980 (4) (McKinney 1993).

98. Minn. Stat. § 253B.03 (d) (as amended by 1991 Minn. Laws, Ch. 148). The statute, however, limits coverage to "intrusive mental health treatment,"

which is defined as psychotropic medications and electro-convulsive therapy.

99. For example, for a number of years the author has prepared living wills expressing preferences concerning psychotropic drugs for people in New York. In New York, a court has upheld the use of a living will to enforce the right of a person institutionalized for mental illness to refuse electro-convulsive therapy. *See* Matter of Rosa M; No. 96965/89, N.Y.L.J. Nov. 26, 1991 (Sup. Ct. N.Y. County). At the time this article was written, there were similar programs to use advance directives for mental disability treatment planning in California and Texas.

100. In a thoughtful analysis of an extreme procedure, a Michigan court held that involuntary commitment was in itself so inherently coercive that a person could not voluntarily consent to participate in experimental brain surgery, which might result in death or possible injury to the brain. The court concluded that the "fact of institutional confinement has special force in undermining the capacity of the mental patient to make a competent decision" about irreversible experimental psychosurgery: "The involuntarily detained mental patient is in an inherently coercive atmosphere even though no direct pressures may be placed upon him. He finds himself stripped of customary amenities and defenses. Free movement is restricted. He becomes a part of communal living subject to the control of the institutional authorities." Kaimowitz v. Department of Mental Health, No. 73-19434-AW, 1 MDLR 147, 150–151 (Mich. Cir. Ct. Wayne County, July 10, 1973). No court has extended this analysis to nonexperimental treatment, such as medication.

101. Psychotropic drugs, or drugs that act on the brain, include antipsychotic drugs; anti-depressant drugs; lithium, for treatment of manic-depression, also known as bipolar disorder; and minor tranquilizers, such as Valium. BRAKEL ET AL., *supra* note 8, at 328–29.

102. Washington v. Harper, 494 U.S. 210, 229 (1990).

103. S.J. Keith, *Drugs: Not the Only Treatment*, 33 HOSP. & COMM'Y PSYCHIATRY 793 (1982). However, the subsequent introduction of a newer class of drugs, most notably Clozapine, provides some promise of alleviating a number of the disabling aspects of schizophrenia.

104. Davis v. Hubbard, 506 F. Supp. 915, 937 (N.D. Ohio 1980) (citations omitted).

105. *See, e.g.*, F.J. Ayd, Jr., *Pre-Treatment Prediction of Responsiveness to Chlorpromazine: Is it Possible?*, 10 INT'L DRUG THERAPY NEWSL. 4 (1975).

106. *See, e.g.*, May Van Putten et al., *Predicting Individual Responses to Drug Treatment in Schizophrenia: A Test Dosage Model*, 162 J. NERVOUS & MENTAL DISEASE 177, 178 (1976).

107. *See, e.g.*, PHYSICIANS' DESK REFERENCE (43d ed. 1989); C.A. Pearlman, *Neuroleptic Malignant Syndrome: A Review of the Literature*, 6 J. CLINICAL PSYCHOPHARMACOLOGY 257 (1986); Sanford Goldstone et al., *Effects of Trifluoperazine, Chlorpromazine and Haloperidol upon Temporal Information Processing by Schizophrenic Patients*, 65 PSYCHOPHARMACOLOGY 119 (1979); Robert Plotkin, *Limiting the Therapeutic Orgy: Mental Patients' Right to Refuse Treatment*, 72 Nw.U.L. REV. 461 (1978).

108. The mild side effects include dry mouth, dizziness, blurred vision, constipation and muscle stiffness. Even a relatively modest side effect such as drowsiness can be a source of acute distress to patients who are struggling to remain alert and to think more clearly.

109. The more severe muscular side effects, known as extrapyramidal symptoms, include akathesia (motor restlessness and agitation); akinesia (physical immobility and lack of spontaneity); dystonic reactions (muscle spasms, irregular flexing, writhing or grimacing movements); and pseudo-Parkinsonian symptoms (tremors, muscle stiffness, drooling, and shuffling gait). Most extrapyramidal symptoms cease when the drugs are discontinued and can be controlled by the administration of drugs such as Cogentin.

110. Neuroleptic Malignant Syndrome.

111. G.E. Crane, *A Classification of the Neurologic Effects of Neuroleptic Drugs, in* TARDIVE DYSKINESIA 188 (W.E. Fann, Jr., ed., 1980).

112. *See* George Gardos & Jonathan O. Cole, *Overview: Public Health Issues in Tardive Dyskinesia*, 137 AM. J. PSYCHIATRY 776 (1980). *See also Guy Chouinard & B.D. Jones, Early Onset of Tardive Dyskinesia: A Case Report*, 136 AM. J. PSYCHIATRY 1323 (1979) (patient developed tardive dyskinesia after only one month of drug exposure).

113. Dilip V. Jeste et al., *The Biology and Experimental Treatment of Tardive Dyskinesia and Other Related Movement Disorders, in* 8 AMERICAN HANDBOOK OF PSYCHIATRY 536 (Berger & Brodie eds., 2d ed. 1986).

114. Early cases, however, frequently go undetected, partly because antipsychotics tend to mask its symptoms and partly through inattention. Many patients do not demonstrate symptoms until they have discontinued the medication, and it is too late to halt the disorder. *See* Jeste et al., *supra* note 113, at 560; *Chouinard & Jones, supra* note 112, at 1323. Even when

symptoms are apparent, psychiatrists may overlook them. In two disturb-
ing studies, psychiatrists failed to notice signs of tardive dyskinesia in some
75% and 90% of the cases, respectively. Hansen et al., *TD Prevalence:
Research and Clinical Differences, New Research Abstracts,* 1986 139th
Ann. Meeting A.P.A., cited in brief for *Amicus curiae* A.P.A. at n. 20;
Washington v. Harper, 494 U.S. 210 (1990); P.J. Weiden et al., *Clinical
Nonrecognition of Neuroleptic-Induced Disorders: A Cautionary Study,*
144 AM. J. PSYCHIATRY 1148, 1150 (1987).

115. *Washington,* 494 U.S. at 230.

116. Jeste et al., *supra* note 113, at 539 (25.6% of chronic psychiatric inpatients
treated with neuroleptics have tardive dyskinesia); G.E. Crane, *Neuroleptics
and Their Long-Term Effects on the Central Nervous System, in* TARDIVE
DYSKINESIA AND RELATED INVOLUNTARY MOVEMENT DISORDERS (Joseph
DeVeaugh-Geiss ed., 1982) ("50% of patients in long-term drug therapy
show evidence of long-lasting neurotoxicity"); Davis v. Hubbard, 506 F.
Supp. 915, 929 (N.D. Ohio 1980) (citing Robert Sovner et al., *Tardive
Dyskinesia and Informed Consent,* PSYCHOSOMATICS, Mar. 1978, at 173);
Rennie v. Klein, 476 F. Supp. 1294, 1306 (D.N.J. 1979) (expert evidence
indicated that 25 to 50% of institutionalized patients have tardive dyskinesia).

117. Alexander D. Brooks, *Constitutional Right to Refuse Antipsychotic
Medication,* 8 BULL. AM. ACAD. PSYCHIATRY & L. 179, 191 (1980).

118. In many states, there is a waiting period of one to several days before a
voluntary patient can leave the hospital, while the facility evaluates whether
to initiate commitment proceedings.

119. *See, e.g.,* Plotkin, *supra* note 107, at 474 –79.

120. Rivers v. Katz, 504 N.Y.S.2d 74, 79 (1986).

121. *Id.*

122. *See, e.g.,* Brooks, *supra* note 117, at 191.

123. *See, e.g.,* Washington v. Harper, 494 U.S. 210, 221–22 (1990) (prisoner
possesses significant due process liberty interest under federal constitution
in avoiding unwanted administration of antipsychotic drugs) (citing, *inter
alia,* Youngberg v. Romeo, 457 U.S. 307, 316 (1982)); *In re K.K.B.,* 609
P.2d 747, 752 (Okla. 1980); *Rivers,* 504 N.Y.S.2d at 78 (common law right
and state constitutional liberty interest to refuse medical treatment); Rogers
v. Commissioner, Dep't of Mental Health, 458 N.E.2d 308, 314 (Mass.
1983) (common law right and state constitutional interest in being free from
"nonconsensual invasion of bodily integrity") (citation omitted).

124. *Washington*, 494 U.S. at 238 (Stevens, J., dissenting).

125. For a detailed analysis of a First Amendment theory of the right to refuse medication, *see* Bruce J. Winick, *The Right to Refuse Mental Health Treatment: A First Amendment Perspective*, 44 U. MIAMI L. REV. 1 (1989).

126. Olmstead v. United States, 277 U.S. 438, 478 (1928) (Brandeis, J., dissenting).

127. In *Washington v. Harper*, 494 U.S. 210 (1990), the Supreme Court adopted a medical model analysis in ruling that a prisoner's liberty interest in refusing antipsychotic drugs can be overridden by a showing that the prisoner has a serious mental illness, is dangerous to self or to others, and the treatment is in the prisoner's medical interests. The Court also ruled that the prison need only prove its case by the minimal "preponderance of the evidence" standard and that due process required no more than an "independent" decisionmaker consisting of physicians on the staff of the institution —not a judicial hearing. Because *Harper* involved a convicted prisoner, who had lesser rights than a civilly committed patient, it can be distinguished from a civil commitment case.

128. 458 U.S. 1119 (1982).

129. Rennie v. Klein, 653 F.2d 836 (3d Cir. 1981) (en banc), *cert. granted*, 458 U.S. 1119 (1982) (judgment vacated and remanded for consideration in light of *Youngberg v. Romeo*, 457 U.S. 307 (1982)). *Youngberg*, a right-to-treatment case based on the finding of a due process liberty interest in avoiding unreasonable restraints, held that treatment decisions are presumptively valid so long as they are made by a professional and were not a substantial departure from accepted professional judgment, standards and practice.

130. 722 F.2d 960, 980–81 (2nd Cir. 1983).

131. These provisions were codified in 14 N.Y.C.R.R. 27.8(b)(d).

132. *Project Release*, 722 F.2d at 989 (citations and emphasis omitted).

133. Youngberg v. Romeo, 457 U.S. 307, 322–23 (1982).

134. The regulations allowed the patient to object to the treating psychiatrist, the chief of service, and the director of the hospital. There was no impartial hearing, right to present evidence or confront witnesses, or right to be present at the deliberations. Where a state facility was involved, there was a further right to object to the regional commissioner of mental health.

135. *See, e.g.*, Rivers v. Katz, 504 N.Y.S.2d 74 (1986).

136. Rogers v. Commissioner, Mental Health, 458 N.E.2d 308 (Mass. 1983).

137. *But see* A.E. v. Mitchell, No. C.78–466 (D. Utah 1980), *aff'd*, 724 F.2d 864, 867 (10th Cir. 1983) (rejecting request for order barring forcible administration of drugs to involuntary patients without a declaration of incompetency on grounds that Utah's commitment law specifically requires finding of incompetency to consent to treatment). This case, however, turns on the unique provisions of Utah's commitment statute.

138. *See, e.g.*, *Rogers*, 458 N.E.2d 308.

139. Matter of Guardianship of Richard Roe III, 421 N.E.2d 40 (Mass. 1981).

140. *See, e.g.*, Rivers v. Katz, 504 N.Y.S.2d 74 (1986).

141. *Id.* at n. 90.

142. Paul S. Appelbaum, *The Right to Refuse Treatment with Antipsychotic Medications: Retrospect and Prospect*, 147 AM. J. PSYCHIATRY 413, 418 (1988).

143. *See, e.g.*, Davis v. Hubbard, 506 F. Supp. 915, 926–27 (N.D. Ohio 1980).

144. *See, e.g.*, Bee v. Greaves, 744 F.2d 1387, 1390 (10th Cir. 1984) (jail inmate forcibly injected with medication "for the express purpose of intimidating him so he wouldn't refuse the oral medication anymore"), *cert. denied*, 469 U.S. 1214 (1985); Mackey v. Procunier, 477 F.2d 877 (9th Cir. 1973); Pena v. New York State Div. for Youth, 419 F. Supp. 203, 207 (S.D.N.Y. 1976); Nelson v. Heyne, 355 F. Supp. 451, 455 (N.D. Ind. 1972), *aff'd*, 491 F.2d 352 (7th Cir.), *cert. denied*, 417 U.S. 976 (1974).

145. *See, e.g.*, (Willowbrook consent decree) NYSARC v. Carey, 393 F. Supp. 715 (E.D.N.Y. 1975), Appendix A, (Q)(4) (to remedy past abusive medication practices at an institution for people with mental retardation, the decree mandated: "Medication shall not be used as punishment, *for the convenience of staff*, as a substitute for program, or in quantities that interfere with the resident's program.") (emphasis added).

146. *See, e.g.*, Matter of Rosa M., No. 96965/89, N.Y.L.J. Nov. 26, 1991 (Sup. Ct. N.Y. County) (court recognizes living will, written while woman was competent, withdrawing consent for electro-convulsive therapy).

147. Paul S. Appelbaum & Thomas G. Gutheil, *Drug Refusal: A Study of Psychiatric Inpatients*, 137 AM. J. PSYCHIATRY 340, 344 (1980). *See also* Brooks, *supra* note 117, at 213 (no adverse effects resulting from right to

refuse drugs decision in *Rennie v. Klein*, 476 F. Supp. 1294 (D.N.J. 1979)); Davis v. Hubbard, 506 F. Supp. 915, 937 n. 31 (N.D. Ohio 1980) (experts testified that in institutions where the right to refuse drugs had been recognized, there were no adverse effects on the operation of the institution or on its treatment goals); Rogers v. Okin, 478 F. Supp. 1342, 1370 (D. Mass. 1978) (Only 12 of 1,000 involuntary patients refused drugs for extended periods during the two years a temporary restraining order was in effect. The court found that "the great majority of patients have not declined their psychotropic medication during the pendency of the T.R.O. [establishing the right of involuntary patients to refuse drugs]. Most of those who did changed their minds within a few days.").

148. Paul S. Appelbaum, *Legal Issues Relevant to Homelessness and the Severely Mentally Ill Population*, 20 BULL. AM. ACAD. PSYCHIATRY & L. 455 (1992), citing S.K. Hoge et al., *A Prospective, Multicenter Study of Patients' Refusal of Antipsychotic Medication*, 47 ARCHIVES GEN. PSYCHIATRY 949 (1990).

149. *See, e.g.*, J. Richard Ciccone et al., *Right to Refuse Treatment: Impact of Rivers v. Katz*, 18 BULL. AM. ACAD. PSYCHIATRY & L. 203 (1990); F. Cournos et al., *Outcome of Involuntary Medication in a State Hospital System*, 148 AM. J. PSYCHIATRY 489 (1991); F.H. Deland & N.M. Borenstein, *Medicine Court, II: Rivers in Practice*, 147 AM. J. PSYCHIATRY 38 (1990); S.K. Hoge et al., *The Right to Refuse Treatment under Rogers v. Commissioner: Preliminary Empirical Findings and Comparisons*, 15 BULL. AM. ACAD. PSYCHIATRY & L. 163 (1987); M.G. Farnsworth, *The Impact of Judicial Review of Patients' Refusal to Accept Antipsychotic Medications at the Minnesota Security Hospital*, 19 BULL. AM. ACAD. PSYCHIATRY & L. 33 (1991).

15

Paternalism and Autonomy in the Ownership and Control of Money and Property by Persons with Mental Disability*

Paul F. Stavis, Esq.

Introduction

Over the past thirty years, persons with mental disabilities have been increasingly empowered by one of the most dramatic social movements for the enhancement of personal civil rights since the desegregation of the public schools: the movement of care and treatment for persons with mental disability from large institutional settings into smaller community ones.

This has greatly enhanced the personal freedoms of formerly institutionalized persons, giving them more opportunities to enjoy, in the words of the Declaration of Independence: "the pursuit of happiness." Essentially this means being given the personal power to control the many choices about their daily lives. Many, if not most, people have at some-time in their lives been subjected to the regimentation of

It is very psychologically intimidating to an individual to be compelled to conform to a monotonous regimen dictated by others. Choice is the essence of freedom.

an institution. For some it might have been military service, and for others a sectarian school, a summer camp, the Boy or Girl Scouts, etc. Having had even a taste of this experience, it is not hard to understand how important it is to be

* Acknowledgment is given to Brenna D. Mahoney, Esq., for her assistance in the research and writing of this article.

able to make the simple, but significant choices of our everyday lives. It is very psychologically intimidating to an individual to be compelled to conform to a monotonous regimen dictated by others. Choice is the essence of freedom.

Government generally provides two kinds of funds for the care and treatment of persons with mental disability: the primary public monies which are used to pay for the care and treatment, and smaller personal needs allowances for expenses of daily living. When these two categories of monies were managed within the close confines of an institution, it was relatively easy to keep track of them and regulate the appropriateness of their expenditure.

Since government, however, must increasingly deal with hundreds of programs and thousands of recipients of services, rather than a few large institutions, it has had a tendency to develop management systems for these monies which accommodate its own convenience and that of its providers, at the expense of eroding the personal decision-making role of each recipient. Thus the dramatic enhancement of personal freedoms that deinstitutionalization has brought, has not been accompanied by similar freedoms to control the primary funds used for care and treatment or for personal expenditures.

Persons with mental disability often have varying degrees of decision-making ability, making problematic uniform reliance on their decisions. One amelioration for this problem has been surrogate decision-makers who generally are court appointed, e.g., a guardian of the person or property. When a person (known in law as the "ward") is determined by a court to lack the capacity to manage property or money, a guardian may be chosen to do so. The guardian, where possible, is usually a close family member or a friend of the mentally disabled ward, since that person would generally know the personal preferences of the ward and likely be trustworthy to act in his or her best interests, especially when it comes to handling money. Depending on the laws of a particular state, there are other forms of guardianship and surrogate decision-making including public guardians, conservators, and committees of the person or property, health care agents, powers of attorney, etc., but the specific characteristics of these are beyond the scope of this article.

> *Since government must increasingly deal with hundreds of programs and thousands of recipients of services, it has had a tendency to develop management systems for these monies which accommodate its own convenience and that of its providers, at the expense of eroding the personal decision-making role of each recipient.*

However, due to the unavailability of persons willing to act as guardians and the relatively high cost and resources it takes to complete this court process, the government has not tended to seek out and help establish such court-appointed, personal surrogates. Rather, for reasons of administrative convenience, it has entrusted possession and control of personal allowance and care and treatment monies to its licensed vendors of services, called "representative payees" under the Federal Social Security Program.

One of the problems with this representative payee model is that a provider of care appointed as representative payee might have somewhat conflicting roles—to sell services to the recipient as well as to pay for them with the recipient's money. In this sense, a provider is not in the best position to defer to the recipient's choices wherever possible since its own economic interests may conflict with the recipient's choices.

The alternative of permitting recipients to control these funds themselves also presents many questions concerning how much control should be given over to a person with mental disability to manage such funds, i.e., whether sufficient protection exists to secure the funds from misuse. These types of questions fall into three categories: (1) the permissible choices and parameters of control of such funds by the consumer-beneficiary; (2) the restraints upon frivolous spending that endangers basic needed services; and (3) the appropriateness of paternalistic protection, employed as mechanisms to strike this balance between full autonomy and appropriate protection. Some examples of these questions are:

- How much choice should recipients have over how such monies are spent by others or on their behalf? How much control should be exercised and under what legal mechanisms should that be done?
- Should a recipient be permitted to expend a great deal of money on something most people would consider frivolous or of a low priority, e.g., jeopardize the recipient's fiscal ability to provide for necessities, including care and treatment, medicine, or rent?
- Should recipients be allowed to "squander" their money, e.g., on excessively expensive goods (e.g., clothes, electronic equipment, etc.), gambling, or, on other frivolous items to a point of endangering their long-term resources or their ability to provide basic necessities? Should there be limitations or prohibitions on injurious items such as cigarettes, junk food (especially if such has particularly bad consequences to a recipient, such as exacerbating a Prader-Willi syndrome) or illicit street drugs?
- Should there be encouragement or even a requirement that a consumer use his or her money for positive purposes such as teaching a person to save for the future?

- Finally, what are the provider's obligations in this regard? Should it, for example, be mandated to hire a truly independent fiscal surrogate for recipient funds?

History of Law: Property Rights vs. Personal Rights

As reflected in the U.S. Constitution, as well as existing generally in the laws of the United States, the laws of western civilization have drawn a distinction between rights of the person and rights of property. Ironic as it may seem to us in the twentieth century with its profound emphasis on personal freedoms, the development in law of individual rights was presaged by concerns over property rights such as its ownership and control. The eminent colonial historian Edmund Morgan wrote:

> For the colonists, as for other Englishmen, property was not merely a possession to be hoarded and admired; it was rather the source of life and liberty. If a man had property, if he had land, he had his own source of food, he could be independent of other men, including kings and lords.... Without property men could be starved into submission. Hence liberty rested on property, and whatever threatened the security of property threatened liberty.[1]

This distinction between rights of property and personal freedom can also be found within the Constitution's Bill of Rights. For example, some amendments establish personal rights such as free speech, freedom of religion, freedom from cruel and unusual punishment, etc., while others specifically address rights of property, such as the Fifth Amendment, which prevents the government from taking property without just compensation, or the Fourteenth Amendment, which prohibits the government from negatively affecting property without due process of law.

Historically, the issue underlying ownership and control of money and property for some persons with mental disability has been their legal or factual competence, capacity, or ability to handle property or money.

Historically, the issue underlying ownership and control of money and property for some persons with mental disability has been their legal or factual competence, capacity, or ability to handle property or money. Persons who were considered unable to act rationally, e.g., children were by definition of law presumed to be incompetent and persons with mental disability, were not permitted to control property, although they could own it and enjoy its profits. In such cases, what was the role of government?

The traditional role of government, the state, the law or the sovereign was the power to take control of property for the good of the child or disabled person. This was a form of paternalism, still known in contemporary law by its Latin name, *parens patriae*, meaning the government's power to act in appropriate circumstances as the parent of anyone in the country.

From the time of ancient law, the philosophy of government called for justice to be dispensed closest to and most preserving of the family.

Laws of Property, Paternalism, and Disability of the Ancient and Middle Ages

In the ancient laws of Greece and Rome, paternalism was considered one of the two great functions of government; the other power was that of enforcement of law and order, known as the "police power." The definition of "paternalism" in terms of government responsibility and authority is:

> the system, principle or practice of managing or governing individuals, businesses, nations, etc., in a manner of a father dealing with his children...[such as] characteristic of or befitting a father [e.g.,] a kind and paternal reprimand....[2]

This responsibility of the state historically and currently is to act as the 'parent of the country" (*parens patriae*) for any and all of its citizens who are in need of such "parental" assistance. Under this traditional power of government, for any person, child or adult, who is in need of care and has no family or friend to provide it, the government as sovereign will act as the parent of last resort for that person.[3]

> [T]he Supreme Court suggested that the *parens patriae* power, like the police power, is rooted in the very nature of the state in modern society. The Court described the *parens patriae* power as "inherent in the supreme power of every state. . . and often necessary to be exercised in the interests of humanity." * * * The *parens patriae* function can thus be viewed as a power which the members of the community have granted for the protection of their future well-being.[4]

From the time of ancient law, the philosophy of government called for justice to be dispensed closest to and most preserving of the family. Thus, for persons with disability (or for any family member with decisional incompetence, such as children), the father of the family had the inherent legal authority to make such decisions. In Ancient Greek law this was called *potestas* (power), and later in Roman law the same principle was known as *pater familia* (father of the family), although Roman law also provided for the appointment of a guardian (known as a "curator") to administer an incompetent person's property.

It is very important to note that for any guardian, it was an essential attribute of his or her behavior to be a "fiduciary" (i.e., to act totally and unambiguously in a selfless way and with complete loyalty to the ward) and to make an accounting to the ward's heirs, a court, or other significant persons with an interest in the ward. This is still the law today.

In England, between 1255 and 1290 A.D., the statute *De Praerogativa Regis* was enacted. It divided persons with mental disabilities into two legal categories based on ability. Persons with mental illness were then called "lunatics" and persons with mental retardation were then called "natural fools" or "idiots." The king was automatically the custodian (i.e., guardian) of the property of both, but could treat such properties differently. For a person with mental illness, the king had a "duty" to manage his property and to use the profits from the land for care and treatment of the ward. The king had to return the property if the mental illness was cured or sufficiently ameliorated.

For a person with mental retardation, whose condition would probably not improve significantly, the king could take and keep the profits from the land once having provided for the ward. Upon the death of the ward, the land had to be returned to his heirs.[5] Of course, both of these cases assume that there is sufficient property and profits therefrom to make intervention by the king worthwhile. Later, upon the refinement of English law with the addition of due process, a person's right to retain control of property and to have his mental status objectively adjudged, a *writ de idiot inquirendo* (the same was done for a "lunatic") was issued, which entitled the person to a trial before a jury of twelve men.

> *The role of the government as the responsible parent has gone from one where the law recognized the nuclear family as the primary care giver and decision-maker, to centuries later, where that role devolved upon the king as the sovereign.*

Early Laws of the United States

In early America, following the precedent of the English law, some states (e.g., New York State) required the same *writ de lunatico inquirendo*, which included a trial by jury, to protect the property of a person with mental illness under principles of due process of law.[6]

Thus, the role of the government as the responsible parent has gone from one where the law utilized the nuclear family as the surrogate care giver and decision-maker, to centuries later, where that role devolved upon the king as the sovereign. As English law democratically evolved, as later in the United States, this *parens patriae* role was given over to the elected government generally and usually exercised by the judiciary as it is today.

Thus, it is ironic that in today's mental hygiene systems the situation seems to have come full circle. From centuries ago up to the deinstitutionalization movement, the sovereign or the government directly provided services in its own institutional settings. Over the last thirty years, control of services has been moving back to the community and to individual control.

Where there is evidence that a person cannot manage or control property competently, the concept of paternalism in our law helps to preserve that property and to devote its profit for the good of its owner.

However, one very important feature that greatly affects ultimate consumer empowerment through choice that has not changed is the way in which monetary resources are spent. Control of the money expended for care and treatment has remained either with the government or with the persons or entities selected and licensed by the government and its officials, i.e., service providers. While this continues to be true in the mental hygiene areas, other government programs have given consumers more freedom of choice, such as the GI Bill, food stamp program, and Medicare and, to an increasing extent, Medicaid, under its "waiver" provisions. In a similar way, it is time that the mental hygiene system truly empowers the recipients of care and treatment by permitting them reasonable control of these benefits and, where necessary, to authorize surrogate decision-makers who are closest to the recipient to make the most personalized decisions possible.

As with other laws, under the existing system there is a general presumption that a person of adult years should control his or her own property. And a child of minor years or an adult who is incapable or unable to make rational decisions may own title to property, but may also have control of it circumscribed or withdrawn in his/her best interests. A surrogate decision-maker is then appointed under law to make such decisions in the best interests of the disabled or child owner of the property. Thus, where there is evidence that a person cannot manage or control property competently, the concept of paternalism in our law helps to preserve that property and to devote its profit for the good of its owner.

Under the well-established principles of "fiduciary" and "paternalism," it has long been the law that a guardian must permit the ward to make all decisions he or she can, as well as to participate in others where that is possible. Even for those where no decisional contribution of the ward is available, decisions should be made as the ward would make them or at least in his or her best interests as determined by a person who best knows and is most loyal to the ward.

Contemporary Rights of Money and Property: Vouchers as a Way to Fiscal Empowerment

Money is equated not only with power, but also with personal freedom. Indeed, for many people, rights of property and economic well-being play a more prominent role in their day-to-day lives than the great personal freedoms in the Bill of Rights.

For the mental hygiene system, it was certainly the highest priority to first transfer care and treatment away from the impersonal institutional settings. But it is now time to follow that with greater freedom in the fiscal areas. Current governmental funding streams recognize such personal fiscal autonomy only in a limited way of granting control over personal allowance funds to permit modest personal choices of daily necessities or luxuries. But, there is no similar consumer empowerment for the bulk of funds presumably used for the most important matters of care and treatment. There is rather an uneasy partnership between the government, formerly the primary provider of care, and its licensees who have assumed that role. Still missing from this equation is the empowerment of persons with mental disability, who are the real beneficiaries, by giving them a reasonable range of choices in these decisions.

Choices of how the primary funds are spent, within appropriate guidelines that are consistent with governmental interests, should be given to persons with mental disabilities so that they can direct the use of such funds as they see fit for their own care and treatment. Giving personal control of these funds inherently brings a sense of ownership of the benefits they purchase. In this way, it is more likely that services will be chosen to better suit the needs of the individual. It is the difference between a free lunch and one that must be paid for; in the former case, a person will not be "fussy"; in the latter case, a person will make sure of its value if his or her resources are individually at stake.

For example, each recipient could be given a government voucher or credit card to spend for any care and treatment deemed acceptable within broad parameters of government interests, much as food stamps can be used for food of any kind, but not alcohol; the GI Bill can be used for a vast variety of education, but not for a car. The voucher should be provided in the context of the development of an individual plan of services and supports with the active participation of interested and caring family and friends. The voucher could be used to buy housing, clinical services, homemaker assistance, job work services, etc., as described in the plan, and even for the services of a personal surrogate to assist the consumer in decision-making.

If a recipient is not able to choose on his or her own or with help from family, friends, or others concerned with his well-being, decision-making should then be supplied by a decision-maker closest to that recipient or at least one who independently has the recipient's best interests at heart, preferably one selected by the consumer himself.

If a recipient is not able to choose on his or her own or with help from family, friends, or others concerned with his well-being, decision-making should then be supplied by a decision-maker closest to that recipient or at least one who independently has the recipient's best interests at heart, preferably one selected by the consumer himself. While the motives of most providers of care cannot be impugned, they nevertheless clearly have legitimate interests other than the recipient's *per se*, which may or may not conflict with the recipient's interests, e.g., meeting payroll, ongoing business activities, turning a profit or a surplus, etc. These multiple interests might well limit a fuller range of choices that should be offered to the recipient.

Who should decide what is the best way to expend the public funds which are used to pay for an individual's care and treatment—a provider of services, the consumer, or someone acting directly and closely with the consumer? Also, is it not self-serving to some extent to have a vendor of services also determine the quality and quantity of those services? Would it be more efficient and effective to use some of these funds to attract competent surrogate decision-makers for recipients, under a process that is not so formalistic and expensive?

In the national best-selling book, *Reinventing Government*,[7] the author discusses "Putting Customers in the Driver's Seat" when it comes to government services:

> Even in competitive service delivery systems, public agencies usually contract with various providers...or allocate budgets between various providers.... Too often, politics interferes with these decisions. The providers with the largest constituencies get the most money, simply because they can bring the most political pressure to bear during budget time.... Few

> politicians get elected because service providers do a good
> job, but many politicians get defeated because a constituency
> rebels.... But when the customers control the resources, no
> legislature can protect inferior providers from the verdicts
> rendered by those customers.[8]

The issue here is whether true empowerment means that the consumers can choose, within appropriate boundaries, the services that best fit their individual lifestyles and life choices. The proposition is that persons with mental disability should be put in the driver's seat of choosing their own services. And even if they can only do so partially or not at all, then that decision should be assisted or made by someone who is a fiduciary and closest to the recipient to help determine what is in his or her best interests or desires.

A voucher system would truly empower persons with mental disability to gain control over their lives and to make the most important decisions for themselves. Consumer-driven systems waste less, match the supply to the demand, empower customers to make choices, and create opportunities for innovation.

Another benefit to government would be a much-needed reimbursement system where the incentive is to purchase only higher quality care. Presently, the link between efficient spending and quality services requires frequent audits and inspections, and that is not happening in the current system. The government has not devoted adequate resources to perform inspections or to account for or follow the hundreds of millions of dollars it pays out to programs. For example, the New York State Office of Mental Retardation and Developmental Disabilities (OMRDD) has approximately six auditors for hundreds of licensed agencies and thousands of programs. OMRDD regulations set up a system which utilizes the audits done by private accountants upon its programs, but this system has legal and other deficits and is easily circumvented with few or no penalties to either the program or the private accountants.

The issue here is whether true empowerment means that the consumers can choose, within appropriate boundaries, the services that best fit their individual lifestyles and life choices.

By empowering recipients or their personal surrogates to monitor both personal allowances and program expenditures, the state would increase the fiscal integrity of a system because there would be a much greater personal self-interest in the expenditure of the funds. That is, now there is no direct cost to a consumer if there is waste and inefficiency; it is like a free lunch. If a limitation of the consumer's own funds are at stake, then there is a cost of receiving inferior services or other opportunity costs.

Presumably, consumers would flock to programs that provide good and desirable services, thereby increasing the resources of good programs.

Presumably, consumers would flock to programs that provide good and desirable services, thereby increasing the resources of good programs. Presumably, there would also be a greater diversity as fits the demands, desires, and needs of recipients. As in private business, bad programs would have to improve or die a natural economic death, i.e., go out of existence for lack of customers, rather than by bureaucratic fiat. Moreover, such programs would not have to rely on the politics of appropriations from the legislature or appeals to the bureaucracy for more money. More money would come from success with consumers and their empowerment to choose, thereby linking exemplary service with compensation. True consumer empowerment means control, choice, and satisfaction. Today's funding system supplies too few of these incentives or disincentives. Instead, it fertilizes a very entrenched provider network which has insufficient economic feedback to improve or diversify.

Appointment of Third Parties to Handle Fiscal Matters for Persons with Mental Disability

Since some of the persons served by mental health and developmental disabilities programs may have questionable competence to manage their own fiscal affairs without assistance, it is useful to examine the types of fiscal decision-making surrogates available under law. Some can be appointed administratively, such as a "representative payee" for Social Security payments, and others are appointed by a court of law.

True consumer empowerment means control, choice, and satisfaction. Today's funding system supplies none of these incentives or disincentives. Instead, it fertilizes a very entrenched provider network which has insufficient economic feedback to improve or diversify.

There are two points of view on the assignment of such a surrogate decision-maker. One is that it significantly reduces the person's autonomy over his or her property and also may impose a substantial financial burden due to the fact that certain fiscal representatives are paid for their services out of the resources of the person with mental disabilities.

The other point of view is that fiscal decision-makers, who behave as proper fiduciaries as all are required to do under law, enhance a person's abilities to control his or her funds to the extent possible, and provide protection and management only where it is needed due to the mental disability. The element common to all is the "fiduciary concept," i.e., to act primarily for another's benefit and to be responsible for any losses due to a breach in selfless loyalty to the beneficiary.

The difference between a fiscal surrogate being a net gain or loss in autonomy usually turns on his or her adherence to the fiduciary principle. Of course, the same problems arise where this principle applies to other common fiduciary relationships such as stockbroker, banker, lawyer, trustee, etc. With less scrutiny of the surrogate, the chances of appointing one who will not be a genuine fiduciary increase. Similarly, where the fiduciary has a potential conflict of interest, as for example if the fiduciary is both provider/vendor of services and a fiscal surrogate, expenditures might not be made in the best interests of the beneficiary. Instances where fiscal surrogates have been highly disloyal, grossly negligent, or have actually misappropriated the beneficiary's funds have been the subject of several investigations and public reports.[9]

The difference turns on the care with which a surrogate is chosen and the training he or she is given to act as a fiduciary and to be accountable for the actions taken.

When properly used, the fiscal surrogate, like a money manager, should be an asset to enhance a person's fiscal autonomy, to assist in the growth of such autonomy where possible and to protect the funds so that they can be put to the benefit of the person with mental disability. But, as happens in the general public, a negligent or unscrupulous stockbroker, lawyer, banker, or fiscal surrogate can do much damage if given a license to control a person's funds. The difference turns on the care with which a surrogate is chosen and the training he or she is given to act as a fiduciary and to be accountable for the actions taken.

A. COURT-APPOINTED REPRESENTATIVES

1. Article 81 Guardianship

Under Article 81 of the Mental Hygiene Law, the court may appoint a guardian for a person if the court determines that: (a) the appointment is necessary to provide for personal needs or to manage the property and financial affairs of the person, or both; and, (b) the person agrees to the appointment or is incapacitated.[10] The powers of the guardian, if appointed, must be specifically set forth in the court's order and must be limited to those which are necessary to assist the incapacitated person.[11] With respect to property, the guardian may be authorized to exercise those powers necessary and sufficient to manage the property and financial affairs of the incapacitated person, to provide for the maintenance and support of the incapacitated person, and those persons dependent upon the incapacitated person.[12]

A determination of incapacity requires clear and convincing evidence that the person is likely to suffer harm because: (1) the person is unable to provide for his or her own personal needs or property management; and (2) the person cannot adequately understand and appreciate the nature and consequences of such inability.[13] In making the required assessment, the court must give primary consideration to the person's functional level and limitations.[14] The standards of due process for the incapacitated person begin with a presumption of competency and only limit it after utilizing a high standard of proof ("clear and convincing") that the appointment of a guardian is in the recipient's best interests.

The proceeding for guardianship may be commenced by the filing of a petition with the court by several persons including any person with whom the alleged incapacitated person resides and any person otherwise concerned with the welfare of the alleged incapacitated person, including a corporation or public agency.[15] A broad category of persons may serve as guardian including an agency or facility which could serve as guardian for several of its recipients.

When presented with a petition for guardianship, the court appoints a court evaluator who is to independently assist the court in its determination of the person's capacity, the availability and reliability of alternative resources, determining the need for legal counsel, and assigning proper powers to the guardian. The evaluator reports to the court and makes recommendations based on the best interests of the alleged incapacitated person.[16] Although the evaluator may serve as a useful source to the court, ultimately the cost of the evaluator may be a significant financial burden to the person with mental disability since if a guardian is appointed, the court may award a reasonable fee to the court evaluator to be paid by the estate of the allegedly incapacitated person.[17] If the petition is denied or dismissed and a guardian is not appointed, the court may order either the petitioner or the allegedly incapacitated person to pay a reasonable fee to the evaluator.[18]

Article 81 does contain extensive provisions regarding notice of the guardianship proceeding.[19] The Article provides for a hearing, at which the alleged incapacitated person has a right to appear with counsel. The person's appearance, however, may be waived if he or she is completely unable to participate in the hearing or no meaningful participation will result from the person's presence at the hearing, or if the person is not present in the state.[20]

2. Guardianship of Property

A guardian for persons with mental retardation and developmental disabilities also may be appointed under Article 17-A of the Surrogate's Court Procedure Act. Unlike an Article 81 guardian, an Article 17-A guardian is granted general authority over the person or property or both.[21] A petition for guardianship may be made by a parent or any interested person, including a corporation.[22] Courts should be cautioned that the choice of a guardian is crucial. Appointment of a guardian who conducts himself or herself properly, effectively enhances the ward's use of his or her property.

In order for the court to appoint such a guardian, it must be satisfied that the mentally retarded or developmentally disabled person is incapable of managing himself or herself and/or his or her affairs by reason of mental retardation or developmental disability and that such condition is permanent in nature.[23] Certification of two physicians or one physician and one psychologist is required.[24] In addition, the court must determine that appointment of the guardian is in the person's best interest.[25]

3. Conservator and Committee

Prior to the 1992 enactment of Article 81 of the Mental Hygiene Law, the court had the authority to appoint conservators and committees under Articles 77 and 78 of the Mental Hygiene Law. Orders made under Articles 77 and 78 remain in force until modified by a judge pursuant to Article 81.[26] Thus, although use of conservators and committees is being phased out, there are still conservators and committees in effect that were appointed before the 1992 enactment of Article 81. A conservator or committee is now also obligated to comply with the reporting requirements of Article 81.[27]

a. Conservator

Any relative or friend, including "a corporate body, social services official, or public agency authorized to act in such capacity which has a concern for the financial and personal well-being of the proposed conservatee" may be appointed conservator.[28] The powers of a conservator are limited by a court order specifying the extent of the income and assets of the conservatee which are to be placed under the conservatorship, and a court-approved plan for the preservation, maintenance, and care of the conservatee's income, assets, and personal well-being.[29] Compensation for the conservator is fixed by the court.[30]

b. Committee

Article 78 of the Mental Hygiene Law permitted the court to appoint a committee of the property of a person who had been lawfully committed or admitted to any mental hygiene facility and who was declared by the court incompetent or unable adequately to conduct his or her personal or business affairs so as to avoid waste or destruction.[31] Compensation for the committee is paid at the same rate as an executor or administrator.[32] If the petition to appoint the committee is granted, reasonable attorney fees also may be awarded. These fees would be paid out of the funds of the incompetent.[33]

B. ADMINISTRATIVELY APPOINTED REPRESENTATIVES

1. Representative Payees

A representative payee is a person appointed for a beneficiary of Social Security or Supplemental Security Income when the Social Security Administration (SSA) determines that the interest of the beneficiary will be served by representative payment rather than direct payment. SSA will make such a determination when it finds that the beneficiary is not able to manage or direct the management of his or her own benefit payments.[34] When a representative payee is appointed, the benefit is mailed directly to the payee who then has responsibility to spend the funds for the beneficiary's maintenance.[35]

Interestingly, four and one-half million Social Security beneficiaries receive their benefits through a representative payee, although only a small portion of them have been determined legally incompetent in state court. Ten percent of all benefits are paid to a representative payee, totaling more than twenty billion dollars.

Interestingly, four and one-half million Social Security beneficiaries receive their benefits through a representative payee, although only a small portion of them have been determined legally incompetent in state court.[36] Ten percent of all benefits are paid to a representative payee, totaling more than twenty billion dollars.[37]

The SSA bases its determination on evidence from a medical professional concerning the nature of the beneficiary's illness, chance of recovery, and a medical opinion concerning his or her financial management abilities.[38] The SSA also considers statements from friends or relatives who have observed and are familiar with the beneficiary's financial management abilities.[39]

The representative payee is chosen by SSA from among interested persons, agencies, or institutions. The controlling factor in the selection is the beneficiary's best interest.[40] The flexible list of preferred payees is as follows: spouse or relative with custody or showing strong concern; legal guardian; friend who has custody or shows a strong concern; public/nonprofit institution; private institution; others who are qualified, able, and willing.[41] Despite this list, one-quarter of those adult beneficiaries who receive representative payment have an institution or public official serving as payee.[42] As a result, beneficiaries may be placed in a position where their funds are controlled by persons or entities responsible for their care. Once again, this dual role by a provider (that is, seller) of care raises a possible conflict of interest and increases the risk of infringing on the autonomy of beneficiaries who may be capable of making some financial decisions, but not others.

Additionally, unlike a person who has a court-appointed representative, the beneficiary is entitled only to written notice that a representative payee has been appointed; no requirement of advance notification to the beneficiary exists.[43] As a result, the beneficiary learns of the appointment of a payee only after SSA's review has taken place and the payee has been chosen. The beneficiary does not have an opportunity to participate in the choice of payee or decision whether to appoint one at all except after the fact, by objecting and providing additional information to the SSA.[44] If the beneficiary does not object, however, the determination to appoint the payee will be issued.[45]

2. OMRDD Regulations

The New York State Office of Mental Retardation and Developmental Disabilities (OMRDD) has promulgated regulations governing the management of recipient funds by an agency or facility.[46] They require an accounting process be established by which the receipt and disbursement of personal allowance funds for each person are recorded, if management of personal allowances is assumed by the agency or sponsoring agency.[47] Additionally, if the chief executive officer of the agency is a representative payee, a record of all monies received must be maintained.[48] No arrangement is permitted that implies current or future ownership of a person's assets by an agency or facility, its employees or volunteers, or by family care providers.[49] OMRDD also provides that agencies and facilities must not withhold personal allowances or demand personal allowances to pay for expenses, supplies, or services.[50] Personal allowances must not be borrowed, pledged, or given or withheld to reward or punish a person.[51]

Nevertheless, the studies and investigations conducted by the New York State Commission on Quality of Care for the Mentally Disabled have found repeated instances of such violations that went

Empowerment essentially means the ability to make choices that reflect one's preferences, personality, and goals.

unnoticed and unpunished.[52] The standards set forth in the OMRDD regulations are in vain if there is insufficient monitoring and enforcement. The result is that persons with mental disability are unable to exercise autonomy in their financial affairs and may be subjected to misuse of their funds.

Conclusion

Empowerment essentially means the ability to make choices that reflect one's preferences, personality, and goals. Not only does choice inure for the benefit of the individual, but it also benefits the system as a whole if the assumption is made that each person chooses available alternatives in his or her own best interests. Currently, while the mental hygiene system has been changing for the enhancement of individual liberties, it would also benefit from a genuine orientation toward consumerism as well. As the consumer movement is revolutionizing private industry's attention to consumer needs and satisfaction, that model should also be tried with consumers of government-financed mental hygiene services. Such a program cannot work if it is singularly centered in the universe of government or provider control; their roles are vital, but their interests are not necessarily the same as consumers. There must be a synthesis which blends all of these interests with an emphasis on or ultimate goal of consumer empowerment.

Thus, the control of funds should be transferred to consumers or as closely to them as possible through fiduciary surrogates. Within such a system, fiscal controls in the form of vouchers or otherwise, can be imposed to ensure that there is purpose and integrity to a system. Current surrogate appointment mechanisms should be considered as modified to provide a practical balance in such a system, where finding and appointing a surrogate is cost efficient and effective, while ensuring proper recognition of the individual and property rights of the recipient of services.

Endnotes

1. E. MORGAN, THE BIRTH OF THE REPUBLIC, 1763–89 16 (Chicago: University of Chicago Press, 1956), as quoted in H.H. WELLINGTON, INTERPRETING THE CONSTITUTION 53, (New Haven, Yale University Press 1990).

2. RANDOM HOUSE DICTIONARY OF THE ENGLISH LANGUAGE 1056 (1st ed. unabridged 1966).

3. The other power is known as the "police power." It is the exercise of the sovereign right of a government to promote order, safety, health, morals and general welfare within constitutional limits and is an essential attribute of government. BLACK'S LAW DICTIONARY 1041 (5th ed. 1979).

4. *Developments in the Law—Civil Commitment of the Mentally Ill*, 87 HARV. L. REV. 1190, 1208 (1979).

5. S. BRAKEL ET AL., THE MENTALLY DISABLED AND THE LAW 10 (3d ed. 1985).

6. *Id*. at 14.

7. D. OSBORNE, REINVENTING GOVERNMENT, (Addison-Wesley Publishing Company 1992).

8. *Id*. at 182.

9. Public Reports of the NEW YORK STATE COMMISSION ON QUALITY OF CARE FOR THE MENTALLY DISABLED: FALLING THROUGH THE SAFETY NET: "COMMUNITY LIVING" IN ADULT HOMES FOR PATIENTS DISCHARGED FROM PSYCHIATRIC HOSPITALS, (Aug. 1993) and EXPLOITING THE VULNERABLE: THE CASE OF HI-LI MANOR HOME FOR THE AGED AND REGULATION BY THE NYS DEPARTMENT OF SOCIAL SERVICES, (June 1992), PROFIT MAKING IN NOT-FOR-PROFIT CARE: A REVIEW OF THE OPERATIONS AND FINANCIAL PRACTICES OF BROOKLYN PSYCHOSOCIAL REHABILITATION INSTITUTE, INC. (Nov. 1986), MISSING ACCOUNTABILITY: THE CASE OF COMMUNITY LIVING ALTERNAIVE, INC. (June 1994).

10. N.Y. MENTAL HYG. LAW § 81.02(a) (McKinney Supp. 1994).

11. N.Y. MENTAL HYG. LAW § 81.15(b) (McKinney Supp. 1994).

12. N.Y. MENTAL HYG. LAW § 81.21 (McKinney Supp. 1994).

13. N.Y. MENTAL HYG. LAW § 81.02(b) (McKinney Supp. 1994).

14. N.Y. MENTAL HYG. LAW § 81.01(c) (McKinney Supp. 1994).

15. N.Y. MENTAL HYG. LAW § 81.06(a) (McKinney Supp. 1994).

16. N.Y. Mental Hyg. Law § 81.09 (McKinney Supp. 1994).

17. N.Y. Mental Hyg. Law § 81.09(f) (McKinney Supp. 1994).

18. *Id.*

19. N.Y. Mental Hyg. Law § 81.07 (McKinney Supp. 1994).

20. N.Y. Mental Hyg. Law § 81.11(c) (McKinney Supp. 1994).

21. *Compare* N. Y. Surr. Ct. Proc. Act § 1750 (McKinney Supp. 1994) *with* N.Y. Mental Hyg. Law. § 81.15(c) (McKinney Supp. 1994).

22. N. Y. Surr. Ct. Proc. Act § 1751 (McKinney Supp. 1994).

23. N. Y. Surr. Ct. Proc. Act § 1750 (McKinney Supp. 1994).

24. *Id.*

25. *Id.*

26. *See* L. 1992, c. 698, § 4; amended L. 1993, c. 32 § 17, eff. April 1, 1993.

27. *Id.*

28. N.Y. Mental Hyg. Law § 77.03(e) (McKinney 1988).

29. N.Y. Mental Hyg. Law § 7719 (McKinney 1988).

30. N.Y. Mental Hyg. Law § 77.27 (McKinney 1988).

31. N.Y. Mental Hyg. Law § 78.01 (McKinney 1988).

32. N.Y. Mental Hyg. Law § 78.21 (McKinney 1988).

33. N.Y. Mental Hyg. Law § 78.03(2) (McKinney 1988).

34. 42 U.S.C.A. §§ 405(j)(1), 1383(a)(2)(A) (West 1991 & 1992).

35. U.S. Dep't of Health and Human Servs., Social Security Admin., Social Security Handbook §§ 1615, 1616, 1617 (11th ed. 1993) [hereinafter Social Security Handbook].

36. Margaret G. Farrell, *Doing Unto Others: A Proposal for Participatory Justice in Social Security's Representative Payment Program*, 53 U. Pitt. L. Rev. 883, 889 & nn.14 & 15, 890 & n.18 (1992) (citing 1989 S.S.A. Annual Report to Congress 28–31; 1990 S.S.A. Annual Report to Congress 23–26).

37. *Id.* at 889 & nn.14 & 15.

38. SOCIAL SECURITY HANDBOOK, *supra* note 35, at §§ 1604, 1605, 1606.

39. *Id.* at § 1604.

40. *Id.* at § 1607.

41. *Id.* at § 1609.

42. Farrell, *supra* note 36, at 889 & n.17 (citing OFFICE OF RES. AND STATISTICS, SSI REPRESENTATIVE PAYEE MI LISTING (1989).

43. *Id.* at 891–92.

44. SOCIAL SECURITY HANDBOOK, *supra* note 35, at § 1611.

45. *Id.* at § 1611.

46. 14 N.Y.C.R.R. §§ 633.14, 633.15. The New York State Office of Mental Health does not have any similar regulations.

47. 14 N.Y.C.R.R. § 633.14.

48. *Id.*

49. *Id.*

50. 14 N.Y.C.R.R. § 633.15.

51. 14 N.Y.C.R.R. § 633.15.

52. *See, e.g.,* NEW YORK STATE COMMISSION ON QUALITY OF CARE FOR THE MENTALLY DISABLED, EXPLOITING THE VULNERABLE: THE CASE OF HI-LI MANOR HOME FOR THE AGED AND REGULATION BY THE NYS DEPARTMENT OF SOCIAL SERVICES, at xi (May 1992).

16

"Dancing in the Sky Without a Parachute": Sex and Love in Institutional Settings[1]

Susan Stefan, Esq.

Few areas present the apparent tension between promoting autonomy and the duty of protection better than sexuality in institutional settings. Clinicians may see themselves in an intolerable bind: mandated to promote normalization and integration, facing demands for the right to privacy and to sexuality, but at the peril of life-shattering consequences to the client and legal penalty to themselves if choice, autonomy, and normalization result in failure or injury.

In some ways this is a correct perception of contradictory demands by the legal system. Fundamentally, however, like many false dichotomies, the tension may not be inherent in the issue, but in the way we frame it. For example, maximizing choice often requires ensuring a safe environment in which to make choices. Giving people education and training is both an empowering and a protective thing to do, and excessive behavioral controls present obstacles to both autonomy and safety.

> *All institutions that isolate people as social or medical problems have an enormous aversion to dealing with issues of sexuality.*

Currently there are ironclad unwritten rules in most institutions against sex of any kind, and very few written policies to deal with any of the multitude of issues that are raised by sexuality.[2] This is not an issue unique to psychiatric institutions or institutions for persons with mental retardation or developmental disabilities, or to community facilities for people in the mental health system. It is a mistake to think that the desire to prevent institutionalized people from having sex is due solely to their mental disabilities. All institutions that isolate people as social or medical problems have an enormous aversion to dealing with issues of sexuality. Many nursing homes are extremely hostile to any notion of sexuality of their residents, even spouses;[3] there are very few shelters for homeless people where families or couples can stay. Rehabilitation centers for people with serious injuries, especially head injuries, share an aversion with mental institutions to even discussing the sexuality of their residents,[4] as do long-term care hospitals.[5] Many prisons also refuse to acknowledge that sex happens within the prison[6] and deny condoms to prisoners despite the high risk of AIDS.

At the same time, everyone knows that sex happens in institutions and always has.[7] It happens as out-and-out rape,[8] or as sexual molestation short of intercourse by professionals or aides of vulnerable patients of all ages and both sexes and across the spectrum of competence.[9] It happens as a result of fear and coercion, it happens for cigarettes, it happens with people who want attention[10] or are self-destructive or who have really fallen in love with each other[11] or who are lonely or who are clearly not competent to have any idea what is going on at all. Often it happens and institutional authorities don't find out until later, when a male or female resident is found to have venereal disease or a woman becomes pregnant. Sometimes she is many months pregnant before her condition is discovered. I am personally aware of at least four cases where a woman in continuous institutional custody was seven or eight months pregnant or gave birth before there was any official recognition that she was pregnant.[12] Patients have sex with each other;[13] with their visitors,[14] and more often than you might think, staff and professionals have sex with patients.[15] While covert sexual episodes raising serious questions about mutuality and consent occur with some frequency, attempts by patients to have more open and continuing relationships with each other, and expressions of affection between patients such as hand-holding and kissing, tend to be strongly discouraged.[16] Such overt relationships between patients are treated by staff with alarm, and are often actively obstructed.

> *This debate is not about whether there should be sex in mental hospitals: there is sex in mental hospitals. It is about the official policy stance towards what everyone knows already exists.*

It is "don't ask, don't tell" in its most virulent form. I think this is a very good analogy. I often heard this debate framed as one about whether the military should allow gay people in its ranks, which was absurd: the military has had gay people in its ranks as long as it has existed. This debate is not about whether there should be sex in mental hospitals: there is sex in mental hospitals. It is about the official policy stance towards what everyone knows already exists.

The Need for Comprehensive Policies on Issues Pertaining to Sexuality in Institutional Settings

Despite knowing that sex of all kinds is a common occurrence at institutions, very few states or institutions have developed comprehensive policies to deal with the many questions raised by sexuality in an institutional setting.[17] Unwritten customs or policies vary from facility to facility and even ward to ward, and many don't make sense; for example, no sexual contact on the ward, but sexual behavior tolerated and even encouraged on hospital grounds.[18] One institutionalized woman said, "At Illinois State Psychiatric Institute they didn't care what we did, as long as no one got pregnant."[19] While there is substantial literature and at least some thoughtful policy-making in the area of sexuality of persons with mental retardation or developmental disabilities,[20] psychiatric institutions and publications remain more silent.[21] The silence does not mean that sex isn't happening; it means that it is covert and, in all likelihood, coercive and that any beneficial aspects of sexuality are eliminated, while most of the harmful ones go unchecked. Meanwhile, HIV rates at institutions are high and rising.

This current state of affairs is dangerous in every way. It is a breeding ground for irreparable psychological damage, legal liability, and death. Clients caught having sex, or even kissing, are put in seclusion and/or restraints;[22] the parties are separated, one is transferred to another ward,[23] and business goes on as usual. Sex education is rare, contraception is handled badly, and client pregnancies are handled worse. Institutions may try to force abortions on women who don't want them,[24] and women who do want them are prevented from getting them.

In the area of patient sexuality, most sensible solutions require intense involvement, not indifference to danger in the name of maximizing autonomy.

Women who have no business being in institutions are kept there simply because they are pregnant,[25] where they are medicated or restrained. As the HIV rate goes up, very little systematic planning is being done to prepare to care for clients as they become increasingly ill.

Inevitably a crisis happens, a sexual assault that cannot be ignored or covered up because the family finds out or the woman gets pregnant or the attacker is a staff member or is HIV-positive, and reactions are institutionally defensive and protective. A policy is developed during or in the aftermath of disaster. At that point there is an impulse to be draconian, or to argue that nothing could have prevented this, or that it was this patient's fault somehow. If a wooden house caught fire in a neighborhood of wooden houses, city officials could argue that they all had to be torn down, because the whole neighborhood was a fire-

We think about what is a disaster in terms of sex and romance, and what is natural human experience, what exactly do we want to prevent or control, and how does our answer to that question fit with goals of integration and mainstreaming?

trap; or that wooden houses are an expression of the residents' choice, inevitably vulnerable to fire, and nothing could or should be done. City officials could blame the residents for having built or chosen to move into a wooden house (and add that they were probably smoking cigarettes or left the stove on). Ideally, however, officials would try to ensure that houses had sprinkler systems, that the neighborhood had fire hydrants, and perhaps offer to assist in fireproofing the wood as much as possible. I would like to suggest this approach in the area of patient sexuality—most sensible solutions require intense involvement, not indifference to danger in the name of maximizing autonomy. Intense involvement is not synonymous with overcontrol, but rather the kind of involvement that seeks to successfully empower rather than issue futile prohibitions, which are themselves a form of indifference.

In order to come up with policies that prevent disasters from occurring, we actually have to think about all of this—what is a disaster in terms of sex and romance, and what is natural human experience, what exactly do we want to prevent or control, and how does our answer to that question fit with goals of integration and mainstreaming? At all times we must keep ourselves from falling into destructive stereotypes or dichotomies between choice and protection.

A recent case that illustrates the harm of the false dichotomy between choice and protection in the worst possible way was the Glen Ridge, New Jersey case. Jurors had a choice between believing on the autonomy side the defense attorney's presentation of a predatory and promiscuous mentally retarded girl and, on the protection side, the prosecution's image of a girl so incompetent as to be unable to exercise any choice or autonomy at all. Both of these images are repugnant to me. The paradigm is wrong. And that is one of the themes I want to underscore. Too often, we frame policy choices in this way, as though there are only two possible models, neither of which is particularly savory and neither of which ultimately reflects reality—either social reality or the reality of the individuals involved in the situation.

The story in the Glen Ridge case is probably more complex than either the prosecution or defense presented, more uncomfortably familiar to the rest of us. To the extent that it focused on the woman's competence as a trait of hers, inherent in her condition and static, and ignored the interaction between her and the boys as partially determinative of the issue, this framework represented a threshold failure.[26] Questions about sexuality are not about static capacities that people carry around inside themselves. All of these issues, right to treatment and to refuse treatment, but sexual issues in particular, are about interactions between people—not just the people who are or may be having sex, but those people and people like you, or like the prosecutor in the Glen Ridge case. As all of you know from your own personal relationship histories, and as some of you must believe by virtue of your chosen profession, we behave differently in different relationships and our competencies change as we learn and grow. The girl in Glen Ridge may be able to have very different relationships with different people. But the need for relationship, connection, affection—all the needs we all have—is our common ground with the girl in Glen Ridge, and with all of us here today.

The Glen Ridge story, and the hundreds of stories involving disabled people, romance, and sex that occur every day, take place in a broader social context than an overriding focus on disability would suggest. For a mental health professional, clients' primary and overriding identities may be as patients, but for the individuals, the experiences of being black, or a woman, or gay, or Catholic, or Jewish, may be as or more important and determinative than their diagnosis in terms of why they behave the way they do and want the things that they want. The Glen

> *When you look at the raging debates over the meaning of rape and consent and sexuality, and at the rate of divorce, don't be too quick to attribute behaviors of clients to illness or pathology, as opposed to the crazy way that we are all socialized to deal with matters of relationships and sex.*

Ridge case may ultimately be about a girl who agreed to do sexual things with boys so that they would like her better and want to spend time with her. Maybe it was only her disability that attracted our attention, that and the number of boys and the nature of the things they did that attracted society's attention. The essence of that story is going on all the time in junior highs and high schools everywhere, and it has much more to do with interactions between men and women and the meaning of sexuality than it does with disability. When you look at the raging debates over the meaning of rape and consent and sexuality, and at the rate of divorce, don't be too quick to attribute behaviors of clients to illness or pathology, as opposed to the crazy way that we are all socialized to deal with matters of relationships and sex. This socialization is replicated everywhere.

I read a great deal of the writings of people who have been through the mental health system to attempt to understand this issue better. These writings, in striking contrast to the professional literature, show first of all that sex and sexual advances are taken for granted on coed wards, particularly in long-term facilities. They show what few professional writings recognize: people in institutions are lonely. Some are attracted to people who reciprocate their affection, and some pursue and harass people who do not reciprocate at all. Some are very much in love, some want to be reassured, some just want sex.

An atmosphere in which true choice can flourish does not exist naturally in any institution or in the mental health system. It has to be carefully thought through and planned and created.

People are tentative, worried about rejection, very much like you and me. Unlike you and me, they also worry about the effects of psychotropic medication on their ability to make love.[27] Unlike you and me, they worry as adults about getting caught having sex because its consequences hold terror for them: being put in seclusion or restraints,[28] something even parents or police who caught us having sex didn't do. As Huey Freeman described his fear about having a sexual relationship in an institution, "We were dancing in the sky without parachutes."[29]

The goal should be to create an environment in which the exercise of true choice can flourish. Please bear with me while I explain all that I mean by this principle.

Many people may believe that true choice cannot coexist with disability. I believe that a far greater obstacle is that true choice is hard to achieve in an institutional setting. This goal is difficult and may be impossible in the mental health and mental retardation systems as they exist today, with massive imbalances of power and coercion. People who are treated as objects, people who are powerless, people who are not listened to, are people for whom concepts like choice and consent simply add insult to injury. At the same time, people who are members of a group that is in many ways loathed and misunderstood and stigmatized, and people who are often caught in poverty, have absences of choice that come from a larger social system and racism and sexism therein.

Of course, an atmosphere in which true choice can flourish does not exist naturally in any institution or in the mental health system. It has to be carefully thought through and planned and created. The current system, I need hardly tell you, is not a system where true choice can flourish with regard to sex.

So the first thing I would like to urge is to go back and immediately start working on formulating a comprehensive policy regarding these issues. Most institutions and state agencies do not have such policies.[30] It is much better from an administrative, clinical, and legal point of view to have a policy than not to have a policy. If no policy exists, different staff will do different things, people will be confused and lack guidance, exploitation and rape will continue unabated, and it will lower the morale of staff and patients. Clinically, sexuality is so clearly a significant area in the treatment of clients, particularly women clients, that any ongoing progress in treatment could be sabotaged by concurrent events at the hospital. Legally, research has shown that one of the best ways to avoid liability for failing to properly protect clients from rape or assault is to have a thoughtful policy in place and to have followed it.[31] Any honest person in authority in an institutional setting will acknowledge that sexual activity takes place within that setting which is potentially harmful—to know that and not to take steps to address it is just a shortcut to liability.

This policy should be a comprehensive policy, because all of these issues—sexual education, AIDS testing, contraception, sexual and romantic activity—are entirely intertwined. The last thing an administrator wants is a policy that recognizes the right to sexual interaction without having a policy on safety from sexual assault or abuse, or to promulgate a policy on education for normal social and sexual interaction without knowing how staff should react if a client then tries to ask for contraceptives or an AIDS test. Policies must address a minimum of three areas: safety from sexual assault (including a clear prohibition on staff sexual activity with patients); sex and health education (including contraception and sexually transmitted diseases); and sexual expression by patients (including sexual and romantic interactions among patients).

Most of the literature I have read strongly recommends that staff be surveyed about their attitudes and undergo thorough training before any policy is implemented.[32] One of the two points of greatest consensus in every article on this subject is that staff are extremely uncomfortable about discussing sexual issues with clients—much more uncomfortable than the clients are with discussing the issues with staff. In addition, staff often have issues of their own.[33] Education takes place not only during program, but at all times, and staff must be knowledgeable about the policy, and firmly directed that their own values should not interfere with its implementation. This will be easier to achieve if they have been consulted and their concerns heard prior to creating the policy.

Sample State Agency and Institutional Policies

As part of the research for this presentation, I sent out a survey to fifty state directors of mental health agencies requesting any policies they might have, whether agency or institutional, and the results of any research done in this area by their state agency.

Of the thirty-one responses received, most reflected an incomplete approach: California, for instance, has a policy about HIV education for patients, but no other written policy. In some states, such as Ohio, some institutions have policies, but the state agency does not. While Minnesota does not have a written policy, its *Client Handbook*, which appears to be used throughout the state, effectively conveys a policy. South Carolina is working on developing a policy. The state of Texas and the Bangor Mental Health Institute in Maine had developed excellent draft policies, but neither has been officially adopted, and the Texas policy has been rewritten beyond recognition. Two responding states, Nebraska and New York, have developed fairly comprehensive policies on sexuality in institutions.

An atmosphere of true choice is not some kind of Darwinian jungle where the strong "choose" the weak, or where disempowered and neglected people are abandoned to a desolate and optionless world. An atmosphere of true choice is one rich in education and information, abundant with respect for the dignity of all people.

As might be expected, policies vary widely. Predictably, policies about AIDS are far more detailed and comprehensive than policies about sexuality—

either consensual or nonconsensual. Also predictably, institutional policies tended to be more restrictive than state policies. Arizona State Hospital discourages sexual behavior between patients, and "if there is a reason to believe patients have had sexual intercourse, behavioral restrictions will be imposed according to each patient's individual treatment needs and the unit policy."[34] Three state policies, by contrast, appear less punitive. Minnesota's *Client Handbook* advises residents against new sexual relationships or new partners while in the insti-

People are no more safe in an atmosphere where sex is hushed up and not discussed than they are in an atmosphere where it is public and unchecked.

tutional settings, but on the same page informs clients that birth control information and contraception is available to them if they are sexually active. New York requires staff to use "careful thoughtful judgment" about sexual activity involving patients, and advises staff to consider the length of the client's stay in the institution, the client's ability to understand his or her right to consent or refuse to participate in sexual activity, the patient's level of comfort with his or her chosen sexual roles and preferences, the patient's level of knowledge regarding safe and healthy sexual activities, any medical condition the patient may have which has significance in relation to sexual activity, and the objectives of the patient's treatment plan. Nebraska will provide a shared room to married patients, although it prefers to discharge patients who marry, as "'normal' marital routines are difficult to establish in an institutional environment."[35] All three states have fairly comprehensive policies, unifying protection against sexual abuse and education regarding sexually transmitted diseases with a policy that both clarifies that different situations may warrant different responses and gives fairly clear guidance to staff members.

The Three Prerequisites of a Comprehensive Policy

A. Recognizing and Preventing Sexual Assault and Sexual Abuse in Institutional Settings

Writings by psychiatric survivors not only take for granted that consensual sex takes place in institutions, they also assume that sexual assault and molestation is common and is often ignored by staff and by the facility. This is obviously not acceptable. An atmosphere of true choice is not some kind of

Darwinian jungle where the strong "choose" the weak, or where disempowered and neglected people are abandoned to a desolate and optionless world. An atmosphere of true choice is one rich in education and information, abundant with respect for the dignity of all people. It is also an environment where people feel safe. People are no more safe in an atmosphere where sex is hushed up and not discussed than they are in an atmosphere where it is public and unchecked. Many states have statutes that explicitly require reporting physical or sexual abuse against persons with disabilities, yet institutions rarely do this.[36] Institutions should make it a priority to discover and eliminate sexual behavior that is not mutually desired—that is, sexual behavior that is unwanted by one of the parties involved. Too much emphasis has been placed on competence to consent, and insufficient emphasis on whether sexual acts are the result of mutual desire. "Consent" does not mean the sexual contact was desired, only that it is tolerated. In a hierarchical and coercive environment, this is not enough.

People who have been taught that their bodies are objects to be used regardless of their wishes, and who have their powerlessness reinforced by being in an institutional setting, are less likely to fight back or to report unwanted sex, and more likely simply to endure it or even to exchange sex for cigarettes or favored treatment.

Before we even come to the question of whether any form of consensual or mutually desired sexual interaction ought to be officially permitted in the institutional setting, therefore, the crucial first step is to make clear to all that sexual abuse and rape will not be tolerated in the institution; to empower patients to say "no" to unwanted attentions; and to give them reason to report immediately when their refusals are not respected. Policies should require that these reports be promptly investigated and that appropriate preventive, corrective, or disciplinary action be taken to assure the safety of all patients.

This cannot be accomplished simply by fiat or announcement. Many patients in institutions have histories of past sexual abuse, which affect them in a variety of ways. Studies uniformly show that if they are raped again, they will suffer a great deal; studies also show that they are at increased risk of being raped again. People who have been taught that their bodies are objects to be used regardless of their wishes, and who have their powerlessness reinforced by being in an institutional setting, are less likely to fight back or to report unwanted sex, and more likely simply to endure it or even to exchange sex for cigarettes or favored treatment. People who are proud of their bodies do not trade sex for cigarettes. "Simply labeling sex for cigarettes, food, or attention as prostitution or promiscuity often fails to deal with the institution's responsibility to meet the needs being expressed in healthier and nonexploitive ways."[37]

At the same time, women in institutional settings are at increased risk of sexual assault because of the isolation of the settings and their lack of credibility. One article outlined five factors in making women vulnerable to sexual abuse: segregation or isolation, lack of decision-making power, lack of self-esteem, lack of access to support and services available to other women in the community, and poverty. Obviously, people with disabilities are at greater risk of sexual abuse in society than nondisabled people, and people in institutions may well be at greater risk than people in the community.[38] The very fact of being institutionalized helps make a woman more vulnerable to sexual abuse because she realistically recognizes herself as powerless and dependent. She knows that her wishes have no real relationship to her circumstances. Victims of sexual assault are often chosen for being unlikely to resist or to report—institutionalized women clearly fall into these categories.

Administrators may be reluctant to inform the police [of sexual assaults], either because of fear of negative publicity, or because of repeated experiences of investigations ending in yet another decision not to press charges.

This is equally true for many institutionalized men. Men in institutional settings may also have been abused as children or adults,[39] and these experiences can be extremely traumatizing because the stigma associated with homosexuality increases the pressures to keep silent.[40] Gay men are particularly vulnerable to assault.[41] Segregation by sexes in many institutions makes males more subject to assault, and similar disincentives for reporting exist.

It is not simply the powerlessness of the patients that impedes reporting of sexual abuse. *All* the incentives are against reporting. Patients may not perceive the experience as abuse; it may be the only way to get attention. Paradoxically, those who do report may be perceived as problems, as manipulative, as seeking attention, out of touch with reality, may be retaliated against, or viewed as problems by the staff. Patients may not perceive that reporting will improve their situation and may be afraid it will just make things worse.

Staff may want to protect each other, feeling more loyal to other staff than to administrators or patients. They, like the patients, may fear retaliation from other staff or from administration if they report. They may realistically think nothing will come of it. They may be uncertain as to exactly what is not tolerated and what should be let go, what is discretionary and what is not.

Administrators may be reluctant to inform the police, either because of fear of negative publicity, or because of repeated experiences of investigations ending in yet another decision not to press charges.

What can be done to make an institutional environment more safe, and to diminish the threat of sexual assault? First, have a policy that addresses this issue. Requiring administrators, professionals, staff, family members, and clients to sit down together and discuss this issue will probably illuminate many of the issues to be addressed. Second, ensure that staff are trained and sensitized to this issue. Perhaps one specific female staff member should be designated on each ward that has women patients. This increases the chances of knowing which women have histories of sexual abuse. In addition, incoming histories of all patients should include questions about sexual abuse, phrased in ways that are likely to elicit accurate responses. Obviously, staff must be prepared to work with patients who disclose histories of sexual abuse on these issues, not merely note it in the charts and ignore it. Some people don't talk about these kinds of issues right away; staff should be alert to this and prepared to work with the individuals if the issues come up later. Women desperately need to talk about what happened to them and be listened to sympathetically. Administrators and psychiatrists should probably not rely completely on standard training in this area. Many places have rape crisis centers or shelters for battered women. It wouldn't hurt to talk to some survivors about what would most help them. Staff who are sensitized are more likely to be trusted by patients who may report more to them.

Of course, any sexual contact by any staff person with any patient is sexual assault, and reported or observed contact should be immediately investigated in accordance with already promulgated procedures. If substantiated to the satisfaction of the administration with an appropriate protective process for the employee,[42] the first incident of sexual assault or abuse should be grounds for immediate dismissal, of professional staff as well as of aides. Administrators may wish to ask Protection and Advocacy representatives, or some other outside group, to conduct investigations. Policies should address the circumstances under which incidents will be reported to the local police or sheriffs. Administrators and mental health professionals alike should understand state reporting requirements of abuse of vulnerable populations, which vary from state to state, and follow them to the letter. This may require explaining to the patient that you have no choice in reporting the staff member's abuse, but will stand by her every step of the way in the investigation.

Another way of preventing sexual abuse, as suggested above, is to empower clients to say no. Institutions may want to form groups around this issue; local women's organizations and rape crisis centers may be helpful in this regard. Many institutions have gymnasiums or places for clients to exercise; self-defense classes could be taught. Many women have commented on the positive effect of such classes on their psychological health.

The chief problem is not a struggle to understand the difference between consensual sex and rape, or the result of good faith efforts to increase autonomy, but simply indifference to repeated warnings, requests for help, and manifest peril.

The institution or agency can promulgate policies that prohibit male aides from being alone with female clients, whether they are doing checks of women in seclusion or restraints, taking them to appointments, or are alone on the ward at night.

Finally, the agency or institution can keep records of reports of sexual assaults and review them to see if there are patterns involving time, place, victim, alleged offender, or method of assault that suggest ways of preventing future incidents. Reading both ex-patient literature and a substantial number of cases suggests that the chief problem is not a struggle to understand the difference between consensual sex and rape, or the result of good faith efforts to increase autonomy, but simply indifference to repeated warnings, requests for help, and manifest peril.

Some people who sexually assault patients—usually low-level staff—get caught and the agency gets sued, or the perpetrator is turned in for criminal prosecution. There have been a number of cases recently brought about by sexually assaulted patients. Let us see what they teach us about what is going on in institutional settings, and what the courts are requiring. The following cases were selected because they represent a typical sample of a large number of cases.

Sumblin v. Craven County Hospital Corporation, 357 SE2d 376 (N.C.App. 1987) involved a woman patient who was harassed for days by a male patient (Gerald). She complained to the nurses; and her family, who visited her and witnessed the molestations, also complained to the nurses. Gerald never raped

Edith Sumblin: the complaint charged that he fondled her and grabbed her legs. When the hospital tried to get her complaint dismissed on the grounds that she had not presented expert testimony on the standard of care in the profession usually required in malpractice cases, the court rejected the argument, stating that a "hospital, much like the proprietor of any public facility, owes a duty to invitees to protect the patient against foreseeable assaults by another patient." The court decided that no special skill was required to protect Edith Sumblin, and that it was up to the jury to decide whether hospital personnel acted as reasonably prudent persons under the circumstances.

In *Alphonso v. Charity Hospital*, 413 So.2d 982 (La.App. 1982), the patient was raped twice; during the first episode she was heavily sedated and unable to struggle very much; the second time she screamed and hospital employees caught her attacker, a patient known to be a "deranged sexual deviant," in the act. The hospital also negligently allowed the rapist—who apparently was not prosecuted—to discover her home address, and to send her a letter at her home threatening to rape her, whereupon she slashed most of her body with a razor to make herself unattractive to him.

> *Many of the people perceived as extremely disabled can convey their distress about unwanted sexual activity in starkly clear terms.*

In most of these cases, the complainant has either complained before, usually repeatedly, or multiple clients have complained. For example, an EEG technician at a state hospital sexually molested at least six women patients.[43] Although the women were medicated before the EEG to "help them relax" and were necessarily recumbent with wires attached to their heads, the court found that two of the women had "willingly accepted" his advances and acquitted him as to those charges.

There are two points to be made here: protection against sexual abuse and assault needs to be established, and fears about confusion between consensual sexual activity and assault—often cited to explain the denial of the right of voluntary sexual activity—are not supported by case law or by the literature. Many of the people perceived as extremely disabled can convey their distress about unwanted sexual activity in starkly clear terms.[44]

B. PROMOTING RESPONSIBILITY AND HEALTH IN SEXUAL ACTIVITY

1. Education

Sexuality is a part of almost everyone's life, including almost every individual in the mental health system. An institutional program that purports to prepare people to be reintegrated in the community and ignores issues of relationships and sexuality is leaving out a huge and vital aspect of a person's life. Psychotropic medication has effects that relate to sexuality, including decreasing sexual desire, impotence, and retarded or premature ejaculation.[45] Even the most conservative authors I read appear to agree unanimously that it is essential to provide information and education on issues such as the effects of medication on sexual functioning, various methods of contraception, and the risk factors for AIDS and other sexually transmitted diseases, as well as information regarding health issues such as menopause, the need for certain medical tests such as Pap smears, and the reactions that patients may have to them. Other information in educational programs include discussions about

An institutional program that purports to prepare people to be reintegrated in the community and ignores issues of relationships and sexuality is leaving out a huge and vital aspect of a person's life.

rape, homosexuality, and sexual values, such as the right to say no discussed in the previous section. All patients should receive full information about sexually transmitted diseases, in contexts where they can feel free to ask questions, and in written materials as well as orally. Much of this information may be vital to protect the patient and others who interact with him or her. To ignore it risks ignoring a crucial part of the patient's life, in many different ways.

Once information is provided, however, it will probably raise issues with a number of clients that will call for sensitivity and listening: issues of the impact of religious beliefs on contraception; issues involving appropriate social roles and behavior. Most importantly, information about contraceptives and sexually transmitted diseases may lead to requests for contraceptives or for testing.

2. Contraceptives

Most of the policies that have been submitted in response to my survey make it clear that contraceptives should be available to the institutionalized individual. At the same time, the way to obtain condoms, for example, is almost universally to ask a nurse or staff member. Some institutions have them available at the nurse's station. These practices create needless barriers to patients' access to and use of condoms. Condoms are a relatively inexpensive item and should be available for free in men's and women's bathrooms.

3. Testing

If the client wishes, tests for HIV seropositivity should be available. These might be conducted by an outside party under strict confidentiality, but obviously they should not be conducted on any client without his or her knowledge or consent unless there are extremely strong indications that the client may have AIDS.

Almost every state has extremely detailed laws and/or policies regarding AIDS testing, and these vary considerably from state to state. Of all areas discussed here, AIDS testing is the one where an administrator is least likely to be writing on a clean slate, and any policies regarding testing should be compared to preexisting policies or law to determine whether current practice is the result of unwritten custom, policies that could be changed, or state legislative requirements.

Condoms are a relatively inexpensive item and should be available for free in men's and women's bathrooms.

4. Protecting Privacy

One of the most frequent complaints in ex-patient writings about hospitalization, especially the writings of women, is the unmet need for privacy and solitude. Since most institutions require clients to share rooms, it is possible for an individual to be institutionalized and never have a moment away from others at any point in the day.

Privacy is more than having a place to go away from the noise and away from other people that is not a seclusion room. Privacy includes not receiving shots in the buttocks in full view of other staff or residents. Privacy includes knocking on doors to clients' rooms.

The concern to provide people with space, quietness, and solitude goes beyond the concerns raised by this article. I believe the absence of privacy is one of the most destructive aspects of institutional life, and its presence is crucial to providing any kind of support to a distressed or disturbed person. The absence of privacy is one of the most prevalent sources of unhappiness and frustration of institutionalized people, and must be addressed for a variety of reasons. One of the reasons for its absence is the pervasive concern with preventing sexual encounters—it should be a priority to meet all reasonable concerns about safety while still providing privacy.

C. THE RIGHT TO SEXUAL EXPRESSION AND VOLUNTARY SEXUAL ACTIVITY

Historically, issues pertaining to patient sexuality were simplified, at least at a theoretical level: all sexual behavior was viewed as dangerous to the mental health of a psychiatric patient because of its potential to stimulate or prolong regression.[46] This attitude has essentially continued to this day, and may have intensified since concerns have been raised over transmission of AIDS. The most progressive literature cur-

> *The most controversial question is whether sexual or romantic relationships between patients, or patients and someone on the outside, will be officially recognized and permitted by institutions, and under what circumstances, and with what limitations.*

rently available involves "permitting" emotional or romantic relationships between some patients (although precluding any physical expression of such a relationship).

The theoretical position that no sexual behavior was to be permitted at all extended to forbidding masturbation, even in private, forbidding any sign of affection between patients, including holding hands or kissing, both of which have been punished quite severely,[47] and maintaining a vast silence about sexual concerns of hospitalized people.

A policy about sexuality in an institutional setting must acknowledge all people as sexual beings, whose sexuality is not shed when they come through the institutional gates. Masturbation should be allowed in private, and simply not permitted in public.[48]

The most controversial question, however, is whether sexual or romantic relationships between patients, or patients and someone on the outside, will be officially recognized and permitted by institutions, and under what circumstances, and with what limitations.

Two things need to be remembered in considering this question: no one is suggesting that institutions bless or condone or permit all sexual relationships between all patients, no matter what; and no one should be suggesting that sex doesn't happen right now on a continuing basis in institutional settings.

One possible attitude is that no institution is a perfect place, mistakes happen, and any time sex occurs in an institutional setting, a mistake has happened which must be prevented from happening again, if at all possible. That is the position taken by many professionals, apparently on the grounds that either sex is always bad for the patients, or at least potentially bad enough that it is not worth taking the chance to see how it turns out.

I am extremely sensitive to the complications raised by a right to sex in a population of women, where the majority of whom have suffered sexual abuse. And I think these must always be remembered in formulating any policy about voluntary and consensual sex. But on the other hand, I don't believe that women who have been raped can never again engage in pleasurable and consensual sex. I don't believe that sex that is engaged in for mixed-up reasons by confused or depressed people should necessarily be banned, or else a lot of us would lead very different kinds of lives. Most of all, the time I have spent around institutions convinces me that a professional who bans sex, but is perfectly willing to have the same patients spend all day long in bed, as long as they are alone, or in a stupor on medication that has wiped out any ability to act at all, or to have patients watch television all day long without saying a word to anyone, is more concerned about order on the ward than the well-being of the people in his or her care. I have a hard time believing that people who spend their days and nights in bed alone are doing better than those who are having consensual sex with each other. Therefore, I am open to the possibility of voluntary, mutually desired sex being permitted institutionally.

When it is suggested that sexual activity be permitted in an institutional setting, or even in a supervised community setting, one of the first issues raised is the question of how to judge the competence of consent. For a variety of reasons, I would like to suggest to you that the consent standard is not the best standard to follow.

Sexuality and love in institutions present excruciatingly difficult questions. There are no easy answers. The only easy thing to know is that failing to address these questions is not the answer.

There is particular reason to be concerned about the consent of an institutionalized woman, not only because of its competence, but because of its voluntariness. As I suggested above, it is not unreasonable to be concerned that an institutionalized woman may have a history of sexual abuse, and studies link past sexual abuse to vulnerability for future sexual abuse. In institutions, as in families, women may feel that they have nowhere to go, nowhere to hide, no way to say no. Institutionalized women are likely to be relatively disempowered regarding their right to say no to unwanted sexual advances. So I would suggest a standard that any sexual interaction, including kissing, be mutually desired. I think this standard is more sensitive to some of the real concerns here than a competence standard, which would inevitably import value judgments about the wisdom of the relationship, and since many relationships are unwise, many women would undoubtedly be found incompetent to consent to protect them from their own folly in wanting to pursue a relationship with a man who might cause them considerable pain.

Even if clients are mutually desiring of a relationship, the institution's legal duty to protect clients would justify a requirement that individuals involved in such relationships be willing to be tested for sexually transmitted diseases, and to disclose the results of those tests to each other, if state law permits the institution or agency to impose such conditions. Each state will have different laws, and agencies or administrators wishing to explore the possibilities suggested here should consult with attorneys familiar with the laws in their own state.

Sexuality and love in institutions present excruciatingly difficult questions. There are no easy answers. The only easy thing to know is that failing to address these questions is not the answer.

Endnotes

1. For this description of a sexual relationship in a mental institution, I am indebted to HUEY FREEMAN, JUDGE, JURY AND EXECUTIONER 172 (1986).

2. For a discussion of some of the policies that do exist, *see infra* pp. 8–9.

3. *See* James R. McCartney et al., *Sexuality and the Institutionalized Elderly*, 35 J. AM. GERIATRICS SOC'Y 331 (1987).

4. Stanley Ducharme & Kathleen Gill, *Sexual Values, Training, and Professional Roles*, 5 J. HEAD TRAUMA REHAB. 38, 39 (1990).

5. Andre Dupras & Marie-Sylvie Poissant, *The Fear of Sexuality in Residents of a Long-Term Care Hospital*, 8 SEXUALITY & DISABILITY, Winter 1987, at 203.

6. *See, e.g.*, Angela Davis, *Angela Davis: An Autobiography, in* BEARING WITNESS: SELECTIONS FROM AFRICAN-AMERICAN AUTOBIOGRAPHY IN THE TWENTIETH CENTURY 204–207 (Henry L. Gates, Jr. ed., 1991).

7. My support for this statement includes innumerable accounts by psychiatric survivors of sex in institutional settings, a startling number of criminal, malpractice and constitutional cases arising out of rape in institutional settings (only a tiny fraction of which must be reported), as well as many honest accounts by professionals in the literature. All of these will be cited as appropriate throughout the rest of this piece.

8. Nieson Himmel, *Rape Suspect with AIDS Virus Held in Attempted Murder Case*, L. A. TIMES, Sept. 11, 1987, at 42 (male patient booked on criminal charges after he sexually attacked a fellow woman patient at County-USC Medical Center "mental ward"); Alphonso v. Charity Hospital, 413 So.2d 982 (La.App. 1982); Porter v. Michigan Osteopathic Hospital Association, 428 N.W.2d 719 (Mich.App. 1988); BRIAN PALMER, ALL THAT HELL ALLOWS, PART II 85, 164 (1993); Alameda County v. Superior Court, 239 Cal.Rptr. 400 (Cal.App. 1987); State v. Mickelson, 848 P.2d 677 (Utah App. 1992).

9. In using the word "patient," I have no desire to offend individuals who consider themselves survivors of the psychiatric system, or those who feel that they are consumers of mental health services. I myself prefer "institutionalized person" or "person in the mental health system" as descriptive and relatively neutral, but they have proven too cumbersome in this essay. I am dissatisfied with all of these terms: "consumer" and "client" do not have the

connotations of coercion and powerlessness that I believe are at the heart of the mental health system; "survivor" does not reflect the benefit that many people testify they have received from mental health treatment. "Patient" is the default winner, in part because of the extensive literature pointing out many commonalities of powerlessness between all patients. Only a few of these are JAY KATZ, THE SILENT WORLD OF DOCTOR AND PATIENT (1984); WILLIAM MAY, THE PATIENT'S ORDEAL (1991); and GEORGE ANNAS, JUDGING MEDICINE (1988).

Source material concerning rape in institutions includes FREEMAN, *supra* note 1, at 157; Dian Cox Leighton, *Being Mentally Ill in America: One Female's Experience, in* TREATING CHRONICALLY MENTALLY ILL WOMEN 63, 66 (Carol Nadelson & Leona Bachrach eds., 1988); PALMER, *supra* note 8, at 164. Many of the principal cases about the right to be free from injury involve young retarded men who were sexually abused, *Shaw by Strain v. Strackhouse,* 920 F.2d 1135 (3rd Cir. 1990); P.C. v. McLaughlin, 913 F.2d 1033 (2nd Cir. 1990). *See also Jackson v. Fort Stanton Hospital and Training School,* 757 F.Supp. 1243, 1275 (D.N.M. 1990) (citing sexual assault by unknown perpetrator resulting in death) rev'd in part, 964 F.2d 980 (10th Cir. 1992), and other cases cited in Susan Stefan, *Leaving Civil Rights to the "Experts": From Deference to Abdication under the Professional Judgement Standard,* 102 YALE L. J. 639, 663 n.113 (1992).

10. Peter Hartocollis, *Hospital Romances: Some Vicissitudes of Transference,* 28 BULL. MENNINGER CLINIC 62 (1964).

11. R. Morgan & Joan Rogers, *Some Results of Integrating Men and Women Patients in a Mental Hospital,* 6 Soc. PSYCHIATRY 113 (1971) (This British hospital study notes that of 506 patients admitted in a five-year period, 18% had relationships with other patients; four marriages occurred, three of which the authors judge as "so far childless but otherwise successful."). *Id.* at 115.

12. Two of these cases were in Chicago, *Rep. Bowman Vows Full Probe of Patient Abuse,* CHI. SUN-TIMES, May 17, 1988 (infant found dead in toilet bowl after being born to woman at Chicago Read Mental Health Center and belated discovery that mentally retarded woman was 7½ months pregnant). There was also one case in Texas and one in Montana.

13. Sanz v. Commonwealth of Puerto Rico, 535 F.Supp. 330 (D. Puerto Rico 1982).

14. SUSANNA KAYSEN, GIRL INTERRUPTED 65 (1993).

15. The New York State Commission on Quality of Care for the Mentally Disabled found that complaints of sexual abuse by clients of the mental health system involved aides or direct care staff more than twice as often as other patients. While most of the attention in this area has gone to cases involving sexual relations between patient and therapist in an outpatient setting, inpatient cases alleging rape and sexual abuse are increasing dramatically.

16. DOUG CAMERON, HOW TO SURVIVE BEING COMMITTED TO A MENTAL HOSPITAL: A TRUE STORY 44 (Vantage Press 1980).

17. The two most common observations in the literature that I read were the discomfort of institutional staff with sexual issues and the absence of clear institutional guidelines or policies for dealing with sexual situations. It seems clear that if staff feel especially uncomfortable about a set of issues, they are in particular need of clear guidelines and policies, and that the absence of clear guidelines and policies can only intensify discomfort.

18. D. Civic et al., *Staff Perspectives on Sexual Behavior of Patients in State Psychiatric Hospital*, 44 HOSP. & COMM'Y PSYCHIATRY 887 (1993).

19. FREEMAN, *supra* note 1, at 174.

20. I have surveyed the field fairly extensively, and oddly enough, there is far more literature regarding the sexuality of mentally retarded and developmentally disabled people than people who are labelled mentally ill. There are more policies, they are more thoughtful, and there are more training programs and educational videos.

21. Virtually the only journal to publish articles regarding this issue is HOSP. & COMM'Y PSYCHIATRY, as can be seen from many of the citations herein.

22. *See* CAMERON, *supra* note 16, at 44; FREEMAN, *supra* note 1, at 183. The accounts of the psychiatric survivors are corroborated by the professionals' accounts of their reactions to discovering sex between patients. Sometimes patients who simply become close friends are separated because of the suspicion of a sexual relationship, JANET GOTKIN & PAUL GOTKIN, TOO MUCH ANGER, TOO MANY TEARS: A PERSONAL TRIUMPH OVER PSYCHIATRY (1992).

23. FREEMAN, *supra* note 1, at 183.

24. LeFebvre v. North Broward General Hospital, 566 So.2d 568 (Fla. App 1990).

25. *See* cases cited in Susan Stefan, *Whose Egg Is it Anyway? Reproductive Rights of Incarcerated, Institutionalized and Incompetent Women*, 13 Nova L. Rev. 405, 443–447 (1989).

25. *See* Susan Stefan, *Silencing the Different Voice: Competence, Feminist Theory and Law*, 47 U. Miami L. Rev. 763 (1993).

27. Freeman, *supra* note 1, at 159.

23. *Id.*

29. *Id.* at 172.

30.   Paul Abramson et al., *Sexual Expression of Mentally Retarded People: Educational and Legal Implications*, 93 Am. J. on Mental Retard'n 328, 331 (1988). New York and Nebraska are two of the few states in the country that do have policies about sexuality in institutions. These policies show thoughtfulness and sensitivity that surely comes from many, many hours of struggling with these difficult issues. I might have drafted a different policy, but those policies meet many of the basic prerequisites which I will outline today. Other states have so far indicated that they have no comprehensive policies on sexuality in institutional settings.

31. Camille LeGrand, *Mental Hospital Regulation and the Safe Environment: Liability for Sexual Assault*, 12 L. Med. & Health Care, Dec. 1984, at 236.

32. Stephen Wolfe & Walter Menninger, *Fostering Open Communications about Sexual Concerns in a Mental Hospital*, 24 Hosp. & Comm'y Psychiatry 147 (1973); Donald Cohen & Richard Tannenbaum, *Sexuality Education for Staff in Long-Term Psychiatric Hospitals*, 36 Hosp. & Comm'y Psychiatry 187 (1985).

33. Gail Richert & Robert A. Canosa, *Sexuality Education in a Partial-Hospitalization Program*, 2 Int'l J. Partial Hosp'n 301, 303–305 (1984); Abramson et al., *supra* note 30, at 331.

34. Ariz. State Hosp. Policy #NSG-I-116. The effective date of the policy is Aug. 21, 1985, and it was last reviewed and revised on Sept. 8, 1993.

35. Neb. Dep't of Pub. Institutions II-A-3(E)(2)(Mar. 15, 1985).

36. In one case in Florida, *Doe v. Walker*, No. 83-1154-7 (Fla.Cir.Ct.Pinellas County, filed July 6, 1987)(second amended complaint), a hospital barred investigating police from the crime scene and prevented them from talking to the victim or to witnesses. The woman collected $450,000 after a week-

long jury trial, and two hospital administrators pleaded no contest to charges of obstructing justice. Stefan, *supra* note 25, at 429 n. 103.

37. Maureen Crossmaker, *Behind Locked Doors—Institutional Sexual Abuse*, 9 Sexuality & Disability, Fall 1991, at 209.

38. It is difficult to draw conclusions about this issue because of the extreme disincentives to report sexual abuse and molestation in institutional settings, and because very few studies are done to document such abuse. For an exception, *see* Judith Musick, *Patterns of Institutional Sexual Assault*, 7 Resp. Violence Fam. & Sexual Assault No. 3, May/June 1984.

39. While substantially more hospitalized women than men have histories of sexual or physical abuse, fifteen percent of hospitalized men reported histories of abuse. Trudy Mills et al., *Hospitalization Experiences of Victims of Abuse*, 9 Victimology 436, 439 (1985). In another study, twenty percent of institutionalized males reported sexual abuse as a child or adult, compared with about sixty percent of the women. Andrea Jacobsen et al., *The Failure of Routine Assessments to Detect Histories of Assault Experienced by Psychiatric Patients*, 38 Hosp. & Comm'y Psychiatry 386, 388 (1987).

40. Craig L. Anderson, *Males as Sexual Assault Victims: Multiple Levels of Trauma*, *in* Homosexuality & Psychotherapy: A Practitioner's Handbook of Affirmative Models (John C. Gonsiorek ed., Haworth Press 1982).

41. *Id.*

42. It is critical to the success of any attempt to eliminate sexual abuse in institutions that staff members know clearly what is expected of them if an individual reports or witnesses sexual abuse, as well as to know what to expect if they are accused of abuse. The policy on sexual abuse must spell out what constitutes abuse. Rules must be clearly written, be perceived by staff as objective and fair, and must target observable behaviors. If staff do not believe that these rules are enforced fairly as to them, the goal of enhanced reporting by staff will not be met.

43. State v. Tonzola, 621 A.2d 243 (Vt. 1992).

44. State v. Mickelson, 848 P.2d 677, 682 (Utah App. 1992)(nursing home resident with senile dementia, organic brain disease, and other severely disabling conditions "emotionally distraught" after sexual molestation); Salsman v. Commonwealth, 565 SW2d 638 (Ky.App. 1978).

45. Richert & Canosa, *supra* note 33, at 302; Salman Akhtar & J. Anderson Thomson, Jr., *Schizophrenia and Sexuality: A Review and Report of Twelve Unusual Cases—Part I*, 41 J. Clinical Psychiatry, Apr. 1980, at 168–171.

46. Cohen & Tannenbaum, *supra* note 32, at 187.

47. Wolfe & Menninger, *supra* note 32, at 150 (two teenagers caught kissing in a hallway were each restricted to their rooms for one full day).

48. Civic et al., *supra* note 18, at 887 (reports lack of privacy as a hindrance to patient's ability to masturbate in private).

17

"Equal Treatment" and "Special Treatment": Considerations in ADA Implementation

Ira A. Burnim, Esq.

My workshop was billed as a "practical" one. But I would like to address the issue of "equal treatment" and "special treatment" from a perspective that is perhaps "impractical," being as much philosophical as it is legal. My thesis is that in our advocacy work we pay too little attention to a central issue: Do we want society to treat people with mental disabilities "like everyone else," or do we want society to treat them differently from everyone else? This question has profound implications for our strategies for promoting the freedom, independence, and integration into society of

> *Do we want society to treat people with mental disabilities "like everyone else," or do we want society to treat them differently from everyone else?*

people with mental disabilities. It is also at the heart of our difficulty in addressing issues about *Choice & Responsibility*, the theme of the conference.

In our discussions about choice and responsibility, we often find ourselves asking: What is the relevance, from the perspective of law and public policy, of the fact that a person has or is labeled as having a mental disability? We tend to respond in two seemingly contradictory ways. On the one hand, we often say that mental disability is irrelevant and that persons with mental disabilities[1] should be treated like everyone else. They should enjoy the same rights and be under no legal constraints merely because they have a mental disability. On the other hand, we often insist that disability status is relevant and demand special accommodations or protections for people with mental disabilities.

When we seek equal treatment, we usually rely on one of two reasons. Sometimes we say that it is illegitimate to label someone as having a mental illness or a mental disability, and thus illegitimate to have any legal scheme take into account a person's status as a person with a mental disability. More often, we assert that a person's having a mental disability does not justify society's treating that person differently with respect to his or her fundamental rights. The equal treatment line of thinking informs the views of many consumers and disability lawyers on such critical issues as forced treatment and civil commitment. It also informs their advocacy for "community placement." At the core of our opposition to forced medication is the notion that competent people with mental disabilities should have the right to refuse medical care, including medication, just like everyone else. At the heart of opposition to civil commitment is the idea that people with mental disabilities should not be confined against their will unless they commit a crime, just like everyone else. In particular, they should not be confined based on a prediction or likelihood that they will act dangerously in the future. Our society, we assert, does not permit other people to be confined on the basis of such a prediction or likelihood; people with mental disabilities should not be treated differently.[2] Similarly, our commitment to "community placement" is based, in large measure, on the view that people with mental disabilities have the right to live in the community and participate in society, just like everyone else.

> *At the heart of opposition to civil commitment is the idea that people with mental disabilities should not be confined against their will unless they commit a crime, just like everyone else.*

The Americans with Disabilities Act (ADA) incorporates the notion of equal treatment. It forbids discrimination—that is, different treatment—based on one's status as a person with a mental disability. It outlaws a variety of policies and practices that amount to "people with mental disabilities need not apply."

The ADA thus attempts to remedy the myriad ways that people with mental disabilities are subjected to discrimination. In only the last several months, we at the Bazelon Center have used the ADA to address the following forms of unequal treatment:

- In some states, people with mental disabilities are denied the right to vote, regardless of their legal competence.
- In some states, people with mental disabilities are not allowed to participate in public programs that provide attendant care services. It does not matter whether or not they require such services; only people with physical disabilities get attendant care services. In some states,

people with physical disabilities who require attendant care services because of their physical disabilities are ineligible solely because they also have mental disabilities.

- An individual working as a merchant marine was recently denied a renewal of his license because of a history of mental illness. The Coast Guard made no effort to determine whether the individual was qualified to work as a merchant marine and was unmoved by the fact that the individual's employer was both satisfied with his work and wanted to keep him on.

- Pursuant to a policy sanctioned by Judge, now Justice, Breyer, *Ward v. Skinner*, 943 F2d 157 (1st Cir. 1991), *cert. denied*, 112 S.Ct. 1558 (1992), the Department of Transportation denies commercial licenses to drive a truck to people with epilepsy who take medication. The Department of Transportation will not consider the fact that an individual's seizures are controlled by medication.

- People are denied homeowner's insurance and driver's insurance merely because they have mental disabilities. These denials are made without knowledge of and without regard to individuals' actual capacities and the actual risks, if any, of insuring them. We once received a call from someone denied a driver's license because, in the course of his work, he used his car to transport people with mental disabilities.

Much of what is most offensive about society's treatment of people with mental disabilities would be remedied if people with mental disabilities were treated like everyone else.

- Several states deny people drivers' licenses merely because of a history of mental illness. Again, these denials are made without knowledge of and without regard to individuals' actual capacities and the risks, if any, from their driving.

- A state's Department of Social Services threatened to revoke a woman's license to provide day care in her home because she sometimes permitted her daughter, who had mental retardation, to assist her by reading to and playing with the children. DSS cited a regulation that child care workers be of "sound health and mind."

- Applications for licenses to practice law or medicine are denied when applicants refuse to answer questions about mental health treatment. There are no questions on the application about other aspects of applicants' health care.

As this litany demonstrates, the principle of equal treatment enshrined in the ADA is critically important. Much of what is most offensive about society's treatment of people with mental disabilities would be remedied if people with mental disabilities were treated like everyone else. The principle that people's mental disabilities are irrelevant and should not be a basis for treating them differently, if comprehensively applied, would end many of the practices that result in the denial of equal citizenship and full participation in society.

But there is a hitch. There are problems with the idea that in formulating law and public policy, disability status should be irrelevant. There are many rules and practices of government agencies, the workplace, and the world of commerce that, when applied without regard to disability status, operate to disadvantage and exclude people with mental disabilities. The rules were written and the practices were developed by and for people without mental disabilities. They may work well for everyone else, but for people with mental disabilities, they create innumerable barriers to enjoyment of government services and equal participation in society.

There are problems with the idea that in formulating law and public policy, disability status should be irrelevant. There are rules and practices of government agencies, the workplace, and the world of commerce that operate to disadvantage and exclude people with mental disabilities.

A classic example is the way in which governments run many public assistance programs. The application process is hard to navigate. Applications must be made in person and only at limited times and locations. The locations are crowded and noisy. Little assistance is available. These conditions discourage many applicants, but they have an especially devastating impact on applicants with a mental disability, many of whom are incapable, without some accommodation, of successfully completing the application process. Another example are workplaces' inflexible policies concerning work schedules or unpaid leave. Often, such policies prevent people with mental disabilities from securing or maintaining employment.

To deal with the fact that in the worlds of government and commerce the standard way of doing things may have the effect of disadvantaging or excluding people with mental disabilities, we have imposed through the ADA an obligation on government to make "reasonable modifications" in its programs and activities and an obligation on employers to make "reasonable accommodations" in the workplace.[3] Both of these sets of obligations are far-reaching. A state or local government[4] under the ADA may not provide an individual with a disability:

- an opportunity to participate in or benefit from [an] aid, benefit, or service that is not equal to that afforded others;[5] or,
- an aid, benefit, or service that is not as effective in affording equal opportunity to obtain the same result, to gain the same benefit, or to reach the same level of achievement as that provided to others.[6]

It is also unlawful for a state or local government agency to impose or apply eligibility criteria that tend to screen out an individual with a disability, or any class of individuals with a disability, from fully and equally enjoying any service, program, or activity being offered.[7]

To avoid these outcomes, state and local government must make "reasonable modifications in policies, practices, or procedures."[8] There is only one limitation on government's obligation to make "reasonable modifications." A public entity need not make a modification, even when that modification is required to provide a person with a mental disability equal access or an equal benefit, if the public entity "can demonstrate that making the modifications

In government and commerce the standard way of doing things may have the effect of disadvantaging or excluding people with mental disabilities, thus we have imposed through the ADA an obligation to make "reasonable modifications" and "reasonable accommodations."

would fundamentally alter the nature of the service, program, or activity."[9] A "fundamental alteration" is a modification that is so significant that it alters the essential nature of the goods, services, facilities, privileges, advantages, or accommodations being offered.[10]

The Bazelon Center, under a grant from the U.S. Department of Justice, is directing a project in South Carolina aimed at identifying "reasonable modifications" that need to be made in public assistance programs. The project is developing a model process for identifying needed modifications, as well as a checklist of modifications that public agencies should consider. The project is a collaboration among consumers, family groups, the protection and advocacy agency, the state public welfare agency, and the state mental health department. The project has identified the following modifications to afford people with mental disabilities equal opportunity to access public assistance programs:

- flexible scheduling, including: avoiding early morning appointments (which are often difficult for people taking medication), permitting breaks during application and interview appointments, and allowing extra time to complete forms and gather documentation;
- assistance in keeping appointments and completing forms, including: having staff make reminder calls, make follow-up calls and visits if an appointment is missed, and make home visits if necessary to complete the application process; and providing information brochures and application forms worded in plain language and available in alternate formats (e.g., audio cassette, Braille, large print);

The only limit on an employer's obligation to make an "accommodation" is that the requested accommodation be "reasonable." This means that it must not impose an "undue hardship" on the employer.

- environmental modifications, including: reducing noise, using partitions and room dividers to minimize distractions and enhance privacy, and improving ventilation and lighting;
- education of staff about the strengths and needs of individuals with mental illness; and,
- education of consumers and family groups about available services, activities, and programs for individuals with mental illness and about the requirements of the ADA.

Employers are required to pay similar attention to the needs of people with mental disabilities. The ADA requires that employers make "reasonable accommodations" to enable a person with a mental disability to secure and hold a job.[11] "Reasonable accommodations" include:

- modifications or adjustments to the job application process that enable an applicant with a disability to be considered for a position;[12] and,
- modifications or adjustments to the work environment, or to the manner or circumstances under which the position held or desired is customarily performed, that enable an individual with a disability to perform the essential functions of the position.[13]

The types of modifications required are extensive. According to ADA regulations, they include not only making a workplace physically accessible, but also: job restructuring, part-time or modified work schedules, reassignment to a vacant position (when the person with a disability must be relieved permanently or temporarily from the person's current position), acquisition or modifications of equipment or devices, and appropriate adjustment or modifications of examinations, training materials, and policies.[14] Other types of accommodations that have proved successful are extra unpaid leave, job coaches, supervisory adjustments, education of co-workers, and providing private or protected work space.[15]

The only limit on an employer's obligation to make an "accommodation" is that the requested accommodation be "reasonable." This means that it must not impose an "undue hardship" on the employer.[16] To determine whether a requested accommodation imposes an "undue hardship," one looks to, among other things, the nature and net cost of the accommodation, the overall financial resources of the employer, and the impact upon the ability of other employees to do their jobs.[17]

The task of persuading society that in a particular situation, people with mental disabilities should be treated like everyone else is made more difficult by our insisting in other situations that people with mental disabilities are entitled to special treatment.

Typically, the types of accommodations needed by people with mental disabilities are low cost and readily achievable. They do not require substantial expenditures, like those sometimes required to make a workplace physically accessible. Most often, what is required of the employer is little more than flexibility and the willingness to be responsive to the expressed needs of persons with mental disabilities.

The obligations imposed by the ADA on government and employers to accommodate the needs of people with disabilities are quite extraordinary, perhaps even revolutionary. I would not give them up. But I believe that like other societal efforts to afford people with mental disabilities special treatment, they have a cost that is important to acknowledge. In many situations, we argue that people with mental disabilities should be treated like everyone else. We argue, in effect, that society should consider disability status irrelevant. Whenever we instead promote the idea that people with mental disabilities are "special" and deserve "special" accommodations or attention, we undermine the force of our claims for equal treatment. The task of persuading society that in a particular situation, people with mental disabilities should be treated like everyone else is made more difficult by our insisting in other situations that people with mental disabilities are entitled to special treatment. In one situation, we claim that disability status is irrelevant; in another, we claim it makes all the difference.

It is important to acknowledge the many ways in which we as an advocacy community have insisted that disability status is relevant. We have created special protections for people with mental disabilities, such as the protection and advocacy agencies. Indeed, the existence of the host of the conference, the Commission on Quality of Care for the Mentally Disabled, is a testament to the idea that disability status is relevant. We have promoted the creation of specialized services, such as special education and special housing programs. We have also secured enhanced income support programs for people with disabilities. I have always found it remarkable that a poor family with a disabled child receives nearly twice the amount of income support that a poor family without a disabled child receives. This is because we have suc-

> *We attempt to ensure through law and practice that the twin notions of "equal treatment" and of "special treatment" are harnessed in service of the goal that people with mental disabilities be full participants in our society.*

ceeded in creating a special welfare program for poor children with disabilities—the SSI program—that is more generous than AFDC.

We have been successful in securing special protections and additional resources for people with mental disabilities, and we have been successful in requiring society to acknowledge and accommodate their special needs. But each time we make a claim for these forms of "special treatment," we unavoidably emphasize the differences between people with mental disabilities and the rest of society. In so doing, we strengthen the justification for different or unequal treatment and undermine our claims that people with mental disabilities should be treated just like everybody else.

This dilemma is what Harvard law professor and Bazelon Center board member Martha Minow has called the "dilemma of difference."[18] I don't know any way out of it. One possibility is that we give up the claim that people with mental disabilities should be protected against discriminatory treatment, but this is clearly unacceptable. The other possibility is that we embrace the view that disability status is never relevant. I have often wondered whether people with mental disabilities might be better off if society adopted this radical notion of equality, and essentially ignored—in law and public policy—the fact that some people have mental disabilities. I am interested in others' views on this. I can't quite figure out how it would work.

This leaves the option of muddling through—the option that, in practice, we have selected. We attempt to ensure through law and practice that the twin notions of "equal treatment" and of "special treatment" are harnessed in service of the goal that people with mental disabilities be full participants in our society. In this endeavor, we have been remarkably successful, as the enactment of the ADA attests. But we need to acknowledge the dangers that are inherent in our approach and that, increasingly, lie ahead.

The principle of different treatment, once unleashed, is difficult to contain. It is the fundamental underpinning of society's claim that it is legitimate to confine people with mental disabilities based on a prediction or likelihood of violence and that it is legitimate to forcibly medicate them. Society concedes that other people are not treated in this fashion, but nonetheless insists that, because of the special nature of mental disability, this form of unequal treatment is both permissible and necessary.

After repeatedly insisting that disability status is relevant, how credible are our claims that it is irrelevant in the context of confinement and forced treatment and that equal treatment should be the rule?

After repeatedly insisting that disability status is relevant, how credible are our claims that it is irrelevant in the context of confinement and forced treatment and that equal treatment should be the rule?

It is commonly suggested that there is a way out of the "dilemma of difference." The solution to the dilemma, it is said, is that we insist on equal treatment when doing so promotes people with mental disabilities' independence and integration into society, and we insist on "special treatment" when doing so would promote those aims. This solution essentially subordinates the question of whether people with mental disabilities will be treated differently or like everyone else, to the question of how to best promote the independence and integration of people with mental disabilities.

The problem with this approach is that there are competing visions of how best to promote independence and integration. Our vision may place a high value on freedom and choice. But other visions are more paternalistic. They focus on the need for treatment. Treatment is viewed, in effect, as the essential foundation for independence and participation in society. Without treatment, it is asserted, people with mental disabilities cannot have meaningful freedom, make meaningful choices, or lead meaningful lives.

We may not agree with this competing view, but my guess is that it is the dominant view of society. For this reason, therefore, it is problematic to say we will choose "equal treatment" or "different treatment" by considering what will best promote independence and integration, freedom and choice, or any other set of values. In addition, it seems unlikely that concepts as broad and ambiguous as independence and integration, or freedom and choice, will provide clear answers to the question of when it is legitimate to insist that people with mental disabilities be treated like everyone else and when it is legitimate to insist they be treated differently.

What I am fairly certain of, however, is that when we make a claim for special treatment, we pay a price. We unintentionally support the claim that the differences between people with disabilities and the rest of society justify unequal treatment.

The case studies prepared for the session "Is 'Equal Treatment' Consistent with 'Special Treatment'?" help place these issues in focus. The one that gave workshop participants the most pause was the case of Ms. Billings, who claimed that it was her mental disability that caused her to embezzle funds from her law firm. If the cause of Ms. Billings' conduct was unrelated to a mental disability, she would have no grounds for being readmitted to the bar. Should she have a claim for special treatment because her misconduct was the product of a mental disability? The ADA provides a basis for asserting that the state bar should make an exception to the rule that embezzlement results in permanent disbarment in Ms. Billings' case. Such an exception, it could be argued, is required to provide her with equal access to employment. But many workshop participants, especially consumers, thought Ms. Billings should not be accorded special treatment.[19]

Ms. Billings brings us back to the issues of *Choice & Responsibility*, the theme of the conference. It is hard to separate issues of choice and responsibility from issues of when it is appropriate to treat people with mental disabilities like everyone else and when it is appropriate to treat them differently. Is Ms. Billings responsible for her conduct if it was caused by a mental disability?[20] If a mental disability was the cause of her behavior, did she make a meaningful choice that she should be punished for? Should Ms. Billings be treated like everyone else and be permanently disbarred, or should she be accorded special treatment and be readmitted to the bar upon a showing that she is unlikely to engage in future misconduct?

I do not know what the correct result is in the case of Ms. Billings— permanent disbarment or readmission to the bar. I suspect that her independence and integration into society would be best promoted by her being readmitted. I do not know whether that result (and precedent) would best promote the independence and freedom of others with mental disabilities. What I am fairly certain of, however, is that when we make a claim for special treatment on Ms. Billings' behalf, and on behalf of clients or friends whose situations are more sympathetic, we pay a price. We unintentionally support the claim that the differences between people with disabilities and the rest of society justify unequal treatment, including subjecting people with mental disabilities to schemes of regulation and control different from those that apply to everyone else.

•

Endnotes

1. I refer often to "persons with mental disabilities." In using the term, I mean it as a shorthand that includes persons "labeled" as having a mental disability.

2. Recent interest has been expressed in the practice of confining people with other disabilities (e.g., people with AIDS, people with tuberculosis) based on future dangerousness. *See, e.g.*, Lawrence Gostin, *The Politics of AIDS: Compulsory State Powers, Public Health, and Civil Liberties*, 49 OHIO ST. L.J. 1017, 1026–38 (1989).

3. In the following discussion of the ADA, I will focus on Titles I and II of the ADA, which apply to employers and state and local government. Of course, the ADA's reach is more extensive. Its antidiscrimination provisions apply to public accommodations, which are, essentially, places of commerce. The ADA also imposes obligations on the telecommunications, transportation, and insurance industries.

4. The ADA does not apply to the federal government. However, Section 504 of the Rehabilitation Act imposes on the federal government obligations similar to those the ADA imposes on state and local government.

5. 28 C.F.R. § 35.130(b)(1)(ii).

6. 28 C.F.R. § 35.130(b)(1)(iii).

7. 28 C.F.R. § 35.130(b)(8).

8. 28 C.F.R. § 35.130(b)(7).

9. 28 C.F.R. § 35.130(b)(7).

10. *See* U.S. DEP'T JUST., THE AMERICANS WITH DISABILITIES ACT: TITLE III TECHNICAL ASSISTANCE MANUAL 27 (1992); Jackson v. Fort Stanton Hosp. and Training Sch., 757 F. Supp. 1243, 1299 (D.N.M. 1990), *rev'd in part on other grounds*, 964 F.2d 980 (10th Cir. 1992).

11. 29 C.F.R. § 1630.9(a).

12. 29 C.F.R. § 1630.2(o)(i).

13. 29 C.F.R. § 1630.2(o)(1)(ii).

14. 29 C.F.R. § 1630.4(o)(2)(i)&(ii).

15. *See, e.g.*, LAURA L. MANCUSO, CASE STUDIES ON REASONABLE ACCOMMODATION FOR WORKERS WITH PSYCHIATRIC DISABILITIES (California Dep't Mental Health & Department Rehabilitation 1993).

16. 29 C.F.R. § 1630.9(a).

17. 29 C.F.R. § 1630.2(p).

18. MARTHA MINOW, MAKING ALL THE DIFFERENCE: INCLUSION, EXCLUSION & AMERICAN LAW (1990).

19. If you hold this view, would it change if Ms. Billings' misconduct had not been criminal, was clearly caused by her disability, and was unlikely to recur? Would an accommodation be appropriate?

20. She may be able to defend her criminal case based on a plea of insanity. Would it make a difference to you in assessing whether she should be readmitted to the bar that she had been excused from criminal liability because her mental disability rendered her unable to conform her actions to the requirements of the law?

18

Mental Disability and Criminal Responsibility

Fred Cohen, Esq.

Introduction

The topic assigned to me is: "Breaking the Law: When Should Persons With Mental Disabilities Be Excused vs. Held Responsible?" The question is framed in such a way as to highlight the insanity defense—the defense most closely associated with the relationship between mental disability, criminal conduct and blameworthiness, and to consider also the appropriate consequences which should follow any decision finding or rejecting blameworthiness.

Clearly, there cannot be a single answer to the question posed by the title. Indeed, it is a question that must be followed by an observation: *It all depends.*

Insanity

In the first instance, it all depends on what purpose, either jurisprudentially, symbolically, or empirically, we assign to the insanity defense. Is it to sort out, however roughly, the seriously mentally ill and mentally retarded from other defendants and keep them out of the penal system? If it is to perform this sorting-out function, then how broad or narrow should the entrance be to criminal irresponsibil-

> *If we did not have something resembling the insanity defense, we would have to invent it.*

ity and, thus, *direct* entrance into the mental health system? Do we also understand that when the insanity defense fails—like a long fly ball caught at the fence—this most likely means only delayed entrance or reentrance to the mental health system, although via a clogged and increasingly legally vulnerable prison mental health system?

Obviously, if the insanity defense is supposed to divert the seriously mentally ill from the peno-correctional process, the defense fails miserably with studies showing anywhere from 8% to 19% of all prisoners having some form of significant psychiatric disability.[1] Unless we are willing to conclude that it is confinement which causes the mental illness, then clearly, the insanity defense does not serve as even a large-mesh screen for blocking the seriously mentally ill[2] from entering and continuing through the criminal justice system.

Where free will does not exist, there is no choice; where there is no choice, there can be no culpability.

The most recent research shows the defense is used in only about 1% of all felony cases; it is successful about one-quarter of the time,[3] and when successful, the acquittees spend about double the amount of time incarcerated in a mental health facility than defendants convicted of similar charges.[4]

As a matter of our criminal jurisprudence, I would assert that if we did not have something resembling the insanity defense, we would have to invent it. Once invented, however, we would confront the policy question of how wide or narrow should we make the path to criminal irresponsibility. There is only one criminal defense that says "I did not do it," and that is alibi. All the other defenses say, in effect, "I did it but...." The insanity defense says, "I did it, but it can be explained *and* ought to be excused by a mental disease or defect which substantially impaired my cognitive or volitional abilities."

Our criminal law punishes persons who are blameworthy and not those who merely cause proscribed harm. Theoretically, we might construct a system of penal law based on a theory of social defense. Under such a system, concepts of *mens rea* and mental states such as intent or recklessness would be abolished, and a person's voluntary, harm-producing acts would serve as the basis for state intervention. After the power to officially intervene is gained, then decisions would be made about the appropriate measures of intervention. For some it might be a dose of punishment for deterrent purposes; others might do a bit of community service for restorative ends; still others might undergo individualized treatment aimed at a reduction of recidivism through individual change; while others might be incarcerated to restrain them from causing further social harm.

This, however, is not our jurisprudence. We assign blame based on individualized notions of responsibility, and blame cannot be assigned where the actor is able to prove that he "believes that he is squeezing lemons when he chokes his wife."[5] We cling to *mens rea* and mental states as the bridge between objective harm and the subjectiveness of blameworthiness.

While much of this may sound like an alchemist's brew, there is at least symmetry here in that our criminal law's construct of personal responsibility rests importantly on the free will posit. Where free will does not exist, there is no choice; where there is no choice, there can be no culpability.

That "free will"—like *mens rea*—may be viewed as an archaic, religiously based myth or as a philosophical stand-in for an unabashedly moral judgment, is not my point. The free will posit serves as the foundational material for our criminal law. A defendant may explain his conduct by arguing that "the Devil made me do it." To succeed, he had better show that the Devil's commands flowed from the right type of mental illness, not merely a religious injunction, and that the illness substantially impaired his ability to rationally choose; that is, to exercise free will.

> *A person may be found criminally irresponsible due to mental disease or defect—the insanity defense—and while that person may be psychotic, it is linguistically and conceptually wrong, confusing, and needlessly stigmatic to label him insane.*

A sociologist may argue that poverty, for example, causes crime. That, however, is not actually a teleological—or means/end directed—statement. It is a statement designed to displace blame from an individual offender and assign it elsewhere, if blame there be. I might not argue with the assertion, but I would insist that its only real significance is in the answer to the question: So what! Is property now to be equalized? And what is to be done pending redistribution?

Poverty, of course, is something external to the actor, while mental illness is viewed as something internal; something for which there is no blame and something which is inseparable from the person. "It" goes where he goes and may serve both to explain and excuse criminal behavior. Poverty may explain, but it will never excuse.

There are many curiosities about the insanity defense, but time and space do not permit me even to list them. I will, however, idiosyncratically select a few from the many as a device to make my further points.

First, there is the linguistic dilemma of referring to an insanity defense based on mental disease or defect and, in the same breath, referring to someone *as* insane. A person may be found criminally irresponsible due to mental disease or defect—the insanity defense—and while that person may be diagnosed—say—as psychotic, it is linguistically and conceptually wrong, confusing, and needlessly stigmatic to label him insane.[6]

Expansion Efforts

Second, in this post-*Hinckley* era of legislative activity to constrict the defense, I detect countervailing moves to expand it, albeit in backdoor fashion and also to transpose it to the area of self-defense. I refer here to such defense variations as pre- and post-menstrual syndrome, sexual addiction,[7] compulsive gambling disorder (or the Pete Rose disease), battered wife syndrome, urban survival syndrome (raised recently in Texas to bolster an apparently weak claim of self-defense), the "black rage" insanity defense (apparently to be offered by attorney William Kunstler on behalf of Colin Ferguson, charged with the Long Island Railroad slaughter in December 1993), and now "adopted child syndrome" (to be raised in a proposed second trial of Joel Rifkin, who has confessed to the murder of 17 women).[8]

> *Given enough time and wit, we may construct an understanding—or at least an explanation—of anyone's criminal behavior, but the policy question is do we then wish to excuse it?*

While there are significant differences and varying degrees of appeal in these efforts to enlarge either insanity or self-defense, they share one characteristic: they are efforts to explain criminal conduct in the guise of justifications or excuses. What may be missed here is the distinction between an *explanation* and a *defense*. Given enough time and wit, we may construct an understanding —or at least an explanation—of anyone's criminal behavior, but the policy question is do we then wish to excuse it? Do we wish to excuse, but then deprive, a person of his liberty in the name of treatment?

If a person kills, let us say, in self-defense or in the defense of others, we do not then commit that person to a mental (or "antiself-defense") hospital. Why? Because the law accepts self-defense as within the range of expected and tolerable activity by a rational person who is himself in a life-threatening situation.

A killing in self-defense, then, is viewed as predictable and tolerable behavior by a "normal" person in some form of extremis, with normalcy a compendium of majoritarian values that a community views as acceptable.

The urban survival syndrome, on the other hand, would argue that the defendant shot and killed two unarmed assailants because they "dissed" him and that if he had retreated, his days were numbered. In the alternative, one might argue that the "urban jungle" provides context for this new version of self-defense and becomes a part of a defendant's reasonable perception of an imminent threat.[9]

The battered wife, black rage, and urban survival syndromes all seek recognition as a basis for self-defense and thus complete exculpation with no "get better" dues to pay.

The "Pete Rose" disease is another matter. Apparently, one cannot have this disorder and also win at gambling. Assuming that there is such a compulsion and that it manifests itself primarily by uncontrollable losing, this creates interesting questions for the chronic gamblers' therapists: Do they strive only to have the victim not gamble—or to gamble, but do so successfully?

Acceptable Mental Disorders

Beyond the various syndromes and compulsions seeking admittance to the world of self-defense or mitigation, we encounter other disorders that seek recognition as an acceptable mental disease to be used as a predicate for the insanity defense. There are, in other words, "good" and "bad" mental disorders and what may be "good" (or acceptable) for one legal purpose (e.g., insurance benefits) is "bad" for another (e.g., insanity defense).

If substance abuse and the various compulsions and syndromes noted earlier served as a predicate for an insanity-type defense, the consequences would be enormous.

Alcoholism and drug addiction, for example, alone will not formally qualify as the mental disease predicate required for the insanity defense. Indeed, neither will they qualify for the "serious illness" predicate that both the Eighth or Fourteenth Amendments mandate for the treatment of the convicted prisoner or detainee.[10]

Vaillant, in his classic work on alcoholism,[11] ultimately decides that calling alcoholism a disease, rather than a behavior disorder, is a useful device for treatment purposes, admission to the health care system, and for purposes of understanding and study. Thus, on pragmatic grounds, he arrives at a verdict of alcoholism-as-disease. Others, with a different agenda, may argue that substance abuse represents moral failure, calling for moral, regenerative measures, or that the disease label may, in fact, be antitherapeutic. Thus, as I stated earlier concerning the overriding question of when persons with mental disabilities should be excused: *It all depends.*

Any expansion of the disease concept to accommodate an enlarged mission for the insanity defense will simply lengthen the line into some type of coercive intervention for treatment purposes.

Vaillant states, "The argument may be legitimately made that there is no more reason to subsume alcohol abuse under the medical model than to include compulsive fingernail biting, gambling, or child molesting in textbooks on medicine."[12] However that may be, if substance abuse and the various compulsions and syndromes noted earlier served as a predicate for an insanity-type defense, the consequences would be enormous.

Do we wish to admit alcoholism or drug addiction into the halls of mental disease for the purposes of the required predicate for an insanity defense? If so, we presumably would not make it a total free pass in that the alcoholic or addict would have to be under the influence of the substance at the time of the harm-producing conduct.

By some counts, perhaps 40% to 80%[13] of the persons entering our prisons are substance abusers. Speaking very broadly here, should we allow being addicted and "under the influence" to serve as a basis for a type of insanity defense, it is clear that society would not simply allow such acquittees to walk out of the courtroom. Rather, any expansion of the disease concept to accommodate an enlarged mission for the insanity defense will simply lengthen the line into some type of coercive intervention for treatment purposes.

We might push the thought even further and consider ushering in the golden age of enlightenment sought earlier by the Gluecks and psychiatrists like Benjamin Karpman who viewed all criminality as symptomatic of abnormal mental states and who, naturally, would revile as anachronistic the "free will" posit and the assertion of official power to punish for that which is inherently an expression of pathology.

In this projected golden age, the criminal conduct would merely be symptomatic of the underlying pathology, and our threshold question of responsibility would be rendered meaningless. There simply could be no responsibility issue, only questions as to the nature, duration, and location of appropriate treatment.

To this point, I have suggested that the insanity defense is the law's primary, albeit clumsy, mechanism for determining the lack of criminal responsibility of persons with mental disabilities. While I believe that the basic premises of our criminal law require something akin to the insanity defense, those same premises do not dictate whether the defense should be broadly or narrowly available. Thus, the mere availability of an insanity defense may satisfy jurisprudential ends, but its narrow basis permits many persons with severe mental disabilities to be confined in the penal system.

> *I can say with confidence that security and treatment staff alike, everywhere, believe that there are more seriously mentally ill in prison than ever before.*

I also briefly reviewed, by way of contrast, a number of recent courtroom efforts to expand eligibility for criminal irresponsibility. Lawyers are presenting as defenses a variety of addictions, compulsions, syndromes, and often compelling socioeconomic explanations for criminal conduct, albeit with little success.

Post-*Hinckley*, the federal government, as well as many states, has narrowed the defense to cognitive impairments only; emphasized the need for a serious mental disease; engaged in procedural and burden-of-proof shifting, designed to narrow the potential for success; moved toward automatic commitment, abetted by the incomprehensible *Jones v. United States*,[14] and made release increasingly difficult.[15]

Expansion of the Mentally Ill in Prison

The combination of an increasingly restrictive insanity defense, rejection of any expansion of the disease concept, and an extremely punitive climate, has created an era characterized by an enormous and expanding prison population which includes a growing number of apparently seriously mentally ill inmates. Having been intimately involved in recent prison mental health litigation in six states, I can say with confidence that security and treatment staff alike, everywhere, believe that there are more seriously mentally ill in prison than ever before; more schizophrenia and clinical depression, and more violently mentally ill.

The more recent epidemiological studies confirm this anecdotal material. For example, in their study of 3,684 New York State prisoners, Steadman, Fabisiak, Dvoskin, and Holohean (1987)[16] used standardized surveys to collect data from health workers and correctional counselors on randomly selected inmates throughout the state. They were interested in determining the presence of psychiatric disability and functional disability. The authors found that 15% of those studied had significant psychiatric disability.

Ron Jamelka and his colleagues did an overview of a number of studies focusing on the prevalence of mental illness in prisons and concluded:

> [P]revalence rates for major psychiatric disorders...have increased slowly and gradually in the last 20 years and probably will continue to increase. Facility surveys suggest that only six to eight percent of adjudicated felons are currently being designated as seriously mentally ill. Clinical studies, however, suggest that 10 to 15 percent of prison populations have a major DSM-III-R...disorder...and need the services usually associated with severe or chronic mental illness.[17]

Based on the studies referred to, and the overwhelming weight of the observational and anecdotal evidence, it seems clear that a large number of persons who are seriously mentally ill[18] are passing through the portals of our criminal justice system and into our jails and prisons. Crowded into those same facilities are large numbers of socially and psychologically dysfunctional people for whom adjustment anywhere is difficult.

The filtering devices utilized at the front-end of the criminal justice system—certainly including the insanity defense—appear to play no meaningful role in diverting many of those who are seriously and not-so-seriously mentally ill from penal confinement.

The filtering devices utilized at the front-end of the criminal justice system —certainly including the insanity defense—appear to play no meaningful role in diverting many of those who are seriously and not-so-seriously mentally ill from penal confinement. Whether or not these devices should perform this function is an entirely different question.

Once an individual achieves captive status, then there is a constitutional obligation to provide treatment for those with a serious medical or mental health condition.[19] Ironically, since it is only those captives with serious ailments for whom treatment is mandated, another sorting out process begins.

At the front-end of the system a narrow search for criminal responsibility may have been conducted. This included separating "good" from "bad" illnesses—mental disease from a parade of syndromes, compulsions, and antisocial personalities—and assigning blame accordingly. The handful of 'irresponsibles" were seen to leave the courtroom for a mental hospital and the undifferentiated mass of "responsibles" left for penal confinement.

For the purposes of constitutionally *mandated* mental health services, those who get off the prison bus must start again and ultimately convince a mental health professional that they are seriously ill. The constitutional command is to not be deliberately indifferent to those with serious illnesses.[20]

The world of penal confinement sets up significant hurdles to the attainment of adequate mental health care. Security staff guards the door to treatment, suspicious of those who are "manipulators." A typically small and often embattled mental health staff

> *The quietly decompensating captive usually is not a problem for security, and he will not likely be sought out by clinicians visiting his cell. His care will come late, if at all.*

opens its door only slightly, guarding against those seeking "secondary gain"—those who are merely violent and not also mentally ill.

Gone for the moment is the search for responsibility, as well as the argot of criminal law. A captive's access to treatment likely will be governed by the treatment resources available in a particular correctional system and not primarily by a clinical assessment of need. In the terribly crowded world of jails and prisons, every unit assigned to treatment (or rehabilitation) will be filled. Thus, we encounter intense competition for scarce resources.

The captive must negotiate the worlds of security and mental health professionals to gain access to the scarce resource of care. For example, the wildly acting out and violent captive is both the best candidate for care and also the one who creates the most suspicion. Is he really "mad" or is he merely "bad?" The quietly decompensating captive usually is not a problem for security—he is quiet and manageable—and he will not likely be sought out by clinicians visiting his cell. His care will come late, if at all.

For some captives, mental health care and placement is a welcome respite, and they are willing to pay the price. The price may include being labeled a "bug" by fellow inmates and either being shunned or victimized; waiting for medication in stigmatizing "bug" pill lines; the denial or delay of parole; or the often terrifying side effects of psychotropic medication.

This paper opened with the assigned topic of the criminal responsibility of persons with mental disabilities which, in turn, was accepted as an invitation to examine threshold questions of criminal accountability. Having negotiated the insanity defense, along with a variety of syndromes and compulsions and their limitations as screening mechanisms, I turned to our swelling prison populations which include significant numbers of persons with mental disorders. Beyond the essential questions of which captives receive what kind of mental health care are some intriguing questions of responsibility, and it is to those I now turn.

Prison Discipline, Mental Illness, and Responsibility

Prisons may be described as asylums, total institutions, or total communities, the latter metaphor being most adaptable to my present purposes. Viewed as a total community, as a place where all of the activities of life are performed under the governance of a single legal authority, we encounter an encapsulated version of some aspects of the free, or segmented, community.[21] All prisons have a disciplinary code which likely will incorporate by reference the jurisdiction's penal code, along with special rules of procedure and rules relating to sentencing or dispositions.

Prison disciplinary proceedings, in perhaps unexpected ways, bring us full circle to our threshold question: When should persons (inmates) with mental disabilities be excused or held responsible? To be more specific, suppose an inmate has been diagnosed as schizophrenic and is undergoing treatment in a prison's residential treatment unit (RTU). Suppose further that the inmate refuses his or her medication and dur-

There will be voices from the prison clinical and security community who will argue that an inmate's mental disorder simply cannot serve as an excuse for rule infractions.

ing that interim slaps a fellow inmate, punches a correctional officer, wanders unnoticed off the RTU without a pass, and appears to violate the prison's rules governing escape?

Suppose, further, that another hypothetical prisoner is housed in the general population of a prison without an RTU, but the inmate is on a mental health caseload with the same diagnosis and treatment as our first inmate and engages in the same "acting-out" behavior?

If either hypothetical inmate is charged with any of the above rule infractions and is found guilty, it is likely that the punishment will be some form of lockdown, and the misconduct will contribute to a tightening of the inmate's security classification. This, in turn, may lead to prolonged disciplinary or administrative segregation, denial of access to those prisons with a more moderate environment, and even delayed or denied parole.

Should the inmate's mental condition be taken into account in a pre-disciplinary hearing process; subsequently, by the disciplinary tribunal? Should there be a formal diversionary process for the inmate whose misconduct is closely related to his or her mental condition?

Should there be rules requiring the disciplinary tribunal to determine the inmate's fitness (or competence) to proceed; to determine if the inmate is not responsible as a result of a mental disorder; to take into account the inmate's mental condition merely for dispositional purposes?

There is something that should at least nag at us about punishing someone being treated as mentally ill and whose offending behavior appears to be intimately related to the diagnosis and treatment.

In my experience, disciplinary infractions escalate during the period of a mentally ill inmate's non-compliance with psychotropic medication. Thus, in the hypotheticals posed, I have made it fairly easy to associate the harm-producing conduct with a mental condition and even the treatment regimen employed.

This, however, merely sharpens the policy dilemma. There will be voices from the prison clinical and security community who will argue that an inmate's mental disorder simply cannot serve as an excuse for rule infractions. To do so, they argue, will create chaos and communicate a kind of "free pass" message to the offender.

Perhaps without realizing it, these voices argue for a prison disciplinary code based on "strict liability"; that is, one where no culpable mental element need be proved. On the other hand, there is something that should at least nag at us about punishing someone being treated as mentally ill and whose offending behavior appears to be intimately related to the diagnosis and treatment. Parenthetically, this problem, and the consternation it causes, exists in similar fashion in psychiatric hospitals.[22]

And, so, what is to be done about this issue of accountability of mentally disordered inmates? The meager caselaw on point is not supportive of inmates' claims to a type of administrative insanity defense.[23]

On the assumption, then, that there is no legal mandate, constitutional or otherwise, to adopt such a defense, is it sound policy to formalize distinctions based on *where* the conduct occurs; i.e., an RTU vs. the general population?[24]

May it be argued that, in fact, institutional safety and discipline are not threatened by harm-producing behavior in an RTU-type setting in the same fashion as it would if the same behavior occurred in another setting?

I will not pretend to have done anything more than raise the mental disorder-responsibility issue in a problem area where it is seldom encountered in the literature. When the issue is occasionally sounded, the debate settles into categories very similar to those encountered when dealing with the insanity defense and the traditional criminal prosecution. The notable difference, of course, is the reality of governing a prison played off against, "Do you want people like that going to a hospital and getting out!"

Some Solutions

If an inmate is unable to understand the charges or muster even a nominal defense or explanation, then it is unseemly—and perhaps unconstitutional—to proceed with a hearing. Surely, if an inmate has a right to be physically present at the hearing, this should include the right to be mentally present—i.e., competent—at the hearing.[25]

Surely, if an inmate has a right to be physically present at the hearing, this should include the right to be mentally present—i.e., competent—at the hearing.

I would argue that, at a minimum, when an inmate is on a mental health caseload or has a relatively recent history of treatment for mental illness, then this should at least be factored into the charging (or diversion) decision and into the dispositional decision.[26]

I would avoid at all costs the spectacle of an obviously mentally disturbed inmate being repeatedly locked down for behavior clearly related to the mental disorder and the attainment of a security designation that virtually assures confinement in close custody in a maximum security prison.

I have painted a consciously incomplete picture of a captive's right to mental health care. Clearly, that is a subject deserving independent and more comprehensive coverage than may be done in the space available to me here. My only point was to emphasize again that, while the issue of mental disability as excuse is of major jurisprudential interest, it is of minor consequence in sorting out the mentally ill from others.

The rare insanity acquittee leaves the courtroom for the mental hospital, while those who merely "hit long fly balls" leave for prison only to begin another series of engagements in the quest for appropriate care. In captivity, one must fight the war of security vs. treatment; malingering vs. authentic illness; scarce resources and heavy demand; and even doing more time because of the reluctance of parole authorities to release inmates who have been treated for mental illness.

Finally, I return to the front-end of the system, but not to debate the niceties of the law and procedure associated with the insanity defense. Rather, I would argue that as a matter of policy, we might use the coercive power of the law and its agencies to divert at least some of the chronically mentally ill who engage in minor criminal conduct from the criminal justice system, but to not then abandon them. We have available a variety of residential and nonresidential options for providing appropriate care in the community for those who are accused or convicted. Surely it makes more sense to halt the criminal process for many individuals who plainly suffer with mental disabilities and to provide care and community protection at the same time.

The Milwaukee Community Support Program, for example, deserves serious consideration by any local government.[27] The Program is operated as an alternative to incarceration, and for about $3,000 a year per client it provides medical and therapeutic services, money management, housing along with casework, and day reporting accompanied with close supervision.

Obviously, this type of program is not appropriate, either politically or programmatically, for all offenders with mental disabilities. It is certainly appropriate to consider as a preventive device for minor offenders on their way to heavier offenses.

For those offenders who are mentally ill and who become captives, it is imperative that we develop back-end programs so that they are not simply released with two weeks of medication or placed on some undifferentiated parole caseload in the community.

While the constitutional duty of care is bounded by the four walls of a penal facility, our best efforts should be aimed at early diversion for some and continuing care for those who come through the system.

Endnotes

1. *See* H.J. Steadman et al., *A Survey of Mental Disability Among State Prison Inmates*, 38 HOSP. & COMM'Y PSYCHIATRY 1086 (1987). *See also infra* note 17.

2. I realize that there are important problems associated with the term *seriously mentally ill*. In my experience, clinicians tend to equate *serious* with psychosis; or with an Axis-I, DSM diagnosis; or with a functional reference to being unable to function with regard to a significant impairment of judgment, behavior, capacity to recognize reality, or to cope with the ordinary demands of life. *See* FRED COHEN, LEGAL ISSUES AND THE MENTALLY DISORDERED PRISONER 58–63 (U.S. Dep't Just., N.I.C. 1988) for a review of the relevant caselaw on point. *See also infra* note 18.

3. L.A. Callahan et al., *The Volume and Characteristics of Insanity Defense Pleas: An Eight-State Study*, 19 BULL. AM. ACAD. PSYCHIATRY & L. 331–338 (1991).

4. Joseph H. Rodriguez et al., *The Insanity Defense Under Siege: Legislative Assaults and Legal Rejoinders*, 14 RUTGERS L.J. 397, 403 (1983).

5. MODEL PENAL CODE, § 4.01 comments.

6. This linguistic and conceptual error leads to such absurd phrases as "presently insane" or "temporarily insane." Clearly, a person may be presently suffering from some mental illness, and the illness may be transient. However, once a person is found not guilty by reason of insanity, that person has been found not responsible for conduct which occurred at a given point in time, and for that time, that person will always be irresponsible.

7. The Supreme Court recently rejected an appeal by a Maine college instructor, Donald Winston, who claimed he was discriminated against when fired due to numerous incidents of sexual harassment. Winston claimed he was sexually obsessive and should receive counseling and not be fired.

8. John T. McQuiston, *Form of Insanity Defense Planned for the Next Rifkin Trial*, N. Y. TIMES, May 11, 1994, at B7.

9. Elijah Anderson, *The Code of the Streets*, ATL. MONTHLY, May 1994, at 81, brilliantly describes the violence associated with deeply ingrained codes followed by the ghetto poor. Manhood and nerve, central to survival, exist around the taking of things one wants, who punches first, or even behaving "properly" when mugged, or risk facing death for not knowing. A set of rules are known, or "should have been known," and rule violators suffer greatly while rule enforcers are elevated to "bad dudes."

10. *See, e.g.*, Fred Cohen, *Captives' Legal Right to Mental Health Care*, 17 L. & PSYCHOL. REV. 1, 7 (1993). The life threatening consequences that may accompany withdrawal will, of course, mandate appropriate care.

In using the term "formally qualify" I mean to save ground for the diagnostic manipulation that may occur in moving the alcoholism or drug addiction to the status of secondary illness and elevating any major mental disorder to the status of primary diagnosis.

11. G.E. VAILLANT, THE NATURAL HISTORY OF ALCOHOLISM: CAUSES, PATTERNS, AND PATHS TO RECOVERY (1983).

12. *Id.* The argument for inclusion of alcoholism, and not the others in the text, rests on a variety of individual, pathological consequences; the need for medical care, as in detoxification; and frequent abuse of loved ones.

13. A study recently conducted of Vermont prisons disclosed that 83.6% met lifetime criteria for alcohol abuse/dependency, and 69% met subcriteria for drug abuse/dependence. THOMAS A. POWELL ET AL., PREVALENCE OF MENTAL ILLNESS AMONG RURAL PRISONERS (forthcoming 1994).

All of the anecdotal evidence I possess leads me to conclude that prison officials everywhere consistently use the 80% figure when estimating the number of inmates in their system who are "substance abusers." With no hard criteria to measure who is a substance abuser, I realize that such estimates are valid only as the perceptions of the source —but I believe there is value in that.

14. 463 U.S. 354 (1983) (upholding automatic commitment after a n.g.r.i. verdict based on a presumption of continuing mental illness and/or dangerousness flowing from the underlying offense).

15. *See* MICHAEL J. PERLIN, THE JURISPRUDENCE OF THE INSANITY DEFENSE (1994) for a superb treatment of these developments.

16. Steadman et al., *supra* note 1, at 1086–90.

17. R. Jamelka et al., *The Mentally Ill in Prison,* 40 HOSP. & COMM'Y PSYCHIATRY 481, 483–84 (1989).

18. Admittedly, neither the designation of an inmate as seriously mentally ill nor the definitions and criteria generally used are wholly objective or always agreed upon. In the author's experience, the following definition is most often agreed upon in litigation: Seriously mentally ill means a substantial disorder of mood or thought which significantly impairs judgment, behavior, capacity to recognize reality, or cope with the ordinary demands of life.

19. *DeShaney v. Winnebago Dep't of Social Servs.*, 489 U.S. 189 (1989) and *Estelle v. Gamble*, 429 U.S. 97 (1976) are the Supreme Court decisions most clearly supportive of the text.

20. *See* Cohen, *supra* note 10, at 1 (for a full discussion of the concepts of "seriousness" and "deliberate indifference").

    Intake screening is an important aspect of the constitutional duty to provide, at least minimally, adequate mental health care. *See, e.g., Ruiz v. Estelle*, 503 F. Supp. 1265, 1332 (S.D. Tex. 1980) (full judicial history omitted) where screening/classification is treated as a constitutional obligation.

21. A crucial difference, of course, is that in prison accountability attaches to all phases of one's life. Failure to follow the rules concerning work, socializing, visiting, eating, resting—and so on—leads to an indivisible accountability.

22. *See* Stephen Rachlin, *The Prosecution of Violent Psychiatric Inpatients: One Respectable Intervention*, 22 BULL. AM. ACAD. PSYCHIATRY & L. 239 (1994).

23. *People ex rel. Reed v. Scully*, 531 N.Y.S.2d 196 (Sup. Ct. 1988) is a most unusual decision urging the availability of an insanity defense in prison disciplinary proceedings involving an inmate with a history of mental illness.

    More typical is *Knight v. Estelle*, 501 F.2d 963 (5th Cir. 1974), *cert. denied*, 421 U.S. 1000 (1975) holding the insanity defense unavailable in probation and parole revocation proceedings and using this, then, as an analogue to prison disciplinary proceedings.

24. Again, in my experience, this is generally what occurs in practice with variations based on who happens to be the victim. That is, slapping the fellow inmate/patient is acting out; punching the officer is likely to be an assault.

25. *Wolff v. McDonnell*, 418 U.S. 539 (1974) does, indeed, give an inmate charged with a serious violation the right to be at a hearing, along with a few other due process safeguards.

26. *See Powell v. Coughlin*, 953 F.2d 744 (2d Cir. 1991) upholding practice of clinical staff holding *ex parte* discussions about an inmate's mental health with members of a disciplinary tribunal.

27. This description is drawn from DOUGLAS C. MCDONALD & MICHELLE TEITELBAUM, MANAGING MENTALLY ILL OFFENDERS IN THE COMMUNITY: MILWAUKEE'S COMMUNITY SUPPORT PROGRAM (U.S. Dep't Just., National Inst. Just. 1994). The $3,000 figure apparently does not include housing costs.

    I use the cautionary term "consider" as a way to signal the fact that I have no information on the program's effectiveness or, indeed, the criteria that might be used in this assessment.

SECTION THREE
QUALITY ASSURANCE

19

Capitalizing on the Safety Net of Incident Reporting Systems in Community Programs

Nancy K. Ray, Ed.D.

Like many states' Protection and Advocacy agencies, the New York State Commission on Quality of Care for the Mentally Disabled most often encounters the dilemma of honoring versus intervening in the personal, but "dangerous" choices of individuals with mental disabilities in its review of serious injuries and incidents reported by community programs. Such incidents are especially common to newer, nontraditional community service programs, including apartment programs, supported work programs, and other innovative day programs or peer support services programs, where consumer autonomy, responsibility, and independence in daily living are important program goals and where, in fact, staff are more often absent than present, and service recipients do make most of their own daily living decisions.

Quite reasonably, concern for responsible and safe recipient decision-making often becomes the paramount concern of administrators and staff members of newer community programs. As one community program administrator recently told me, "Every day recipient 'free choice' brings some poor choices. The problems are generically the same—unsafe sex, poor money management, drugs, and just plain carelessness." This administrator continued explaining that keeping one step ahead of poor choices, trying to remedy the adverse outcomes which they have wrought, and trying to make sure that they do not recur has become his main, and not always very satisfying, occupation.

This administrator's plea struck a responsive chord. For while it is plainly true that newer community service programs place service recipients in the more desirable position of being able to direct their own lives to a much greater extent, in so doing, they also place service recipients in more situations where they encounter risks that most of us never considered when we first conceived of the benefits of closing institutions and promoting integrated, community services for persons with mental disabilities. Just as plainly, although community program administrators may feel responsible for service recipients' poor decisions and their adverse outcomes, alone they are not in very powerful positions to address either, however much time these concerns may take from their workdays.

It is also clear that the quality assurance mechanisms that we have historically exported from institutional settings to traditional community service programs, with 24-hour staff supervision, are not effectively structured to help program administrators and service recipients cope with the heightened risks inherent to the newer community service programs. Among the most unsuited traditional quality assurance mechanisms are incident reporting systems, most of which were designed specifically for state institutions and later transported (usually with few modifications) to traditional community residences, with 24-hour staff coverage.

> *Although community program administrators may feel responsible for service recipients' poor decisions and their adverse outcomes, alone they are not in very powerful positions to address either.*

These systems, which were developed largely to address issues of staff abuse, mistreatment, neglect, and misconduct and which focused primarily on sorting out issues of staff responsibility and culpability for resident injuries and other untoward events—have some, but marginal, relevance in newer community programs. The operating practices of these systems—from their reporting guidelines to the staff-heavy composition of their incident review committees to the staff- and program-responsibility focus of their special investigations and recommendations for corrective actions—are also clearly out-of-synch with the consumer empowerment mission and values of newer community service programs.

Creating Consumer-Driven Incident Reporting Systems

The purpose of this article is to propose an alternate perspective on incident reporting systems for newer community service programs. This perspective encourages community service administrators to recreate their systems as consumer-centered risk management safety nets for their program enrollees who may be independent in negotiating many aspects of their daily lives, but who may still need support, assistance, and protection from time-to-time in making good personal choices, which are consistent with their self-interests and which also ensure their safety and well-being.

This perspective recognizes that in newer community service programs, more unusual and untoward incidents will be linked to the recipients' rather than the staff's personal choices

In newer community service programs, more unusual and untoward incidents will be linked to the recipients' rather than the staff's personal choices and decisions.

and decisions. In these programs, the expanded role of the incident review committees is not to sit in judgment of recipients' decisions, but to consider strategies which may help service recipients avoid similar ill-advised choices, decisions, and adverse outcomes in the future. This is clearly a more difficult and more challenging undertaking.

Achieving this undertaking requires retailoring both the design and operation of incident reporting systems to be more consistent with the different goals of community services programs. Most centrally, if incident reporting systems are to be effective teaching and learning tools for service recipients and staff in promoting the cardinal goals of recipient empowerment and independence, administrators will need to rethink the composition of the programs' incident review committees. Having just one or two token current or former service recipients on the committee will no longer be sufficient. Ensuring truly effective consumer-centered incident reporting systems mandates that service recipients have many voices on these committees. Meeting this challenge will also require rethinking most other

Ensuring truly effective consumer-centered incident reporting systems mandates that service recipients have many voices on incident review committees.

aspects of traditional incident reporting systems from what constitutes a reportable incident, to who should be notified of reports, to how incidents should be investigated and reviewed, to what constitutes responsible corrective and preventive actions.

In deliberating on each of these decisions, program administrators should involve current and former service recipients. Listening, responding, and incorporating service recipients' views will not only result in the remaking of incident reporting systems more consistent with program goals of recipient empowerment, it will also provide the foundation for effective and constructive recipient participation in incident review committees.

Guidelines for Reportable Incidents

Deciding what should constitute a reportable incident should be a group decision of program administrators, staff, service recipients, and where applicable, the program's board of directors. Each group will likely have their own priority incidents, and consideration of the views of all groups should promote reasonable decision-making. Preexisting state laws, regulations, and policies should also be reviewed—as these will form the uncontested minimum standards for what constitutes reportable incidents.

> *Deciding what should constitute a reportable incident should be a group decision of program administrators, staff, service recipients, and where applicable, the program's board of directors.*

As shown in Figure 1, most states have legal mandates which require the reporting of untoward events and injuries which implicate staff responsibility; which result in serious injuries requiring medical care in an emergency room, urgent care center, or hospital; which involved (or are alleged to have involved) possible criminal conduct; or which involved intentional, self-inflicted injuries. Using this schema, committees are encouraged to delineate with appropriate specificity those untoward events and injuries—which they *must* include as reportable incidents.

Determining what other untoward events should constitute reportable incidents in community programs is more difficult, and less likely to be defined with precise definitions. Common sense and good judgment will serve as primary guideposts—as administrators, staff, and recipients seek to focus their incident reporting systems on important incidents, which present serious risks to service recipients and programs, and at the same time, ensure that incident reporting systems do not become so flooded with minor, inconsequential injuries and untoward events that they lose their effectiveness, and in the process, also become intrusive management tools, which tread heavily on service recipients' privacy and legitimate desires to take risks and learn from their own mistakes.

> *One would not want to prescribe the reporting of all events which were potentially dangerous, but where good fortune helped the service recipient through the misadventure without harm.*

Typical Legally Mandated Reportable Incidents

I. Incidents Which Implicate Staff Responsibility

All untoward events and injuries where staff responsibility is implicated should constitute a reportable incident. These include among others, allegations of staff physical or sexual abuse, staff neglect, staff mistreatment, or staff exploitation of program enrollees.

Specific incidents might include a staff person hitting or swearing at a program enrollee; a case manager failing to seek clinical help for a suicidal client; a staff person having sex (consensual or nonconsensual) with a program recipient; or a staff person charging a $10 service fee for a cashing service recipient's entitlement check.

II. Incidents Where Program Enrollees Are Seriously Hurt

Injuries which require treatment in a hospital, emergency room, or urgent care center—regardless of the cause of the injury—should be reported. These serious injuries warrant review to ensure that appropriate immediate medical care was ensured, that specific safeguards and supervision for the injured individual are in place, and that appropriate corrective and preventive actions are taken.

III. Injuries Involving Criminal Conduct

Untoward events which suggest or allege criminal conduct by program enrollees, including prostitution, theft, illegal drug possession or sales, or assaults, should be considered reportable incidents, regardless of law enforcement involvement. All incidents involving potential criminal behavior present serious risks to the program enrollee; many also present risks to other program enrollees, to the program itself, and to neighbors and other community members. (See pp. 287–289 for a discussion of the more perplexing question of when programs should notify law enforcement officials of these incidents.)

IV. Incidents Involving Intentional, Self-Inflicted Injuries

Intentional, self-inflicted injuries, even when the injury may not have been serious, are also usually legally mandated reportable incidents. Suicidal gestures and self-abusive behaviors may signal that a service recipient needs more support or supervision, special counseling, a medication change, or simply more attention from his or her case manager. In serious cases, they may signal a need for hospitalization or a move to a higher level of care.

Figure 1

Community service programs will find it difficult to list all of the types of untoward events and injuries which may fall in the realm of these more discretionary reportable incidents, but consideration of five general categories of potentially reportable incidents is helpful (Figure 2).

Classes of High-Risk Untoward Events Common to Community Service Programs

✓ Untoward events, which may not have resulted in a serious injury, but which posed a likely and immediate risk of serious injury

✓ Untoward events which have recurred many times and which are likely to result in serious and immediate harm to the individual or others

✓ Untoward events which threaten an individual's enrollment in the program

✓ Untoward events which result in serious property damage

✓ Untoward events which spur community animosity toward the program and/or its service recipients

---

Figure 2

❑ **Incidents Which Present a Risk of Serious Harm**

Fortunately, most of us manage to escape serious injury from most of our risky and ill-advised decisions. The same holds true for most individuals with mental disabilities who are served by community service programs, and one would not want to prescribe an incident reporting system which mandates the reporting of all events which were potentially dangerous, but where good fortune helped the service recipient through the misadventure without harm.

The exceptions to this general rule, however, are those untoward events and decisions where serious injury was not only possible, but likely, and/or where there is good reason to believe that the individual may still be unaware of the riskiness of the situation from which he/she may have escaped unscathed. Thus, an incident whereby a program recipient recklessly ran into a major intersection should be reported, even when no injury resulted, because it was *likely* that a serious injury would have resulted. Similarly, an incident whereby a program enrollee engaged in unsafe sex with a neighborhood drug addict may warrant reporting if program staff have reason to believe that the individual is not fully aware of the health risks

> *In considering recurring untoward events and their reportability, it is important, however, to protect the boundaries of program enrollees' privacy and rights to "bad habits."*

he/she may be taking. If, on the other hand, it is clear that the service recipient was well aware and appreciative of the risks he/she was taking, but chose to continue the relationship, this would not be a reportable incident.

❑ Recurring Untoward Events

Some recurring untoward events and injuries, even when they have not yet led to any serious recipient injury, may also warrant reporting if there is good reason to believe that they will continue to recur, perhaps with more serious harm. These incidents may include residents who repeatedly fail to lock apartment doors, who repeatedly leave stoves on when they are not being used, or who repeatedly go outside in very cold weather inadequately dressed. Other recurring dangerous behaviors which may warrant attention by incident review committees may include residents who repeatedly engage in unsafe sex with multiple partners or who frequently fail to maintain minimally adequate nutrition, because they spend too much of their limited funds on alcohol and cigarettes.

In considering recurring untoward events and their reportability, it is important, however, to protect the boundaries of program enrollees' privacy and rights to "bad habits." All of us have such bad habits—which by definition both recur and are bad for us. And, all such bad habits do not have a place in an incident reporting system. Some bad habits, like smoking cigarettes, not exercising, eating no

> *Key criteria in discriminating "reportable" bad habits include the seriousness and immediacy of the likely harm to the individual, the individual's understanding of the risks involved, and whether the bad habit presents a serious risk of harm to others.*

vegetables, being somewhat chronically in debt, are common to many Americans. Key criteria in discriminating "reportable" bad habits include the seriousness and immediacy of the likely harm to the individual, the individual's understanding of the risks involved, and whether the bad habit presents a serious risk of harm to others.

Thus, one would not usually report chain cigarette smoking, even in instances where the individual suffers from respiratory problems which are badly aggravated by his smoking, if the individual understands the risks involved, but asserts his personal choice to smoke. In contrast, in this same situation, if the individual were leaving burning cigarettes unattended in his apartment or falling asleep while smoking in his apartment causing burns to furnishings and his clothing, the potential immediate and serious risk to other apartment residents, and the resident himself, would suggest the need to report the individual's dangerous smoking habits, even if the individual acknowledges the problem and affirms that he understands the risks of fire.

The risk of program expulsion is itself a serious potential harm to the individual and warrants reporting and discussion by the incident review committee.

❑ Untoward Events Which Threaten Program Enrollment

Another subclass of untoward events which usually warrant reporting are those which may threaten the individual's continued enrollment in the program. Such incidents include instances where service recipients repeatedly come to work programs drunk, chronically fail to pay their rent, verbally harass and threaten neighbors or other program enrollees, or refuse to comply with other important program rules. Oftentimes these untoward events and incidents result in no immediate harm to the individual—but the risk of program expulsion is itself a serious potential harm to the individual and warrants reporting and discussion by the incident review committee.

These discussions have the primary purpose of trying to identify strategies which may help the individual with the behavior which is threatening his or her program enrollment. Additional training, counseling, support, or opportunities for structured leisure activity may all be effective interventions. Incident review committee discussions of these incidents also help ensure that rules governing program expulsion are fairly implemented and that, when appropriate, these rules are revised to protect service recipients' rights.

These discussions will also help program managers better appreciate how certain untoward recipient behaviors affect their other service recipients and the quality of their daily lives. These understandings can encourage program staff to address service

Incidents where a service recipient's actions result in serious damage to property or which present a significant risk of serious damage should be considered reportable incidents.

recipient behaviors, which may have otherwise seemed less serious to them, as they were less directly affected.

❑ Untoward Events Resulting in Property Damage

Because of their actual or potential harm to the individual or other program enrollees—and their repercussions for the program itself—incidents where a service recipient's actions result in serious damage to property or which present a significant risk of serious damage should be considered reportable incidents. These incidents may include apartment or building fires, broken doors or windows, smashed walls, and burglaries facilitated by a consumer leaving doors or windows unlocked. Reporting such incidents ensures that the recipient's need for additional services, support or counseling, or even a different residential setting, are addressed. Incident reviews also provide a forum for program staff to consider thoughtfully other possible program responses to a service recipient's willful destructive behavior. Such responses may include fines to cover repair costs, apologies to neighbors, and/or requesting the recipient's assistance in making the needed repairs.

❑ Untoward Events Which Foster Community Animosity

Events and individuals' behaviors which cause community opposition or hostility, even when these occurrences may not have led to any direct harm to anyone, also warrant consideration by a community program's incident reporting system. Examples of such behaviors may include residents urinating in the street, loitering in local stores, begging small amounts of money or cigarettes from other customers, or discarding their garbage inappropriately.

Incidents which threaten a program's reputation and welcome in the neighborhood should be considered and addressed as reportable incidents.

Even when these incidents are isolated to one or two individuals, they can compromise the program's welcome in the neighborhood and adversely impact on the community's reception to other programs' enrollees. Allowing such behaviors to go unchecked, may threaten an individual's program enrollment or lead to his/her arrest for disorderly conduct or some other charge. Without attention, these incidents can also fuel community protests against the program.

For all of these reasons, incidents which threaten a program's reputation and welcome in the neighborhood should be considered and addressed as reportable incidents. While programs want to ensure that their interest in these events does not begin to prescribe a higher standard of community behavior for their program recipients than others in the community, programs do want to promote good citizenship. It is also important for program administrators to recognize that when these incidents are "overlooked," their ill-effects often fall most directly on their other service recipients, who may be unfairly stigmatized or shunned by community members due to the objectionable and offensive behaviors of a few. Peers who share residence in an apartment building where a program enrollee is discarding garbage in the corridors, or coworkers in a supportive employment site whose own work is disturbed by an individual who comes to work drunk and disorderly may believe that there is much more immediacy to the need to tell the individual that his/her offensive behavior must stop and that if it does not, fair but direct consequences will result.

Legal requirements governing external notifications vary markedly across states, and all community service agencies need to ensure that they fully understand and comply with these requirements.

When to Notify External Parties

In recreating their incident reporting systems, community programs also need to consider guidelines for external notifications to law enforcement officials, regulatory and funding agencies, and family members, guardians, and significant friends of the involved service recipient. Legal requirements governing external notifications vary markedly across states, and all community service agencies need to ensure that they fully understand and comply with these requirements.

In most cases, however, these requirements offer incomplete guidance to new community service programs where issues of criminal liability for program enrollees, as well as appropriate family member and guardian involvement and notification, can be considerably more complex and controversial. On the one hand, newer community service programs often shy away from external notifications as they seek to protect the privacy of their service recipients and sometimes also to shield them from legal liability. On the other hand, in some situations, external notifications can be especially helpful as community programs embrace the mutual concepts of choice and responsibility for their service recipients and as they reach out for the support of family members, guardians, and law enforcement officials who may be able to be more persuasive in communicating the danger of certain recipient choices or behaviors.

Some states, like New York, require community service agencies to report all knowledge of possible criminal acts; most, however, do not, leaving many of these decisions to the discretion of community agencies themselves.

Correspondingly, legal mandates for notifying external regulatory and funding agencies of reportable incidents are often too narrowly construed for the variety of incidents which may be reported in newer community services programs. While many community program administrators will shirk from calling state regulators in the case of any reportable incident not clearly mandating such notification, such calls can serve as a valuable risk management strategy for the program—as state officials can also be asked their advice for handling and responding to the incident. These calls are especially warranted when law enforcement officials are involved, when the incident has triggered adverse program publicity, and when the community program frankly does not know the best way to respond to the incident.

Notifying Law Enforcement Officials

Law enforcement notifications often present the most difficult program decision-making. Some states, like New York, require community service agencies to report all knowledge of possible criminal acts; most, however, do not, leaving many of these decisions to the discretion of community agencies themselves. Not unreasonably, most program administrators often avoid law enforcement notifications, except in cases of serious criminal conduct. Fearing adverse repercussions for service recipients and for their programs, program administrators will often not inform law enforcement of "minor" suspected or known criminal acts, including shoplifting; assaultive behavior, which results in no serious personal injury; nonserious property damage; prostitution; possession of small amounts of illegal drugs; etc.

Developing clear and explicit program guidelines governing law enforcement notifications promotes the accountability of these notifications and is in the best interest of service recipients and the program.

While there is much disagreement among clinical and legal experts in the field of mental disabilities regarding the above decisions, it seems clear that where legal mandates do not specify the obligation of service providers to report suspected or alleged criminal acts, community service agencies are well-advised to formalize their decision-making for these rulings. Developing clear and explicit program guidelines governing law enforcement notifications promotes the accountability of these notifications and is in the best interest of service recipients and the program. Formal guidelines also ensure that law enforcement notifications are made consistently and fairly—and that they do not become unpredictable "punishments," which recipients sometimes accurately perceive as matters of highly personal staff discretion.

Programs may seek to prescribe law enforcement notifications for some types of suspected or alleged criminal behavior. For example, most programs require that suspected criminal conduct which results in a serious injury to an individual or others and/or which involves serious criminal behavior, which may constitute a felony, should be shared with law enforcement officials. Yet, programs also need other guidelines to assist them in consistently making law enforcement notifications in instances

In formulating guidelines for law enforcement notifications, program administrators should also meet with local law enforcement officials.

of less serious alleged criminal conduct. Two useful general guidelines for programs to consider in guiding this decision-making include:

- requirements for law enforcement notification for alleged criminal conduct, regardless of the actual harm to the offender or others, if the risk of more serious harm to the offender or others was great; and,
- requirements for law enforcement notification in cases of recurring criminal conduct where the offender's behavior has not abated, despite program staff counseling, training, and support.

Thus, when a program enrollee, with a history of violent behavior, is illegally carrying a firearm, even when no one has yet been threatened, the program should seriously consider notifying law enforcement officials. Likewise, if a program enrollee is repeatedly shoplifting from the local Woolworth's despite counseling and warnings from staff,

When finalized, programs should ensure that all service recipients and staff are fully briefed about required law enforcement notifications when they join the program.

law enforcement notification may be warranted, although the purchase price of the stolen items is nominal.

In formulating guidelines for law enforcement notifications, program administrators should also meet with local law enforcement officials to discuss these reports, how they will be made, and if possible, cooperative arrangements governing the interrogation of service recipients and other aspects of criminal investigations. Such meetings should be held as often as needed to ensure strong working relationships with law enforcement officials.

Due to their importance, programs should clearly document their standards related to law enforcement notifications. In programs which have boards of directors, the board should also have an explicit role in reviewing and approving these guidelines. When finalized, programs should also ensure accountable procedures which guarantee that all service recipients and staff are fully briefed about required law enforcement notifications when they join the program. Consequences for failing to report these incidents and ensure that such notifications are made should also be clearly spelled out for all program administrators and staff.

Oversight of these notifications can place program enrollees, staff, and community members at severe risk of harm. These oversights—especially when they are detected in the wake of more serious criminal activity—can also have serious negative repercussions for the program and its other program enrollees, as the oversight may encourage community fears and mistrust of the program's ability to safely manage the risks presented by its enrollees.

Notification to Families, Guardians, and Friends

When to notify service recipients' family members, guardians, and significant friends of reported incidents is also usually a difficult program decision. Whereas notification requirements to parents and guardians are often clear in institutional and more traditional 24-hour staff supervised community residential programs, in newer community service programs, program enrollees are much more likely not to have legal guardians and/or appointed guardians are more likely to have limited, narrowly defined decision-making jurisdiction. At the same time, regardless of guardianship status, the notification, support, and assistance of these individuals who are close to the service recipient and care about his/her well-being are often desirable as community programs seek to address reportable incidents.

Community service programs should discuss family/guardian notifications with their enrollees at the time of their admission to the program, seeking a mutual agreement.

In the best case scenario, community service programs should discuss family/guardian notifications with their enrollees at the time of their admission to the program, seeking a mutual agreement of when (and which) family members and friends are to be notified of significant incidents. These agreements should be signed by the individual and, where applicable, by his/her legal guardian, and they should be communicated to case managers and maintained in the individual's program record. Periodically, but at least annually, these agreements should also be reviewed and re-signed and dated.

Like other advance directives, these prearranged agreements are especially helpful for individuals with mental health problems—who at the times they may most need the help of family members or friends, they may not be able to think clearly. These agreements are also beneficial for individuals with compromised cognitive abilities who may not always appreciate the seriousness (or potential seriousness) of situations they are experiencing or the help that family members and friends may be able to offer.

These agreements can also help community service programs as they seek to establish constructive relationships with family members and close friends. They help to clarify expectations up front and minimize misunderstandings. They also help to ensure that the programs can capitalize on the informal supports of family members and friends of individuals whom they serve, while at the same time, respecting their service recipients' privacy rights and needs to establish some independence.

Investigating Reportable Incidents

Many guidelines for special investigations of reportable incidents in newer community service programs are similar to those in institutional and 24-hour supervised community residential programs. For example, special investigations in both groups of programs seek basic fact-finding about the incident—focusing on what happened, when it happened, where it happened, why it happened, and who was involved.

In newer community service programs, like in other more traditional programs, special investigations are also uniformly warranted when there are allegations of staff abuse, neglect, mistreatment and exploitation, as well as in incidents which result in serious harm to residents or which appear to reflect program liability or staff culpability.

At the outset, it is likely that a greater percentage of the reportable incidents in these programs may warrant special fact-finding simply because staff usually are not present when incidents occur.

Yet, beyond these common attributes, guidelines for special investigations in newer community service programs also have their unique characteristics. At the outset, it is likely that a greater percentage of the reportable incidents in these programs may warrant special fact-finding simply because staff usually are not present when incidents occur, and more frequently, there are open questions about exactly what did occur, when it occurred, where it occurred, and who was involved. Much more often, staff will rely on "hearsay" information in filing their initial reports, and special investigations will be warranted to ensure that what was initially reported reflected what actually occurred.

The nature of the fact-finding surrounding reported incidents in newer community service programs is also likely to take on a different character and focus. In traditional programs, special investigations usually focus on program liability and staff culpability for the reported incident. This focus is also appropriate for some reported incidents in newer community service programs (i.e., incidents of alleged staff abuse, neglect, or other misconduct), but in these settings the issues of *direct* program and staff accountability for reportable incidents are more often quickly resolved.

In these programs—where service recipients more often self-determine the chain of events that lead to reportable incidents—special investigations often have a much more targeted consumer focus.

Instead, in these programs—where service recipients more often self-determine the chain of events that lead to reportable incidents—special investigations often have a much more targeted consumer focus. These investigations must probe much more deeply into: (1) the service recipient's choices and behaviors that led to the incident; (2) the individual's understanding of these choices and behaviors and their implications; and (3) the reasonableness of the staff's efforts (or lack thereof) in ensuring that the individual's personal choices and decisions were truly voluntary and informed, and in his/her best interest.

It is simply inconsistent for program administrators and staff to sit alone in reviewing and deliberating on incidents, many of which involve recipient choices, behaviors, and decision-making.

Central to resolving each of these issues is the primary role of service recipient testimony and the testimony of others who know the individual well. There is simply no way to resolve these questions without extensive interviews with the service recipient and those staff, family members, and friends who know him/her well. These interviews are also often much more complex than the simple what, where, when, and who fact-finding of special investigations in more traditional programs. Figure 3 provides some examples of interview questions which can be especially helpful in these investigations.

Incident Review Committees

Incident review committees also find their mission altered toward a greater consumer-centered focus in newer community service programs. As noted in the beginning of this article, the membership of incident review committees in newer community service programs must well represent program enrollees. In these programs which espouse service recipient empowerment and community independence as primary goals, it is simply inconsistent for program administrators and staff to sit alone in reviewing and deliberating on incidents,

Strict standards for confidentiality of committee discussions must be clearly explained and enforced. Any committee member who violates these standards should be immediately removed from the committee.

many of which involve recipient choices, behaviors, and decision-making.

Yet, involving current and former program enrollees on these committees will require far more than making careful committee membership selections. It is critically important that formal training programs and user-friendly training materials be developed for all incident review committee members, including service recipients. These materials should start with the basics, explaining the agency's policies and procedures for incident reporting, review, and investigation, as well as the role and responsibilities of incident review committees and their members. They should also clearly delineate any state legal mandates related to incident reporting, investigation, and review—including any mandated involvement of law enforcement officials.

Consumer Choice Investigation Inquiries

❏ How did the individual's personal choices and decisions lead to the incident? How likely was the adverse consequence given the individual's choices and behaviors?

❏ Were the individual's choices and decisions which led to the incident truly informed and voluntary? Was he/she influenced by another or others who encouraged unwise decisions? Did he/she comprehend the possible adverse consequences of the decisions made? Did he/she understand that there were other options which may have been less dangerous?

❏ Assuming that the individual's choices and decisions were informed and voluntary, did he/she intentionally pursue these decisions with the objective of harming himself/herself?

Alternately, were the risky choices and behaviors chosen because the individual believed that the risk was worth other potential benefits? If so, was the individual's assessment of the potential benefits logical and reasonably sound (i.e., might a nondisabled adult make a similar decision given the same circumstances)?

❏ Were program staff aware that the individual was considering making a potentially dangerous choice or decision? If so, what did they do to try to prevent the dangerous choice or mitigate its potentially adverse outcome? Were these actions appropriate and consistent with program's expectations?

❏ If program staff were aware of the pending risk to the individual, did they take appropriate actions in notifying (or not notifying) their supervisor?

Figure 3

Confidentiality requirements will require extra attention, as well. Wherever possible, the identities of service recipients and program staff involved in reported incidents should be redacted from circulated documents, and they should be concealed from committee members. In addition, strict standards for confidentiality of committee discussions must be clearly explained and enforced. Any committee member who violates these standards should be immediately removed from the committee. Committee members who have personal relationships with individuals involved in a reported incident should also remove themselves from any committee deliberation of the incident.

The focus is less directly on what the program or staff may have done wrong, as on what the program or staff could have done better *. . this task of contemplating opportunities lost, or simply not noticed, is a more difficult deliberation and judgment.*

Incident review committee members of newer community service programs will also find that as they expand their reviews beyond the issues of staff and program direct responsibility or culpability for reported incidents, they will be confronted by complex considerations and deliberations. Frequently they will be asked to look beyond the immediate circumstances of the incident and consider how staff may have intervened in the long chain of events and service recipient personal choices and behaviors which led up to the adverse incident.

Here, the focus is less directly on what the program or staff may have done wrong, as on *what the program or staff could have done better* to empower the individual in making voluntary, informed choices and decisions which may have resulted in more positive outcomes and better safeguarded his/her well-being. Clearly, this task of contemplating opportunities lost, or simply not noticed, is a more difficult deliberation and judgment. Figure 4 provides a listing of questions that may be especially helpful to review committee members as they attempt to shift their deliberations both to a more consumer-centered and quality improvement focus.

Conclusion

Re-creating incident reporting systems to address issues of consumer choice and program responsibility in newer community service programs is a management reform whose time has come. While untoward events emanating from staff misconduct and poor judgment unfortunately continue in commu-

Inquiries for Incident Review Committees
Community Service Programs

☐ Was all needed immediate and follow-up medical and mental health treatment afforded to the individual? If not, why not, and what can be done to prevent such lapses in the future?

☐ Were all required and warranted external notifications made to regulatory bodies, law enforcement officials, and family members and legal guardians?

☐ What assistance and support should be given to the individual in handling any long-term adverse physical, emotional, social, or financial consequences of the incident?

☐ Has sufficient program staff support been offered to ensure that the individual fully understands and appreciates the adverse consequences of his/her unwise and dangerous choices or behaviors?

☐ What additional training and/or staff assistance and support should be offered to the individual in avoiding similar future incidents?

☐ Are there other sources of support or assistance available to the individual from friends, family, or neighbors which may help to preclude future incidents?

☐ If the individual has resisted needed support, assistance, and/or training, why has he/she resisted this help? Can the needed assistance or training be packaged or delivered in another manner which the individual may find more acceptable?

Figure 4

nity programs, the far more common and perplexing protection from harm issues in newer community service programs are those which require program review to help service recipients avoid dangerous personal choices and to make better choices which promote their self-interests.

As the sphere of the protection from harm issues shifts in newer community programs, so must program administrators reorient their incident reporting systems, creating more viable risk management safety nets for their consumers. Many of these changes will challenge conventional views of quality assurance in services for persons with mental disabilities. This transformation, most fundamentally, will require that program administrators recenter their incident reporting systems on consumer interests, establishing new and more significant roles for service recipients in cooperative program risk management, quality assurance, and other oversight activities for their programs.

Both program staff and service recipients will need training and ongoing administrative support and direction as they make these changes. As detailed in this article, many procedural changes will also follow, as community service programs refocus their incident reporting systems to be more compatible with program goals of consumer empowerment and independence in daily life. In short, re-creating incident reporting systems to fit newer community service programs will require administrative, staff, and service recipient effort, but in the end, it will also yield a much more viable forum for consumer growth and independence in daily living choices which promote their best self-interest.

SECTION FOUR
CASE STUDIES

20

In the Matter of Jeff Kerwin: What Would You Have Done?

Thomas R. Harmon

Introduction

This is the story of Jeff Kerwin (a pseudonym), whose life and death—at age 37 due to complications from Prader-Willi syndrome—are testimony to the very real service delivery dilemma: when client rights and choices clash with professional responsibilities.[1]

Prader-Willi syndrome (PWS) is a developmental disability afflicting between four to ten people out of every 100,000. A complex disorder with multiple physical, cognitive, and behavioral characteristics, PWS was identified as a clinical entity and a birth defect only in the late 1950s. Since then, genetic studies have linked PWS to anomalies in chromosome #15 in a majority of cases; in others, the disorder's etiology is less clear.

Jeff Kerwin's life and death are testimony to the very real dilemma: when client rights and choices clash with professional responsibilities.

Among the key clinical characteristics of PWS are:

☐ **Hyperphagia and Obesity**

Although at birth infants with PWS have a poor sucking ability, difficulty swallowing, and little interest in feeding, within the first years of life food becomes their dominant, compelling interest. Young children, adolescents, and adults with PWS will consume any food in sight. Never feeling satiated, the person with PWS will continue to eat as long as food is available and, if left unchecked, will search for more: raiding cupboards, rummaging through garbage cans, and sometimes even stealing from stores or neighbors' houses. Uncontrolled, the person with PWS, even as a child, will become obese to the point that mobility is impaired and life jeopardized.

❑ **Impaired Cognitive Ability**

Almost all individuals with PWS (97%) have some degree of mental retardation, although some have been found with IQs as high as 100. Typically, IQs range between 20 and 90, and the average IQ is 65. Most individuals with PWS fall within the mild mental retardation/borderline intelligence strata.

❑ **Physical Anomalies**

In addition to uncontrollable hunger, obesity, and retarded mental development, people with PWS share other unique physical characteristics including hypotonia (poor muscle coordination and tone) which affects mobility and respiratory and skeletal systems; hypogonadism (underdeveloped or disordered primary and secondary sexual characteristics) which affects fertility, sexual identity, and self-esteem; and other physical anomalies including short stature, abnormally small hands and feet, unusual facial features, and a tendency to bruise easily, compounded by a propensity to pick at skin injuries—often leading to infections.

> *There is no cure for Prader-Willi syndrome. Treatment focuses on addressing its symptoms, chiefly the excessive weight gain. Absent interventions, the prognosis is bleak and promises early death from obesity-related problems.*

❑ **Behavioral/Social Difficulties**

Although described as generally having pleasant dispositions, persons with PWS are prone to episodes of emotional, violent outbursts and temper tantrums, as well as bouts of depression. Contributing factors include: frustration over inability to obtain food, social rejection by peers, and a sense of "needing to be in control," usually related to food intake. Episodes of manipulation, property destruction, stealing or foraging for food, and depression are mingled with periods of "naive friendliness, docility, and affability," as described in the literature.

There is no cure for Prader-Willi syndrome. Rather, treatment focuses on addressing its symptoms, chiefly the excessive weight gain and associated problems, through strict environmental and dietary controls and behavior modification. Absent these interventions, the prognosis for individuals with PWS is bleak and promises early death from obesity-related problems (diabetes, heart or kidney failure, etc.), or possibly poisoning (stemming from food foraging activities), or infection (associated with poor circulation, skin-picking behavior, and reduced sensitivity to pain).[2]

The Early Years

Jeff Kerwin was born in 1957, one year after Prader-Willi was identified as a clinical syndrome by the Swiss physicians for whom it was named.

Clinical records are silent on many aspects of his early years; however, they revealed that he was the product of a full-term pregnancy and normal delivery, but as an infant had poor sucking reflexes and muscle tone. He was described as a "floppy baby" and had delayed developmental milestones. Soon after his birth, Jeff's parents divorced, and his mother eventually remarried.

Throughout his childhood and adolescence, Jeff lived with his mother and stepfather in upstate New York and attended special education programs. The records reviewed did not shed much light on Jeff's weight or eating habits during these years, or

Jeff was diagnosed as having Prader-Willi when he was in his 20s. To control his eating, the family locked cupboards and chained the refrigerator shut.

when Prader-Willi syndrome was entertained as a possible diagnosis. It is documented, however, that Jeff tested in the borderline range of intelligence and was obese.

According to Jeff's mother, Jeff was not diagnosed as having Prader-Willi syndrome until the early 1980s when he was in his 20s. Until then, she knew he was "different" and had emotional, behavioral, and learning difficulties, but the cause was not clear.

Primary among his problems, according to his mother, was his uncontrollable eating and excessive weight. Less than 5 feet tall, Jeff's weight fluctuated between 200 to over 400 pounds. To control his eating, the family locked cupboards and chained the refrigerator shut. As Jeff would unscrew hinges or handles to gain access to food, or steal from neighbors' houses, someone had to be with him almost constantly, and it was nearly impossible to take him out to social functions or to visit relatives or friends. Mrs. Kerwin reported that neither she nor her husband had much of an out-of-home life as all of their energy was spent trying to limit Jeff's access to food, a constant struggle in which Jeff usually prevailed.

Following completion of his special education school program and receipt of his General Education Diploma, Jeff continued to live with his parents. For a brief period he attended a sheltered workshop, but dropped out and spent his days at home.

Sometime after the diagnosis of PWS was made, Jeff was admitted to a nutritional rehabilitation program in Connecticut. The year was 1983, he was 26 years old and, at 4 feet 10 inches tall, weighed 390 pounds. The placement was short-lived, however, and Jeff was discharged due to his frequent emotional outbursts and tendency to victimize other residents—stealing their food and money (to buy food).

Upon discharge, Jeff entered a community residence for developmentally disabled persons near his family in upstate New York. However, he was soon discharged due to his tantrums and refusals to follow staff directions and the rules of the house. For several months, Jeff lived independently. According to family members, he did not care for himself properly and gained additional weight. During this period he also developed severe and recurrent leg ulcers, due to poor circulation. Treatment of the ulcers required inpatient care at a local hospital. Following discharge from the hospital, Jeff lived with his parents and received outpatient services from the local district office of the State Office of Mental Retardation and Developmental Disabilities. The services, which consisted of counseling and family supports, were conducted in the home, as Jeff refused to leave the family residence for work, social, or recreational programs.

At age 30 he was admitted to a community residence developed to serve individuals with PWS.

A Special Placement

By 1986, Jeff's family was unable to manage him at home, and at age 29 he was admitted to an eight-bed community residence developed by the Office of Mental Retardation and Developmental Disabilities to serve individuals with PWS. It was located more than 200 miles from his home.

The residence provided strict environmental controls to limit food access (including locked cupboards and refrigerator), as well as special nutritional and exercise regimens and behavior modification and counseling services. It was also the expectation that all residents would engage in, and be challenged and rewarded by, meaningful daytime activities. All aspects of daily life were highly controlled and monitored to ensure health—including smoking, which was one of Jeff's pleasures, but is strongly ill-advised for persons with PWS.

Entering the residence weighing over 400 pounds, over the next five years through environmental and behavior controls, diet, exercise, and counseling, Jeff lost approximately 250 pounds, coming within 30 pounds of his ideal body weight (IBW) of 95–121 pounds. He also began attending a sheltered workshop where he earned over $50 a week, when he was willing to work.

During this period, genetic testing revealed deficiencies in chromosome #15, confirming the PWS diagnosis, and intelligence testing resulted in a full-range IQ score of 71, indicating that Jeff was of borderline intelligence. Health-wise, Jeff suffered a number of the side effects of his obesity/PWS,

According to his mother and residence staff, the years Jeff spent in this facility were among his healthiest.

including high blood pressure, congestive heart failure, and poor circulation. Excessive fat tissue and recurrent leg ulcers prompted several surgical interventions (liposuction and skin grafts).

According to his mother and residence staff, the years Jeff spent in this facility were among his healthiest—he tended to health issues, engaged in work activities and, for a period of time, kept his weight down to about 150 pounds. However, according to his mother and facility staff, he also developed a sense of what were his "individual rights" and an increased determination to exercise his views on this matter.

Admitted to the residence on a voluntary basis, in time, Jeff began to rebel against its regimented structure. He would elope from the program, only to be returned; sneak food into the residence; demand to be allowed to smoke; etc. While on visits to the family home on holidays, to which he could travel independently, Jeff would break from his special diet regimen and gain excessive amounts of weight, sometimes up to 20 pounds in a two-week period.

After more than five years in the residential program, Jeff demanded to be discharged. He was transferred to a developmental center. The purpose of the placement was to provide respite—it was hoped that Jeff would return to the PWS residence voluntarily.

The Placement Ends, October 1991

Eventually, in October 1991, at age 34 after more than five years in the residential program and increasing elopements and complaints about the home's rigid rules, Jeff demanded to be discharged. He was transferred to the local state developmental center in whose catchment area the residence was located. The center is a several-hundred-bed institution serving a population by and large far more disabled and lower functioning than Jeff. The purpose of the placement was to provide Jeff respite—a safe haven and a cooling-off period of several weeks—after which, it was planned, or rather hoped, that Jeff would return to the PWS residence voluntarily.

While in the center, however, Jeff stole food from other residents and engaged in property destruction, assaults, and self-injurious behavior. He disagreed with the plan to return to the PWS residence and, asserting his right not to be held in the center against his will, formally demanded his release/discharge. He stated that he wanted to live independently in his own apartment. Although Jeff was fairly high functioning—able to read and write on a third-grade level, travel independently, and manage money to some extent—clinicians were concerned that he had little insight or motivation to manage his PWS and related health care needs. It was felt that if he lived independently, he would not adhere to his special diet or care for his recurrent leg ulcers and infections, and thus his health would be severely compromised.

In October 1991, the facility applied to the Supreme Court for an order authorizing Jeff's involuntary retention and treatment at the center. Citing Jeff's diagnosis of Prader-Willi syndrome, his borderline intelligence, his history of gaining excessive weight resulting in compromised health while living independently, and his resistance to proper dietary and exercise regimens which would benefit him, as well as his resistance to medical attention for recurrent leg ulcers, the facility indicated that Jeff was at risk for a variety of medical complications and death. The facility posited that Jeff required care and treatment for his developmental disability and that his judgement was so impaired that he was unable to understand the need for such care and, as a result, posed a substantial threat of physical harm to himself or others. The Court authorized Jeff's involuntary retention for a period of 60 days.

> *Jeff agreed to a plan: placement in a supervised community residence, but not a Prader-Willi residence. He agreed to a voluntary transfer to a developmental center near his parents from which he could be placed in a community residence.*

During the next two months, facility staff worked with Jeff to try to develop a viable treatment and placement plan. It was clear to staff that the developmental center was not the most appropriate placement for Jeff, given his abilities. Staff also noted that there was no compelling evidence that Jeff's condition posed an *immediate* danger warranting the restrictive setting and services of the center, and that if a court hearing was held at the end of the 60-day involuntary retention period, the judge might order his immediate release. Staff appreciated, however, that once on his own, Jeff's overeating might eventually result in life-threatening health problems.

Jeff, on the other hand, was adamant that he would never return to the Prader-Willi residence, with all its restrictions and rules, asserting that he knew his rights and nobody could make him. He also protested (and broke) the rules of the developmental center, particularly those pertaining to smoking and eating. For example, upset with the "no smoking" plan staff developed for him, Jeff secured the assistance of a legal service which fashioned a compromise agreement that Jeff could smoke, but only five to eight cigarettes a day.

> *He would demand his personal allowance and spend it as he saw fit, sometimes purchasing and eating up to 15 candy bars at a time.*

Toward the end of the two-month involuntary retention period, as staff were preparing an application for a one-year, court-ordered involuntary commitment, Jeff agreed to a plan: placement in a supervised community residence, but not a Prader-Willi residence. As he also wanted to live closer to his family, he agreed to a voluntary transfer to a developmental center near his parents from which he could be placed in a community residence, once a bed became available. His family was agreeable to the plan.

At the New Center, March 1992

Jeff arrived at the new developmental center, a several-hundred-bed facility in upstate New York, in late March 1992. At that time he was 34 years old and weighed 178 pounds.

From the time of arrival, Jeff tended to be isolative and manipulative, according to the center's records. He refused to follow a special diet designed to address his PWS. (The diet consisted of three regular daily meals totaling 1,000 calories, with several snacks in between consisting of salads and Jello.) Claiming, "It is my money, and I have a right to it," he would demand his personal allowance funds and spend as he saw fit, sometimes purchasing and eating up to 15 candy bars at a time. He also broke the facility's smoking rules, stole from others, and engaged in property destruction and self-abuse if staff attempted to set limits. At one point he opened one of the skin grafts on his leg with a nail clipper when he felt staff were infringing on his rights. (Initially, he refused to allow staff to tend to his ulcerous legs, but in time relented and even became proficient in caring for them himself.)

Although Jeff participated productively in a workshop where he earned money, he refused to cooperate with professional staff, even those responsible for conducting assessments. He refused to speak with psychologists, social workers, and the nutritionist.

As he refused to speak, attempts to conduct full-scale intelligence testing, last completed in 1986, were futile. On the basis of staff observations, however, an Adaptive Behavior Scale was performed.

Almost two months after admission, Jeff had gained over 30 pounds and weighed 210 pounds.

This indicated that Jeff's daily living skills were on par with those of an adult, but that his socialization skills were the equivalent of a ten-year-old child, largely due to his poor coping abilities. His communication skills were about on the same level. But his fine and gross motors skills were on par with those of a five-year-old child, largely due to physiological problems associated with his PWS.

After weeks of attempted assessments and observations, Jeff was assigned the diagnoses of borderline intelligence, Prader-Willi syndrome, conduct disorder, and passive-aggressive disorder. Although considered, it was not felt that he suffered from a psychotic disorder. Medically, he was diagnosed as having a number of problems associated with his PWS, including morbid obesity, chronic leg ulcers, circulatory problems, and a history of hypertension and congestive heart failure.

By mid-May 1992, almost two months after admission, Jeff had gained over 30 pounds and weighed 210 pounds. Consultants were called in on the case. It was their impression that the developmental center, given its size and population mix, was not the most appropriate environment to afford the degree of structure Jeff required, given his unique needs, and that he would best benefit from a smaller, highly structured community residence or a behaviorally oriented family care home. They also noted, however, that the center should target the most important behaviors which *must* (emphasis theirs) be controlled, such as Jeff's stealing, food scavenging and aggression, while he remained in the center.

The consultants recommended that a very highly structured behavior management plan be developed to begin to address the target behaviors and that a search for a small, but very structured, community-based program be initiated.

About two weeks after the consultants' report was received, Jeff eloped from the facility.

Discharge Planning, June 1992

Within three days Jeff was found and returned to the center, whereupon he demanded to be released.

Senior clinicians conducted assessments and conferred, concluding that Jeff was not in immediate danger. They also concluded that Jeff suffered no clinical condition which would warrant petitioning a court for his involuntary retention: while he was overweight and prone to ulcers, his medical condition, including blood pressure and ulcers, was stable; he suffered no infections; he was able to care for his skin condition; and, on interview, he indicated that he would "assume responsibility" for reasonable caloric intake.

Jeff was agreeable to staff's suggestions that he stay at the facility for a couple of days so that placement and discharge plans could be arranged. However, he resisted all suggestions of supervised community residences which, in staff's opinion, offered the structure needed for management of his PWS.

Jeff demanded to be released. Senior clinicians conducted assessments and conferred, concluding that Jeff was not in immediate danger.

The only option Jeff would agree to, short of living independently, was a home for adults, which essentially offers room and board and a minimal degree of supervision (regulations require one staff person for every 40 residents).

On June 10, 1992, Jeff was released to a 375-bed adult home which he had visited and liked.

The discharge plan called for Jeff to live in the adult home temporarily, until he was willing to move to a more supervised setting. For his health needs, Jeff was to attend a family practice clinic of a local hospital. He was also to be referred to the State's Office of Vocational and Educational Services for Individuals with Disabilities (VESID) to be assessed and trained for vocational/daytime activities.

According to the plan, staff of the developmental center's outpatient services, including a case manager and a nurse, were to visit Jeff regularly to monitor his status and intervene or advocate for additional services when the need arose.

The discharge plan noted that these were not the most desirable or appropriate arrangements for Jeff, but the best ones possible given his resistance to other service options, including staying at the center until alternative arrangements could be made, and the absence of clinical conditions which would justify his involuntary retention.

The plan also noted that Jeff's mother was consulted on the matter and reluctantly agreed to the discharge while citing concerns over his PWS and his inability to independently manage this condition.

Five months after Jeff's death, his mother told investigators that she cried and begged center staff not to release her son. She claimed facility staff advised her that they had no legal recourse but to let him go, and counseled her on "rights and dignity" issues. She told investigators that she questioned, "What about his right to live? Where is the dignity in being allowed to eat impulsively, with no controls, to the point of death?" But, she relented to the plan, she said, because, "They knew the law, they were the professionals...but they didn't know my son."

From the onset, Jeff's attempt at independent living was fraught with problems.

Freedom and Death, June 1992–August 1993

From the onset, Jeff's attempt at independent living and life in the community was fraught with problems.

He refused referrals to VESID, as he did not want to be associated with programs which served "the retarded." His relationship with the family practice clinic quickly ended after he was reportedly demanding, yet non-compliant. Depending on whom one spoke with, Jeff either "wore out his welcome at the clinic," due to his behaviors, or just plain refused to go to the clinic.

More significantly, Jeff's residential arrangement fell apart. Upon arrival at the adult home, he soon got into altercations and arguments with staff and fellow residents. He was ridiculed by the home's clientele over his appearance and taunted with questions like: "Are you a man or a woman?" He reportedly stole money from residents and, when he didn't get his way, threatened others with harm. When arguments escalated to the point of becoming physical, police were called. Within 60 days, the adult home management initiated eviction proceedings against Jeff, as his behaviors threatened the well-being of other residents and substantially interfered with the orderly operations of the facility.

Following eviction in August 1992, Jeff moved through a succession of placements in welfare hotels and one brief, five-day stay in a community residence. During this period, he was robbed, arrested for shoplifting candy and cigarettes, and neglectful of his personal hygiene. He was noted, by staff in the respite community residence, to be malodorous and spending his allowance on bags of junk food.

From the time of Jeff's discharge from the developmental center in June 1992, the case manager from the center maintained nearly daily contact with him. Many of the contacts were of a crisis nature: trying to mediate problems in the adult home; assisting Jeff secure new housing; resolving Jeff's legal problems; and helping Jeff secure entitlements or extra money when he was short of funds. But during the calm between storms, the case manager maintained just as frequent contact with Jeff: taking him to dinner or food shopping (to ensure, to some degree, he was eating a healthy diet); reminding him to bathe; socializing with him; and encouraging

Jeff appeared to be gaining weight, and periodically his leg ulcers were infected.

him to become involved in VESID services or other daytime activities, including volunteer work, in which Jeff expressed a fleeting interest. By early November, the case manager found an apartment for Jeff, so he would no longer have to live in a spartan hotel room. Together they furnished and decorated it, shopping for furniture, curtains, cleaning and cooking materials, etc.

The nurse from the developmental center also visited Jeff regularly to monitor his health status. During visits by the nurse, or even to the doctor's office, Jeff refused to be weighed; the nurse, however, noted that he appeared to be gaining weight. She also noted that while grocery shopping, Jeff would buy pie and pudding, in addition to excessive amounts of meat. (It appears, based on the comments of others who visited Jeff and found empty pizza boxes and other food containers, that he also called for take-out deliveries.)

Periodically, the nurse would find that Jeff's leg ulcers were infected, draining purulent fluid. On these occasions, she would arrange for a visit to the doctor. Although Jeff would not comply with the physician's requests and advice concerning his weight, the nurse noted he would follow the physician's orders (topical antibiotics and fresh dressings) for the leg infections which, in time, would improve.

By December 1992, Jeff had begun to experience other problems. Due to his increased weight and ambulation problems, he had difficulty using the bathroom in his apartment. He needed a toilet raiser, grab bars to ensure safety getting in and out of the shower/tub area, and a hand-held shower head so that he could more thoroughly wash. He was also informed that the developmental center was planning to transfer his outpatient services to a not-for-profit agency in the area which would continue his case management services, a change that made Jeff uneasy. And, on occasion, he was lonely; he would call the developmental center's Administrator on Duty, who in turn would call the case manager who would promptly visit Jeff.

Jeff's case manager and others from the developmental center worked on securing adaptive equipment for his bathroom. But they also encouraged him to return to the developmental center, or move to a community residence, or agree to admission to a rehabilitation center in Pennsylvania which specialized in the treatment of PWS. Jeff refused. He stated he was happy and that he would rather have one year of life in his apartment, than ten years in a residential program. He even refused offers to return to the developmental center, even on a periodic basis, to use its facilities for showering, socializing, etc.

He stated he was happy and that he would rather have one year of life in his apartment, than ten years in a residential program.

Over the next six months (January–June 1993), Jeff continued to gain weight. Although he refused to be weighed, staff saw an obvious increase in his size to the point where it was difficult to find and purchase clothes which fit; they also noted that while shopping, Jeff would load up on bread, nuts, and other ill-advised food items. He refused to listen to their suggestions on healthy choices. He experienced mood swings and periods of sadness and sleeping difficulties; but he rejected his physician's suggestion of trying the medication Prozac to treat his emotional difficulties, as well as his rigidity/compulsive eating. He also experienced periodic problems with his leg ulcers, which he would only sometimes allow nursing staff to treat. And he continued to reject suggestions that he move to a more supervised setting or seek admission to the PWS rehabilitation facility in Pennsylvania.

During this period, Jeff's case management services were transferred from the developmental center to the private developmental disabilities service agency. This occurred gradually over period of several months so that Jeff could become accustomed to his new case managers; as developmental center staff started to reduce and eventually fade-out their visits, staff from the private agency began to visit Jeff and increase the frequency of their visits.

Jeff continued to gain weight; he had difficulty walking even 10 feet and was taken to the hospital on two successive days for shortness of breath. It was felt that his episodes of shortness of breath were associated with his morbid obesity.

The plan called for staff from the private agency to visit Jeff ten hours weekly to help him with nutritional issues, housekeeping, and attending medical appointments. As Jeff was having increased difficulty ambulating due to his weight, the plan called for purchasing a scooter so he could get around outside his apartment and go to stores. Due to budget constraints, however, the private agency never received funding for a full ten hours of weekly staff service or for the scooter. Nevertheless, the agency's case manager visited Jeff nearly every other day. Arrangements were made for a nurse from the county health department to periodically assess Jeff's legs and overall health status.

The new case manager recorded her concerns about Jeff's failure to maintain his diet, as well as his gaining weight and refusing to allow the nurse to conduct assessments.

By the end of June 1993, the case manager notified her supervisor of her concerns over Jeff's health. He had difficulty walking even 10 feet. At about the same time, Jeff was taken to the hospital on two successive days for shortness of breath. On the first day he refused to be examined by anyone. His private physician was called by the hospital and attempted to speak with Jeff in the emergency room by phone. Jeff refused to speak to him and left the hospital against medical advice.

On the second day, Jeff allowed an assessment: his vital signs were within normal limits, his lungs were clear, and his respiratory status was normal. It was

Staff expressed their concerns over Jeff's life and safety. He rejected their suggestions of placement in a supervised residence, but agreed to admission to a Prader-Willi syndrome rehabilitation program in Pennsylvania.

felt that his periodic episodes of shortness of breath were associated with his morbid obesity, and he was referred to his private physician.

In early July, the case manager and her supervisor met with Jeff. By this point, his weight (believed to be in excess of 400 pounds and possibly closer to 500) impaired his ability to do simple tasks around his house; he even had difficulty standing and walking in his apartment. He was so large that he could no longer get into the shower/tub area, and it was felt he needed a specially designed shower area into which he could be rolled on a chair. He could no longer use the toilet, but he refused to discuss how he was managing this need. (The agency initiated a bidding process for bathroom renovations.)

During the meeting, agency staff expressed their concerns over Jeff's life and safety. He rejected their suggestions of placement in a supervised residence, but agreed to admission to a Prader-Willi syndrome rehabilitation program in Pennsylvania. By this time, according to some people who knew him, Jeff was afraid and knew his PWS was out of control. However, in the opinion of others, including Jeff's private community-based physician whom Jeff had allowed to treat his leg ulcers on occasion, but not the PWS-related issues, Jeff did not really understand the nature and consequences of his PWS.

Staff of the private agency promptly sent out an application to the Pennsylvania program and followed this up with letters to his private physician seeking additional clinical information to facilitate admission and to Medicaid officials requesting permission for out-of-state treatment.

On August 27, 1993, Jeff died in his sleep. Prader-Willi syndrome was identified as a contributing factor. Days later, his case manager received notice that Jeff's admission to the center in Pennsylvania had been approved.

Staff also arranged for daily aide service in Jeff's apartment to assist in housekeeping tasks, etc. But Jeff, who was now essentially bed- or chair-bound, refused to allow anyone (i.e., visiting nurses) to assess his physical condition. He also refused to see his doctor, although by August he was complaining about his leg ulcers and feeling worse with every passing day.

Anticipating that Jeff would be approved for admission to the Pennsylvania program, staff started to make arrangements for his transportation to the program. However, on the morning of August 27, 1993, Jeff died in his sleep. His death was attributed to congestive heart failure; Prader-Willi syndrome was identified as a contributing factor.

Several days later, Jeff's case manager received notice that Jeff's admission to the rehabilitation center in Pennsylvania had been approved.

Discussion

The universal reaction to Jeff's death among those who knew him well—including family, nurses, clinicians, and case managers—was profound sadness. But this was accompanied by anger on the part of some who rued the day Jeff was released from the protective, yet restrictive, environment of supervised living; and discontent on the part of others who, while believing they acted on Jeff's behalf by respecting, even facilitating, his wish to live independently, were uncomfortable with the outcome—his death.

All, many in tears during interviews, questioned whether things could have, or should have, been done differently. Even with the clarity of hindsight which tragedy often brings, each wrestled with what should have tipped the balance in decision-making: clinical opinions of what would be in Jeff's best interest, or Jeff's preference. Each wrestled with the dilemma posed when professional responsibility and client choice clash.

Decisions which expose individuals to little or no risk of harm do not warrant rigorous scrutiny or vigorous intervention by service providers.

Increasingly, providers are facing this dilemma as the service system evolves from a very paternalistic mode—in which clients' choices and wishes played a back seat role to "professional wisdom" about what is in their best interest—to one in which service recipients are seen as equal partners in steering the course of service delivery and whose wishes and choices should be as valued as the wisdom and advice of professionals.

While there are no easy answers as to what to do when partners in the service compact disagree over which direction their shared venture should go, there are guideposts to aide professionals in difficult decision-making. They call for: assessing whether the choice being expressed by the consumer is consistent with what is known to be his or her stable or persistent values, preferences, and interests; and assessing the probability, severity, and duration of harm, if any, associated with the choice being expressed by the consumer.

Decisions which expose individuals to little or no risk of harm and are clearly consistent with the known values and interests of the individual, even if they are ill-advised choices (such as a person with Prader-Willi syndrome going off his or her diet once a month), do not warrant rigorous scrutiny or vigorous intervention by service providers. However, as the risk of harm associated with an individual's choices increases, in terms of its probability, severity, or duration, or as it becomes less clear whether a choice expressed is consistent with the individual's values or best interests, the need for careful professional scrutiny and intervention likewise increases.

As the risk of harm increases, or as it becomes less clear whether a choice expressed is consistent with the individual's values or best interests, the need for careful professional scrutiny and intervention likewise increases.

Jeff consistently and clearly expressed his wishes; some—such as not wanting to be associated with "retarded people"—posed little danger or risk and were not counter to his best interests. Others, such as his wanting to smoke, did not pose an imminent risk of harm. Yet others, chiefly his desire to live without constraints over his food intake, posed a high probability of serious harm which, left unchecked, would also pose imminent harm.

Jeff's legacy is a challenge to all service providers to reflect upon his life—his disabilities, his abilities and wishes, the services provided, and the decisions made—in

Jeff's diagnosis of Prader-Willi syndrome carried with it an early death sentence.

order that they are better prepared to respond to a conflict for which there are no easy answers: when clients' rights and choices clash with professional responsibilities.

- Jeff's diagnosis of Prader-Willi syndrome carried with it an early death sentence, unless his eating could be controlled by external parties. His history confirmed he was unable to independently control his food intake, and consequently he gained excessive amounts of weight and suffered health-related problems prior to admission to a facility with a controlled environment in 1986. Should he have been allowed to leave a controlled environment and live independently? Should staff have made more vigorous efforts to use involuntary commitment to keep him in a developmental center? What other alternatives did they have?

- His diagnosis of Prader-Willi syndrome was also accompanied with limited cognitive abilities, impaired mobility, and stunted emotional, social, and physical development. Although developmentally disabled, Jeff, with an IQ of 71, was not "technically" mentally retarded. But was he, based on his clinical condition and history, suffering from a developmental disability about which he lacked

Should he have been allowed to live independently? Should his opinions and choices have been given the deference that they were?

an understanding of the need for treatment? Should his opinions and choices have been given the deference that they were?

- During an eight-month period, between October 1991 and June 1992, two state developmental centers arrived at two different decisions about Jeff's clinical capacity to consent to treatment. The first center believed he lacked the ability to understand his need for treatment and secured a court order for involuntary care when Jeff demanded to be discharged; the second center, confronted with the same clinical picture/information and Jeff's demands for release, discharged him. Should a court-ordered retention have been attempted?

- Were the discharge and aftercare plans for Jeff appropriate once he left the developmental center, was evicted from an adult home, and eventually settled into his own apartment? Should his noncompliance with plans to maintain his health while in the community—such as weight monitoring, compliance with dietary and medical regimens, etc.—have triggered additional action, including involuntary retention and treatment?

- When Jeff left the developmental center in June 1992, his health was relatively stable. Although overweight, his hypertension was under control; his skin condition was good; he had no infections, and he demonstrated an ability to tend to recurrent ulcers; and he asserted he would assume responsibility for reasonable caloric intake. Over the next 14 months, Jeff's weight more than doubled, his ulcers worsened and were periodically infected, he had difficulty walking even 10 feet, suffered respiratory difficulties, became bed- or chair-bound as he could not

He wanted the opportunity of at least one year of living in freedom over the alternative of continued incarceration. Were the agencies which facilitated this wish assisting or harming Jeff?

walk, and eventually died. Clearly, he left the developmental center in relatively good health, claiming he could care for himself; but in the ensuing months, his health declined to a life-threatening degree, illustrating his inability to properly care for himself. Should staff have intervened to ensure he received the services he required, even on an involuntary basis? At what point? When should concerns over his rights and choices have been overridden by concerns for his life and health? Who should have been involved in making this determination?

- Jeff, despite having Prader-Willi syndrome, associated health problems and limited cognitive abilities, wanted his freedom. He did not want to be associated with "retarded" people. He did not want his refrigerator locked, and cigarettes counted, or be denied the opportunity to go to a grocery store to buy what he wished. He did not want people inspecting his body or inquiring about his weight, which he already knew was too much, different, and embarrassing. After seven years in the controlled environments of developmental centers or community residences, he did not want to be associated with programs which made those demands or monitored his compliance. He wanted the opportunity of at least one year of living in freedom over the alternative of continued incarceration. Were the agencies which facilitated this wish assisting or harming Jeff?

- What would you have done?

Endnotes

1. Jeff Kerwin is a pseudonym for an individual whose August 1993 death was brought to the Commission's attention by one of the service agencies with which he had been affiliated. This case study was developed based on a review of Mr. Kerwin's residential and outpatient records and interviews with his mother and staff of agencies which provided him care.

2. See Cassidy, S. B. (1987). Prader-Willi syndrome: Characteristics, management, and etiology. *Alabama Journal of Medical Sciences*, *24*(2), 169–175; Mitchell, L. (1980). *An overview of the Prader-Willi syndrome* (rev. ed.). Edina, MN: Prader-Willi syndrome Association; Welfare Research, Incorporated. (1984). *An introduction to neuroloical impairments in New York State*. Albany, NY: Author.

Case Studies on Personal Choice and Professional Responsibility

Introduction

These case studies were prepared in conjunction with the symposium, *Choice and Responsibility: Legal and Ethical Dilemmas in Services for Persons with Mental Disabilities*. This symposium included 16 workshop sessions, each targeting situations and issues where consumers' choices and the obligations of service providers to meet consumers' needs and to protect them from harm came into conflict. The case studies were used for discussion purposes. In this volume, the case studies have been organized in eight topic areas: (1) Residential Services, (2) Day Services, (3) Criminal Justice, (4) Health Care–Medical, (5) Health Care–Psychiatric, (6) Money Management, (7) Sexuality, and (8) Discrimination.

Of note, these case studies emanate from real cases drawn from the files of the NYS Commission on Quality of Care. Although the names of individuals and certain details of the cases have been changed to protect the confidentiality of the individuals involved and, in many cases, the actual outcomes of cases have been omitted, all cases tell of real issues and dilemmas.

The purpose of these case studies is not to suggest that the problems have single right answers or solutions. Indeed, most of these cases came to the Commission as there was a debate among reasonable persons as to the right approach or solution to the problem presented.

The intention of this compilation of case studies and their discussion across a series of workshop topics was to structure a learning experience for providers, consumers of services, family members, and advocates which could be helpful in bringing some structure to our deliberation of these cases. The case studies are intended to challenge us to consider in a more ordered way the values for personal choice, independence, and normalization for persons with mental disabilities and the legal and ethical obligations of service providers, guardians, and advocates.

In short, the case studies are designed as a vehicle to help "clear our heads" on these difficult dilemmas, many of which seem at first glance to be almost without a responsible solution. As the Commission has encountered these cases, we have become aware that while these dilemmas may not have one right answer or one "best approach," there are wrong answers and there are wrong approaches; and there are better answers and better approaches. In considering these case studies, agency administrators, program managers, staff members, consumers, family members, and advocates may be able to move toward better answers and better approaches.

I.   Residential Services

Mr. Antonellis

Mr. Antonellis is 38 years old, and he is moderately retarded. Mr. Antonellis lived at home until he was 20, at which point he moved to a state developmental center. For the past three years, he has lived in a community residence. His parents have recently begun visiting Mr. Antonellis regularly in the community residence, and they have expressed concerns that Mr. Antonellis is frequently not clean, his toe nails are extremely long, and he has not seen a dentist since he moved into the residence.

Residential staff say that they have encouraged Mr. Antonellis to shower and wear clean clothes, and they have provided the opportunity for him to go to a podiatrist and to the dentist, but he is not interested. Residential staff report that when they push these issues, Mr. Antonellis becomes upset and tells them that they have no right to bother him about these issues because he is not hurting anyone. Mr. Antonellis works at a sheltered workshop, where his work skills are good, but his poor hygiene has held him back from a possible supported work placement. These issues have been discussed with Mr. Antonellis who states he doesn't mind staying at the workshop.

Does Mr. Antonellis have a right to keep his bad personal hygiene habits? Should residential and/or workshop staff be more aggressive in getting Mr. Antonellis to comply with their recommendations? How should residential staff respond to Mr. Antonellis' parents?

Mr. Gomez

Mr. Gomez is a young man with borderline intelligence and a borderline personality disorder. He lives in a supportive apartment, and receives vocational counseling. Over time, Mr. Gomez has secured, and then promptly lost, several jobs as a busboy and a messenger, because he spent too much time socializing with the customers.

Recently, Mr. Gomez met and "fell in love" with a young woman, Ms. Dale. Tenants from Mr. Gomez's apartment building alerted agency staff that Ms. Dale was a known crack addict and a prostitute. Staff talked to Mr. Gomez, but he denied any problem with Ms. Dale and soon afterwards, allowed her to move in with him. Whenever program staff visit Mr. Gomez, the apartment is full of "street people." During one visit, staff found a glassine envelope commonly used for drugs.

Staff do not believe that Mr. Gomez is abusing drugs, but they do believe that Ms. Dale and her friends are drug abusers. Staff also believe that Mr. Gomez is being exploited by Ms. Dale and her friends, who eat his food and "crash" in the apartment. Additionally, they fear that Mr. Gomez may not be aware of the health risks associated with his relationship with Ms. Dale.

When staff advised Mr. Gomez not to let Ms. Dale and her friends in his apartment, he retorted, "They're my friends and it's my apartment; I can do what I want."

What should the agency do?

Mr. Bryce

Mr. Bryce is moderately retarded, and he lives with his mother, who is mildly retarded and has trouble supervising him. Mr. Bryce has a childhood history of sexual abuse, and recently he exposed himself in public and made sexual advances to peers in the workshop. The workshop has tried to arrange a residential placement where Mr. Bryce can be better supervised and provided consistent training, but none of the community providers will accept him because of his sexual behaviors.

Recently, Mr. Bryce allegedly exposed himself to two eight-year-old girls. The families of the girls were willing to drop charges if Mr. Bryce was moved to a setting away from their neighborhood, where he would be supervised. As this was Mr. Bryce's first criminal charge, the District Attorney was in agreement, but the Office of Mental Retardation and Developmental Disabilities could not find a community placement for Mr. Bryce. These officials stated that the only placement available was in a secure state facility many miles from Mr. Bryce's home. Neither Mr. Bryce nor his mother wants this placement. The workshop administrator has appealed to OMRDD, stating that Mr. Bryce's rights to appropriate services are being denied, and that Mr. Bryce may not have even gotten into this trouble if community services had been appropriately responsive.

How should the Office of Mental Retardation and Developmental Disabilities respond to this appeal?

Ms. Palmer

Ms. Palmer is a 35-year-old Hispanic woman living in a community residence. She has been diagnosed with mild mental retardation and cerebral palsy. She has been a model resident of her home and a great worker at her day program. Ms. Palmer's parents have been her legal guardians since she was 18.

Ms. Palmer has been asking her treatment team if she can be moved to a less structured setting, like a supportive apartment. Her best friend, Ms. Bran, recently moved from Ms. Palmer's house to a two-person supportive apartment, and when Ms. Palmer visits her, she returns asking staff why she can't move also. Ms.

Palmer initially was told that she needed to develop certain skills to move, and she has done so, meeting all of her goals for independent living, including budgeting and cooking. At the last team meeting, Ms. Palmer's social worker presented the idea of a supportive apartment for Ms. Palmer.

Mr. and Mrs. Palmer, who were at the team meeting, were very opposed to the idea, and they would not sign anything to have their daughter referred to the supportive apartment program. They have not changed their minds. Ms. Palmer was very upset by her parents' decision and told the entire team that she wanted to move and that she should be given the same chance her friend was given to be independent. The agency agrees with her.

What are Ms. Palmer's rights, the agency's obligation, and her guardians' limits?

Mr. Johnson

Mr. Johnson had been homeless for several years and refused all residential services. Last year, after much encouragement from his case manager, Mr. Johnson moved into a supportive apartment. He has been doing relatively well, but he has not paid his rent in the past two months preferring to use his money for his own purposes. Mr. Johnson's roommate angrily tells his peers at the workshop that everyone treats Mr. Johnson like he's special.

Program staff are concerned because Mr. Johnson's roommate is also threatening not to pay the rent. What should they do?

II.   Day Services

Ms. Lensky

Ms. Lensky, whose family immigrated to the United States from Poland in 1990, is moderately mentally retarded. Ms. Lensky has always lived at home, and she never attended any formal programming until very recently, when she began attending a sheltered workshop program. At the workshop, Ms. Lensky is not very attentive to her job, and she prefers to socialize with her new friends and several of the staff members.

Workshop staff have told Ms. Lensky that she cannot take breaks whenever she likes and that she must do her work. Although Ms. Lensky seems to understand the workshop staff, she does not take them very seriously; she smiles, tentatively returns to her work station, but then soon moves off again. Workshop staff have also solicited Ms. Lensky's parents' support, but they speak little English and, in any case, they do not seem to have much appreciation for the staff's concerns.

There is a workshop rule that individuals who take extended breaks or who willfully don't do their jobs are to be suspended, and Ms. Lensky's supervisor has warned her that she will be suspended for three days the next time she takes an extended break. Several workshop staff, however, think this is not the best approach for Ms. Lensky, especially as her parents are not inclined to reinforce the program's perspective.

How should workshop staff intervene? What special efforts should be considered in working with Ms. Lensky's family?

Ms. Martin

Ms. Martin attends a workshop which requires compliance with psychiatric treatment regimes. Recently, Ms. Martin has refused to take her psychotropic medication, prescribed for "impulse control," complaining of the side effects of the medication. To date, there are no noticeable ill effects of Ms. Martin's decision. Her performance at the workshop is good, and Ms. Martin is not psychotic. Her workshop supervisor has told Ms. Martin, however, that unless she agrees to take her medications, she will be terminated from the workshop.

Is this policy legal? What options does Ms. Martin have?

Ms. Serena

Ms. Serena has a supported work position as a maid at a local hotel. She was recently arrested for allegedly shoplifting at the local mall. As soon as the hotel learned of the arrest, they asked the agency to remove Ms. Serena from her position.

Should the agency comply with the hotel's request?

III. Criminal Justice

Mr. James

Mr. James has a diagnosis of borderline personality disorder, and he drinks excessively, which often leads to his abuse of his elderly mother, with whom he lives, and confrontations with neighbors. Although the psychiatric center had in the past hospitalized Mr. James when his behavior became dangerous, after a recent episode of his verbally threatening two neighborhood children, the center refused to admit Mr. James, and he was taken to jail. Mr. James preferred this response, and he told his public defender that he wanted to enter a guilty plea to a misdemeanor, serve his time in jail, and get out.

Mr. James' story has played prominently in the local media, and public opinion is running high that Mr. James' behavior is a threat to the entire neighborhood. There is much uneasiness among the community service providers about Mr. James' pending release from jail, as well. At a recent meeting, there was consensus that Mr. James would benefit from a supportive apartment, a support group for persons with drinking problems, and an intensive case manager. But, although providers sponsoring these programs were present at the meeting, none were eager to serve Mr. James, as they feared his presence may threaten their other clients.

Does anyone have an obligation to serve Mr. James when he gets out of jail?

Mr. Rickert

Mr. Rickert is moderately retarded and has little concept of money, but he has a long history of petty theft from neighborhood stores. Over time, a pattern has developed where he is caught for stealing, his residential provider makes restitution, and criminal charges are dropped. At these times, Mr. Rickert's freedom to roam the neighborhood independently is restricted temporarily, as a consequence of his behavior, and he is counseled about his stealing and warned that it will result in more serious consequences if he does not stop.

His shoplifting, however, has not abated, and his provider now requests advice on whether it may be better to let Mr. Rickert spend a few weeks in jail the next time he is caught. The county jail has no services for Mr. Rickert, however, and his case manager fears that he will be victimized during his incarceration. Mr. Rickert's service providers have asked for help in structuring their deliberations on what to do next, and particularly if there are any other options for Mr. Rickert.

Next time, should Mr. Rickert go to jail? Can residence staff do anything to prevent a next time?

IV. Health Care–Medical

Mr. Santiago

Mr. Santiago is 59 years old; he has borderline intelligence, mental health diagnoses of personality and adjustment disorders, and diabetes. He lived at home with his elderly mother until her death three years ago when he was admitted to a community residence, and for the first time in his life, he began attending a day program.

Since moving to the community residence, Mr. Santiago has become more independent—travelling in the neighborhood, going to church services and enjoying community events—things he rarely did in the past. Generally, Mr. Santiago has done extremely well in the residence, and he reportedly is "very happy" with his life.

Residence staff make sure that Mr. Santiago goes to his medical and mental health appointments, and they also monitor his medications and diet in the residence. While out in the neighborhood, however, Mr. Santiago uses his personal funds to purchase foods not on his diet. Staff have tried to stop this in various ways, including limiting his access to his personal funds, but Mr. Santiago is so well-liked by local merchants, that they give him free food if he is short on cash. As a result, Mr. Santiago has gained over 50 pounds since entering the residence, and he consistently has high blood sugar levels.

Mr. Santiago's doctor is concerned about his diabetes and says that the only way to control Mr. Santiago's diet would be to "lock him up." Residence staff have spoken with Mr. Santiago's brother, who is also his guardian, about the possibility of transferring Mr. Santiago to a more restrictive setting, but his brother refuses, saying Mr. Santiago has never been so happy.

Residence staff acknowledge that Mr. Santiago is happy, but they are worried about the doctor's warning and that without better diet control, Mr. Santiago's eating habits could lead to serious and even fatal health consequences. What should residence staff do?

Ms. Stock

Ms. Stock was a 24-year-old woman who suffered from a major affective disorder, borderline intelligence, and behavioral difficulties. For a year prior to her death, Ms. Stock lived in a community residence and was treated with a variety of psychotropic medications. Ms. Stock also suffered from hypertension, obesity, and diabetes. Community residence staff were aware of these problems, and Ms. Stock was linked with a local health clinic. On admission, community residence staff and Ms. Stock discussed her medical problems and treatment, and Ms. Stock stated that she wanted to manage her health care personally and did not want staff to accompany her to appointments.

What residence staff did not know, however, was that Ms. Stock was noncompliant with the recommendations of the health clinic regarding her diet and high blood pressure. At times, Ms. Stock wouldn't even attend the clinic; she would tell residence staff that her next appointment was in "three months" when it was really the next day or week. Two weeks after Ms. Stock's last missed appointment at the health clinic, she complained of not feeling well, and she vomited. Staff asked her if she wished to go to an emergency room, but she declined. The next morning she was found dead in bed. The death was attributed to her diabetes and hypertension.

Were community residence staff negligent in following up on Ms. Stock's health care? Are there procedures that the community residence could put in place to provide a more reasonable safety net for residents like Ms. Stock?

Mr. Stevens

Mr. Stevens is a 65-year-old man with a diagnosis of mental illness. He resides in a community residence and attends a day treatment program. Mr. Stevens is generally considered to be amiable, and he usually agrees to most treatment suggestions. For many years he has tolerated a hernia condition which continues to worsen. Mr. Stevens is not considered an appropriate candidate for a truss or support since he does not like to be bothered with it and often "forgets" to put it on.

His treating physicians now determine that it is in his best interests to have an operation to repair the hernia even though Mr. Stevens objects to the operation. They consider Mr. Stevens' objections to be incapacitated due to his inability to understand the risk of strangulation which could lead to complications, even death. They also think that he is having a severe panic reaction to the recommended operation and general anesthesia.

A complaint has been filed in court to obtain informed consent for the proposed hernia operation. Mr. Stevens' attorney agrees that the operation is in his best interests and that he probably is not capable of making the decision to consent or refuse the treatment in an informed manner. Should the attorney oppose the proposed operation in court, even though Mr. Stevens needs it and may not fully appreciate the negative consequences of not having it?

V.   Health Care–Psychiatric

Mr. Smith

Mr. Smith is 40 years old, and he has had a long history of depression, with repeated hospitalizations. In the past, Mr. Smith had been treated with antidepressants and lithium with reasonable success. Most recently, however, Mr. Smith has developed a serious heart condition, and his cardiologist recommended discontinuation of Mr. Smith's psychotropic medications due to their adverse effects on his heart, which the doctor believed were potentially life threatening. Mr. Smith agreed with this recommendation, but within three months he became severely depressed and was hospitalized. Upon consultation with Mr. Smith's cardiologist, his psychiatrist and a consulting psychiatrist on the hospital's staff strongly recommended ECT treatment to Mr. Smith.

Mr. Smith, however, strongly objected to ECT treatment, noting his observations of patients during previous hospitalizations before and after ECT treatment. Mr. Smith remained adamant in his objection to ECT treatment, even after lengthy discussions with his psychiatrist, his primary therapist, and his wife. These discussions transpired over a full week.

Over the next two weeks, Mr. Smith's psychiatrist, therapist, and wife continued, however, to try to persuade him to change his mind, emphasizing that he had no other viable treatment choice. Finally, after three weeks of being in the hospital, Mr. Smith reluctantly signed an ECT consent form for a series of eight treatments. After the first ECT treatment, Mr. Smith told his psychiatrist, therapist, and wife that he did not want to have any more treatments. They tried to persuade him to accept additional ECT treatments, stressing that there was no other treatment available. After refusing ECT for two days, Mr. Smith relented saying, "I don't want it, but I have no choice, so I will accept it."

After the second ECT treatment, Mr. Smith again refused to have any more treatments. Again, his psychiatrist, therapist, and wife tried to persuade him to change his mind. After several days, Mr. Smith reluctantly agreed to a third ECT treatment. This pattern of refusal, intense efforts at persuasion, and reluctant acceptance followed Mr. Smith's third and fourth ECT treatments. After his fifth ECT treatment, however, Mr. Smith firmly refused any additional treatments and would not relent. He asked to leave the hospital and was discharged against medical advice. He now receives outpatient treatment from a community psychiatrist and is taking medication for depression. The medication has not had an adverse effect on his heart.

Did Mr. Smith give voluntary informed consent to ECT? If no, what aspects of the informed consent process were compromised? What boundaries and principles should professionals consider when attempting to encourage psychiatric patients to accept treatments which they initially refuse?

Mr. Alger

A lawyer is contacted by a friend of an elderly man in a nursing home, Mr. Alger. He has a diagnosis of early Alzheimer's disease, and schizophrenia-like symptoms. His only family member is estranged, will not assist with his care, and adamantly feels he should be in a nursing home. Since entering the nursing home, Mr. Alger has been receiving psychotropic medication and his condition has improved, but he complains constantly about being in the nursing home and expresses the desire to return home. A consulting psychiatrist feels that Mr. Alger would be safer and more comfortable in the nursing home; he also feels Mr. Alger may be able to live at home with a home health aide. Mr. Alger also has a court-appointed guardian who adamantly feels that Mr. Alger should stay in the nursing home, and who believes that the psychiatrist is crazy to permit him to return home.

Mr. Alger's lawyer obtains a court hearing, and the court orders the guardian to return Mr. Alger to his home, with a 24-hour-a-day home health aide. Mr. Alger is not happy with the aide, but begrudgingly accepts her as the price of being in his home. He tells his lawyer that being at home is the "most important thing" for him.

After being at home successfully for a month, however, Mr. Alger begins to refuse to take his psychotropic medication. His mental condition begins to deteriorate, and the home heath aide has difficulty getting him to bathe and dress appropriately for the weather. On one occasion, he wanders away from the house and is returned hours later by the police who find him lost and disoriented.

The home health aide begins to put the psychotropic medication in ice cream, which Mr. Alger eats voraciously. This ploy is effective, and Mr. Alger's difficult behaviors quickly subside.

Mr. Alger's lawyer learns that her client is being secretly medicated after this ploy has been used successfully for several months. Her investigation reveals that, without the medication, Mr. Alger will likely decompensate again and be involuntarily placed in a nursing home. Mr. Alger is unaware he is receiving unwanted medication, and has never sought his lawyer's help regarding medication refusal. Should the lawyer do anything to inform Mr. Alger what is going on or just leave well enough alone?

Mr. Martin

Mr. Martin was admitted to an inpatient psychiatric service. According to his wife, Mr. Martin's condition had began to deteriorate when he stopped taking his antipsychotic medications and he started to demonstrate threatening behaviors at home and to have increasingly serious delusions of persecution. When offered medication to control his symptoms in the hospital, Mr. Martin told the staff that he will not take any pills because they inhibit his artistic talents. Although Mr. Martin has not been dangerous since his admission to the hospital, in the past, when he stopped taking his medications, he had assaulted a policeman, hospital staff, and his wife.

Mr. Martin's wife wants him to be involuntarily medicated because, in the past, medications have been successful in controlling these symptoms. She has discussed this with his psychiatrist, who recommended a long-acting injectable form of medication. Mr. Martin does not agree, and he refuses both oral and injectable medications. Mr. Martin's treatment team anticipates further decompensation based on his history and plans to petition the court to medicate Mr. Martin against his will.

Are Mr. Martin's rights to refuse medication being respected? Is it appropriate for the treatment team to petition the court on "anticipatory" dangerousness? Should they wait until his condition actually deteriorates before acting?

Ms. McCarthy

Ms. McCarthy is a patient on the local hospital's psychiatric unit where she has been a patient several times before. Upon admission with a diagnosis of a bipolar disorder, she was in a highly agitated state and accepted treatment with lithium, but refused adjunct therapy with Haldol. During the next several days, before the positive effects of lithium took hold, she was often loud and seldom slept through the night. She was rude to staff and often irritated other patients with her provocative behavior. Although Ms. McCarthy had objected to Haldol, her psychiatrist who knew of this objection, ordered STAT intramuscular doses of Haldol when her behavior became disruptive to the unit milieu. Ms. McCarthy has made a complaint to the hospital administration and a Mental Health Legal Services lawyer, stating that she was medicated without justification. She feels she posed no danger to herself or others and should not have been subjected to the intramuscular doses of Haldol.

Has Ms. McCarthy's psychiatrist bent the law in ordering emergency administrations of Haldol when she was disruptive to the unit, but not a clear danger to herself or others? What other alternatives did the psychiatrist have? What types of disruptive behaviors would meet the legal test for emergency administrations of a psychotropic medication over a patient's objections?

Mr. Judd

Mr. Judd was admitted to a psychiatric center in an acute, psychotic state, hallucinating, experiencing delusions of a religious nature, and behaving in a bizarre manner (i.e., vomiting and eating the vomit). He was placed in seclusion and offered oral medication which he refused. Despite his resistance, after two days of not eating any food, Mr. Judd was medicated on an emergency basis against his will with an intramuscular injection of Haldol. The rationale for involuntary medication was the danger he was to himself because he had not eaten.

The medication was administered despite pleas from family, friends, and members of his "church" who claimed that he was "with the spirits." They told staff that the medication would interfere with Mr. Judd's religious experience and he just needed to be protected from harm. Several days later Mr. Judd "cleared," was discharged, and went back to work. He was very angry with the treatment he received and assured the treating clinicians that he would never be brought back as a patient again. He also refused to take any medications as an outpatient.

Should the hospital have medicated Mr. Judd against his will? Or should they have listened to his objections, which were reinforced by family and friends?

Mr. Allen

Mr. Allen is 42 years old, and he has a long history of mental health problems and many hospitalizations. Currently, he is a patient at a state psychiatric center. Two months ago, Mr. Allen eloped from the center and was picked up by the police for stealing a car, driving without a license, and abandoning the car after sideswiping a telephone pole. This episode is just one of many where Mr. Allen's elopements have led to his getting into trouble with the law.

Due to Mr. Allen's recklessness and criminal behavior, he has been remanded to the state psychiatric center for a psychiatric evaluation. At the center, because of his elopement risk and the public sensitivity around his case, Mr. Allen is restricted to the unit. He is not allowed to go outside, participate in any off-unit activities, or attend church services at the on-campus chapel. Due to staff shortages, there are few, if any, therapeutic activities on the ward.

Mr. Allen has complained to his treatment team that he is being treated unfairly, that he would have more privileges in jail, and that he is getting no treatment. Are staff justified in their decisions? What alternatives could they have considered?

Julio

Julio is an eight-year-old child of a migrant farm worker who has been displaying symptoms of attention deficit disorder with hyperactivity (ADHD). Over the past year, his behavior and school achievement have deteriorated to a point where he is failing most subjects, he is a constant disruption in his class, and he is routinely ridiculed by his peers. The school nurse and the school psychologist have suggested that Julio may benefit from Ritalin (a stimulant medication which often produces dramatic improvements in children with ADHD), and they have recommended that Julio be evaluated by a child psychiatrist.

Julio's mother consulted with a local physician, who warned her of the side effects of Ritalin, especially its potential to stunt Julio's physical development. Based on this discussion and her personal reservations, Julio's mother is refusing to take Julio to a psychiatrist. She feels the school should be able to deal with Julio's behavior without medication. She also thinks that Julio's hyperactivity is a result of his difficulty in understanding English and keeping up with his peers.

Should school officials take any further actions or should they accede to Julio's mother's wishes? What options does Julio's mother have?

Mr. Davidson

Two years ago, Mr. Davidson's parents placed him in the ABC Residence after 25 years at home. They had become his legal guardians at age 18. Mr. Davidson, who is developmentally disabled, is known to have very challenging behaviors, and the agency has been writing behavior plans. Recently, it seems to the Davidsons that the agency has given up trying to manage Mr. Davidson with behavior plans and has called upon their psychiatrist who has prescribed medications. The parents are very opposed to this approach as Mr. Davidson has reacted poorly to medication in the past, and they are not satisfied that all other options have been explored.

The agency has recently told Mr. and Mrs. Davidson that if they do not agree with putting their son on medication, the agency will seek to discharge him. Last night, the agency called 911 after Mr. Davidson's outburst, which they had never done in the past, and Mr. Davidson was admitted to the psychiatric unit of the local hospital.

What rights do Mr. and Mrs. Davidson have to make treatment decisions regarding their son? Is the agency justified in the ultimatum they gave the Davidsons?

Ms. Sommers

Ms. Sommers is 22 years old. Since her early adolescence, she had lived in a children's mental health treatment program, but six months ago she moved into an adult community residence program for persons with mental illness. Initially, Ms. Sommers did well in the community residence, but her condition worsened after a few months, and she has spent the last three weeks in an inpatient psychiatric unit.

Hospital staff are trying to plan Ms. Sommers' discharge. The community residence director has called several times stating that he will hold a bed for Ms. Sommers for 30 days, only if he is ensured that she will be discharged to their program. Hospital staff believe this would be the best placement for Ms. Sommers, who appears immature and naive and who has almost no money management or community survival skills. Ms. Sommers, however, wants to live more independently and is refusing to move back to the community residence.

How should hospital staff proceed with discharge planning for Ms. Sommers?

Mr. Jarrell

Mr. Jarrell, who is Hispanic, has a history of drug and alcohol abuse, and he was involuntarily admitted to an inpatient psychiatric unit. Initially, Mr. Jarrell did not participate in any unit activities due to the acute nature of his illness. As his condition improved, however, Mr. Jarrell continued to refuse to participate, stating that the activities were meaningless, culturally irrelevant, and he did not choose to be there anyway.

After his admission, Mr. Jarrell repeatedly asked his doctor for unescorted grounds privileges, but his requests were denied on the basis of his refusal to participate in any unit activities. As the days passed, Mr. Jarrell became angrier and angrier and refused to do just about anything staff asked. After a 30-day stay, he was ultimately discharged.

Was staff's approach to Mr. Jarrell's refusal to participate in activities appropriate? Should staff have discharged Mr. Jarrell without resolving the dispute? Would another approach have yielded better outcomes for Mr. Jarrell?

Ms. Katz

Ms. Katz immigrated to this country five years ago, and she has attended an outpatient clinic at a municipal hospital for several years. Ms. Katz's behavior can be very difficult to tolerate, as she is prone to angry outbursts of salty language at the slightest provocation. These outbursts can be directed at secretaries, doctors, people in the clinic waiting room, etc.

Recently, the municipal hospital did some renovation work, and now both the children and adult clinics share the same waiting room. After several warnings, Ms. Katz has been told that she is being terminated from the clinic, as her psychiatrist and other clinic staff believe that her outbursts traumatize children sitting in the waiting room.

Is Ms. Katz receiving fair treatment? Is her dismissal from the clinic legal?

VI.   Money Management

Mr. and Mrs. Davis

Debbie and Seth Davis are a married couple in their 30s. Mrs. Davis is mildly retarded, and Mr. Davis is moderately retarded. They currently live in an adult home, although they had previously lived in a supportive apartment. Mrs. Davis is able to read, and she is very resourceful in contacting agencies and individuals for services the couple needs.

Mr. and Mrs. Davis do not always accept the help and guidance they request, however. Four months ago, Mrs. Davis called Social Security and petitioned to have the supportive apartment agency's status as her representative payee revoked and to have herself appointed as Mr. Davis's representative payee.

For the next two months, Mrs. Davis did not pay any rent to the agency. Although the agency did not take any action against Mr. and Mrs. Davis, one Sunday, they abruptly vacated their supportive apartment and moved into a "garage" apartment. Agency staff discovered that Mrs. Davis found this garage apartment through a newspaper ad, and she rented it because it was so much less expensive than their supportive apartment. Apparently, Mrs. Davis did not understand that her SSI check would be reduced substantially if she moved out of the supportive apartment.

Since then, Mr. and Mrs. Davis have been evicted from the garage apartment, lived in a shelter, and two adult homes. They have experienced a variety of problems in each of these settings—but in all, they have not paid their rent. Presently, Mr. and Mrs. Davis are about ready to be evicted from their second adult home for not paying their rent and, as the operator puts it, "for generally being difficult residents."

The adult home operator has called Mr. and Mrs. Davis's case manager stating that the couple will most likely end up in a shelter, where they may be victimized. The operator is sympathetic to their plight, but she reports that she cannot tolerate residents not paying their rent—if she did, she would lose her livelihood.

As Mr. and Mrs. Davis's case manager, what should you do next?

Ms. Oliver

Ms. Oliver is 27 years old and mildly mentally retarded. For the past year she has lived in a supportive apartment operated by Webster's Services. According to all who know her, Ms. Oliver is very capable of managing most of her daily affairs. She has a part-time job, she can independently use buses to travel many places in the city, and she buys most of her own clothes and other personal items independently.

One day, staff of Webster's Services changed the locks on Ms. Oliver's apartment door when she was not home. Staff packed some of Ms. Oliver's belongings into two garbage bags and placed them in the hallway. Reportedly, this was done because Ms. Oliver had not paid her rent in several months.

Ms. Oliver's parents are outraged at how this matter has been handled. They have complained to the agency director, noting that no one had informed them of the planned eviction and that Webster's Services had failed to follow up on their requests that their daughter be offered money management training and that a representative payee be appointed to manage her Social Security checks.

Webster's Services report that they did offer Ms. Oliver money management training, but she never attended. They state that they did not file for representative payee status, as they believe Ms. Oliver is capable of managing her money, and that she just does not want to pay her rent and would rather use her money for clothes, cigarettes, and alcohol. Agency staff acknowledge that they did not inform Ms. Oliver's parents of the eviction date, but they add that her parents were well aware that this action was pending and that they contribute to Ms. Oliver's problems by always jumping in to rescue her from her own irresponsible behavior, even though they are not her legal guardians.

Who is right here—Webster's Services or Ms. Oliver's parents? What steps should be taken next to resolve this situation in Ms. Oliver's best interest?

Ms. Darling

Ms. Darling is a 28-year-old independent woman with mild/borderline mental retardation. She lives in a supportive apartment with a roommate, and for seven years she has worked for IBM in the mailroom. Her parents are vigilant advocates for her.

Last year, Ms. Darling became involved with a man who lives in her building. They are together most of the time, and Ms. Darling has become noncompliant with apartment rules and her work plan, often missing several days of work every month. She is now in jeopardy of losing her job. It is believed that she is giving away most of her money, as she is often broke and without enough money to purchase food or travel to work.

The agency has tried counseling Ms. Darling, but she refuses to answer questions about her relationship and usually misses her counseling sessions. Her parents are frantic, and the agency is at its wits' end on how to deal with this situation. The man involved with Ms. Darling does not want anything to do with the agency or any outsiders. Ms. Darling wants everyone to just leave her alone.

Ms. Darling's parents have always believed that she was capable of making her own decisions and, therefore, have never petitioned the court for guardianship. They are now reassessing their original decision and have sought the advice of lawyers and advocates. Should Ms. Darling's parents seek guardianship? Should they leave her alone to take the consequences of her decisions?

Mr. Harold

Mr. Harold is 30 years old, he has a diagnosis of borderline personality disorder, and he has been residing in a supportive apartment operated by Hooper's Place. During the months of September 1992 through January 1993, Mr. Harold made numerous long distance telephone calls resulting in monthly phone bills of over $150. Many of these phone calls were to various 900 numbers.

In cooperation with the telephone company, Hooper's Place restricted Mr. Harold's phone from access to 900 numbers and long distance calls, but Mr. Harold still had a $700 outstanding telephone bill. The agency subsequently paid the bill to secure Mr. Harold's access to the telephone for emergencies, but it is assessing Mr. Harold $15 a week to pay the agency back. This assessment comes out of Mr. Harold's weekly $50 food and personal needs allowance, leaving him with $35 a week for all his personal expenditures, including food.

Mr. Harold has appealed to Hooper's Place and the Commission stating that the agency's assessment is too high and that it will take him almost a year to get out of debt. The agency believes that Mr. Harold should be held responsible, but it is also concerned that he will need to live on so little for so long.

Are there other alternatives open to Hooper's Place? Could the agency develop new policies which might prevent or mitigate such problems in the future?

VII. Sexuality

Ms. Julian

Ms. Julian is a 33-year-old woman who is currently living in a community residence. She has been treated for manic-depressive illness since the age of 19. Ms. Julian has a history of promiscuity, especially during her manic episodes. Ms. Julian has terminated two pregnancies, and she has an eight-year-old daughter who has been placed in foster care.

Recently her promiscuous behavior has increased significantly; she has been having sexual relations with numerous partners, some of whom she has just met. To complicate matters, Ms. Julian does not take her birth control pills consistently and rarely asks her partner to use a condom.

Ms. Julian is receiving human sexuality counseling from the community residence staff; however, the residence staff do not confront Ms. Julian regarding her sexual behavior. They believe she is exercising free choice. She also does not want to talk about it. She says it is none of their business. Residence staff consider Ms. Julian competent to give consent in sexual matters, although they acknowledge that her capacity in this regard may be questionable when she is in an extreme manic phase of her illness.

Should community residence staff take any actions regarding Ms. Julian's sexual behavior and choices? Should these issues be addressed in Ms. Julian's treatment plan, even if she objects to their inclusion?

Mr. Frederick

Mr. Frederick has been living on the coed unit of a state hospital for the past year. He frequently elopes from the hospital, but always comes back in a day or two. Mr. Frederick usually leaves the hospital for sex because, according to Mr. Frederick, "...the hospital ain't no place for a good time." Upon his return to the unit, Mr. Frederick usually tells staff and other patients of his latest sexual liaisons.

Mr. Frederick is HIV positive, and although he has attended sexual education groups and has received private counseling from staff about his sexuality, he continues to engage in high-risk sexual behavior (e.g., he refuses to use a condom, he has multiple partners, he refuses to tell his partners about his HIV status, etc.).

Last month, Ms. Gwen was transferred to Mr. Frederick's unit, and during the past couple of weeks, Mr. Frederick has been seeking out Ms. Gwen's company. Staff have also heard from other patients that Mr. Frederick wants to have sex with Ms. Gwen. Staff are very concerned about this situation because, although both Mr. Frederick and Ms. Gwen have the capacity to consent to sexual activity, Ms. Gwen doesn't know about Mr. Frederick's health condition, and Mr. Frederick is not about to tell her.

What actions, if any, can the unit staff take to protect Ms. Gwen?

Ms. Janeski

Ms. Janeski is 24 and in love for the first time in her life. She's been off drugs and alcohol for the past year, has stayed out of the psychiatric hospital for the past six months, and hasn't thought about killing herself since she fell in love with Mr. Allen.

Ms. Janeski met Mr. Allen, a case manager, at the continuing treatment program she used to attend. Although Mr. Allen's and Ms. Janeski's relationship has been kept a secret, one of Ms. Janeski's neighbors in the supportive apartment program spotted Ms. Janeski leaving Mr. Allen's apartment and is spreading the word around the program that Ms. Janeski and Mr. Allen are sleeping together.

Ms. Janeski is scared to death that Mr. Allen won't see her anymore. The continuing treatment program administrators have gotten word of this development, and they are considering terminating Mr. Allen from his position due to his relationship with Ms. Janeski. Mr. Allen, meanwhile, is taking a few days sick leave, trying to decide what to do next. He is considering hiring a lawyer to protect his job.

Should staff of Ms. Janeski's supportive apartment program get involved in this dilemma? If so, how? What actions should Mr. Allen's employer take? Is it ethical for a case manager to maintain a romantic relationship with a former client?

Mr. Jamison and Mr. Walton

Mr. Jamison and Mr. Walton are both in their 30s; they are both profoundly retarded; and both have legal guardians. They live in the same community-based ICF-MR. For the past two months, Mr. Jamison and Mr. Walton have had a sexual relationship. Residence staff are aware that this relationship involves intimate sexual activity, including anal intercourse.

Staff have tried to talk to the men about their activities; however, neither is capable of verbalizing his feelings. Mr. Jamison's vocabulary consists of only a few words, and Mr. Walton hides his face and giggles when staff bring up the topic of sex. Attempts have been made to teach them to use condoms, but staff are not confident that either understands this.

After an interdisciplinary team meeting, staff decided to allow this activity to continue because both men willingly seek each other out, appear to enjoy their interactions, and are not aggressive towards each other or other residents of the residence.

Was this an appropriate decision by the team? Does the team have an obligation to notify the guardians of Mr. Jamison and Mr. Walton regarding their decision? Would the staff be responsible for any harm that resulted to either resident?

Ms. Laurin

Ms. Laurin is 18 and Mr. May is 32, and they both live in an eight-bed community residence. Ms. Laurin is described by staff as immature and naive. She also has difficulty relating to her peers and has few friends, but she is eager to be liked and accepted.

Mr. May, on the other hand, is mature and well-liked by other residents and staff. He has a steady girlfriend whom he visits on most weekends. This relationship, however, has its ups and downs, and during the "down" time, Mr. May's girlfriend refuses to see him.

Since they've been living at the residence, Ms. Laurin and Mr. May have become friends. During the past week, Mr. May and his girlfriend had a disagreement, and she refused to see him. Mr. May has since asked Ms. Laurin to spend the night at a local motel. Residence staff are aware of this development and are concerned that Ms. Laurin is being used by Mr. May and that she may not be able emotionally to cope with the loss if Mr. May abruptly leaves her for his old girlfriend.

Should residence staff actively discourage Ms. Laurin from meeting Mr. May at the motel or should they stay out of it and let Ms. Laurin and Mr. May make their own decisions?

Ms. Betters

Ms. Betters is a 30-year-old woman with moderate mental retardation and cerebral palsy. Ms. Betters lives with her grandmother; she has a case manager affiliated with a nearby provider agency and attends a local day training program. Ms. Betters and her grandmother also live with an older gentleman, a close friend of the family, with whom Ms. Betters has developed a close attachment. Recently, Ms. Betters' grandmother arrived home unexpectedly and found Ms. Betters and the gentleman together in a sexually intimate situation. Although Ms. Betters clearly likes this man and welcomes his advances, her grandmother is very concerned because she has tried to broach the subject of sex on several occasions with Ms. Betters, to no avail. Ms. Betters does not seem to understand what her grandmother is talking about and wants to continue this relationship. Her grandmother has talked to Ms. Betters' case manager about this and has enlisted her assistance in deciding what to do.

Does the case manager have any responsibility to help the grandmother? Should she be guided by Ms. Betters' expressed wishes?

Ms. Sarafini

Ms. Sarafini, a 23-year-old woman with Down's syndrome and a resident of a community residence, has expressed interest in dating and possibly having an intimate, sexual relationship. Ms. Sarafini has told residential staff that she wants to attend the "dating" group the agency has recently established. The young woman's parents, who are very involved and concerned with their daughter's safety and well-being, are very skeptical that, even with training, she would be able to handle a sexual relationship safely. The residential staff are not sure either. The parents want their daughter sterilized to protect her and completely remove the possibility of her becoming pregnant. While clear about not wanting to go against her parents' wishes, Ms. Sarafini has not come out and expressed a preference as to what she does or does not want.

How should residential staff respond to Ms. Sarafini's parents' request? To her request?

Mr. Jung and Mr. Burton

Ever since his mother died when he was 17, Mr. Jung, who is 25 years old and mildly retarded, has lived in a community residence. Mr. Jung is a very happy person; he works competitively in a supermarket down the street, bagging groceries and performing maintenance-type tasks; and he pursues several interesting hobbies. Recently, Mr. Burton, a severely retarded young man who is around Mr. Jung's age, moved into the community residence. Mr. Jung and Mr. Burton seemed to get along right from the start and began doing things together. Six months after Mr. Burton had moved in, he and Mr. Jung approached the house staff and told them that they loved each other, and they wanted to share a bedroom. They asked the residential staff if they would help them with this request and provide them with the privacy they want.

Should residential staff honor this request?

Mr. Stevens

Mr. Stevens is developmentally disabled and has a history of sexually abusing both adults and children. He currently lives in an apartment program, and the agency believes he is well supervised. Two of his apartment mates have complained that Mr. Stevens has forced himself on them sexually. In response, the agency has required staff to check on Mr. Stevens' whereabouts every 15 minutes. Despite the required increased supervision, however, Mr. Stevens recently sneaked out his window and was found "stalking" a 12-year-old girl swimming in her backyard pool. The girl's parents were upset by this event, and filed a police report. The families of the two men who share Mr. Stevens' apartment were outraged and demand the agency discharge Mr. Stevens.

What should the agency do?

Mr. Mitchell, Mr. Williams, and Ms. Sanders

Mr. Mitchell, Mr. Williams, and Ms. Sanders are mildly retarded, and they have been friends and worked together in the sheltered workshop for several years. During lunch hour one day, all three were found in the men's bathroom engaging in dangerous sexual activity. In fact, Ms. Sanders was injured after being tied to a toilet stall.

Is it necessary to report this incident to the police? Should the program do anything to protect Ms. Sanders from future injuries?

VIII. Discrimination

The Brigwater Community Residence

The Brigwater Community Residence is located in upstate New York, and it serves ten men and women, most of whom are severely mentally retarded and four of whom are also nonambulatory.

After the residence opened, the neighbors began to raise complaints about the parking of the residence staff members' vehicles on the street after dark. Unbeknownst to the voluntary agency operating the residence, the local town has an ordinance which forbids all on-street parking after 5:00 pm through 8:00 am from October 15 to April 15. Justified as both a safety precaution in the narrow town streets, unlit by street lamps, and to ease snow removal in the winter, the ordinance has been in place for years and was universally enforced. The only exceptions were made for evening parties.

Staff of the Brigwater Community Residence, however, frequently parked their cars in the street because there was usually insufficient space in the driveway, and parking staff cars in the driveway made it inconvenient to use the residence van which is parked there. (Although the home has a garage, it cannot accommodate the agency van, because various furnishings and pieces of adaptive equipment for residents are stored there.) Neighbors have brought this violation to the Brigwater Town Superintendent, urging that action be taken. The voluntary agency sponsoring the residence has also appealed to the Brigwater Town Superintendent, arguing that their residence should be granted a waiver from the ordinance, due to the special handicapping conditions of its residents and their need for a specially accommodated van and considerable staff support.

Who should prevail in this case, the neighbors or the voluntary agency?

Ms. Thomas and Mr. Rhode

Ms. Thomas and Mr. Rhode are both in their 30s, and they are both mildly mentally retarded. They share a small subsidized apartment with their three-year-old daughter, Sally. By order of Family Court, the family receives many support services from caseworkers and home health aides who visit a few hours daily and a visiting nurse who comes in weekly "to check on things."

Before these services were in place, Ms. Thomas had been cited for neglect of Sally, who sometimes wandered outside alone, usually appeared dirty, and was very thin. Since these services have been in place, things are going better for the family and especially for Sally, but the child preventive worker acknowledges that Ms. Thomas and Mr. Rhode often don't talk with Sally, that they frequently forget or skip meals, and that they forget Sally's anticonvulsant medications, which contributes to her frequent seizures. When asked what will happen next, the worker candidly reports, "Well, if this were any other family, the child would already be in foster care, but we allow differential treatment in these cases in view of the parents' limitations."

Is the caseworker (or her supervisor) making the right decision?

Ms. Billings

Ms. Billings is an attorney, with a diagnosis of a manic depressive disorder. Last year, she embezzled a large sum of money from the law firm where she was working. In the legal proceedings, she was found guilty, but mentally ill. After several months, Ms. Billings has sought representation to be readmitted to the bar—arguing that she should not be held responsible for her acts as they occurred during a manic episode when she was not taking her psychotropic medication.

Partners in the public interest law firm are ambivalent about taking on Ms. Billings' case. Several partners believe that Ms. Billings should not be readmitted to the bar both because her professional competence and character cannot be assured (due to her mental disability) and because her choice in not taking her medications was volitional, and she should face the consequences for her behavior. Other partners, however, believe that Ms. Billings has a legitimate claim to special treatment, given her disability.

Should Ms. Billings be excused due to her mental illness and readmitted to the bar?

Mr. Jones and Mr. Craft

Mr. Jones, age 72, lives alone on his social security income in a downtown apartment. He has recently met his neighbor, Mr. Craft, a man of about his own age, who has had periodic bouts with depression. In a discussion over coffee at the corner diner, Mr. Jones discovered that Mr. Craft lives in what is called a "supportive apartment," and because of this (and his disability), Mr. Craft's social security check is nearly twice the amount of his own—and his neighbor is able to keep nearly $100 a month just for spending money—much more spending money than Mr. Jones has.

Mr. Jones does not begrudge Mr. Craft his apartment or the help of the social worker who stops by every few days. Mr. Jones doesn't even mind that the agency that helps Mr. Craft has provided much nicer furniture in the apartment than he has. Mr. Jones doesn't think it's right, however, that Mr. Craft should have more spending money than he does.

Does Mr. Jones have a valid claim for equal treatment?